Transforming
Young Adult
Services

ALA Neal-Schuman purchases fund advocacy, awareness, and accreditation programs for library professionals worldwide.

Transforming Young Adult Services

SECOND EDITION

Written and edited by Anthony Bernier

Foreword by John M. Budd

CHICAGO :: 2020

© 2020 by the American Library Association

Extensive effort has gone into ensuring the reliability of the information in this book; however, the publisher makes no warranty, express or implied, with respect to the material contained herein.

ISBNs
978-0-8389-1774-9 (paper)
978-0-8389-1935-4 (PDF)
978-0-8389-1933-0 (ePub)
978-0-8389-1934-7 (Kindle)

Library of Congress Cataloging-in-Publication Data
Names: Bernier, Anthony, editor, author. | Budd, John, 1953- author of foreword.
Title: Transforming young adult services / edited by Anthony Bernier; foreword by John M. Budd.
Description: Second edition. | Chicago : ALA-Neal Schuman, 2020. | Includes bibliographical references and index. | Summary: "This revised and expanded second edition updates a provocative collection of 14 expert contributions to the debate inaugurated in 2013 addressing LIS's historic avoidance in defining and envisioning its young adult users by offering readers a diverse set of possible responses to how LIS should define YAs for its own professional, institutional, and research purposes"—Provided by publisher.
Identifiers: LCCN 2019024013 (print) | LCCN 2019024014 (ebook) | ISBN 9780838917749 (paper ; alk. paper) | ISBN 9780838919330 (epub) | ISBN 9780838919347 (kindle edition) | ISBN 9780838919354 (pdf)
Subjects: LCSH: Young adults' libraries. | Young adults' libraries—United States. | Libraries and teenagers. | Libraries and teenagers—United States.
Classification: LCC Z718.5 .T73 2020 (print) | LCC Z718.5 (ebook) | DDC 027.62/6—dc23
LC record available at https://lccn.loc.gov/2019024013
LC ebook record available at https://lccn.loc.gov/2019024014

Book design and composition by Karen Sheets de Gracia in the Cardea and Acumin Pro typefaces.
Cover image © Laurin Rinder.

⊚ This paper meets the requirements of ANSI/NISO Z39.48-1992 (Permanence of Paper).

Printed in the United States of America
24 23 22 21 20   5 4 3 2 1

Contents

FOREWORD TO THE FIRST EDITION *by John M. Budd* vii

PREFACE: **Young Adult Services at the Crossroads** *by Anthony Bernier* xi

ACKNOWLEDGMENTS *xxiii*

INTRODUCTION: **Making the Case for Transforming** *by Anthony Bernier* xxv

PART I   Betweenness

1   Envisaging Young Adult Librarianship from a Teen-Centered Perspective 3
by Denise E. Agosto

2   Diverse Identity in Anxious Times 17
Young Adult Literature and Contemporary Culture
by Karen Coats

3   Students or Learners? 27
Conceptualizing Youth in School Libraries
by Mary Ann Harlan

PART II   Intellectual Freedom

4   Misfits, Loners, Immature Students, and Reluctant Readers 35
Librarianship in the Construction of Teen Readers of Comics
by Lucia Cedeira Serantes

5   Identity at Odds 49
The Sometimes Conflicting Viewpoints about Young Adults' Rights in Libraries
by Cherie Givens

6   Situating Youth Voice 61
Moving from Understanding to Action through Critical Theory
by Jeanie Austin

PART III Confronting Convention

7 **Crossing Over** *77*
The Advent of the Adultescent
by Michael Cart

8 **Storytelling, Young Adults, and Three Paradoxes** *93*
by Kate McDowell

9 **"The Library Is Like Her House"** *111*
Reimagining Youth of Color in LIS Discourses
by Kafi D. Kumasi

PART IV Emergent Roles

10 **Beyond Coaching** *121*
Copiloting with Young Adults
by Wendy Schaetzel Lesko

11 **LIS's Vision of Young Adults** *129*
Some Historical Roots for Current Theories and Practice
by Mary K. Chelton

PART V From Citizenship to Membership

12 **Tribalism versus Citizenship** *139*
Are Youth Increasingly Unwelcome in Libraries?
by Mike Males

13 **Imagining Today's Young Adults in LIS** *151*
Moving Forward with Critical Youth Studies
by Paulette Rothbauer

14 **Moving Beyond YAs as "Citizens"** *163*
The Promise of Membership
by Anthony Bernier

Conclusion: **Membership's Promise for Praxis** *by Anthony Bernier 183*

About the Editor *191*

About the Contributors *193*

Index *197*

Foreword to the First Edition

It is tempting to begin prefatory remarks by asking, What is a discipline? This of course is not a new question, although potential answers may have become even more elusive in recent years. As Anthony Bernier observes in his introduction, the core audience for services, the focal points of the service dynamics, and the institutional context of study present questions that the essays in this volume attempt to address. If readers will allow me a digression, I would like to situate some initial thoughts within the locus of disciplinary inquiry. I ask for forbearance because any discussion of transdisciplinary inquiry (note that I do not use the more familiar, though nearly bereft of meaning, term *interdisciplinary*) depends on a definition of *discipline*. Also, the relevance of the inquiry presented here is founded on efforts to render the thought and research into young adult services as accessible as possible. That also relies on definitional beginnings. With some trepidation I invoke the name of Thomas Kuhn (1970), who in *The Structure of Scientific Revolutions* argued that a discipline (or subdiscipline) is built around a paradigm, or "the entire constellation of beliefs, values, techniques, and so on shared by members of a given community," and "the concrete puzzle-solutions which, employed as models or examples, can replace explicit rules as a basis for the solution" of scientific questions (175). What happens when the constellation expands, when the boundaries of past inquiry no longer obtain?

Many formerly well-defined disciplines, even in the natural sciences, broke through those boundaries some time ago. In then rather nascent areas such as psychology, individuals like William James helped to create the kinds of questions that could be addressed. Psychology has changed markedly since James's day, but his groundbreaking thought should not be forgotten (and may find resonance in young adult services). At this point it may be useful to return to Kuhn (1970, 180): "A paradigm governs . . . not a subject matter but a group of practitioners." Up until this point one may think that I am denying the avowed purpose of this reader. The foregrounding must be clarified now. The transdisciplinary purpose of library and information science (LIS) is, specifically, to achieve the goals set out for and in this volume; that is, LIS cannot be constrained by the limitations of the past—limitations that too narrowly bound the scope of research and the envisioning of institution.

Bernier urges inquiry that emerges from LIS *as* a discipline. Fair enough. We return to the question of definition, this time with specificity, and ask, What is LIS? At the risk of being presumptuous, allow me to suggest some elements of a disciplinary framework within which young adult services can be examined and formulated. One element that many people dispute at the current time is the institutional locus of the services. Rather than irrelevant or peripheral, the institutional is essential. The institution itself is misunderstood and all too facilely dismissed by some who would deny that humans gravitate to places that embody meaning for them. Libraries are such a place; most importantly, they are places of human engagement and—dare I say it—construction. One need not be a social constructionist to accept that institutions are particularly human constructions, designed and created for purposes of interaction, exploration, and discovery. In other words, the library is a counterpoint to any naive solipsism that omits the interdependence that characterizes the human condition (if I can be permitted a bit of lofty language). There is no denying that "library as place" is a rather recent notion, but it does in some ways represent a return to ideas of the library as a learning environment. An excellent treatment of the library as place is the collection of essays edited by Buschman and Leckie (2007). Some of the essayists who contributed to that volume are also represented in this reader. The concept of the institution pervades all of the sections of the present volume and should be taken as something of a first principle for inquiry and practice in LIS. In fact, the institution is a locus for critical inquiry and practice.

Another and actually related idea is community. Institutions should not exist merely for self-perpetuation; their being has a foundation of connections among people. Institutions of specific types have specific kinds of connections as components of their essential natures. Communities look to institutions in some important ways as extensions of what they seek to be and do. Here a complex dynamic has to be introduced: Communities have multiple identities that should be recognized by the people who operate within institutions. Communities include embodied linguistic, cultural, and other groups that share one or many characteristics. To some extent the sharing is situational and can be recognized by physical and cultural environment. In other ways there are choices made by people, or what Michael Walzer (1983) calls "association." There is a serious challenge to institutions and those who work in them here; the positions many people make are based on skepticism and suspicion when it comes to official institutions, regardless of stated missions or services of the institutions. LIS as a discipline must have as a facet the understanding of the tensions that can exist between communities and institutions, and the research and praxis in the field must address the challenge directly. Services, including young adult services, are not abstractions; they are pragmatic, even as they should have sound frameworks.

Insofar as communities are individuals who share some binding ties, librarians (within the institutions of libraries) have to embrace the inevitable sharing and difference that will occur in all interactions. Librarians must learn to accept the community members as other selves who have qualities that are commonly human, that can be commonly occurring with themselves, and as unique individuals who have cognitive, linguistic, cultural, political, and other qualities that set them apart. The understanding librarians must aspire to is that difference: Young adults, for example, are not adults. African-American young adults are not Asian-American young adults. Those who live lives of affluence are not those who live in poverty. Acceptance of these ideas necessitates accepting a phenomenological foundation for LIS. That said, youth (while an essential but not totalizing characteristic) is a component of lifeworld. Services as phenomenological actions must embrace lifeworld as simultaneously a shared mode of being and a fact of individuality.

Thinkers who include Edmund Husserl, Maurice Merleau-Ponty, Emmanuel Levinas, and Paul Ricoeur have detailed precisely what these foundations entail. There is another essential characteristic of phenomenological intentionality (in addition to the acceptance of *I* and *Thou*): "Our consciousness—including of the mental acts that accompany many of our perceptions—is not merely a blank slate on which the phenomena write. Consciousness is intentional; it is directed; it has a purpose. Since consciousness is active, phenomenology must account for intentionality, for the realization that our perceptions are perceptions of something" (Budd 2005, 46–47). Intentionality applies to the librarian and the community member equally; each has an active consciousness. An implication of intentionality is consciousness of one's own experiences. Young adults are subjects (in the sense of being reflective selves); they are not objects of professional service. It is appropriate to assume that the language of service should be able to embrace the selfhood and subjectivity of the patrons (see Zahavi 2005). What the librarian can do, and young adult services demonstrates the point starkly, is help shape what that young adult is conscious *of*, what that person *perceives*.

A third principle, referred to by Bernier, is a particular species of ethical action. Communication and discourse are naturally components of young adult services. Communication carries an ethical necessity; freedom is one element of the necessity. This is customarily referred to as intellectual freedom in librarianship; in young adult services it can mean avoidance or negation of any paternalistic protection of individuals. The readers/information users are presumed to have sufficient agency that they are able to take responsibility for what they access, see, hear, and read. There has tended to be a sort of orthodoxy of official positions regarding intellectual freedom and freedom to read and view. Orthodoxy is not always bad and is not always to be resisted; however, it should be examined critically. For example, some statements that may be taken as orthodox in particular settings could hold that gaming is deleterious to young adults. Such a claim has no merit on its face since it is not reasoned. The communicative ethics of young adult services should have a rational component, which includes the examination of what it is to be a young adult at this point in time and in the complex society. The ethical foundation in this context shares a goal with many ethical standpoints; the good life for young adults can be enhanced by services offered *in* libraries *by* librarians. The ethical responsibility of scholars and professionals is not to adopt a prescriptive model and apply it universally. The communicative ethics forms the third leg of the stool, along with the institution and phenomenology, to create the possibilities for a genuine LIS inquiry into young adult services.

I began with a question, and I attempted to answer it with some specificity. The question is well addressed by the authors who have contributed to this reader. The answer in this short foreword is primarily my own, but it is derived not simply from solitary contemplation, but also through discussion with colleagues, including some of the authors here. Hence, it is intended to be at least somewhat reflective, showing what is in the best inquiry today as well as what can be in future study. There is little doubt that the work presented in these pages is a breakthrough; it is something unique in young adult services scholarship. It deserves a wide and critical audience.

John M. Budd

REFERENCES

Budd, J. M. 2005. "Phenomenology and Information Studies." *Journal of Documentation* 61, no. 1: 44–59.
Buschman, J. E., and G. J. Leckie. 2007. *The Library as Place: History, Community, and Culture*. Westport, CT: Libraries Unlimited.
Kuhn, T. S. 1970. *The Structure of Scientific Revolutions*. 2nd ed. Chicago: University of Chicago Press.
Walzer, M. 1983. *Spheres of Justice: A Defense of Pluralism and Equality*. New York: Basic Books.
Zahavi, D. 2005. *Subjectivity and Selfhood: Investigating the First-Person Perspective*. Cambridge, MA: MIT Press.

PREFACE

Young Adult Services at the Crossroads

The first edition of *Transforming Young Adult Services* advanced the following claim: "The study and practice of young adult (YA) services within the context of library and information science (LIS) appears to be quickly approaching a crossroads."

Several things have changed since publishing this claim. Thousands of new professionals entered the field. Communities opened new or renovated library buildings by the hundreds—many including new YA spaces, some with spaces called "makerspaces." Some libraries adopted a new category of human development called "tween." The American Library Association's Young Adult Library Services Association (YALSA) issued many statements, guidelines, and calls for action. Librarians published many new practitioner titles, appeared on hundreds of panels and in workshops, and posted to many blogs. Libraries all over the country began to stretch more decisively toward user-defined outcomes to articulate, document, and demonstrate their public value.

On the other hand, many things did not change. The domain of professional YA services, for example, continues to languish in the backwater of broader LIS consciousness rather than receive acknowledgment as one of its crown jewels. While YA services has become an increasingly productive and dynamic subfield among LIS practitioners over the past 25 years, especially regarding the adaptation to rapid technological change, innovations in civic-engagement programming, and the introduction of equitable YA spaces in libraries, actual evidence-based research on YA services has only sporadically shown signs of life. YA services remains among the least researched aspects of LIS.

Another thing not exhibiting much change remains LIS's stubborn refusal to acknowledge and incorporate YA service interventions, innovations, and creativity into the profession's overall story. Introductory LIS texts in professional and graduate-level courses, for example, scarcely mention YA services.

A further critique exhibited throughout this second edition remains LIS's continuing reluctance to engage the contributions of interdisciplinary youth studies. These include many potent contributions and influences from critical social theory to LIS and YA services.

Instead of exploring these potential benefits, however, LIS currently remains mired in a dated conceptual framework about the human experience. This prevalent framework, borrowed nearly exclusively from developmental psychology, includes roots stretching back to the eighteenth-century Age of Enlightenment.

This view, when applied to contemporary young adults, defines the innocuous sounding "youth development" paradigm. Youth development embodies a totalizing theory, a hegemonic vision of "youth" as a naturally imperfect, embattled, inadequate, transitory life "stage," exclusively defined in opposition to fully flowered fantasies of ill-defined "mature adulthood." According to this paradigm, achieving such a mystical "adult" status occurs only if assisted by very particular types and kinds of interventions. One need go no further to find broad institutional affirmation of these claims than the division of the American Library Association dedicated to serving YAs, the Young Adult Library Services Association. YALSA's current strategic concepts, prominent in the association's aspirational documents and statements, too quickly elide member value for presumptuous claims about "alleviating" YA "problems." LIS's uncritical implementation and recalcitrant dedication to youth development, and only youth development, reveals that libraries promote themselves as numbering among these particular interventions. LIS maintains this claim, however, without evidence to support it.

In response, the work advanced in this edition of *Transforming Young Adult Services* collectively instigates a debate among LIS students, LIS instructors, practitioners, and researchers. It asks the field to consider alternatives to this historical default and dedication to youth development and advocates articulating an LIS-specific vision of today's YAs to transform and reorient the daily practice of professional YA librarianship.

Such a project promises to focus and elevate the profile of YA work rather than extend its current position in LIS's backwater. It will raise awareness of the effectiveness and meaning of libraries' contributions with young people. It can recast and revalue the contributions professionals make to not only YAs but also their institutions, and thus society. And because scholars contributed most of the material for this collection, it partially meets scholarship's responsibility to constantly examine professional practice and offer new and innovative ideas for how libraries can increase the well-being of their communities.

In order to achieve these aspirations, *Transforming Young Adult Services* brings together some of the field's best YA researchers and evidence-based practitioners who write from their specialized experiences, perspectives, and strengths. Collectively these contributors demonstrate facility with the most applicable scholarship and writing on YA librarianship, broader youth studies, and critical social theory.

On the way to articulating their respective interpretations about how LIS should envision YAs, these experts cull and synthesize LIS literature to produce a resource identifying many essential topics pertinent to the application of daily YA services. These topics include youth identity formation (including racial identity and gender identity), YA materials and collections, youth development, models of intergenerational youth participation, critical perspectives on youth studies, storytelling and programming, public and school librarianship, YA services history, intellectual freedom (in various institutional contexts), and professional ethics. Together, this collection conceptually and historically interrogates the field's conventional categories to examine how they currently produce and manifest an inadequate and derived institutional imagination of today's youth.

In *Transforming Young Adult Services*, readers will discover research articles and studies that augment the many up-to-date and sufficiently detailed lists of resources that currently inform LIS and professional YA practice (resource guides, manuals, collection building references, sample forms and documents, program and outreach models, and tips for using technology, for instance). More importantly, this collection poses hard and even uncomfortable questions about LIS's current assumptions regarding youth and what it often defines as "best practice"—as opposed to what it can actually prove as *being* best practice. Thus, this collection inaugurates what should become a new and much needed foundational debate about how LIS conceives of today's young adults.

WHO SHOULD READ *TRANSFORMING YOUNG ADULT SERVICES*

While no single collection can legitimately claim to address all relevant topics, or even to cover the most important topics to the same degree, *Transforming Young Adult Services* attempts to introduce critical social theory to the broadest, most compelling, most practical aspects of YA librarianship.

As mentioned earlier, however, this collection does not attempt to offer readers another resource guide. The profession already produces prodigiously on that score. Nor does it claim to offer final answers to all of the vexing questions it raises. This collection nevertheless does attempt to articulate the conceptual contours that explain, underlie, and frame how LIS currently perceives, positions, delivers, and values YA work. It aims to help students, instructors, and professionals define YA users for their own institutional purposes and thus better understand how their institutions can apply these perceptions in daily practice and research.

For LIS students, *Transforming Young Adult Services* concentrates on fundamental aspects of YA librarianship that currently go unaddressed in daily practice. It offers to enrich critical appreciation of the history and traditions of YA services, identify some of the current challenges in delivering YA services, and encourage making informed decisions about the YA users students are preparing to serve. It will also help students become better interpreters of LIS research and more reflective consumers of information related to the incessant moral panics about youth that pervade today's culture through popular parlance, media, and public policy. Moreover, students will come to understand the potential for dynamic innovation through debate (not mere lists of prescriptions) and the creativity that YA professionalism truly offers.

Transforming Young Adult Services also promises to benefit professionals, paraprofessionals, and administrators currently responsible for YA services. This collection connects and contextualizes larger concerns that color and inform the legacy practices and daily assumptions they have inherited and will help them better evaluate the choices still before them that can easily go unrecognized. Many of these choices offer to influence all aspects of YA service formation, innovation, delivery, and evaluation. School library and media specialists, particularly those working with youth in middle school and high school, will also find a great deal of this material applicable to pursuing the curricular missions of their host institutions.

LIS faculty and instructors will likewise find this a rich collection of diverse concepts and arguments to spark lively discussion and productive assignments with which to prepare students for becoming deliberative professional practitioners. Each section addresses different categorical approaches to YA services that, like the individual studies, lend themselves to comparing and contrasting engagements. Instructors can combine and parlay various configurations of chapters and essays into different conceptual and applied exercises.

A RISING DEBATE IN FIVE SECTIONS

Transforming Young Adult Services organizes chapters into five parts meaningful to LIS students, professional librarians, and instructors as well as to scholars. To one degree or another, all of these studies and essays challenge prevailing LIS approaches and seek to transform YA services professionalism by interrogating the need for a more LIS-specific vision of its end user.

The collection opens with "Introduction: Making the Case for Transforming," a contextualizing historical analysis of the crossroads YA services is rapidly approaching.

Part I, "Betweenness," presents a topically conventional yet provocative collection of studies. In the first chapter, "Envisaging Young Adult Librarianship from a Teen-Centered Perspective," LIS scholar Professor Denise E. Agosto, of Drexel University, conducts a content analysis of three years of LIS research and practitioner writing about YA services. Agosto uncovers a pattern of professional discourse that, despite the past decade's intense policy-level discussion about "youth involvement," continues, in actual practice, to project itself as "adult-centered." This contribution inaugurates the discussion by urging LIS professionals to become more self-aware of the homilies they speak and write about and to move beyond a systematic concentration on youth experience.

In chapter 2, "Diverse Identity in Anxious Times: Young Adult Literature and Contemporary Culture," English Professor Karen Coats, of Illinois State University, offers an updated essay from the first edition. Coats extends Agosto's investigation by reaching deep into contemporary YA fiction to derive and advocate for a fluid LIS vision of today's youth—one oscillating between the benefits she sees in youth development as well as more dynamic social constructions of youth identity. Coats filters the question of how youth are constructed through literary criticism and arrives at a theoretically sophisticated analysis to argue the importance of understanding how youth identity is "dialogically engaged" in a project of individual "self-fashioning." Mobilizing the postmodern concentration on fluid meanings of the self, Coats suggests that research and practice on that front would better serve LIS than does the prevailing modernist interpretation of the self as static and solid.

Chapter 3's contribution, new to the second edition, by Dr. Mary Ann Harlan, Assistant Professor and Coordinator of the Teacher Librarian Program at San José State University's School of Information, plainly lays out the challenge of envisioning a betweenness in YA users for LIS professionals in schools in "Students or Learners? Conceptualizing Youth in School Libraries." Highlighting a theme that emerges repeatedly in *Transforming Young Adult Services*, this study explores the nature of how YA identity emerges from negotiations in—sometimes cooperating with and sometimes competing against—conflicting institutional visions. In this instance, Harlan grapples with the dynamic relationships of education's institutional vision of itself and the information professional's identity and commitments as an ethical practitioner.

While all of the contributions in part I ostensibly address conventional and fundamental categories of daily LIS practice and research, they more importantly interrogate cardinal and legacy practices from different perspectives. These topics may appear familiar at first. Careful reading, however, will yield critical insights suggesting increasingly radical departures from common daily practices. After many years of lectures, workshops, conference presentations, books, and articles about the need for LIS to more deeply engage "youth participation" and youth-centric services, as Agosto and others point out, these notions have failed to gain broad or sufficient institutional penetration into daily practice. It is also clear that what constitutes LIS's current definition of "youth" also at least partly obstructs the emergence of more flexible and diverse approaches—concepts more contested or negotiated despite the long-standing impulse for LIS to borrow a static and simplistic age-based definition. The field must confront this dilemma head-on and imagine its own LIS-specific vision of young people.

Part II, "Intellectual Freedom," opens with another common theme emerging throughout the collection in arguing for the inclusion of YA literature itself as a meaningful indicator of how LIS envisions YA library users. These contributions appear particularly well-timed to respond to today's cacophony of unleashed information. While information appears on the surface to be ubiquitous, forces both inside and outside the library strain against YA access issues. What do these competing forces teach about how LIS should envision young library users while at the same time reconciling professional ethics?

Dr. Lucia Cedeira Serantes, Assistant Professor and Coordinator of the Certificate in Children's and Young Adult Services of the Graduate School of Library and Information Studies, City University of New York, probes that question in chapter 4. In "Misfits, Loners, Immature Students, and Reluctant Readers: Librarianship in the Construction of Teen Readers of Comics," Cedeira Serantes presents historical analysis reflecting how the field has manifested its visions of library users through its reception, and rejection, of particular literary genres. This study's content analysis critically engages LIS's historical reactions against comics, tracking all the way back through the 1930s. Cedeira Serantes documents the systematic and institutional marginalization of both the literary form and its readers as it coexisted with the form's enthusiastic reception by those readers—all this despite the profession's traditional espousal of values supporting freedom of access. The materials sitting on library shelves, as well as those that never make it to the shelves in the first place, tell an unfortunate and lingering tale of how LIS has envisioned YA users. Few observers have so clearly drawn connections between library collections and the ways in which LIS deploys its vision of youth as has Cedeira Serantes.

The author of chapter 5, "Identity at Odds: The Sometimes Conflicting Viewpoints about Young Adults' Rights in Libraries," is Dr. Cherie Givens, attorney, LIS scholar, and lecturer at San José State University's School of Information and author of *Information Privacy Fundamentals for Librarians and Information Professionals (2014)*. In light of the preceding chapters, Givens's study (updated from the first edition) continues the questioning of how LIS should envision today's youth and further prefigures the crossroads the profession is quickly approaching. Givens asks how the field should align itself ethically in advancing the rights and intellectual freedom of contemporary youth. Here the conflicting paradigms of modernism's static and universal conflating of chronological age and maturity "development" chafe against postmodernism's increasingly urgent questions regarding the socially constructed meaning of chronological age itself. Givens's thesis is that LIS must constantly weigh the legal status of youth (with all its inconsistencies, ironies, contradictions, and complexities) against professional virtues, aspirations, and ethical commitments.

Dr. Jeanie Austin, a recent PhD from the iSchool at the University of Illinois at Urbana-Champaign, in another new contribution to the second edition, extends Harlan's chapter 3 study. Austin presses for an LIS-specific vision of YAs within the relational context of a complex host institution in chapter 6, "Situating Youth Voice: Moving from Understanding to Action through Critical Theory." Austin applies postmodernism's concern with identity and power relations to the tensions between the juvenile detention system on one hand and racial privilege and heterosexual normativity on the other. Austin brings together powerful factors of identity formation inclusive of youth of color, LGBTQ youth, and gender-non-conforming youth with an institutional host not known for supporting LIS's ethical commitments to information access or intellectual freedom.

This second part, "Intellectual Freedom," certainly points to the difficulties LIS faces when attempting to define its young adult user. On one hand, considering the more open public library (as addressed by many authors), institutions such as schools (as addressed by Harlan), and centers of juvenile detention (as addressed by Austin), it is easy to identify at least three entirely different missions—each seeking its own institutional outcomes. On the other hand, however, the very complexity of this dilemma points directly to the value in recognizing the master's degree in library and information science as capable of producing *one* profession that addresses all of these (and other environments, such as libraries in religious institutions or on Native American reservations). Grappling with the complex vision of YA users emphasizes how important it is that professionals engage this question for their own respective communities and contexts.

Michael Cart, well-known YA literature critic and columnist, past president of YALSA, and the first recipient of the YALSA/Greenwood Publishing Group Service to Young Adults Achievement Award, begins part III, "Confronting Convention." Cart revisits youth identity to confront convention in a particularly provocative way in chapter 7, "Crossing Over: The Advent of the Adultescent." This study examines historical and contemporary texts in youth psychology and sociology to reevaluate concretized chronologically based notions of how LIS categorizes young library users in light of current economic exigencies. In Cart's analysis, today's social conditions suggest that the prevailing LIS category of "youth" itself now requires redefinition based not upon a conventional chronological notion of "teen" but on an "emerging," more prolonged process toward adulthood. Cart explores the institutional implications of this insight through the LIS practice of book reviewing and collection development procedures.

The second chapter in part III, "Storytelling, Young Adults, and Three Paradoxes," another new contribution to this edition, is by Dr. Kate McDowell, Associate Professor, School of Information Sciences at the University of Illinois at Urbana-Champaign. McDowell accords with Cart in reexamining chronological age but goes further in critically assessing prevailing notions of the youth development paradigm for obstructing the articulation of an LIS-specific vision of YAs within the dynamic triangular processes and relationships otherwise available through storytelling.

In chapter 9, Dr. Kafi D. Kumasi, Associate Professor and youth scholar at Wayne State University's School of Library and Information Science, employs critical race theory (CRT) in "'The Library Is Like Her House': Reimagining Youth of Color in LIS Discourses." Kumasi provokes questions about the implications of white racial privilege in defining today's YA library-using population. However, unlike other authors who argue that we must concentrate greater resources on youth experience, Kumasi argues that because the current construction of YA library users in the LIS imagination remains coded racially as white, the first order of business requires greater reflection on the meanings of the white privilege of LIS *professionals*. Moreover, while the critique of an underacknowledged racial privilege among professionals in LIS is not new, it is certainly a new question to raise when assessing YA services specifically. In this insightful and provocative turn, Kumasi challenges the intellectual and conceptual efficacy of the illusionary "color blind" cliché.

Part IV of *Transforming Young Adult Services*, "Emergent Roles," not only builds upon a largely forgotten history of competent and active youth community engagement but also extends study into current youth activism. Youth in large numbers, LIS professionals should recall, were productive farmers of urban victory gardens during the 1940s. Youth were activists in gaining African Americans access to public facilities (like libraries!) in the 1950s and 1960s and throughout the larger civil rights and antiwar movements of the 1970s. They have played gainful roles as protestors against harsh anti-immigration policies since the mid-2000s. They constitute active participants and leaders in recent Occupy, youth voter enfranchisement, police misconduct, and gun reform movements. Part IV parlays and translates these legacies of youth agency into critical studies to inform a new vision of YAs for libraries.

Wendy Schaetzel Lesko, Executive Director of Washington, DC's Youth Activism Project (YAP), contributes chapter 10, "Beyond Coaching: Copiloting with Young Adults." Lesko points out how YAP's intergenerational School Girls Unite effort serves as yet another demonstration (this time on the international stage) of the influence youth can make upon civil society and public policy—not in some abstract future, as promoted under youth development, but in the here and now young people live in. While the rhetoric promoting "youth participation" is not new, few researchers and institutions have mined or implemented the intergenerational partnership model illustrated by Lesko. Perhaps by reaching for successful experiences of other youth-serving efforts, beyond simply the psychology department, LIS might achieve an interdisciplinary sophistication capable of articulating a vision of youth more relevant to its own institutional aspirations and professional obligations.

Chapter 11 features one of the most decorated practitioners and influential scholars in YA services. Dr. Mary K. Chelton, Professor Emeritus, Graduate School of Library and Information Studies, City University of New York, cofounder of *Voice of Youth Advocates* (*VOYA*), and the second past president of YALSA to appear in *Transforming Young Adult Services*, contributes a new study in "LIS's Vision of Young Adults: Some Historical Roots for Current Theories and Practice." Chelton recuperates and reflects upon several generations of YA library services history to acknowledge not only some of the qualified benefits the youth development paradigm has offered LIS, defending LIS's importation of it from outside the discipline, but also LIS's "fixation" on it to the exclusion of other approaches. In responding to conversations she detects surfacing in LIS, Chelton explores notions of a dynamic YA identity already at play.

The fifth and final part of *Transforming Young Adult Services*, "From Citizenship to Membership," critically addresses the degree to which youth development hegemony continues to serve or inhibit LIS in general and YA services in particular. The chapters in this section continue to deepen engagement with YA services history and the consequences of its traditional avoidance of critical social theory and deconstructionism.

Sociologist and former University of California faculty Dr. Mike Males, Senior Researcher with San Francisco's Center for Juvenile and Criminal Justice, addresses how LIS should envision today's YAs in chapter 12. In this revised version of "Tribalism versus Citizenship: Are Youth Increasingly Unwelcome in Libraries?" Males introduces LIS to the work of classical anthropologist Margaret Mead. Unlike the pro-youth development positions represented in some of this collection's studies, Males's investigation shows how today's youth demographics, and patterns of technological adoption, constitute much of why youth studies scholarship demonstrates increasing skepticism of the explanatory power of the dominant youth development paradigm. Further, as in many other essays in this collection, Males takes issue with the assumed youth/adult bifurcation at the ideological core of youth development. Also in accord with other essays, Males contends that YA identity stems from youth and adult interaction ("synergetic" relationships), not simply from inherent or biological opposition. Ignoring this binary youth/adult tradition, he asserts, risks concretizing "adult tribalism" and unnecessarily hardens social institutions like libraries against the possibility of age integration or intergenerational possibilities. Instead, like Chelton and others, Males continues to examine what the notion of "citizen" holds for LIS practice and research.

In chapter 13, Paulette Rothbauer, Associate Professor in the University of Western Ontario's Faculty of Information and Media Studies, engages the question of how LIS should envision today's YAs in "Imagining Today's Young Adults in LIS: Moving Forward with Critical Youth Studies," a revision of her study in the first edition. By extending concerns opened here by Chelton, Males, and others, Rothbauer more deeply probes the historical assumptions of youth as an "essential stage" in human development rooted in the field of psychology since the late nineteenth century. In the essay's direct engagement with the long-dominant paradigm of youth development in LIS research and practice, Rothbauer examines many of the stereotypes that LIS has long taken for granted and through which YA services have largely been, and continue to be, defined. Rothbauer resolves that "our heavy reliance on theories of human development is, perhaps, unwarranted." In Males and in Rothbauer, in particular, we continue to see a rising tide of critical youth studies scholars who are no longer willing to abide a strict and unquestioned LIS commitment to the developmentalist apparatus.

Contributing chapter 14, "Moving Beyond YAs as 'Citizens': The Promise of Membership," is Dr. Anthony Bernier, professor at San José State University's School of Information, former member of the American Library Association's Committee on Accreditation, and Chair of the SJSU iSchool Youth Services Program Advisory Committee. Bernier builds upon the criticism of what he coins as the "youth development industrial complex," introduced earlier and variously throughout *Transforming Young Adult Services*. This study offers a systematic evaluation of the pros and cons of defining YAs as citizens and ultimately comes to rest upon a more robust valuation of how a vision of YAs, cultivated explicitly as members of local community, can enhance YA services praxis across the library's entire institutional profile.

This second edition of *Transforming Young Adult Services* concludes with "Membership's Promise for Praxis," also by Bernier, a systematic reflection on a vision of YAs as local community members applied to a comprehensive YA service profile. Thus, the final chapter synthesizes many of the collection's themes and culminates with several specific ways in which to combine critical social theory, LIS practice, and a relevant yet dynamic vision of young people into a responsive and contemporary praxis (theory plus practice).

THE CROSSROADS AHEAD: PRACTICE *AND* THEORY

LIS rapidly approaches a conceptual "crossroads." The notion of youth development continues to come under increasing scrutiny in broader youth studies analysis (in history, anthropology, and sociology; in feminist, race, and gender studies; in postmodernism and deconstructionism; among others). Its fundamental assumptions about youth, however, stubbornly continue seemingly cemented into LIS orthodoxy and practice.

Yet the rift widens. The gap continues to expand between increasingly moribund assumptions, on the one hand, and a diverse variety of approaches informed by critical social theory propelling analysis of contemporary culture, scholarship, and practice capable of producing a vibrant and complex vision of young adults, on the other.

What should happen if LIS remains unwilling or incapable of crafting its own vision of YAs? Will the institutional pronouncements, ethical guidelines, or other aspirational documents to which professionals point, the ritualistic incantations about "intellectual freedom," for example, or references to the American Library Association's Library Bill of Rights, or even the U.S. Constitution itself, resolve the concerns raised throughout this work?

By introducing and exploring more explicit theoretically informed approaches, the contributions in *Transforming Young Adult Services* boldly begin to separate from the prevailing and popular LIS modernist framework (one preoccupied with experience as the major mode of analysis). Instead these contributions pursue questions associated with postmodernism (analytical modes concentrating more on varying and diverse meanings and dynamic power relations).

Currently, LIS concentrates nearly exclusively on determining, measuring, and drawing understanding from questions derived from hardened institutional assumptions focusing on only the differences between youth and adults. Conversely, this collection seeks to understand how LIS should envision YAs by questioning the *meanings users themselves derive* from libraries through the negotiations of identity and power relations between libraries, YAs, and society.

In perhaps still the most seminal observation made to date about LIS research on YA services, Christine A. Jenkins notes, "If . . . library programs and services for children is insufficiently studied . . . [research on] programs and services for young adults is nearly nonexistent."[1] At long last, LIS needs to reconcile why this statement remains true. The authors in this collection have begun answering.

A FINAL WORD ABOUT THIS COLLECTION

The essays in this collection attempt to both analyze LIS's default vision of today's YAs and inaugurate new questions, approaches, and ideas to fuel a long-needed debate. Readers will encounter authors with differing positions. Some continue to mine and exploit the youth development paradigm for what it might still contribute to library work with young people. Some demonstrate ambiguous or conflicted opinions about this prevailing approach. Readers will also encounter authors increasingly calling into question what I term the youth development industrial complex (YDIC) to advance more decisive and critical perspectives.

The chief intention of this collection is to instigate debate, not resolve these matters for all libraries or for all professionals or for all young adults. Readers expecting clear "answers" to the issues posed here may be disappointed. On the other hand, readers may find validity in, and be persuaded by, the importance of this conversation to the health and advancement of LIS work, the institution, and its connections with young people and their communities.

Transforming Young Adult Services does not endorse one particular view or replace one hegemonic vision of YAs with another. Instead, it acknowledges the present interregnum the field is currently entering. There is always a hinge time after the king dies and a new order emerges. The collection does intend, however, to open up important questions from all of the positions and concerns advanced here and to propel forward a debate about that new order.

A thriving professional community should value the diversity represented in these views. But there is nothing alchemical or magical in combining and contrasting these works against one another. The contributors present them here precisely to open debate.

At base, however, beyond posing questions and proposing responses to the core concern about how LIS should envision today's young people, this collection lodges a profound concern that the profession, in near derelict avoidance and incuriosity about its own legacies, contributions, and impacts, fails to identify the larger conceptual continuities underlying library work. Nor does it currently offer evidence in response to the consequences. LIS, with respect to the social theory challenges swirling around academic and professional circles for at least the past half century, nearly ignored critical engagement about service to YAs.

Mature and influential professions produce the visions of youth they need to make viable contributions to society. Psychology produces youth as patients, clients, and research subjects. Education envisions youth as students and pupils. Criminal justice imagines youth as suspects and perpetrators. Communities of faith envision congregants. Even the physical education department envisions youth as athletes. Yet, uninformed by more recent critical social theory, LIS allows others to perform its intellectual labor and define young library users.

LIS, as a profession, invests too completely in the models furnished by developmental psychology, a discipline with vested intellectual and ideological commitments devoted to its own institutional agenda. Much of this has manifested in LIS's viewing young people against a backdrop of perpetual sentimentality or exaggerated threat. Why has LIS reclined so long in the shadow of another discipline? Why do other youth studies fields ignore LIS contributions?[2] Why has LIS exhibited such an incurious consensus about envisioning youth?

This misguided institutional legacy obscures and deflects the emergence and advance of LIS's knowledge and vision of young people at the expense of serving a much wider array and deeper scope of ordinary youth. It prevents other scholarly and service traditions from regarding LIS professionals more seriously as contributors to knowledge or research about youth and even as aspirants to institutional leadership and management.[3] Further, it no doubt contributes to why YA services does not even register in LIS's broader self-conceptualizations.[4]

Transforming Young Adult Services demonstrates that LIS is capable of fitfully engaging earnest debates about different ways to envision the young people it seeks to serve. It argues that LIS should, and is capable of, articulating its own vision of what libraries should be in the life of YAs, rather than perpetually defining them as needy youth in the life of the institution. It holds out the possibility that the nature of LIS's ethical obligations to the communities it serves need not be limited to uncritically deploying derived visions. It advocates that these professional obligations extend to and include robust intellectual engagement with the larger ideas of our age. Youth historian Philip Graham characterized part of the problem this way:

> Now that women have been liberated, the grey power of the elderly has been asserted, racism is publicly ostracized, and facilities for the disabled are legally required in all public places, the teens have become the last group whose disempowerment is invisible because it is so much taken for granted.[5]

LIS ought not number among the professions that take youth volition, history, and culture for granted. LIS students and professionals are entitled to a challenging deliberation over envisioning youth. The authors appearing in this collection welcome you to this discussion and to the coming debate.

Anthony Bernier

NOTES

1. C. A. Jenkins, "The History of Youth Services Librarianship: A Review of the Research Literature," *Libraries and Culture* 35, no. 1 (2000), 119. Of course there are many reasons why LIS research on YA services remains in this debilitating state. Jenkins's work in this article begins to identify some of them, but a more comprehensive assessment both exceeds the scope of this project and remains unaddressed.
2. For a selection of contemporary youth studies monographs that simply ignore LIS, see A. Lange, *The Design of Childhood: How the Material World Shapes Independent Kids* (New York: Bloomsbury

Publishing, 2018); J. Conner and S. M. Rosen, eds., *Contemporary Youth Activism: Advancing Social Justice in the United States* (Santa Barbara, CA: Praeger, 2016); R. G. Gonzales, *Lives in Limbo: Undocumented and Coming of Age in America* (Oakland, CA: University of California Press, 2015); D. Macallair, *After the Doors Were Locked: A History of Youth Corrections in California and the Origins of Twenty-First Century Reform* (Lanham, MD: Rowman & Littlefield, 2015); R. D. Putnam, *Our Kids: The American Dream in Crisis* (New York: Simon & Schuster, 2015); R. Burrow Jr., *A Child Shall Lead Them: Martin Luther King Jr., Young People, and the Movement* (Minneapolis: Fortress Press, 2014); S. Costanza-Chock, *Out of the Shadows, Into the Streets! Transmedia Organizing and the Immigrant Rights Movement* (Cambridge, MA: MIT Press, 2014).

3. LIS has not contributed meaningfully to critical youth studies despite a century of working at close hand with youth. On the other hand, critical youth studies scholarship continues to innovate not simply conceptually and ideologically but methodologically as well. See, for instance, these examples illustrating how critical youth scholars incorporate even the most marginalized youth populations into the center of their research agenda: N. Mirra, A. Garcia, and E. Morrell, *Doing Youth Participatory Action Research: Transforming Inquiry with Researchers, Educators, and Students* (New York: Routledge, 2016); E. Tuck and K. W. Yang, eds., *Youth Resistance Research and Theories of Change* (New York: Routledge, 2014); N. Lesko and S. Talburt, eds., *Keywords in Youth Studies: Tracing Affects, Movements, Knowledges* (New York: Routledge, 2012); M. Kellett, *Rethinking Children and Research* (London: Continuum International, 2010); T. M. Brown and L. F. Rodriguez, *Youth Participatory Action Research* (San Francisco: Jossey-Bass, 2009); S. Heath, R. Brooks, E. Cleaver, and E. Ireland, *Researching Young People's Lives* (Los Angeles: Sage, 2009); A. L. Best, ed., *Representing Youth: Methodological Issues in Critical Youth Studies* (New York: New York University Press, 2007); J. Cammarota and M. Fine, eds., *Revolutionizing Education: Youth Participatory Action Research* (New York: Routledge, 2007); M. Delgado, *Designs and Methods for Youth-Led Research* (London: Sage, 2006); S. Fraser, V. Lewis, S. Ding, M. Kellett, and C. Robinson, eds., *Doing Research with Children and Young People* (London: Sage, 2005).

4. In none of these standard LIS survey texts, among some of the most cited and respected treatments of the field, do YA services play a significant role: K. Haycock and M. Romaniuk, *The Portable MLIS: Insights from the Experts*, 2nd ed. (Santa Barbara, CA: Libraries Unlimited, 2018); S. Hirsh, *Information Services Today: An Introduction*, 2nd ed. (Lanham, MD: Rowman & Littlefield, 2018); and R. E. Rubin, *Foundations of Library and Information Science*, 4th ed. (Chicago: American Library Association, 2017); J. L. Ayala and S. Guerena, eds.. *Pathways to Progress: Issues and Advances in Latino Librarianship* (Santa Barbara, CA: Libraries Unlimited, 2012); J. Pateman and J. Vincent, *Public Libraries and Social Justice* (Surry, England: Ashgate, 2010); G. M. Eberhart, ed., *The Whole Library Handbook 2: Current Data, Professional Advice, and Curiosa about Libraries and Library Services* (Chicago: American Library Association, 1995).

5. P. J. Graham, *The End of Adolescence* (New York: Oxford University Press, 2005), 1. Also see P. S. Fass, "How the Old Can Learn from the Young," *The American Historian*, no. 8 (May 2016), 21-25.

Acknowledgments

Being a faculty member at San José State University's iSchool, our nation's largest Graduate School of Information, has furnished me with the good fortune of contributing to the professional preparation of progressive students eager for and capable of mounting influential roles in YA services, LIS, and beyond. The promise they exhibit and the support they need to assume leadership continually fuel my own pedagogical and scholarly endeavors. I am particularly grateful to my annual INFORMATION 261A and INFORMATION 285 students.

I am extremely proud of my role as Faculty Advisor of SJSU's only double-blind, graduate-level, open-source *Student Research Journal*, where it is my privilege to work with exemplary students serving as our Editorial Team. Three of these talented LIS students went above and beyond their *SRJ* roles to help me edit this manuscript. I would like to thank in particular Rachel Greggs, Stephanie Akau, and Lisa Lowdermilk.

I would also like to thank an array of friends, colleagues, and associates. Among these are colleagues of the Youth Services Special Interest Group of the Association of Library and Information Science Educators; the iSchool's Youth Services Program Advisory Committee (which I chair); the Advisory Board of *Voice of Youth Advocates* and its Editor-in-Chief, Rose-Mary Ludt; Rachel Chance of ALA Editions and copyeditor Amy Knauer; Dr. Mike Males, and Zenas Bliss.

I would also like to take this opportunity to acknowledge legacy debts I owe to a few people who inspired my continued commitment to YA professional practice and research since the day I entered the field: The Honorable Patrick Jones, Dr. Mary K. Chelton, and "The Chief" Cathi Dunn McRae. These three became the principal igniters of my professional interests, endorsers of my frequent dismay, and perpetual models of integrity and dedication to public service, and, most especially, advocates for advancing professional-grade library service to young people.

INTRODUCTION

Making the Case for Transforming

Anthony Bernier

Every generation of American professional experts sends up "clear-cut" answers, its own doctrinal certainties and Olympian universalisms, about "youth." In stepping back to examine the history of the "child sciences" since their invention, largely in the late nineteenth century, two competing visions or discursive constructions about young adults (adolescents, teenagers) have dominated library and information science (LIS). One expert discourse articulates the degree to which society should exercise *power and control* over the young; the other favors a particular notion of *freedom*. Together, however, they form a powerful consensus view of young adults.

Each doctrine advances its own governing vision of youth rooted in assumptions and truth claims tethering goals to particular procedures, techniques, policies, methods, strategies, and resources for achieving them. This introduction to the second edition of *Transforming Young Adult Services* contextualizes and coheres the essays to argue that while there certainly are distinctions to be drawn between late-nineteenth-century and contemporary visions of youth, these distinctions share more than may at first be apparent. Another insight percolating up in analyzing visions of young adults (hereafter "YAs") is that LIS has only ever *borrowed* from these early discourses; it has yet to advance a vision of its own.

Stated more specifically, today's LIS vision of YAs largely echoes the influence of developmental psychology advanced originally over a century ago rather than having developed its own vision rooted in contemporary thinking or its own institutional obligations and responsibilities.

This introduction, and the studies that follow, trace this legacy. This collection inquires after the implications and consequences these assumptions visit on LIS's strategic and institutional imaginations in delivering YA services. The analysis grows from an assessment that LIS has primarily pursued its connection to youth focused mainly on how YAs fit within the life of the library rather than examining how the library can matter in the life of youth.[1] The collective analysis emerging from these essays attempts to cultivate and prefigure future LIS teaching, practice, and research about whom libraries feel they serve when they seek to serve YAs.

A core argument advanced here is that perpetuating and uncritically reproducing dated and derivative views of youth constitute an ongoing intellectual failure of LIS to incorporate theoretical and contemporary approaches.[2] In avoiding engagement with critical social theory in general, and YA librarianship in particular, LIS has defaulted into borrowing essentially unchallenged century-old visions of youth rather than constituting a vision more suited to its own distinct mission in the here and now.[3]

This collection thus applies directly to YA services the observations of Gloria Leckie and John Buschman that "there is a tendency in LIS to adapt theoretical perspectives from other disciplines, often doing so without a critical or complete understanding."[4] This debilitating avoidance has delayed and deflected LIS's institutional advancement and the development of its professional capacities, has visited decades of dated approaches on the nation's young people, and has thus contributed to LIS's lagging far behind today's best thinking on youth.

THE NINETEENTH CENTURY AND THE WALLPAPER THREAT

Why, I have seen wallpaper which must lead a boy brought up under its influence to a career of crime; you should not have such incentives to sin lying about your drawing-room.

—Oscar Wilde, 1882

Historical analysis of Western civilization's emerging views about distinguishing young people from adults properly points back as far as the late seventeenth century's Enlightenment. Prior to that time children received about the same treatment as adults.

Two key figures began to establish a new and fundamentally distinct role for young people within the family and society: English philosopher John Locke and French political philosopher Jean-Jacques Rousseau. In ways not too distinct from prevalent contemporary views of youth, Locke argued that parental (adult) intervention was required to impart and model intellectual reasoning to children/youth assumed to be inherently "incomplete, inadequate, and imperfect."[5] In contrast to Locke, Rousseau argued that youth should rather be left alone, in their "natural" innocence, to discover and make sense of the world at their own pace. Rousseau proposed that children represented a *tabula rasa* (a blank slate) upon which experience would inscribe a coherent and rational interpretation of the world.

The strategies advocated by Locke and Rousseau differed, of course. However, more important for our purposes is to understand what they *share*: a growing preoccupation with the inherent and natural differences youth represented vis-à-vis adults.

Still, it is not until the late nineteenth century when Western culture began to increasingly aspire to influential claims of "scientific" certitude about these presumptively essential differences. Science rendered its claims through empirical or positivist inquiry (today we might call it "modernist" inquiry) and tried through this approach to rationalize and become "professional" about raising the young. This period, too, produced two intellectual giants, both, significantly, psychologists: G. Stanley Hall and the less well-known Emmett L. Holt.[6]

Separately and together, Hall and Holt successfully influenced child rearing for generations of mothers, nurses, caregivers, social workers, faith leaders, journalists, criminologists, educators, and policy makers. Together they sought in particular to steel mother and child against the unnerving influences of rapidly industrialized urban life. Together they reflect the discourse on youth that continues to reverberate down through today's LIS practice and research.

On the one hand, G. Stanley Hall, echoing Rousseau, represents the more famous "freedom and intimacy" child-rearing and "child-saving" discourse of the late nineteenth century (see table I.1). Freedom and intimacy's positivist claims to "expert knowledge" emerged to exercise influential cultural power flowing from them. Considered more a "romantic"

TABLE I.1 G. Stanley Hall's Universal Claims about the Needs of Youth

G. STANLEY HALL / "FREEDOM AND INTIMACY"	
• Autonomy	• "Liberty" and experimentation
• Nature	• "Child-centered"
• Love and "bonding"	• Progressive/evolutionary

than a rationalist, Hall combined something of a post-Darwinian biology (nature adapts and evolves) with a proto-Freudian psychology (unconscious energies). He defined adolescence in particular as a "developmental turning point, a larval stage" in human experience.[7] Hall's views, it should be noted, included strong doses of those particularly Freudian preoccupations with gender and sex.

Hall parted company with the Rousseauian tradition, however. Where Rousseau advocated that youth be left largely on their own to discover the world, Hall advanced a powerful and increasingly popular notion about specific kinds of adult interventions he felt youth required to achieve productive adulthood.

In Hall's view, youthful passions required channeling. In one of his several appearances before national audiences of librarians, for instance, he warned attendees at the 1919 American Library Association conference that girls' books must be "calculated to fit them for domestic life or womanly vocations." More generally he wrote that all youth were "emotionally unstable, and must have excitement" or the consequences would result in youth seeking excitement on their own in "sex or drink."[8] For Hall, unlike for Rousseau, youth "nature" required taming.

Here we can clearly observe the birth of what I have termed today's youth development industrial complex (hereafter YDIC). The YDIC agenda, promoting a vision of youth virtually indistinguishable in youth services today, represents an ever-burgeoning institutional paradigm constituted in an elaborate and sprawling apparatus of career interests, pedantic ideology, and age-segregationist procedures ostensibly intended to deflect the biological "instability" (or nature) hard-wired, Hall argued, into all youth.

Consistent with other soaring tropes of the nineteenth century, Hall also coined the provocative term "adolescent race." Conflating pseudo-Darwinian notions of racial and adolescent inferiority (compared to only idealized white "adulthood"), he argued that society needed to "civilize" youth in ways not too dissimilar from the ways in which other "childlike and savage races" were thought to require "civilizing" during this time. This nineteenth-century age/race/gender synthesis reverberates endlessly in today's views of presumed antisocial youth behaviors regarding "youth violence," "teen pregnancy," "teen substance abuse," "the teen brain," and a seamlessly endless list of moral panics, including today's hot-button issues surrounding so-called "youth cyberbullying" and "sexting" and the growing screeds of "screen abolitionists." According to Hall's science, without constant adult surveillance and civilizing programming efforts, such as those promulgated even in today's YDIC, society would suffer the consequences of innate youthful savagery.[9]

In contrast to Hall, psychologist Emmett L. Holt launched the "power and control" regime. Echoing Locke from the late seventeenth century, Holt advanced a rubric of child-rearing strategies rooted in rationalized scientific management. But unlike Hall's "softer" approach, Holt advocated a strict and didactic catechism of adult controls, routines, regulations, and rules (see table I.2).

TABLE I.2 Emmett L. Holt's Universal Claims about the Needs of Youth

EMMETT L. HOLT / "POWER AND CONTROL"	
• Conformity	• Prevention
• Nurture	• Parent-centered
• Hierarchy of authority	• Traditional/conventional

This "harder" approach deployed a rhetoric that, in effect, particularly elevated middle-class mothers from conventional domestic roles—effectively promoting bourgeois motherhood from the familiar sphere as a domestic manager to a more powerful, semipublic, and paraprofessional child-rearing specialist. It was mothers the young required, according to Holt, to model and teach "steadiness to fortify them against a disorderly—and ever more materialistic, distracting world." "In these days," wrote Holt, "of factory and locomotive whistles, trolley cars and automobiles, music boxes and the numberless mechanical toys in the nursery, door-bells and telephones in the house," sensory bombardment threatened youth maturation into adulthood and thus threatened the order of Victorian society itself.[10]

For Holt, only a strong, consistent, rational, and regular regimen ensured that youth yielded up "compliance without conflict" in the face of modern society's demands. If achieved, however, Holt promised that youth would mature into sturdy and independent middle-class adults.

Recognizing Holt's "harder" approach as an early predecessor of today's "zero tolerance" attitudes and policies does not require much imagination. Where G. Stanley Hall wished to nurture youth into compliance with Victorian middle-class propriety, Holt meant to extract compliance and conformity through the raw assertion of adult power.

While Holt's views clearly differed in the definition, intensity, and degree of control he urged adults to apply to youth, his greater resonance with Hall is apparent but frequently overlooked (see table I.3). Both built their theoretical foundations on nineteenth-century scientific positivism aimed at rationalizing cultural practices. They shared confidence in the capacity of empirical science to identify and implement universal and biological patterns. Both Holt and Hall viewed youth as inherently flawed and unfit for society. They both perceived youth as dangerously susceptible to behaviors closely associated with the great unwashed masses of laborers and immigrants then teeming in American cities as well as to the problems posed, they felt, by the "darker" races and women. Both envisioned youth maturing or successfully "civilized" only with unqualified dependency on adults.

Here again, however, it is important, especially for an analysis of LIS's vision of YAs, to make significant historical connections. As was true of Locke and Rousseau, both Hall and Holt advanced different strategies to deliver youth into adulthood. They all concentrated their various interventions upon imagining youth in the same way: as inherently, biologically, naturally, different and "other" from adult society. All viewed young people necessarily as a breed apart, as inherently compromised, damaged, and deficient *sub*adults.

Holt and Hall differed from each other only in how they proposed to fix or "solve" the problems they assumed were a natural and universal challenge to youth maturation. Ultimately, the innovation they advanced in the late nineteenth century was confidence that they had discovered, respectively, how to "fix" these problems.

Examining these centuries-old concepts and contemporary practice in light of more recent and burgeoning critical theory and scholarship on the history of youth, however,

TABLE I.3 The Nineteenth-Century Origins of Scientific "Youth"

G. STANLEY HALL AND EMMETT L. HOLT "FREEDOM AND INTIMACY" MEETS "POWER AND CONTROL"
• Based theories on nineteenth-century positivism and empirical modernist science • Claimed to have found universal and biologically determined patterns • Created visions of youth consistent with similar visions of marginalized populations (Native Americans, women, African Americans, immigrants) • Focused on only differences of youth compared to adults (white, middle-class adults)

makes it easy to detect the similarities between them.[11] Unfortunately, LIS has exercised little scrutiny of, or even curiosity about, the service implications of these legacies for daily practice or research.

THE TWENTIETH CENTURY: A CONTINUING CONSENSUS OF DEFICIT AND DIFFERENCE

The "success" or "failure" of all these aspirations, to dilute or deflect the presumptive bestial instincts lurking within all youth, remains debatable among historians, policy makers, and youth studies scholars. What has not been interrogated until rather recently, however, is the consensus that impugns such *natural* impulses to youth in the first place.

There has been even less critical commentary on the ways in which institutions like libraries have been enlisted to implement services encrusted with these assumptions.[12] The exercise of institutional authority and adult power (as manifested in the YDIC) continues, viewed as a necessary, rational, and scientific response to exorcising the Manchurian demons threatening to erupt at a moment's notice in any youth. In connecting this earlier nineteenth-century vision of youth to today, historian Stephen Mintz observed this:

> We may cling to the idea in the abstract [that youth is valuable in and of itself], but in practice American culture—oriented toward mastery and control—views childhood as a "project," in which the young must develop the skills, knowledge, and character traits necessary for adulthood success. . . . Those who cannot adjust are cast adrift. . . .[13]

Throughout the twentieth century and into the present, professionals in youth work closely adhered to this foundational youth-as-breed-apart construction. Clergy, early in the twentieth century, representing the "soft" approach, as it were, advocated training and competitive boxing programs to divert the otherwise presumptive wayward drift of urban boys. Teachers, perhaps ironically, dispensed the "hard" approach through corporal punishment. Other "solutions" to deflect the inherent savage tendencies in youth included the inventions of groups such as the Boy Scouts, Girl Scouts, Woodcraft Rangers, Campfire Girls, YWCA's Y-Teens, and a wide variety of extracurricular programs.[14]

While the specific history of an LIS response to YA service since the late nineteenth century remains largely unstudied, libraries did certainly provide services to young people. And while the notion of what constituted "service" varies a great deal, the scant scholarship on historical LIS YA services largely recalls the experiences of children's librarians as they, chiefly middle-class white women, sought to carve out professional status from within the institution. For historical treatments of library services provided specifically to YAs, however, we possess even less scholarly analysis.[15]

What evidence we do have about services for YAs points to how it was not until late in the second half of the twentieth century when LIS began to institutionally question the unchanging nature of youth embedded in the universal and ahistorical assumptions promulgated by Hall, Holt, and developmental psychology in general. Indeed, youth practitioners in many fields and various occupations began to see a more varied landscape in which *some* youth adjusted better to adult society than did others.

Professionals responsible for working with youth, those continuing in the "soft" tradition, began to develop an arsenal of programmatic responses and interventions to assist youth. Those continuing in the "hard" tradition, on the other hand, began implementing their own lexicon of age-based municipal injunctions, codes, curfews, and truancy ordinances, among other statutory measures, to punish the others.

Neither approach, however, questioned the core assumption about youth as inherently flawed social beings or the preoccupation with only the differences between youth and idealized adulthood. Some youth were perceived to require merely less supervision to become mature adults while others required more punishment, or programming, to keep them on the straight and narrow.

Thus, as in many domains of rapidly professionalizing youth services (social work, psychology, education, and criminology, among others), librarianship gradually adopted the "youth at risk" and "prevention" discourse to manifest and rationalize their interventions with the youth they feared were walking that razor's edge between middle-class propriety and the uncivilized abyss.[16]

LIS also adopted this "soft" approach and engineered service techniques, skills, methods, and practices based on that programmatic model. Libraries aligned resources to civilize youth by deploying the cultural weapons at their disposal: an arsenal of moral suasion we might consider as something of a "second curriculum" (one subordinate to school) delivered through the culturally superior claims afforded them through the promotion of literacy, reading, and books, as well as their relatively unchallenged powerful command of library space.

In the latter portion of the nineteenth century, library luminaries such as Frederick Perkins articulated the library's broad social mission with youth: "while not expressly a school of manners and morals," the library was "much and closely concerned in maintaining a high standard in both."[17] Contemporary service, however, continues to parrot the tradition, as William Lukenbill accurately observes: "Understanding this to be a *primary social responsibility*, librarians easily condemned as harmful to youth certain types of literature and other forms of mass entertainment . . . while at the same time supporting only literature judged by them to be of higher cultural value."[18]

More recently, and particularly since the late 1980s, YA librarians set out to produce their own brand of "at risk" program and service offerings. In partial response to the 1983 U.S. presidential report, "A Nation at Risk," libraries moved to address the mounting panic about the educational performances of the nation's young. Here the basic programming model recruited youth, largely to serve as polite audiences for enlightened or even rogue adult presentations (often by librarians themselves), to receive curricular content reminiscent of classroom instruction and bent, as always, toward the preoccupations of adults. Programs sought to help youth stay in school, stay off drugs, get better test scores, eschew violence and gangs, avoid sex, pregnancy, smoking, and, most recently, focus on "learning" and gaining "skills."[19]

The claims and aspirations embedded in LIS's programmatic assumptions (focus on only the differences between YAs and adults, for example, and the belief that antisocial behaviors in youth are natural) remained obvious and explicit. These assumptions, however, cannot bear up under questioning, especially as evidence documenting actual and unprecedented national levels of academic achievement and behavior revealed how little youth actually are "at risk" (see chapter 12). Kids were not behaving badly. Indeed, as critical youth scholar Mike Males (among growing numbers of others) has been assessing for decades, "It does not seem to matter that the wild scares and save-the-kids remedies do not turn out to be justified by a reasonable examination of information available."[20]

Nevertheless, evidence proved unpersuasive, indeed irrelevant, to the unfurling youth-at-risk juggernaut. Moreover, LIS exhibited little evidence that it knew very much about producing youth-at-risk programs, knew even less about how to evaluate them, and has never causally linked particular library programming with specific behavior outcomes—good or bad. All this goes largely unremarked upon to this day. What we do know, in the few instances of actual research, is that the field continues to claim far more than it can prove.[21]

Subsequent innovations and changes since the late 1980s witnessed library YA service professionals pledged to another emerging wave of seemingly different but nevertheless borrowed discourse—slightly different discourse; same basic assumptions. During this period, rather than continuing to view youth as at-risk recipients of professional commitments and aspirations, LIS institutionally adopted an intervention paradigm widely known as "youth development," wherein adult experts carefully cultivated, arrayed, and deployed community "assets" so that access to these "building blocks" would guide youth toward maturing as "healthy adults."[22]

As alluded to earlier in reference to the YDIC, the concept of youth development, an innocuous-sounding term, performs as a means to define generally a beneficent process of preparing young people for the challenges of adolescence and adulthood through particular activities and experiences promoting social, ethical, emotional, physical, and cognitive competencies. As with many innocuous-sounding agendas, the particulars remain difficult to pin down by definition or in measurements demonstrating validity.

More to the point in this discussion about LIS's vision of YAs, however, are underlying assumptions about young people, institutions, and society that endure unquestioned decade after decade. Further, this approach is so totalizing and normalized in LIS, so accepted, so unquestioned, that the term "youth development" itself need not even appear in the indexes of the profession's foundational texts and resources even as its hegemonic dominance appears on nearly every page.[23] The youth development paradigm also appears prominent in all of the policy, resource, and aspirational documents advanced by YALSA, the American Library Association's young adult division.[24] In no instance, however, does the concept engage analytical attention or critical contextualization.

Under the youth development approach, LIS practitioners, assumed to be more progressive, pursued a strategy wherein selected youth would play more "participatory" or "partnership" roles in their libraries.[25] Of course, these terms, like youth development itself, serve more as free-floating signifiers by seldom offering clear definition, measurement, or evaluation.

Still, for LIS, youth development represented a rather radical shift. No longer would progressive institutions imagine all youth as "at risk" but, rather, as valuable community "partners" and resources—resources, nevertheless, requiring training in and acquisition of discrete, predetermined, prescriptive priorities, opportunities, and, most especially, "skills."

Libraries subsequently instigated various schema in which some young peoples' participation and involvement were, to varying degrees, actively solicited. This is the era of burgeoning teen advisory groups, teen leadership councils, and other configurations in which small and tentative clusters of selected youth directly engage library staff in various discussions about the delivery of YA services.[26]

While more progressive institutions began to adopt youth development, the transition across LIS moved slowly and unevenly. Indeed, confusion, conflation, and ignorance regarding the ideological transition this paradigm represented remain widespread. One is as likely to encounter libraries deploying the "at risk" approach as those using the youth development paradigm. Some deploy both simultaneously without recognizing the difference.[27]

Those libraries informed by the YDIC agenda attempt to fortify youth with skills and positive attributes.[28] The so-called ideological shift introduced by LIS's growing adoption of the youth development model, however, one ostensibly inverting the youth-at-risk approach's exclusive concentration on preventing negative youth behaviors, bears further examination.[29]

THE YOUTH CONSENSUS AND "PATH DEPENDENCY"

The key term in LIS's still uneven transition, from the "at risk" model to youth development, however, remains *ostensible*. Because in addition to the ideological patterns cited earlier, the century-old positivist master narrative governing LIS's broad and deeply rooted consensus about youth persists as an overarching conceptualization of young people as defined only through difference from adults and if not dangerous then irreducibly and essentially "other." Youth continue to be envisioned as an entire demographic category forever plagued by crisis, turmoil, need, and difference.

The totality of youth identity remains defined by their universal, essentialized, and troubled difference from adults. Be they viewed as biologically different from adults (Locke and Rousseau); be they undeveloped and uncivilized subadults (Hall and Holt); be they partially or even sporadically damaged ("youth at risk"); or be they lacking the requisite tools and skills to compete in today's economy as thriving mature adults (youth development), youth are nevertheless viewed as living a fundamentally different and marginal experience—one presumably always less-than and ever at odds with normative and idealized adult community. And this "difference" has been interpreted nearly always (as was true historically regarding nonwhites, women, immigrants, and the non-gender conforming) in opposition to and conflict with mainstream society.[30]

It was, after all, G. Stanley Hall's study of youth in the late nineteenth century that characterized youth itself as a phase of "storm and stress" (from the German *Sturm und Drang*) to fuse developmental biology with the social experience of young people. The operative feature of this continuing view assumes that conflict between youth and parents, youth and other adults, youth and authority, radical mood swings, and risk-taking behavior (including latent predilections toward violence and disruptive behaviors) are normal.

As detailed earlier, more recent interpretations envision all youth, during this "storm and stress" conflict mode, in a symmetrical paradox—rendering a view of youth either, sentimentally, as biological innocents (i.e., "It's not their fault; their brains are not yet developed") or as beings consciously imbued with supervolition, -power, and -agency (i.e., "They're dangerous and they make poor choices"). One week it is panic about being victimized by homicidal bullying; the next, assertions rationalizing risk taking due to biological differences (such as the "teen brain" discourse).[31]

After more than a century of these unquestioned assumptions of youth deficiency and less-than status, there is little evidence that LIS even notices these naturalized and essentialized characterizations of youth in today's popular media, culture, and scholarship.[32] Yet LIS incorporates this consensus seamlessly into instruction, practice, policy, and research.

Thus, as if hopping from one foot to the other, we continue to marginalize and relegate youth within this bifurcated world of false binary opposites: innocent/guilty, immature/adult. In either case, the consistent focus on the inherent and essential deficiencies of youth continues unquestioned.

In beginning to critically evaluate and historicize the operative assumptions at the heart of this continuing consensus, it is useful to ask: In what field of social science or professional practice have universal claims over a century old remained unchallenged? And what consequences ensue when an entire profession continually reproduces and implements those assumptions systematically in daily practice and research? This reaction is reminiscent of Daniel Macallair's observation of the remarkable resistance to change he found in the institutional history of youth corrections. He characterized the circumstances as "path dependency" in which a traditional practice continues even when more effective alternatives have been identified.[33]

Table I.4 illustrates some of the ways in which the rhetoric on youth discourse plays out in current language.

TABLE I.4 Contemporary Language Describing Century-Old Assumptions about Youth

RHETORIC OF THE YOUTH CONSENSUS	
Sentimental View of Youth	**Youth as Superagents**
Innocent	Dangerous
Dutiful	Entitled
Passive	Aggressive
Truthful	Deceitful
Precious	Frenetic
Victim	Perpetrator
Needy	Headstrong
At-risk	Privileged
Asset	Liability
Creative	Unimaginative
Individual	Peer predators
Private/secretive	Exhibitionist
Self-conscious	Calculating
Rudderless	Plotting and cunning
"Gifted"	Underperforming

Taken together the consensus on youth (YDIC) remains alive and well in LIS. Indeed, while there have been slight changes in tactics over time, LIS has uncritically enjoined over a century of child science grounded in dated modernist approaches.

More important still, rather than developing its own vision of youth, grounded in research aimed at achieving its own legitimate institutional mission, LIS has unquestioningly and nearly exclusively relied on the influence of only one field of scholarly inquiry: developmental psychology. The consequence of this dependency led LIS to adopt and reproduce universal, ahistorical, biologically determined, and socially inept assumptions about its putative youth user.

Literary critic and scholar Kent Baxter connected these conceptual and historical dots well when he observed, "These commonplace beliefs about the developmental stage construct adolescence as a significant threat unless the energies and desires associated with it are correctly funneled into a productive, and morally acceptable, activity."[34] Baxter's research leads to the conclusion that since publication of the *Ragged Dick* series of fictional stories in the nineteenth century, libraries have positioned reading and library use among these "funneling" strategies.

Engaging these historic and contemporary concerns with the aid of critical social theory, such as that offered by Baxter and others, might better explain why, decade after decade, so many young people report how little libraries matter to them.[35] How, given the vision the institution holds of them, could another outcome even appear plausible?

LIS suffers hitherto unacknowledged liabilities in reclining exclusively on the dated assumptions ricocheting from developmental psychology. Such an approach hinders LIS's connections with today's YAs and ignores the growing theoretical influences and insights of critical youth studies. Unless and until LIS applies new theoretical insights to how it envisions YAs, such thinking will never be better incorporated into the mainstream of LIS, in general, nor will LIS research be likely to contribute to broader youth studies. Instead, this dated approach would explain why youth studies scholarship continues to ignore LIS interventions with young people even after well over a century of serving them.[36]

CRACKS IN THE CONSENSUS: APPROACHING YA SERVICES CRITICALLY

While deserving of much critical interrogation, evolutions in the youth sciences since the late eighteenth century have not been negligible. True, early theorists from John Locke to G. Stanley Hall viewed all youth as inherently damaged; still, they generally shared optimistic views about saving youth from their assumed biological flaws and protecting them from dangerous influences. "Youth at risk" viewed only selected youth as damaged. And the more contemporary paradigm of "youth development" gestures at constituting youth as "partners" in building "assets" toward achieving mature adulthood—though even this vision nevertheless requires careful cultivation by institutions and adult interventions before youth can achieve maturity in the competitive marketplace.

Thus, this historical master narrative about youth came to understand that biology does not *necessarily* foreclose on the future of all youth to grow, learn, mature, and "develop." These innovations certainly rolled back views of youth prior to the eighteenth century's envisioning youth as unchanging creatures with little differentiation between the teenage years and adulthood.

Consequently, LIS and other youth-serving professions owe these early ideological influences a great debt.[37] Where LIS, for instance, formerly sought to justify YA services by identifying and quantifying particular skills through "output measures," for example, progressive institutions today look to "out*come* measures" to defend and advance programmatic offerings and resource allocations.[38]

Nevertheless, the institution continues to be rooted only in envisioning and addressing institutionally defined user "needs" and deficits and in the teaching of clinically predetermined and curricular-oriented skills.[39] This compulsion adheres as well to recent notions of the "makerspace," in which skill development is even more targeted—this time toward technical dexterity.[40]

What LIS has not done, however, is take full and critical measure of this prevailing consensus (i.e., what coheres the youth sciences and its assumptions). It has failed to acknowledge the hegemonic vision of youth it adopted wholesale from the YDIC paradigm. Further, it fails to engineer a vision more responsive to its own institutional mission. Even the more recent rendition of the YDIC, "*positive* youth development," manifests this consensus and continues to ignore unexamined assumptions about youth across these many decades.[41] The YDIC hegemony, no matter its name, ever imagines youth only as half empty and unprepared for future adulthood. It is a consensus baked deep into LIS teaching, practice, policy, and research. Indeed, these assumptions persist as the prevailing assumptions. And they dramatically contrast and obstruct the evolution of a vision of youth as fully embodied in their present here-and-now moment.

While the youth consensus remains strong, it is also rapidly approaching a conceptual crossroads in facing the liabilities inherent in its derived vision of today's youth.[42] Thus, it remains incumbent upon the profession, particularly students engaged in the study of YA librarianship, to recognize that despite the not unimportant changes wrought by historical assumptions, there is much more cohering these seemingly different approaches than there is separating them.

The following section reflects on some of the major liabilities LIS sustains because of its uncritical symbiosis with the YDIC. Also, through examination of more recent critical social theory, it addresses a substantial list of questions and concerns about the YDIC. These concerns and issues promise to equip LIS students, practitioners, and researchers to address the fundamental question about how LIS should envision today's young people. Addressing this question promises also to help LIS pursue its own institutional mission and to articulate an LIS-specific vision of today's youth.

GRAND TRUTHS EXAMINED: EIGHT LIABILITIES

Numbering among the liabilities inflicted on YA services because of its reliance on the YDIC are eight chief concerns. Further, to the matter addressed in this collection, it should be noted that LIS does not conduct actual primary or evidence-based research on the psychological, biological, neurobiological, anthropological, sociological, or historical experiences of young people. These activities lie outside of LIS's professional and disciplinary boundaries and should thus require some measure of modesty about the claims that libraries make regarding their impacts on young people. More importantly still, neither does LIS conduct research on the efficacy of library services (or lack thereof) in contributing to the stated goals of the youth development approach. Thus, it should be incumbent upon LIS to exercise caution in measuring its claims, language, concepts, models, and generalizations in envisioning young people.[43]

Youth for All Time

The first liability LIS suffers under YDIC hegemony is that few grand transhistorical or pancultural generalizations, such as those articulated in youth development, hold up under universal or historical scrutiny. Further, LIS currently advances no evidence about youth to the contrary. The sweeping and universal generalizations LIS thus indulges to describe or envision "youth" or "young adults" or "teens," and the discrete skills LIS assumes they need, must be contingent and qualified by historical circumstances.[44] Yet in simply adopting YDIC's agenda, LIS perpetuates the reproduction of systematically pathologizing, objectifying, and problematizing nearly every nook and cranny of all youth experience throughout history.

Young people as a group are as dynamic, complex, and diverse as any broad demographic population. Not all youth require the same skills, for instance, or value as essential identifying "neighborhood boundaries," as called for in the Search Institute's "40 Developmental Assets," the single most-relied-upon institutional source in YA services.[45] Nor have all youth "needed" or desired many of the other experiences that document prescribes. Yet LIS's legacy consensus on youth development holds fast to these assumptions and prescriptions, particularly the list of "assets" the Search Institute prescribes for all youth, in all cultures, in all communities, and under all material circumstances.

This consensus also leads LIS to ignore even the agency young people have exhibited in library history. Recent historical scholarship illustrates, for example, how high school-aged youth built a successful movement to racially integrate public libraries in the early 1960s.[46] LIS might thus first consider revising its dependency on the current and simplistic ahistorical constructions of all youth embedded in the YDIC.

Youth as Ever "Other"

A second concern defining this century-old ideological consensus about youth is, of course, that young people continue to be envisioned as inherently deficient—a "problem" population—by adult society, rendering youth susceptible to a process sociologists refer to as "othering."[47] Where G. Stanley Hall and Emmett L. Holt viewed all youth as biologically flawed specimens, the more contemporary discourse of youth service experts and professionals largely views youth as inherently lacking the "skills" and knowledge necessary to succeed in the competitive adult world.

This is not a new or original critique. As early as the 1990s, critical youth scholars Allison James and Alan Prout began to see the conceptual contradictions inherent in the youth development approach. In their critique, they wrote, youth were portrayed "like the laboratory rat, as being at the mercy of external stimuli: passive and conforming."[48] More recently, and informed by anthropology, sociology, and critical social theory, youth studies scholars increasingly share the following critique: "Developmental psychology foster[s] images of the child as an incomplete, malleable organism."[49] In the LIS derivation, youth are constructed as inherently and especially *informationally* flawed.[50]

Youth Always of the Future

A third concern with LIS's youth consensus remains its obsession with an idealized future. Informed only by the YDIC, the youth consensus parses and evaluates all behavioral, cognitive, and skill "development," indeed all youth experience, through an established and linear sequence pointed exclusively at future status. All experience is filtered through and directed toward some distant and imagined mature adulthood. Desired skills include developing "responsibility," "planning and decision making," "resistance skills," and something called "restraint."

As with other developmentalist assumptions, the focus on the future contains little recognition of the present moment youth actually inhabit. In this particular criticism, the notion of "youth development" is revealed to be not chiefly concerned with the lived experience or meanings of youth at all—but only the future of an idealized self-actualized adulthood. As Sandy Fraser, from England's School of Health and Social Welfare has put it, youth "have been valued and understood in term of being 'a work in progress' towards adulthood, concerning what they might become and not who they presently are."[51]

Educational critic Jonathan Kozol expresses skepticism about this assumption more poetically when he writes, "Childhood . . . [should not be] merely basic training for utilitarian adulthood. It should have some claims upon our mercy, not for its future value to the economic interests of competitive societies but for its present value as a perishable piece of life itself."[52]

Developmental Psychology's Dominion

A fourth concern defining the liabilities for LIS regarding this ideological consensus, of youth serving as only a training ground for the future, emanates from the undue and nearly unchallenged dominance of youth services and youth studies research by the field of developmental psychology.[53] Both Hall and Holt were renowned psychologists (as were their mentors and successors). Little of the power that psychology wields over the agendas in today's youth studies research and practice, however, has diminished since those nineteenth-century origins.

The manifestations and deep consequences of this particular circumstance in LIS are many. One readily observable component of how psychology dominates youth work is how it is tethered to nearly an excessive focus on pathological youth behavior. Youth behavior is measured nearly exclusively against a mythical "norm" of idealized values such as complete abstinence from drinking, violence, smoking, drugs, sex, and impure thoughts. Any cursory examination of popular *or* scholarly publications, going back decades, reveals an unbroken legacy obsessed with destructive, antisocial, and counterproductive behaviors—in other words, behaviors subversive of or in conflict with idealized adult culture and adult preoccupations.

In the meanwhile, the far more prevalent daily prosocial behaviors and achievements of the vast majority of ordinary youth go almost unremarked upon. Research nearly ignores the contributions youth make to society.

For its part, LIS research has largely lashed itself to psychology's disciplinary assumptions. Consequently, LIS's own vision concentrates nearly exclusively on the informational deficits youth presumably must overcome for some future self-actualization.[54]

LIS has not, however, merely limited its psychology-dominated vision of youth to serve as targets for intervention, instruction, and remediation. It has also promoted psychology's pathological view of youth to all library users. Library shelves bulge with these psychology-influenced titles (collected ostensibly to "support homework and school assignments" as well as for the general reader), and there is little evidence that libraries even exhibit awareness of this seemingly ever-present collection bias.[55]

It may, at long last, prove useful to pursue alternatives in imagining YAs as *subjects* in their own rights and on their own terms. This may prove more beneficial in achieving LIS goals than forever viewing them merely as objects of clinical diagnoses.[56]

Another dimension of psychology's dominance in shaping LIS's consensus on youth is the nearly unbroken concentration on youth as individuated beings.[57] For all its recent gestures toward advancing a more "positive" vision of young people, the YDIC paradigm does not seek, for instance, to develop critical consciousness about young peoples' own *collective* or shared roles, opportunities, or meanings in society.[58] Rather, it parses youth into individual experiences connected to seemingly universally neutral and normative assumptions of private behavior and achievement. LIS research and practice continue to envision young users largely as singular individuals seeking discrete access to information such as through summer reading programs, college readiness courses, or skills-based programs like after-school tutoring and examination preparation.[59]

This is a discourse presently on nodding terms with the culture's current neoconservative political agenda fetishizing private individual effort and eschewing the collective resources of civil society. In this worldview, private experience trumps any consideration of social or collective contexts and ignores disparate material circumstances, history, and cultural pluralism.

Consequently, we find YDIC ideology layered thick with requirements for proving how specific and ever more discrete activities and programs are necessary to impart particular utilitarian goals, objectives, and, most especially, measurable skills to "improve" or "prepare" individual youth. The YDIC exhibits little value for the ways in which youth collectively contribute to broader culture.[60] Critical youth scholar Sarah Zeller-Berkman encapsulated this particular notion well:

> This model [youth development] does not portray young people as assets to society, but only in need of society's attention, protection, guidance, and development. Although it is valuable to meet young people's needs, by not recognizing that young people are able to contribute to their own development *and that of others*, including adults, the model maintains traditional representations of youth.[61]

Indeed, libraries have, with few arguable exceptions, effectively resisted youth culture and its own demonstrated preferences for collective experience, group identity, building social capital through peer or family associations, or even community or social identity.[62] Libraries vividly manifest their view of youth in public space through the nearly universal library policy forbidding the sharing of a computer screen: the infamous "One Butt to a Chair" commandment. This policy, enforced daily by libraries across the nation, runs directly counter to the ways in which youth constantly demonstrate how they prefer to use library resources and occupy public space.[63]

Neither is this concentration on LIS's individuating the service vision unique to the current LIS youth consensus. In 1979, historian Miriam Braverman observed this propensity explicitly as reaching back to the beginning of YA services: "young people's librarians saw the book as a force contributing to individuality and to the making of better human beings through books."[64]

Material Circumstances: Social Class

A fifth concern about LIS's youth consensus, one growing from the YDIC's blinkered view on individuation, is that youth services professionals deploy this developmentalist discourse freighted with the ultimate aim of imparting particularly instrumental skills promoting a normative middle-class orientation. Child rearing for conscription or assimilation into the settled middle class encapsulates the ambition of the child sciences since their inception. The current paradigm, no matter its name, does not depart from that ambition.

Hegemonic YDIC values, dispensed either from the library or from other youth-serving agencies, attempt to reproduce idealized middle-class values, practices, behavior, and worldviews. This consensus, for instance, privileges middle-class views about the institutions of family, education, and work and about strict obedience to adult authority for setting and "monitoring" youth behavior.[65] It does not promote cultivating or valuing alternative experiences or opportunities, such as might come to pass in the experience of foster youth, for instance, or youth interested in pursuing occupations not requiring higher education, or those who participate in political movements to improve police conduct, advocate for gun control, or reform immigration policy.

Further, failure to consider material conditions highlights how the YDIC paradigm ignores critical systemic, social, or environmental links to assessing what youth "need." Consequently, LIS grapples little with the complexities of structural economic inequality or the material circumstances challenging youth on a daily basis. This pattern persists despite shamefully high rates of child poverty, youth unemployment, and grotesque income disparities translating into a nearly 20 percent poverty rate for the nation's youth.[66]

Beyond the already too narrow "digital divide" concept (worn conceptually threadbare with ubiquitous portable digital communication devices), there is little direct LIS response to neoconservatism's attack on public resources, massive deindustrialization, intergenerational poverty, or unemployment. As popular Harvard public policy professor Robert Putnam notes, "No serious observer doubts that the past 40 years have witnessed an almost unprecedented growth in income inequality in America."[67] The implications of these circumstances for YA services remain largely ignored by professionals coming nearly entirely from relative privilege.[68]

Social Identity

Concern regarding LIS's uncritical compliance with YDIC hegemony is that this middle-class vision is also rather silent on this sixth relevant aspect, social identity, such as racial and gender constructions. Despite decades of broader critical youth scholarship documenting the vagaries of sexism, misogyny, and racism, LIS's youth consensus remains essentially silent on such matters as cultural humility.[69]

Unless we assume that immigration status, gender identity, and racial oppression do not impact youth in libraries at all, we must systematically question the omission of the daily and enduring impacts of these influences upon young people and their connections, or nonconnections, with libraries. Nor does the LIS youth consensus address the impacts of the overwhelming predominance of white librarians on service to increasingly diverse youth populations.[70] And this concern, of course, does not even take into account the many abuses of adult power, on daily public display in social and political institutions. Is that the "mature adulthood" to which YDIC aspires for all youth?

Bringing the State Back In

Not unrelated to the YDIC's blindness to the impacts on youth of social class and material circumstances is a seventh conceptual liability for LIS: an inexplicable avoidance of the role the state plays (for good and for ill) in the experience of ordinary youth. Government enormously figures into how youth understand society—starting with the local schools they are compelled to attend from kindergarten through high school, to the extracurricular programs in which they participate, to the parks and other amusements sponsored in part or in whole by local, state, or county government, to the very libraries in their communities. Government also plays important roles in protecting youth from various harms and dangers.[71] Further still, the YDIC also fails to enter into a critical engagement with the ways in which the state increasingly *withdraws* or even fails to provide support for youth, such as in current immigration policy.[72]

In relying so thoroughly and uncritically on hegemonic YDIC assumptions, LIS thus also sidesteps its responsibility for analysis regarding the library as an actor with state authority. Local, city, and county governments fund libraries. They receive federal subsidies and grants.

All of this, of course, constitutes librarians and support staff as government workers. As such, there may well be implications for professional YA practice worth investigating. What proportion of publically supported library resources compose an equitable share devoted specifically to YA services? How would that portion be calculated and evaluated? What professional roles determine these calculations and measures? What professional obligations exist for librarians (and support staff), as government workers, in perpetuating, reproducing, complying with, or confronting inequitable YA resource allocations?

Youth Compared to What?

Finally, an eighth liability for LIS appears in how the YDIC constructs youth's putative opposite: adulthood. Inasmuch as LIS's unwavering commitment to how youth development hegemony freezes a universal vision of all youth as other and different from adults across all time and space, it also necessarily freezes its universal binary opposite. Not only does this consensus lock in a static deficit position with respect to culture and history for youth; it also constructs a static notion of infallible and idealized adulthood. The YDIC's exclusive concentration on "youth" avoids consideration of or context for adult influence (either individually or collectively) on youth other than as objective and benign facilitators for dispensing and supporting skill acquisition and wisdom. Neither, of course, does YDIC hegemony allow for youth influence on adults.

More careful attention to headline news might council how not all adults deploy their age-based privilege and power with wisdom and equanimity. Perhaps "scrutinizing adult authority" might be added to the Search Institute's list of 40 Developmental Assets?

Taken together the YDIC's hegemonic dominance vastly overemphasizes the shady side of youth. It envisions youth as only ever a project in progress. Further, it focuses exclusively on differentiating youth from the adult community. The LIS consensus, in adhering so closely to this paradigm, thus ignores the implications of institutional, historic, material, and cultural realities that also daily shape the lives, experience, and identities of youth as individuals as well as in groups. LIS's near ecumenical implementation of this paradigm does little to systematically acknowledge the complexities of youth experience or contribute to the well-being of the youth community. Nor does it advance the institution's value to youth studies. Consequently, masses of ordinary youth daily disregard libraries as offering them access to information services to create their own meanings or contribute cultural moments about their lives in the here and now.

NOTES

1. This metaphor applies a more general LIS critique rendered by Wayne Wiegand; see W. Wiegand, "To Reposition a Research Agenda: What American Studies Can Teach the LIS Community about the Library in the Life of the User," *Library Quarterly* 73, no. 4 (October 2003): 369–82.
2. Indeed, librarianship does not exist alone in failing to theorize the category of "age." "But unlike race and gender, age has been a largely undertheorized and unchallenged category"; see K. Baxter, *The Modern Age: Turn-of-the-Century American Culture and the Invention of Adolescence* (Tuscaloosa: University of Alabama Press, 2008), 17.
3. By critical social theory, I mean the systematic analytical interventions included in considering everyday social and structural inequalities regarding institutions, services, arrangements, and social relations. Critical social theory provides tools for examining underlying assumptions about the allocation of institutional resources and the production of authority, power, and meaning.
4. G. Leckie and J. Buschman, "Introduction: The Necessity for Theoretically Informed Critique in Library and Information Science," in *Critical Theory for Library and Information Science: Exploring the Social from Across the Disciplines*, ed. G. J. Leckie, L. M. Given, and J. E. Buschman (Santa Barbara, CA: Libraries Unlimited, 2010), xi.
5. Quoted in R. Cox, *Shaping Childhood Themes of Uncertainty in the History of Adult-Child Relationships* (London and New York: Routledge, 1996), 62.
6. A good deal of this essay's historical analysis of Hall and Holt comes from A. Hulbert, *Raising America: Experts, Parents, and a Century of Advice about Children* (New York: Alfred A. Knopf, 2003).
7. G. S. Hall, *Adolescence: It's Relation to Physiology, Anthropology, Sociology, Sex, Crime, Religion and Education* (New York: D. Appleton, 1904). Others may recognize this vision of youth in the work of psychologist Erik Erikson; see E. Erikson, *Identity, Youth, and Crisis* (New York: Norton, 1968).
8. G. S. Hall, "What Children Do Read and What They Ought to Read," *Public Libraries 10 (1905):* 391–92, and "Children's Reading as a Factor in Their Education," *Library Journal 33 (1908):* 123–28, as cited in D. Garrison, *Apostles of Culture: The Public Library and American Society, 1876–1920* (Madison: University of Wisconsin Press, 1979), 212.
9. For a rare departure from the near uniform treatment of youth antisocial behaviors, see C. G. Vera Sanchez and E. B. Adams, "Sacrificed on the Altar of Public Safety: The Policing of Latino and African American Youth," *Journal of Contemporary Criminal Justice* 27, no. 3 (2011): 322–41.
10. Quoted in Hulbert, *Raising America*, 71–72.

11. P. S. Fass, *The End of American Childhood: A History of Parenting from Life on the Frontier to the Managed Child* (Princeton, NJ: Princeton University Press, 2016); P. S. Fass and M. Grossberg (eds.), *Reinventing Childhood after World War II* (Philadelphia: University of Pennsylvania Press, 2012); P. Kasinitz, J. H. Mollenkopf, M. C. Waters, and J. Holdaway, *Inheriting the City: The Children of Immigrants Come of Age* (Cambridge, MA: Harvard University Press, 2008); M. R. Klapper, *Small Strangers: The Experiences of Immigrant Children in America, 1880-1925* (Chicago: Ivan R. Dee, 2007); K. Sanchez-Eppler, *Dependent States: The Child's Part in Nineteenth-Century American Culture* (Chicago: University of Chicago Press, 2005); B. Soland, *Becoming Modern: Young Women and the Reconstruction of Womanhood in the 1920s* (Princeton, NJ: Princeton University Press, 2000).
12. W. B. Lukenbill, "Helping Youth at Risk: An Overview of Reformist Movements in American Public Library Services to Youth," *New Review of Children's Literature and Librarianship* 12, no. 2 (2006): 197-213.
13. S. Mintz, *Huck's Aft: A History of American Childhood* (Cambridge, MA, and London: Belknap Press of Harvard University Press, 2004), 383. Mintz numbers among a growing group of historians critical of the developmentalist approach. See also S. Olsen, *Juvenile Nation: Youth, Emotions and the Making of the Modern British Citizen, 1880-1914* (New York: Bloomsbury, 2014).
14. For historical treatments of these programming strategies, see B. R. Jordan, *Modern Manhood and the Boy Scouts of America: Citizenship, Race, and the Environment, 1920-1930* (Chapel Hill: University of North Carolina, 2016); K. Baxter, *The Modern Age: Turn-of-the-Century American Culture and the Invention of Adolescence* (Tuscaloosa: University of Alabama, 2008); A. A. Van Slyck, *A Manufactured Wilderness: Summer Camps and the Shaping of American Youth, 1890-1960* (Minneapolis: University of Minnesota Press, 2006); P. Boyle, "How FDR's New Deal for Youth Got Decked," *Youth Today* 13, no. 1 (December/January 2004): 1-40.
15. C. A. Jenkins, "The History of Youth Services Librarianship: A Review of the Research Literature," *Libraries and Culture* 35 (2000): 103-40; M. Braverman, *Youth, Society, and the Public Library* (Chicago: American Library Association, 1979).
16. The Drug Abuse Resistance Education (D.A.R.E.) program—originating in the Los Angeles Police Department—has become the internationally emblematic model for this approach. In this program, all youth require massive intervention efforts to avoid presumed susceptibility to drug abuse. Despite consistent and independent research findings that no-use programs such as D.A.R.E. are likely ineffective, they continue to thrive in schools, paid for by federal dollars. See D. C. Des Jarlais, Z. Sloboda, S. R. Friedman, B. Tempalski, C. McKnight, and N. Braine, "Diffusion of the DARE and Syringe Exchange Programs," *American Journal of Public Health* 96, no. 8 (2006): 1354-58; J. H. Brown, "Youth, Drugs, and Resilience Education," *Journal of Drug Education* 31, no. 1 (2001): 83-122.
17. F. Perkins, "Public Libraries and the Public with Special Reference to the San Francisco Free Public Library," *Library Journal* 10 (1885), as cited in Garrison, *Apostles of Culture*, 40.
18. Lukenbill, "Helping Youth at Risk," 197 (emphasis added). For a much more thorough and critical historical treatment of the connection between reading and the moral agenda of libraries and librarians, see S. Honeyman, *Elusive Childhood: Impossible Representations in Modern Fiction* (Columbus: Ohio State University Press, 2005), especially 113-14.
19. Although virtually all YA service manuals, practitioner-produced monographs, and aspirational documents from professional associations engage in this approach to one degree or another, here is a sampling: D. P. Tuccillo, *Library Teen Advisory Groups*, 2nd ed. (Lanham, MD: Rowman & Littlefield, 2018); L. Braun and S. Peterson, *Putting Teens First in Library Services: A Roadmap* (Chicago: American Library Association, 2017); J. B. Pierce, *Sex, Brains and Video Games: Information and Inspiration for Youth Services Librarians*, 2nd ed. (Chicago: ALA Editions, 2017);

M. P. Fink, *Teen Services 101: A Practical Guide for Busy Library Staff* (Chicago: American Library Association, 2015); M. D. Starkey, *Practical Programming: The Best of YA—YAAC* (Chicago: American Library Association, 2013); M. Gorman and T. Suellentrop, *Connecting Young Adults and Libraries: A How-To-Do-It Manual*, 4th ed. (New York: Neal-Schuman, 2009); P. Brehm-Heeger, *Serving Urban Teens* (Westport, CT: Libraries Unlimited, 2008); R. J. Cohen, "Sex Education and the American Public Library: A Study of Collection Development, Reference Services, and Programming for Young Adults," *The Journal of the Young Adult Library Services Association* 6, no. 3 (2008): 40–45; A. J. Alessio and K. A. Patton, *A Year of Programs for Teens* (Chicago: American Library Association, 2007); C. Mediavilla, *Creating the Full-Service Homework Center in Your Library* (Chicago: American Library Association, 2001); S. B. Anderson, ed., *Serving Older Teens* (Westport, CT: Libraries Unlimited, 2004); R. V. McGrath, ed., *Excellence in Library Services to Young Adults*, 4th ed. (Chicago: American Library Association, 2004); J. G. Mondowney, *Hold Them in Your Heart: Successful Strategies for Library Service to At-Risk Teens* (New York: Neal-Schuman, 2001); R. V. McGrath, *Bare Bones Young Adult Services: Tips for Public Library Generalists* (Chicago: American Library Association, 2000).

20. M. Males, *Teenage Sex and Pregnancy: Modern Myths, Unsexy Realities* (Santa Barbara, CA: Praeger, 2010), 11; A. Ibrahim and S. R. Steinberg, *Critical Youth Studies Reader* (New York: Peter Lang, 2014); also see K. Sternheimer, *Connecting Social Problems and Popular Culture: Why Media Is Not the Answer* (Boulder, CO: Westview Press, 2010); L. Camino and S. Zeldon, "Adult Roles in Youth Activism," in *Youth Activism: An International Encyclopedia*, ed. L. R. Sherrod (Westport, CT: Greenwood, 2006): vol. 1, 34–38; K. Sternheimer, *Kids These Days: Facts and Fictions about Today's Youth* (Lanham, MD: Rowman & Littlefield, 2006); S. L. Nichols and T. L. Good, *America's Teenagers—Myths and Realities: Media Images, Schooling, and the Social Costs of Careless Indifference* (Mahwah, NJ: Lawrence Erlbaum, 2004; M. A. Males, *Framing Youth: Ten Myths about the Next Generation* (Monroe, ME: Common Courage, 1999).

21. See the following research on the claims for two marquee programs: R. Willett, "Making, Makers, and Makerspaces: A Discourse Analysis of Professional Journal Articles and Blog Posts about Makerspaces in Public Libraries," *Library Quarterly: Information, Community, Policy* 86, no. 3 (2016): 313–329; R. Lyons, "Overstating Summer Reading Impacts: The Dominican Study," *Public Library Quarterly* 30 (2011): 54–61.

22. S. Flowers and the Young Adult Library Services Association, *Young Adults Deserve the Best: YALSA's Competencies in Action* (Chicago: American Library Association, 2011); E. Meyers, "Youth Development and Evaluation: Lessons from 'Public Libraries as Partners in Youth Development,'" in *Urban Teens in the Library: Research and Practice*, ed. D. F. Agosto and S. Hughes-Hassell (Chicago: American Libraries Association, 2010), 129–42; Institute of Museum and Library Services, *Museums, Libraries, and 21st Century Skills* (Washington, DC: IMLS, 2009), www.imls.gov/sites/default/files/publications/documents/21stcenturyskills.pdf; Gorman and Suellentrop, *Connecting Young Adults and Libraries*; V. A. Walter and E. Meyers, *Teens and Libraries: Getting It Right* (Chicago: American Library Association, 2003); P. Jones and the Young Adult Library Services Association, *New Directions for Library Service to Young Adults* (Chicago: American Library Association, 2002); Wallace Foundation, *Public Libraries as Partners in Youth Development* (New York: Wallace Foundation, 1999).

23. K. Haycock and M. Romaniuk, *The Portable MLIS: Insights from the Experts*, 2nd ed. (Santa Barbara, CA: Libraries Unlimited, 2018); S. Hirsh, *Information Services Today: An Introduction*, 2nd ed. (Lanham, MD: Rowman & Littlefield, 2018); and R. E. Rubin, *Foundations of Library and Information Science*, 4th ed. (Chicago: American Library Association, 2017).

24. Young Adult Library Services Association (YALSA), *Teen Services Competencies for Library Staff* (Chicago: American Library Association, 2017), www.ala.org/yalsa/guidelines/yacompetencies.

25. J. Spielberger, C. Horton, L. Michels, and R. Halpern, *New on the Shelf: Teens in the Library* (Chicago: Chapin Hall, University of Chicago, 2005). This turn toward the youth development paradigm in libraries mirrors the adoption of this approach earlier and much more broadly across other direct youth service occupations.
26. It is instructive to note here that for all the guidelines, "best practices," and advice literature promoting such participatory and partnership-oriented practices, there has been precious little LIS research demonstrating the value of these activities to libraries or even to youth themselves. Indeed, "youth participation" remains elusive and without a solid basis in research. In some instances, libraries might define that the minor clerical tasks performed by YA volunteers qualify as youth participation. In other settings, mere attendance at a YA program or event qualifies. In more rare circumstances, youth participation includes such activities as contributing to the planning and design of new library facilities or informed YA representations before governing and policy-making bodies. This is not necessarily meant to diminish the importance of such materials or practices in developing a professional dialogue. But these efforts must be differentiated from systematic, methodologically sound, scholarly research capable of providing supportable evidence and generalizable conclusions. See Tuccillo, *Library Teen Advisory Groups*; K. M. Gillespie, *Teen Volunteer Services in Libraries* (Lanham, MD: Scarecrow, 2004).
27. D. Scott, "The Language of Library Services for 'At-Risk' Youth." *Feliciter* 60, no. 4 (2014), 36–38.
28. From among the many examples of near consensus with the youth development paradigm, see YALSA, *Teen Services Competencies for Library Staff*; Young Adult Library Services Association (YALSA), *The Future of Library Services for and with Teens: A Call to Action* (Chicago: American Library Association, 2014); P. Brautigam, "Developmental Assets and Libraries: Helping to Construct the Successful Teen." *Voice of Youth Advocates* 31, no. 2 (June 2008): 124–25; Alessio and Patton, *A Year of Programs for Teens*; D. Weinberger, B. Elvevag, and J. N. Giedd, *The Adolescent Brain: A Work in Progress* (Washington, DC: National Campaign to Prevent Teen Pregnancy, 2005); M. T. Lerch and J. Welch, *Serving Homeschooled Teens and Their Parents* (Westport, CT: Libraries Unlimited, 2004); R. J. Vaillancourt, *Managing Young Adult Services: A Self-Help Manual* (New York: Neal-Schuman, 2002).
29. The field still lacks a history of LIS's widely accepted adoption of the youth development paradigm. It would be valuable to have a critical evaluation of this decision—to trace its origins, identify its advocates, and examine how it was decided upon to serve the field.
30. For one example among many, see the seven-part harangue against teen boys in E. Rockefeller and R. Welch, "Seven Nasty Things Guys May Bring to the Library: Rude Language, Challenging Authority, Physical Violence." *Voice of Youth Advocates* 34, no. 6 (February 2012): 574–75.
31. For only a few examples demonstrating how the neurobiological basis behind the so-called "teen brain" is strenuously contested, see M. Kloep, L. B. Hendry, R. Taylor, and I. Stuart-Hamilton, eds., *Development from Adolescence to Early Adulthood: A Dynamic Systemic Approach to Transitions and Transformations* (East Sussex, UK: Psychology Press, 2016); H. Sercombe, "Risk, Adaptation and the Functional Teenage Brain," *Brain and Cognition* 89, no. 2 (2014): 61-69; F. Gabriel, "Reasonable Unreason: The Limits of Youth in the Teen Brain," in *Deconstructing Youth: Youth Discourses at the Limits of Sense* (New York: Palgrave Macmillan, 2013), 70–101; M. A. Payne, "'All Gas and No Brakes!': Helpful Metaphor or Harmful Stereotype?" *Journal of Adolescent Research* 27, no. 1 (January 2012): 3–17; P. Kelly, "An Untimely Future for Youth Studies," *Youth Studies Australia* 30, no. 3 (2011): 47–53.
32. A. Bernier, "Representations of Youth in Local Media: Implications for Library Service," *Library and Information Science Research* 33 (April 2011): 158–67.
33. D. Macallair, *After the Doors Were Locked: A History of Youth Corrections in California and the Origins of Twenty-First Century Reform* (Lanham, MD: Rowman & Littlefield, 2015), 247.
34. Baxter, *The Modern Age*, 7.

35. Thus, we continually read about how YA patrons find our services lacking: V. Howard, "What Do Young Teens Think about the Public Library?," *Library Quarterly* 81, no. 3 (2011): 321–44; J. Abbas, M. Kimball, K. Bishop, and G. D'Elia, "Youth, Public Libraries, and the Internet: Why Youth Do Not Use the Public Library, Part IV," *Public Libraries* 47, no. 1 (January/February 2008): 80–85; S. L. Cook, S. Parker, and C. E. Pettijohn, "The Public Library: An Early Teen's Perspective," *Public Libraries* 44, no. 3 (2005): 157–61; M. K. Chelton, "The 'Problem Patron' Public Libraries Created," *The Reference Librarian* 36, nos. 75–76 (2002): 23–32; H. Fisher, "A Teenage View of the Public Library: What Are the Students Saying?," *Australasian Public Libraries and Information Services* 16, no. 1 (2003): 4–16; L. Hill and H. Pain, "Young People and Public Libraries: Use, Attitudes, and Reading Habits: A Survey of 13-16-Year-Olds in Nottinghamshire," *International Review of Children's Literature and Librarianship* 3, no. 1 (1988): 26–40.

36. Note how libraries, trumpeting themselves as democratically open and well-regarded institutions, do not figure as positive community assets in critical youth studies scholarship. In none of the following works are libraries even mentioned: J. Conner and S. M. Rosen, eds., *Contemporary Youth Activism: Advancing Social Justice in the United States* (Santa Barbara, CA: Praeger, (2016); N. Lesko and S. Talburt, eds., *Keywords in Youth Studies: Tracing Affects, Movements, Knowledges* (New York: Routledge, 2012); C. Macleod, *"Adolescence," Pregnancy and Abortion: Constructing a Threat of Degeneration* (London: Routledge, 2011); J. K. Taft, *Rebel Girls: Youth Activism and Social Change across the Americas* (New York: New York University Press, 2011); M. E. Thomas, *Multicultural Girlhood: Racism, Sexuality, and the Conflicted Spaces of American Education* (Philadelphia: Temple University Press, 2011); C. Wright, P. Standen, and T. Patel, *Black Youth Matters: Transitions for School to Success* (New York: Routledge, 2010); E. Luhr, *Witnessing Suburbia: Conservatives and Christian Youth Culture* (Berkeley: University of California Press, 2009).

37. A caveat here is that developmental approaches might well afford positive impacts on the ways in which young children mature. Evaluating these claims far exceeds the scope and expertise represented in this collection of studies on adolescents.

38. Young Adult Library Services Association (YALSA), *Teen Programming Guidelines* (Chicago: American Library Association, 2015), www.ala.org/yalsa/teen-programming-guidelines; E. T. Dresang, M. Gross, and L. E. Holt, *Dynamic Youth Services through Outcome-Based Planning and Evaluation* (Chicago: American Library Association, 2006); V. Walter, *Output Measures and More: Planning and Evaluating Public Library Services for Young Adults* (Chicago: American Library Association, 1995). This is, of course, not to denigrate the collection of data about YA services per se, only to call into context the assumptions undergirding them. The Public Library Association's current "Project Outcome" attempts to realign the measures libraries generally take into account when evaluating their programs and services, but these efforts do not focus on serving young adults.

39. LIS refers to these skills as "bibliographic," "information seeking," "information behaviors," "information literacy," or similar terms reflecting the acquisition of library-determined procedures, techniques, or habits of mind.

40. J. J. Burke and E. Kroski, *Makerspaces: A Practical Guide for Librarians* (Lanham, MD: Rowman & Littlefield, 2018); T. Willingham, *Library Makerspaces: The Complete Guide* (Lanham, MD: Rowman & Littlefield, 2018); YALSA Makerspace Resources Task Force, *Making in the Library Toolkit* (Chicago: Young Adult Library Services Association, January 2015), www.ala.org/yalsa/making-library-toolkit; T. McLees, *YALSA's Top Reads: STEM and Making* (Chicago: American Library Association, 2017); E. Kroski, ed., *The Makerspace Librarian's Sourcebook* (Chicago: American Library Association, 2017).

41. "*Positive* youth development," of course, begs questions about what it might have thus been *previously*. N. Deutsch, *After-School Programs to Promote Positive Youth Development: Integrating Research into Practice and Policy* (Cham, Switzerland: Springer Verlag, 2017); S. Intrator and

D. Siegel, *The Quest for Mastery: Positive Youth Development through Out-of-School Programs* (Cambridge, MA: Harvard Education Press, 2014); R. Travis Jr. and T. G. Leech, "Empowerment-Based Positive Youth Development: A New Understanding of Healthy Development for African American Youth," *Journal of Research on Adolescence* 24, no. 1 (2014): 93–116; R. M. Lerner, J. B. Almerigi, C. Theokas, and J. V. Lerner, "Positive Youth Development: A View of the Issues," *Journal of Early Adolescence* 25, no. 1 (2005): 10–16; W. Damon, "What Is Positive Youth Development?" *Annals of the American Academy of Political and Social Science* 591, no. 1 (January 2004): 13–24.

42. For further acknowledgment about youth services at the "crossroads," see A. K. Long, "Youth Services in Public Libraries: History, Core Services, Challenges, and Opportunities," in *Introduction to Public Librarianship*, 3rd ed., ed. K. de la Peña McCook and J. S. Bossaller (Chicago: American Library Association, 2018), 229–56.

43. The values, precepts, strategies, and goals of youth development appear (explicitly or implicitly) in virtually all YALSA documents and resources informing professional conduct; see Young Adult Library Services Association (YALSA), *Core Professional Values for the Teen Services Profession* (Chicago: American Library Association, 2015), www.ala.org/yalsa/core-professional-values-teen-services-profession; YALSA, *Teen Services Competencies for Library Staff*; YALSA, *The Future of Library Services for and with Teens*.

44. A similar sentiment appears in many of the studies in this collection.

45. P. L. Benson, *Parent, Teacher, Mentor, Friend: How Every Adult Can Change Kids' Lives* (Minneapolis, MN: Search Institute Press, 2010); Search Institute, "Developmental Assets Framework," Search-Institute.org, accessed November 2018, www.search-institute.org/our-research/development-assets/developmental-assets-framework/.

46. For a rapidly growing scholarship on the history of library racial segregation, particularly regarding African Americans, and the young adult activism that led to its demise, see W. A. Wiegand and S. A. Wiegand, *The Desegregation of Public Libraries in the Jim Crow South: Civil Rights and Local Activism* (Baton Rouge: Louisiana State University Press, 2018); C. Knott, *Not Free, Not for All: Public Libraries in the Age of Jim Crow* (Amherst: University of Massachusetts Press, 2015); D. M. Battles, *The History of Public Library Access to African Americans in the South, or Leaving the Plow Behind* (Lanham, MD: Scarecrow Press, 2009); P. T. Graham, *A Right to Read: Segregation and Civil Rights in Alabama's Public Libraries, 1900–1965* (Tuscaloosa: University of Alabama Press, 2002).

47. "Youth researchers spend their lives researching and writing about inequality, exclusion, non-participation, disadvantage and disengagement, in other words treating youth research as research on youth related problems." See G. Holm and H. Helve, "Introduction," in *Contemporary Youth Research: Local Expressions and Global Connections* (Burlington, VT: Ashgate Publishing, 2005), xi. "Othering" is the "process by which a group . . . is marked as fundamentally different from what is perceived to be normal or mainstream." See G. Dimitriadis, *Studying Urban Youth Culture* (New York: Peter Lang, 2008), 1. See also M. K. Chelton, "The 'Overdue Kid': A Face-to-Face Library Service Encounter as Ritual Interaction," *Library and Information Science Research* 19, no. 4 (1997): 387–99.

48. A. James and A. Prout, eds., *Constructing and Reconstructing Childhood* (London: Routledge, 1997), 13.

49. A. Clark, R. Flewitt, M. Hammersley, and M. Robb, eds., *Understanding Research with Children and Young People* (Los Angeles: Sage, 2014), 20.

50. A. Bernier, "Not Broken by Someone Else's Schedule: On Joy and Young Adult Information Seeking," in *Youth Information-Seeking Behavior: Theories, Models, and Issues*, ed. M. K. Chelton and C. Cool (Lanham, MD: Scarecrow Press, 2007): xiii–xxvii.

51. S. Fraser, "Situating Empirical Research," in *Doing Research with Children and Young People*, ed. S. Fraser, V. Lewis, S. Ding, M. Kellett, and C. Robinson (London: Sage, 2005), 16.

52. J. Kozol, *The Shame of the Nation: The Restoration of Apartheid Schooling in America* (New York: Crown Publishing, 2005), 95.

53. For a large and growing critique of the developmentalist paradigm, see Clark, Flewitt, Hammersley, and Robb, *Understanding Research with Children and Young People*; F. Gabriel, *Deconstructing Youth: Youth Discourses at the Limits of Sense* (New York: Palgrave Macmillan, 2013); N. Lesko, *Act Your Age! A Cultural Construction of Adolescence*, 2nd ed. (New York: Routledge, 2013); R. Gilchrist, T. Jeffs, J. Spence, and J. Walker, *Essays in the History of Youth and Community Work: Discovering the Past* (Lyme Regis, Dorset, UK: Russell House Publishing, 2009); Baxter, *The Modern Age*; A. Best, "Teen Driving as Public Drama: Statistics, Risk, and the Social Construction of Youth as a Public Problem." *Journal of Youth Studies* 11, no. 6 (2008): 651-69; C. Heywood, *A History of Childhood: Children and Childhood in the West from Medieval to Modern Times* (Cambridge, UK: Polity Press, 2006); S. Honeyman, *Elusive Childhood: Impossible Representations in Modern Fiction* (Columbus: Ohio State University Press, 2005); A. S. Waterman, "Reflections on Changes in Research on Adolescence from the Perspective of 15 Years of Editorial Experiences," *Journal of Adolescence* 28, no. 6 (2005): 681-85. For an international perspective critical of modernist youth developmentalism, see C. Macleod, *"Adolescence," Pregnancy and Abortion*.
54. Bernier, "Not Broken by Someone Else's Schedule."
55. D. A. Wolfe, *Adolescent Dating Violence: Theory, Research, and Prevention* (London: Academic Press, 2018); R. F. Marcus, *The Development of Aggression and Violence in Adolescence* (New York: Palgrave, 2017); L. Damour, *Untangled: Guiding Teenage Girls through the Seven Transitions into Adulthood* (New York: Ballantine Books, 2017); C. James, *Disconnected: Youth, New Media, and the Ethics Gap* (Cambridge, MA: MIT Press, 2014); G. Neufeld and G. Mate, *Hold On to Your Kids: Why Parents Need to Matter More Than Peers* (New York: Ballantine Books, 2014); R. Contreras, *The Stickup Kids: Race, Drugs, Violence and the American Dream* (Berkeley: University of California Press, 2013); K. Seifert, *Youth Violence: Theory, Prevention, and Intervention* (New York: Springer, 2012).
56. To sample a burgeoning specialization of interdisciplinary scholarship particularly focused on youth studies research methods, see N. B. Elliott, *Youth Engagement and Community-Based Participatory Research: The Bipolar Youth Action Project* (London: Sage , 2017); N. Mirra, A. Garcia, and E. Morrell, *Doing Youth Participatory Action Research: Transforming Inquiry with Researchers, Educators, and Students* (New York: Routledge, 2016); Clark, Flewitt, Hammersley, and Robb, *Understanding Research with Children and Young People*; E. Tuck and W. Yang, eds., *Youth Resistance Research and Theories of Change* (New York: Routledge, 2014).
57. S. Zeller-Berkman, "Critical Development? Using a Critical Theory Lens to Examine the Current Role of Evaluation in the Youth-Development Field," *Critical Social Theory and Evaluation Practice: New Directions for Evaluation* 2010, no. 127 (Fall 2010): 35-44.
58. A rare exception is S. Ginwright, P. Noguera, and J. Cammarota, eds., *Beyond Resistance! Youth Activism and Community Change* (New York: Routledge, 2006).
59. For broader critical youth studies treatments of individuation, see N. Eliasoph, *Making Volunteers: Civic Life after Welfare's End* (Princeton, NJ: Princeton University, 2011); D. Farrugia, "Homeless Youth Managing Relationships: Reflexive Intersubjectivity and Inequality," *Young* 19, no. 4 (2011): 357-73; W. T. Armaline, "'Kids Need Structure': Negotiating Rules, Power, and Social Control in an Emergency Youth Shelter," *American Behavioral Scientist* 48, no. 8 (2005): 1124-49.
60. The YDIC is very good at pointing out such things as "boundaries" but never acknowledges how youth build experience with and among each other or, in focusing entirely on the differences between youth and adults, finds cultural meaning intergenerationally with them.
61. Zeller-Berkman, "Critical Development?," 40 (emphasis added).
62. For a rare, evidence-based examination of the prosocial peer experience of most youth, see R. Taffel, *The Second Family: How Adolescent Power Is Challenging the American Family* (New York: St. Martin's Griffin, 2001).
63. A. Bernier and M. Males, "YA Spaces and the End of Postural Tyranny," *Public Libraries* 53, no. 4 (2014): 30-40.

64. Braverman, *Youth, Society, and the Public Library*, 244. One may perceive some daylight between the library's compulsion to individuate young adult users and youth as active agents in the larger culture in Margaret Alexander Edwards's 1969 LIS classic *The Fair Garden and the Swarm of Beasts*. This is a clear response to the era's famous student activism. Nevertheless, the larger thrust of her work does not break stride with the LIS legacy. Edwards's treatment focuses on individualization and deficit views of youth and what they need to become successful middle-class adults. See M. A. Edwards, *The Fair Garden and the Swarm of Beasts: The Library and the Young Adult* (Chicago: American Library Association, 1994), 72–74.
65. LIS largely shares this avoidance of social class awareness, awareness of its own social position as a middle-class-oriented institution, and the implications issuing from these assumptions. See J. Pateman and J. Vincent, *Public Libraries and Social Justice* (Surrey, UK: Ashgate, 2010).
66. Between 2015 and 2016, the poverty rate for children under age 18 is 18 percent. See J. L. Semega, K. R. Fontenot, and M. A. Kollar, *Income and Poverty in the United States: 2016* (U.S. Census Bureau Current Population Reports, P60-259), Census.gov, accessed November 2018, www.census.gov/content/dam/Census/library/publications/2017/demo/P60-259.pdf. In the wealthiest state in the union, California, child poverty has risen to over 23 percent; see R. A. Walker and S. K. Lodah, *The Atlas of California: Mapping the Challenges of a New Era* (Berkeley: University of California, 2013). For a thorough examination of the role social class and material circumstances play in the lives of contemporary youth, see R. White and J. Wyn, *Youth and Society: Exploring the Social Dynamics of Youth Experience* (Oxford, UK: Oxford University Press, 2004).
67. R. D. Putnam, *Our Kids: The American Dream in Crisis* (New York: Simon & Schuster, 2015), 36.
68. For an excellent critique of the role that public youth professionals play in serving the conservative objectives of the state, see B. Belton, *Radical Youth Work* (Lyme Regis, Dorset, UK: Russell House Publishing, 2010).
69. K. Clonan-Roy, C. Jacobs, and M. Nakkula, "Towards a Model of Positive Youth Development Specific to Girls of Color: Perspectives on Development, Resilience, and Empowerment," *Gender Issues* 33, no. 2 (2016): 96–121; P. R. Camangian, "Teach Like Lives Depend on It: Agitate, Arise, and Inspire," *Urban Education* 50, no. 4 (2015): 424–53; Vera Sanchez and Adams, "Sacrificed on the Altar of Public Safety"; P. Boyle and L. Lutton "Youth Development's Racial Challenge," *Youth Today* 14, no. 8 (2005): 1–31.
70. See particularly the studies of Kumasi (chapter 9) and Austin (chapter 6) appearing in this collection.
71. Recent scholarship of childhood history and protective legislation are now not only tracing these back through to federal Progressive Era reforms but even earlier at local and state levels as well. See S. J. Pearson, *The Rights of the Defenseless: Protecting Animals and Children in Gilded Age America* (Chicago: University of Chicago Press, 2011).
72. S. Costanza-Chock, *Out of the Shadows, into the Streets! Transmedia Organizing and the Immigrant Rights Movement* (Cambridge, MA: MIT Press, 2014); R. G. Gonzales, *Lives in Limbo: Undocumented and Coming of Age in America* (Oakland: University of California Press, 2016).

PART I

Betweenness

CHAPTER 1

Envisaging Young Adult Librarianship from a Teen-Centered Perspective

Denise E. Agosto

Young adult library services were founded on the idea of meeting teens' needs and interests, yet an adult-centered perspective dominates both the research and practice in this area. This chapter presents a small-scale content analysis of professional literature as proof of the prevailing adult-centered perspective. It then suggests that a teen-centered perspective for public library research and practice is a better approach in terms of benefits to the target population. A truly teen-centered perspective means that we must change our thinking to (1) conceptualize adolescents as "teens" instead of "young adults"; (2) focus on teen development; (3) focus on teens as individuals first and foremost, and as members of their age and other demographic groups second; and (4) make teens—not information resources—the center of our work.

Library services for teens were founded on the idea of providing information resources to meet teens' needs and interests, yet since their inception much of the related research and practice has been conducted from an adult-centered perspective. For example, a great deal of the scholarly and professional writing relating to teens and libraries has taken the form of theoretical or thematic analyses of young adult literature, with the goal of enabling librarians to encourage youth to read the highest quality books. Certainly, there is value in encouraging teens to read (or watch or listen to or play) high-quality materials, but this approach is an adult-centered approach, with adult scholars and adult librarians assuming that they know what kinds of resources teens need and want and that they can identify the best books (or websites or video games) to meet teens' needs and interests.

This concept of adults determining what is "best" for teens has also led to an emphasis on collecting and recommending award-winning materials, with adults serving as the driving forces behind award designations. There are literally hundreds of youth literature awards, many of which are for young adult (YA) materials (Hilbun and Claes 2010). Even in the case of youth choice awards, librarians still typically select the short lists, and adults still determine what is best for teens.

"Teen-centered" refers to (1) direct youth participation in program and service design, (2) research that uses teens as research subjects or participants, and (3) library programs and services based on research that uses teens as research subjects or participants. In a more teen-centered approach to library research, teen behaviors, thoughts, and preferences would serve as the main sources for research data, as opposed to information resources serving as the most common data for analysis. In a more teen-centered approach to library practice, teens themselves would serve as the experts of their own thoughts, behaviors, needs, and preferences, and teens themselves would determine what resources and services are the best fits to their needs and interests. This is not to suggest that current library research and services for teens are exclusively adult-centered. There is an element of the teen-centered approach in both practice and research, with a growing number of public libraries setting up teen advisory boards and other mechanisms for enabling teens to provide input on program and service design (Tuccillo 2010), and with a small but significant body of teen-centered library and information science (LIS) research being disseminated via academic outlets each year (see, for example, some of the entries on the Young Adult Library Services Association Research Committee's research bibliography [YALSA 2009]).

The concept of a teen-centered approach to public library services is not new. Librarians have been encouraging teens to participate in library services on a limited basis for decades. Tuccillo (2010) traced teen participation in both public and school libraries back as far as the early twentieth century, and she argued that librarians have placed importance on fostering teen participation ever since. What is new is the *level* of teen participation that is required to achieve the vision of a truly teen-centered approach.

The question that drives this chapter is, What should be the central focus of today's library research and services for teens? I will argue that the teen-centered focus is the best approach for creating the public library research and services that can best benefit teens. With this goal in mind, I will show how we must change our thinking in order to lead the field toward a truly teen-centered approach. My intention is not to suggest the elimination of the adult-centered approach but to nudge us further into teen-centered thinking, with the goal of making the teen-centered approach the guiding perspective of library research and services for teens. In this vision, the adult-centered approach does not disappear, but it does become less of a focus, falling beneath the broader teen-centered umbrella guiding library services and research for teens.

AN ANALYSIS OF REPRESENTATIVE LITERATURE IN LIBRARY SERVICES FOR TEENS

Before I can outline necessary changes for making the teen-centered vision a reality, I need to provide some proof of my contention that the adult-centered perspective is dominant. One way to determine the prevailing perspective of a field is to analyze its professional literature. Looking at the current LIS professional literature for teen librarians, many of the articles focus on analyzing information resources, programs, and services from the adult authors' perspectives, without gathering data or input directly from teens. As an example of how the adult-centered perspective dominates the current teen librarianship professional literature, I will analyze the most recent three complete years of articles published in *Young Adult Library Services*.

Young Adult Library Services is, of course, the member journal for YALSA. It is edited and run by active YALSA members, most of whom are teen librarians working in public libraries. Its writers' guidelines explain: "*Young Adult Library Services* is a vehicle for continuing education of librarians working with young adults (ages 12–18) that showcases current research and practice relating to teen services and spotlights significant activities and programs of the division" (YALSA 2011). Thus, the target audience of the journal is teen librarians, and the intent is to provide them with the most relevant and significant research, lessons from practice, and YALSA news and activities. It is not intended to be a research journal read by academics, but a continuing education resource for practitioners. For many teen librarians, it is their main external connection to the field of youth librarianship after completing graduate school.

I used the Library Literature and Information Science Full Text database to gather all of the articles published in *Young Adult Library Services* for the period 2008–2010, a total of 220 articles. I hypothesized that authors of research articles were more likely to include direct input from teens in the form of data than were authors of practice-based articles. To calculate the percentage of research-focused and practice-based articles within the dataset, I defined *research* very broadly as any article that (1) included analysis of some form of data, defining data in the broad sense of any text, such as a book or website; any information collected via a survey, interview, experiment, or other data-gathering means; any information collected systematically about a library program or service, such as attendance or circulation figures; or any use of a theoretical or conceptual framework; and (2) included at least one scholarly reference. All other articles, such as descriptions and announcements of information resource awards, program reports that described programs but did not analyze program success or impacts, editorials, and so on, were considered practice articles.

I used standard qualitative content analysis techniques to analyze the main topics of the articles in the dataset, coding each article for one main topic, iteratively collapsing the emerging list of topics into broader categories until there were eight distinct topic categories for the practice-based articles and five topic categories for the research articles. In some cases, an article could have fit into two or more categories. I chose just one main category per article to simplify analysis and reporting. I used simple descriptive statistics to calculate the quantitative findings.

Practice-Based and Research-Based Articles

Table 1.1 shows the percentages of practice and research articles in the dataset. Of the 220 articles published during the three-year period, 21 (9.5 percent) could be considered research using the very broad definition of *research* above. The remaining 90.5 percent were practice-based articles. As a journal aimed at practitioners and intended partly as a vehicle for dissemination of professional association news, it makes sense that the majority of the

TABLE 1.1 Practice/Research Breakdown of Articles Published in *Young Adult Library Services*, 2008–2010

CATEGORY	2008	2009	2010	TOTAL
Practice (nonresearch)	64 (91.4%*)	53 (84.1%*)	82 (94.3%*)	199 (90.5%)
Research	6 (8.6%*)	10 (15.9%*)	5 (5.7%*)	21 (9.5%)
TOTAL	70 (100%*)	63 (100%*)	87 (100%*)	220 (100%)

* Percentage of total articles published for that year.

articles were nonresearch pieces. However, this analysis indicated that teen librarians who keep up with the field only through professional journals such as this one were exposed to only a small body of the relevant research, just five to 10 items per year for this particular journal during the period of analysis.

Main Topics of Articles

Data analysis of the practice articles yielded eight main topics, as shown in table 1.2. The most frequent main topic was "teen book/resource awards," accounting for 43 of the 199 total practice articles, or 21.6 percent. Articles falling into this category were announcements of award winners, discussions (as opposed to scholarly analyses, which were considered research) of award-winning books and other information resources, texts of teen resource award acceptance speeches, and descriptions of teen information resource awards.

An additional 18 (9.0 percent) practice articles discussed "books and other resources for teens," such as bibliographic essays of recommended teen books about a particular topic or representing a particular genre. Combining the information resource awards category with the other information resources category, a total of 61 (30.7 percent) of the practice articles were discussions relating to teen information resources, most commonly fiction books. This means that nearly one-third of the practice articles focused on teen resources.

The other most common practice topics included "programs and services" (33 articles, or 16.6 percent), "editorials/columns/professional advice" (27 articles, or 13.6 percent),

TABLE 1.2 Categories of Main Topics for Practice Articles Published in *Young Adult Library Services*, 2008–2010

TOPIC	2008	2009	2010	TOTAL
Teen book/resource awards	18 (28.1%)	14 (26.4%)	11 (13.4%)	43 (21.6%)
Other awards/grants	3 (4.7%)	4 (7.5%)	3 (3.7%)	10 (5.0%)
Programs (e.g., book clubs) and services (e.g., reference)	9 (14.1%)	9 (17.0%)	15 (18.3%)	33 (16.6%)
Editorials/columns/ professional advice	10 (15.6%)	9 (17.0%)	8 (9.8%)	27 (13.6%)
Books and other resources for teens	7 (10.9%)	4 (7.5%)	7 (8.5%)	18 (9.0%)
Professional books/other professional resources	10 (15.6%)	2 (3.8%)	15 (18.3%)	27 (13.6%)
Conferences and professional associations	3 (4.7%)	5 (9.4%)	18 (22.0%)	26 (13.1%)
Administration/budgeting/ advocacy/marketing/ collaboration	4 (6.2%)	6 (11.3%)	5 (6.1%)	15 (7.5%)
TOTAL	65 (100%*)	53 (100%*)	82 (100%*)	199 (100%)

* Column does not add up to 100% due to rounding.

"professional books/other professional resources" (27 articles, or 13.6 percent), and "conferences and professional associations" (26 articles, or 13.1 percent).

Table 1.3 shows the five categories of main topics found in the research articles. Again, articles relating to teen books and other information resources accounted for the largest combined category. Together, "analyses of books and other resources for teens" (9 articles, or 42.9 percent) plus "analyses of teen book/resource awards" (2 articles, or 9.5 percent) total 11 articles, or 52.4 percent of the research articles. This means that more than half of the research articles were analyses of information resources for teens.

Teen Input Represented in Articles

Table 1.4 shows the number and percentage of practice and research articles that included some form of direct input from teens. I defined "input" as *any* mention of teens' words, thoughts, or behaviors, such as quotes from verbal conversations or e-mails, anecdotal tales of direct observation of teen behaviors, or more formal data collected via surveys,

TABLE 1.3 Categories of Main Topics for Research Articles Published in *Young Adult Library Services*, 2008–2010

TOPIC	2008	2009	2010	TOTAL
Analyses of teen book/resource awards	1 (16.7%)	0 (0.0%)	1 (20.0%)	2 (9.5%)
Analyses of programs (e.g., book clubs) and services (e.g., reference)	2 (33.3%)	1 (10.0%)	0 (0.0%)	3 (14.3%)
Analyses of books and other resources for teens	2 (33.3%)	6 (60.0%)	1 (20.0%)	9 (42.9%)
Analyses of professional books/other professional resources	0 (0.0%)	1 (10.0%)	(0.0%)	1 (4.8%)
Analyses of teen behaviors/health/development	1 (16.7%)	2 (20.0%)	3 (60.0%)	6 (28.6%)
TOTAL	6 (100%)	10 (100%*)	5 (100%*)	21 (100%*)

* Column does not add up to 100% due to rounding.

TABLE 1.4 Articles Including Teen Input Published in *Young Adult Library Services*, 2008–2010

CATEGORY	NUMBER	PERCENTAGE
Practice articles with teen input	4	2.0% (of 199 practice articles)
Research articles with teen input	4	19.0% (of 21 research articles)
TOTAL ARTICLES WITH TEEN INPUT	8	3.6% (OF 220 TOTAL ARTICLES)

interviews, and so on. Of the 199 practice-based articles, just 4 (2.0 percent) included teen input. Of the 21 research articles, just 4 (19.0 percent) included any data or input from teens. The hypothesis that a greater percentage of research articles than practice articles would include direct input from teens was correct, but the numbers were still very low overall. Just 8 (3.6 percent) of the 220 articles in the entire dataset included any input whatsoever from teens, and again the definition of teen participation was very liberal.

Analysis of the Teen-Centered Perspective in Articles

The goal of this analysis was to examine whether a youth-centered or adult-centered perspective dominated in the recent teen librarianship professional literature, based on content analysis of one representative journal. The analysis showed that the most common article topic in *Young Adult Library Services* between 2008 and 2010 was a discussion or analysis of teen information resources, most often books. Only a small percentage of practice or research articles included any direct input from teens, even casual mention of one single e-mail or conversation excerpt. Again, of the 220 total articles published during this three-year period, just 8 articles (3.6 percent) included any direct input from teens in the form of quotes, survey responses, interviews, e-mail communications, casual observational data, conversations, anecdotes, and so on. The remainder of the articles (96.4 percent) were written from the adult perspective, such as bibliographic essays or reports of library programs presenting the authors' assessments of literary quality or program success. Some of these authors might have taken into account teens' opinions and viewpoints, but if so this was not discussed and readers would be unable to determine any teen input.

Thus, based on this small-scale analysis, it seems that little teen-centered work is making its way into the journal. For many teen librarians, professional journals such as this one are their main source of information about developments in the field of teen librarianship. To move to a more teen-centered approach across the field as a whole, one important step is increasing teen input in the professional writing.

I want to stress here that my purpose is *not* to criticize this journal. It reflects the prevailing perspective of its field and can publish youth-centered work only if potential authors—mainly librarians and library school faculty—write and submit youth-centered work. My point is that based on analysis of the items published in the field's member journal, very few librarians, university faculty, and others are submitting work based on teen input or research data collected from teens. Change needs to take place within the field before the professional literature can reflect it. I should note here that YALSA has recently begun a new journal devoted to publishing research, *Journal of Research on Libraries and Young Adults*. It remains to be seen the extent to which the journal will publish a higher percentage of teen-centered research. Regardless, *Young Adult Library Services* stands as a good example of the kinds of research and professional writing that teen librarians and teen LIS researchers publish in the professional literature, and this body of work has been shown to be overwhelmingly adult-centered.

CHANGING OUR THINKING TO A TEEN-CENTERED PERSPECTIVE

Focus on "Teens," Not "Young Adults"

The purpose of this book is to start a conversation about how students, practitioners, and scholars should conceptualize young adults, as well as to shape the future of library services for this population. The analysis just presented leads me to conclude that we must change our thinking to make teens the central focus of our practice and research. To move toward a truly teen-centered approach, we need to include teens in the conversation, to include teens as much as possible in the process of designing and delivering teen library programs and services, and to make teens themselves our most frequent sources of research data.

Related to the question of what should be the central focus of today's library research and services for teens is what we should we call this population. The answer to that question comes easily for me: *teens*. A truly teen-centered approach to library research and services means replacing the term *young adult* with a term that teens understand and appreciate. We should call this population *teens* because this is a term that they understand and use. For our work to be truly user-centered, we must use, as much as possible, the language that our population identifies with and uses to describe itself.

I learned the importance of using language that teens can understand and appreciate as I have learned virtually every important lesson about teens—from a teen. Years ago I was the head of the children's and young adult departments of a medium-sized public library. A few weeks before I began my new job, the library where I worked had created a new young adult fiction section, a long wall lined with YA paperbacks perched on painted metal shelves. A neon sign above the shelves read "Young Adult Paperbacks." One day, not long after I had begun working, I noticed a teenage girl staring at the sign. "What do you think of this new section?" I asked her.

She answered my question with a question: "Who are these books for? I might read some of these books, but I can't figure out who they're for."

"They're for people your age," I explained.

"Then I think you should do this," she said, removing her coat and holding it up to the sign to cover up the words *Young Adult*. Now the sign read simply "Paperbacks." "It's confusing. We're not adults yet, you know," she added, shaking her head as she walked away empty-handed.

She was right, of course. *Young adult* is a term known only to librarians (and publishers) to mean "adolescents." As Aronson (2002) explains, "The term YA is an odd one; it refers to no clear developmental age group. If anything, it seems to apply to people in their 20's who are just leaving college, beginning careers, and starting families" (82).

Cart (2010) points out, "The amorphous part [of the term *young adult literature*] is the target audience for the literature: the young adults themselves. For it's anybody's guess who—or what—they are!" (3). He cites YALSA's "Two Hundred Years of Young Adult Library Services History" bibliography (Bernier et al. 2010), which traces the use of the term in the professional library literature back as far as 1944.

In my many years of research with teens I have found them to voice consistent objections to the term. So why then do librarians, library researchers, and publishers use this term to refer to teens and sometimes to preteens? Pulliam (2010) suggests that publishers adopted the term *young adult* in the 1960s since "the term 'adolescent' was perceived by teens as condescending and necessarily denoting immaturity" (2). The term had to have been in use in the library field earlier, as the American Library Association's (ALA) Young Adult Services Division began in 1957 (Cart 2010). Regardless of the specific date it entered usage in library research and practice, the intent behind adopting the term seems to have been to give teens respect as full-fledged human beings by calling them adults who just happen to be young. But teens *are* full-fledged human beings, just as babies, children, adults, and senior citizens are all full-fledged human beings, regardless of their ages. We do not have to call teens adults to lend them human legitimacy.

I choose to use the terms *teens* and *teenagers* because they are widely used and understood by both teens and adults. The teens I conduct research with also often call themselves "kids." I do use the term *kids* when speaking with teens, but I don't use the term in academic and professional writing because it is not as specific as teens or teenagers.

The point here is not the specific term that we use. It's not the actual words that matter; it's the thinking behind the use of the words that matters. In a few years or decades, the terms *teens* and *teenagers* might fall out of fashion with the target population, and they might start calling themselves something else. If that happens, I hope I'll be astute enough to pick up on the change and to adopt the new term. If we want to serve teens' best interests, we need to place them at the center of our work and to communicate with them as partners in designing and delivering library research and services. We need to use language that they understand, and language that other adults outside of the field of librarianship understand. We must think of teens as the experts of their thoughts, behaviors, and lives, and we must use their language as much as possible to give authentic voice to this population.

Making teens the central focus in our work also means broadcasting our lessons and messages about what we have learned from teens to a wider audience than just other librarians and LIS researchers. We need to broaden the target audience for our academic and professional writing and presenting to other adults outside of the library field—to adults with influence over teens' lives and livelihoods, such as parents, guardians, teachers, informal educators (such as museum professionals and religious group leaders), government officials, program funders, and so on. We can teach these other adults about the importance of listening to teens and about the importance of respecting teen cultures.

Focus on Teen Development

Since most developmental theories and concepts were developed based on data collected from teens as research subjects, they offer us a teen-centered basis for designing library research and services by enabling us to mold our work in ways likely to optimize developmental benefits for teens. I have argued for a number of years that public and school library services can, and should, promote teens' healthy development. Based on my research with Sandra Hughes-Hassell, I have argued that public and school libraries can and should promote teen development in seven areas: the social self, the emotional self, the reflective self, the physical self, the creative self, the cognitive self, and the sexual self (Agosto and Hughes-Hassell 2006a). I have further argued that we need to broaden our view of the developmental benefits of public library services beyond the traditional focus on homework and leisure reading to support a much fuller range of developmental areas (Agosto 2007, 2010).

Moving from the research literature to the professional literature, longtime teen services librarian Tuccillo (2010) lists a number of benefits of greater teen participation in program and service design and delivery, including promoting positive youth development at the community level:

> Some essential rationales for offering youth participation opportunities include the fact that they provide a catalyst for teenagers to enter adulthood as readers, learners, and library supporters; they promote reading and the library by teen participants to their adolescent peers, who in turn will hopefully also partake in what the library has to offer; they proliferate library usage by helping teens to eventually pass on their love of books and libraries to their offspring; they uphold the concept of positive youth devel-

opment in our communities; and they affirm the prospect of librarianship as a career option for young people. (14)

These are important benefits to teens, but they are not the only benefits. We need to think of potential benefits on a much broader scale than just turning teens into more avid readers, library users, and possibly future librarians. We need to talk to teens about their goals for using library resources and services and make these our goals as well. As seen in this quote, in teen library practice, the philosophy behind encouraging teen participation has been grounded in the belief that library use is inherently good and that increased library use is the goal in itself. We need to move away from this library-centered focus to the teen-centered focus in which the goals of library services are not increased use of library services and resources but increased social, intellectual, creative, and entertainment opportunities, especially for teens with economic, educational, physical, social, cognitive, and other disadvantages.

As my past work has shown, teens turn to public libraries for much more than just information-related purposes. Public libraries commonly play three roles in teens' lives: (1) the library as information gateway, (2) the library as social interaction/entertainment space, and (3) the library as beneficial physical environment (Agosto 2007, 2010). Moving beyond just focusing on the library as information provider to focusing on these three categories of benefits enables us to serve a much wider range of needs.

Focus on Teens as Individuals

Still, the question of whether theories and concepts of youth development should drive teen library research and practice cannot be answered by a simple "yes." Developmental theories must be viewed as general guidelines—general patterns of growth and development. They should not be viewed as exact rules outlining all teens' behaviors, nor should they be seen as immutable laws for planning library programs and services.

We must remember that a theory is a lens for looking at something, be it library services, human behaviors, or anything else. In the social sciences, theory is rarely an absolute law or an absolute truth. With respect to teens and developmental theories and concepts, we must always remember that humans are first and foremost individuals and secondly products of their environments. Teens live and grow in many environments, including cultural, socioeconomic, age-related, racial, ethnic, linguistic, and other contexts. These environments, as well as teens' individual personalities, physicalities, intellects, and life experiences, make them individuals—individuals who in some cases might not represent general developmental patterns. As helpful as developmental theories and concepts can be, they can be dangerously misleading if we accept them to the point of forgetting about basic human differences (as in the digital native discourse described below).

Thinking of developmental theories as rough guidelines, not immutable rules, means remembering that each teen, each person, is unique. Teens' needs and interests vary radically from one person to the next, and as a result, each library needs to turn to its own teen population to discover its unique needs and interests as the basis for designing library services.

As researchers, librarians, and students we stand outside as concerned—deeply concerned—adult observers, but we adults are merely interpreters of teens' thoughts, behaviors, preferences, and needs, as well as designers and promoters of the research and services that can identify and fulfill them. This means that we must constantly talk to teens via formal and informal avenues to follow changes in how they think, behave, and interact—not how adults *expect* them to think, behave, and interact.

Indeed, Kunzel and Hardesty (2006) explain that in the public library teen-centered approach to practice, program and service design should begin with asking teens for ideas:

> Teen-centered means that the first point of reference for every decision and plan and action is teens' longings and desires and interests, stated and unstated. Teen-centered means going to the source—asking teens questions and listening—and then putting the answers to work. (5)

Now a cautionary note: We stand as adult outsiders looking into the teen world, but as librarians and researchers who work with teens, we must be careful not to create an "us versus them" narrative, a "teens are different than we are" attitude. Sure, teens are members of distinct youth cultures, but teens are people first and youth second. Perhaps nowhere is this dangerous "us versus them" narrative more prevalent than in the digital natives (Prensky 2001) discourse. This discourse is not the sole purview of the library field, but it has taken a strong hold in library research and practice (see Biladeau 2009; Gilmore-See 2007; Harris 2009; Ojala 2008). Yes, those with more experience online tend to be more advanced, more comfortable technology users. However, these advanced digital skills are largely results of the effects not of *age* but of the *information age*. We must be careful to challenge the widely accepted digital natives view of all teens as technology experts and enthusiasts because it simply doesn't hold true for all teens (Agosto and Abbas 2010). Similarly, media portrayals often lump teens into one big group—often one big troublesome group (Bernier 2011). These portrayals are dangerous stereotypes that we must challenge while promoting awareness that teens are individuals first and members of their age group second.

Focus on Teens over Information Resources

The monolithic digital natives view of all teens as technology enthusiasts and digital whizzes is largely a resource-centered view: it defines teens by the resources that they use. In the field of library services much of the scholarly and professional writing has taken a similar resource-centered view, most commonly a YA literature-centered view. In the professional literature analysis presented at the beginning of this chapter, for example, by far the most common article topic was teen information resources, particularly books. Certainly it is legitimate and important for LIS students and librarians to be familiar with the wide range of books and other information resources available to today's teens, but it's not enough as a human-centered field for us to focus on literary quality, or on analyzing information resources to identify the "best" ones. Focusing on teens and their information needs first, and on the kinds of resources that can fulfill those needs second, arms librarians, LIS students, and researchers with longer-lasting knowledge that they can apply for decades to come as they work with teens.

From an educational standpoint, LIS educators should focus first on teaching students about teen information needs and behaviors. After students understand the kinds of needs that information resources can fulfill for teens, we can then use specific information resources (everything from print novels to social network sites to online newspapers to video games) to show how these resources can fulfill teens' needs. We need to remember that books and other information resources are not just creative works to be appreciated for their literary and artistic qualities, but tools for meeting teens' varying needs and interests. Popular titles will come and go, but teens' needs and interests are more static. Thinking about information resources from the teen-centered perspective equips us to better serve teens and to serve them for the longer term.

CONCLUSION

Going back to the question of what should be the central focus of today's library research and services for teens, I want to repeat the major themes that I have discussed in this chapter. First, moving toward a truly teen-centered perspective means respecting teens as the experts of their own thoughts, behaviors, preferences, and needs. This means including teens as research participants, as partners in library services design, and basing teen library services on research that gathers data directly from teens. Second, developmental concepts and theories continue to be useful for providing general lenses and explanations of teen behaviors, but they must be seen as general guidelines within which there is wide individual variance. Teens are individuals first and members of their age groups second. We must recognize, respect, and honor individual differences and avoid stereotypes. Third, we need to approach our study of information resources for teens not with the goal of determining the "best" resources from a literary and artistic standpoint but with the goal of learning how resources can best fulfill teens' needs and interests.

Based on the small-scale analysis discussed in this chapter, it seems the adult-centered perspective dominates the current professional writing, as just 3.6 percent of the articles analyzed include any type of teen input, from direct teen input in the form of casual verbal feedback on library programs and services to service design based on teen-centered research. Placing teens more squarely at the center of research and practice can be fairly simple, such as incorporating teen input into analyses of YA literature via focus groups, online literature circles, and other conversations with teens, or designing library programs based on research into teens' information needs, uses, and behaviors. Of course, more teen-centered research is needed in the first place to enable librarians to build programs around it, and teen services librarians need more exposure to the teen-centered research that is being conducted. This is one way that professional journal editors can help to move the field more toward the teen-centered perspective—by publishing brief reports and discussions of the practical applications of this research.

Again, it is important to point out the limitations of the small-scale study presented in this chapter. I examined only one of several journals that publish professional literature relating to library services for teens. Much of this work is also disseminated via books, blogs, and other venues, none of which were included in the analysis. Further, the analysis covered just three years and therefore did not afford historical analysis or examination of trends over time. Future investigations could examine a wider range of publication venues and longer time periods. Even more useful would be the examination of library school curricula to determine the extent to which the teen-centered approach is presented in course topics and readings. The examination could consider questions such as the following:

- To what extent do courses across institutions address library services and research from a teen-centered focus?
- To what extent do they present a literature-centered approach?

- How many institutions offer courses in teen information needs and behaviors? In youth development?

An understanding of prevailing educational approaches could lead to additional suggestions for moving the field more toward the teen-centered approach advocated throughout this chapter.

The good news is that based on "YALSA's Competencies for Librarians Serving Youth," YALSA (2010, 2017) at least is advocating a more teen-centered focus. Six of the seven areas of competencies mention at least briefly the importance of including teens in designing library services. As Flowers (2011) interprets the competencies, "Youth participation in library decision-making is important as a means of achieving more responsive and effective library and information services for this age group" (14). If we keep in mind the important underlying concepts of individuality, view teens as the experts of teen cultures and needs, and maintain an emphasis on teens over information resources as the central focus of the field, we can follow this important movement toward more teen-centered library services for teens and take fuller advantage of our potential for improving teens' lives.

REFERENCES

Agosto, D. E. 2007. "Why Do Teens Use Libraries? Results of a Public Library Use Survey." *Public Libraries* 46, no. 3: 55–62.

———. 2010. "Urban Teens and Their Use of Public Libraries." In *Urban Teens in the Library: Research and Practice*, edited by D. E. Agosto and S. Hughes-Hassell, 83–100. Chicago: American Library Association.

Agosto, D. E., and J. Abbas. 2010. "High School Seniors' Social Network and Other ICT Preferences and Concerns." In *Proceedings of the 2010 American Society for Information Science and Technology Annual Meeting (ASIST)*, in Pittsburgh, PA, October 22–27. www.asis.org/asist2010/proceedings/proceedings/ASIST_AM10/submissions/25_Final_Submission.pdf.

Agosto, D. E., and S. Hughes-Hassell. 2006a. "Toward a Model of the Everyday Life Information Needs of Urban Teenagers: Part 1, Theoretical Model." *Journal of the American Society for Information Science and Technology* 57, no. 10: 1394–1403.

———. 2006b. "Toward a Model of the Everyday Life Information Needs of Urban Teenagers: Part 2, Empirical Model." *Journal of the American Society for Information Science and Technology* 57, no. 11: 1418–26.

———. 2010. "Revamping Library Services to Meet Urban Teens' Everyday Life Information Needs and Preferences." In *Urban Teens in the Library: Research and Practice*, edited by D. E. Agosto and S. Hughes-Hassell, 23–40. Chicago: American Library Association.

Aronson, M. 2002. "Coming of Age: One Editor's View of How Young Adult Publishing Developed in America." *Publishers Weekly* 249, no. 6: 82–86.

Bernier, A. 2011. "Representations of Youth in Local Media: Implications for Library Service." *Library and Information Science Research* 33, no. 2: 158–67.

Bernier, A., M. K. Chelton, C. A. Jenkins, and J. Burek Pierce. 2010. "Two Hundred Years of Young Adult Library Services History." *VOYA*. www.voyamagazine.com/2010/03/30/chronology.

Biladeau, S. 2009. "Technology and Diversity: Perceptions of Idaho's 'Digital Natives.'" *Teacher Librarian* 36, no. 3: 20–21.

Cart, M. 2010. *Young Adult Literature: From Romance to Realism*. Chicago: American Library Association.

Flowers, S. 2011. "Leadership and Professionalism: Competencies for Serving Youth." *Young Adult Library Services* 9, no. 2: 10–15.

Gilmore-See, J. 2007. "Kids 2.0." *School Library Media Activities* 24, no. 3: 55–58.

Harris, C. 2009. "Excuse Me. Do You Speak Digital?" (Interview with J. Palfrey). *School Library Journal* 55, no. 9: 30–33.

Hilbun, J. W., and J. Claes. 2010. *Coast to Coast: Exploring State Book Awards*. Westport, CT: Libraries Unlimited.

Kunzel, B., and C. Hardesty. 2006. *The Teen-Centered Book Club: Readers into Leaders*. Westport, CT: Libraries Unlimited.

Ojala, M. 2008. "Social Media, Information Seeking, and Generational Differences." *Online* 32, no. 2: 5.

Prensky, M. 2001. "Digital Natives, Digital Immigrants." *On the Horizon* 9, no. 5: 1–5.

Pulliam, J. 2010. "Monstrous Bodies: Femininity and Agency in Young Adult Horror Fiction." Unpublished doctoral dissertation, Louisiana State University, Baton Rouge.

Tuccillo, D. P. 2010. *Teen-Centered Library Service: Putting Youth Participation into Practice*. Santa Barbara, CA: Libraries Unlimited.

YALSA (Young Adult Library Services Association). 2009. "Current Research Related to Young Adult Services, 2006–2009: A Supplement Compiled by the YALSA Research Committee." www.ala.org/yalsa/sites/ala.org.yalsa/files/content/guidelines/research/09researchbibliography_rev.pdf.

———. 2010. "YALSA's Competencies for Librarians Serving Youth: Young Adults Deserve the Best." www.ala.org/yalsa/guidelines/yacompetencies2010 (no longer available).

———. 2011. "Young Adult Library Services Author Guidelines." www.ala.org/yalsa/products&publications/yalsapubs/yals/authorguidelines.

———. 2017. "Teen Services Competencies for Library Staff." www.ala.org/yalsa/guidelines/yacompetencies.

CHAPTER 2

Diverse Identity in Anxious Times

Young Adult Literature and Contemporary Culture

Karen Coats

Young adults fashion their identities from the images and discourses that culture makes available to them as well as the imperatives culture imposes in terms of value and recognition. This chapter examines the texts and contexts through which young adults form their identities in contemporary culture and argues that the library must preserve a confident pluralism in the face of calls for narrowly positivist representations of diversity. In addition, this chapter argues that library professionals should stay abreast of current developmental research in psychology and neuroscience that provides information about general capacities, while they must also view their teen clients as individuals with complex, intersectional histories and traits. By applying this theoretical knowledge to programming, librarians can encourage perspective taking that supports multifaceted diversity among young adults.

In an article in the *New York Times Magazine,* cultural critic Wesley Morris (2015) dubbed 2015 "The Year We Obsessed about Identity." Posing the question "Who do we think we are?," he avers that we are

> in the midst of a great cultural identity migration. Gender roles are merging. Races are being shed. In the last six years or so, but especially in 2015, we've been made to see how trans and bi and poly-ambi-omni- we are.

Morris highlights both the optimism and the anxiety that attends this sense of fluidity and merging of identities in contemporary culture. Citing multiple cases from film, books, and celebrities that indicate our desire to transcend categories of race and gender, he also notes the seemingly intractable position of blackness in America as a limit to mutability and autonomy when it comes to choosing one's identity. He ends, however, by drawing attention to Andrew Solomon's *Far from the Tree* (2012), a collection of stories about how people claim horizontal identities—that is, identities formed through affiliations of choice—over and against the vertical ones of race, ethnicity, and cultural tradition they inherit from their parents.

As Morris (2015) notes, a vast representational field has opened with respect to possibilities for identity construction, and he does not even cite the half of it. In addition to challenges to the binary stability of gender and the expanded categories through which to define it that have claimed media attention in recent years, we have also seen the cultural and legal sanction of gay marriage; expanded opportunities and respect for neurodiverse individuals; the revaluation of working-class, nerd, and fandom-based cultures; a resurgence of youth activism; and satiric as well as earnest explorations of how white privilege, toxic masculinity, microaggressions, and trauma affect identity. Moreover, and perhaps more importantly, Morris highlights that

> [f]or more than a decade, we've lived with personal technologies—video games and social-media platforms—that have helped us create alternate or auxiliary personae. We've also spent a dozen years in the daily grip of makeover shows, in which a team of experts transforms your personal style, your home, your body, your spouse.

All of these public conversations have found their way into books for young adults that probe, extend, and deepen their consequences for teen identity formation (see this chapter's appendix for a list of recommended titles). The upshot has been to foreground the fact that who we think we are is a result more of changing modes of social interaction and cultural recognition than of inborn traits, with authenticity redefined as choice rather than fidelity to one's biological or social origins.

Like Morris, I believe that cultural fictions, including celebrity personas as well as films, TV shows, books, and even Internet memes, are a good indicator of our ambivalences and anxieties with regard to identity. But I would go further in asserting that these fictions are more than mirrors that passively reflect existing circumstances or even call those circumstances into question through caricatured distortions. Instead, especially for adolescents, such representations offer expanded possibilities for constructing an identity that will earn them recognition in a social world that they find desirable. As I argued in the first edition of this volume, the way we live now, that is, the way we negotiate our identities in postmodern culture as both adults and teens, is through dynamic interaction with cultural models and the discourses they produce, enable, sustain, and challenge. Therefore, as these models and discourses are in flux, so too are our identities. This state of provisionality and experiment has always been the territory traversed by teens as they seek to define a self that makes sense to them and has uptake with others, but the cultural maps they have to guide them have proliferated to a greater extent than ever before, as has the speed at which teens are expected to adapt to new cultural trends and concerns. It is therefore vitally important for those of us who work with teens to understand our own relationships to these maps in order to help orient the youth we serve. The purpose of this essay is to explore the theoretical contexts of how identity is shaped and informed in and through contemporary culture, in hopes that such exploration can offer some practical insights into what the LIS vision of today's teens can and perhaps should look like so that we might serve them better.

As I outlined in the chapter included in the first edition of this volume under the title "Dialogism, Development, and Destination: Young Adults in Contemporary Culture" (Coats 2013) our understanding of teen identity has undergone philosophical shifts as well as material changes prompted by parenting styles, all of which can be traced through trends in YA literature. In that chapter, I elaborated on the contours of these ideological shifts through examples from specific novels. Here, I want to explore the intense focus on identity in YA literature as it has been highlighted by Morris and, more specifically, through the ways youth literature has become something of a cause célèbre in online discourse. I will briefly reiterate, however, that while our ideologies of the self emerge and change over time, we do not wholly abandon perspectives from earlier periods; instead, they form part of the pluralistic framework that dominates postmodern culture. Thus, from the Romantic teen, innately innocent, desperately vulnerable and yet guided by incorruptible goodness, to the modernist teen, progressing steadily toward a rational adulthood as understood through an ideology of white heteronormativity, to the postmodern teen, untethered from tradition and finding his or her own way while suffering under the onus of a mandate to be fabulous, each has multiple exemplars in contemporary YA fiction. However, most people's current ideological commitments to each position—that is, who we think teens are—tend to exist along a continuum rather than assuming a fixed and final stance, and they are often affected by the quality of the story being told as well as by our desire to believe in the efficacy of our efforts, and the efforts of the books we recommend, to intervene for what we consider good in young people's lives. We want to believe, for instance, that Harry Potter was not damaged by his abusive upbringing (Rowling 1997); that Melinda from Laurie Halse Anderson's (1999) *Speak* will make a full recovery once she has confronted her rapist; that every wallflower like Charlie will find his versions of Sam and Patrick to help him confront his demons and survive high school (Chbosky 1999); that all open-hearted teens will find acceptance for their gender identity and maybe even a soulmate who gently ushers them into the wonders of positive sexual experiences; and that confused teens like Steve Harmon will find redemption while unrepentant ones like Archie Costello will get their comeuppance (Myers 1999; Cormier 1974). We might even find our hearts and minds opened and changed by these books, and if that happens for adults, how much more so might it happen for teens, whose attitudes and experiences are less overdetermined and more open to change to begin with?

TWO CONTEXTS FOR DIALOGIC IDENTITY FORMATION

Why, then, are teens so open to the influence of these cultural fictions? Or, rather, is the idea that they are a valid assumption and how do we know? To answer this question, we need both a social theory of identity and a robust understanding of the cognitive and affective psychology of adolescence. So we will begin with what is happening inside the teenage brain.

Affective-Cognitive Development

One of the reasons why teens are so open to the influence of cultural images and other social inputs is because they do not yet have a coherent sense of self. Both neuroscientists like Rosalind Ridley (2016) and developmental psychologists like Kurt W. Fischer (1980) and Susan Harter (2012) have found that a coherent, stable sense of self, including the capacity to reflect on and evaluate our actions and values, is the result of a process that evolves throughout the teen years into adulthood. Harter specifies that, "[i]n fact, it is not until *late adolescence* if not early adulthood that the abilities to construct . . . a self-portrait potentially emerge" (9). Instead, "the young adolescent is desperately trying to figure out what others think of the self in order to make decisions about which perspectives to internalize as defining features of the self" (76-77). If we read that carefully, we note that the perspectives are initially external to the self, publicly available as costumes to be tried on and scripts to be performed if you will, prior to being internalized. As teens observe the recognition others give them as a result of their performances, they consciously and unconsciously adopt or abandon those scripts as part of their own identities.

The process, according to Harter (2012) and others, goes something like this: Children develop the cognitive capacity to use social comparison in order to evaluate themselves in middle childhood, around ages 8 to 10. Their self-esteem can take a hit at this point, as they can begin to discern both positive and negative attributes in themselves and differentiate between their real and ideal abilities. As their sense of interiority and their capacity for introspection develop into early adolescence, they also come to realize that they behave and are perceived differently in different social situations; in other words, they begin to construct and recognize multiple selves that vary according to context. This is the stage, then, roughly and normatively from ages 11 to 16, when experimentation with identity construction is at its peak, and when teens are most vulnerable to compelling cultural fictions as they seek selves to try on, so to speak. It is also the time when teens feel most confused or fragmented when those selves come into conflict with one another. As Harter notes,

> The creation of multiple selves, coupled with the emerging ability to detect potential contradictions between self-attributes displayed in different roles, naturally ushers in concern over which attributes define the true self. However, from a normative perspective, the adolescent at this level is not equipped with the cognitive skills to fully solve this dilemma. (97)

While most youth services professionals have rejected G. Stanley Hall's (1904) "storm and stress" perspective on adolescence in favor of a positive youth development (PYD) model, there is little consensus as to what qualities will best serve the emerging adults among us over the long haul (see, for instance, King et al. 2005). Do they need the stick-to-itiveness of "grit," or the ability to walk away from relationships and projects that are not working for them? The independence to solve their own problems, or the humility to ask for help? Because of the proliferation of authority figures offering contradictory advice, teens become aware that knowledge and identity themselves are contextual, relative, and implicated in structures of power, open to negotiation and change, offering no clear basis on which to make decisions, other than one's own sense of what constitutes a true or a false self.

Understanding this stage of development has implications for readers' advisory. In general terms, books offer a self-contained, complete world in which actions and their consequences are carefully plotted, unlike the indeterminate, relativistic real one in which teens themselves have to act and take their chances. But the books that resonate most strongly more often than not zero in on characters realizing the costs of engaging in false-self behavior, that is, concealing genuine feelings and saying and doing things the character doesn't believe before emerging as a true self. And while many characters in YA texts are idealized, models of true-self characters are complex; even once they have overcome their false-self behaviors, they retain both positive and negative character traits, and they have credible limitations. Books thus provide one of the linguistic supports that both neo-Piagetians and cognitive developmentalists argue are necessary for teens to develop the higher-order abstractions that serve to integrate their self-portraits; in other words, as the characters reflect on their arcs, the terminology and metaphors authors employ can promote active reflection and new language through which readers can consider their own traits and attributes.

Figured Worlds

The psychology behind teen identity construction is an incomplete model if it is not wedded to a social theory. Hence, a second context for understanding how and why teens are particularly susceptible to Morris's (2015) "great cultural identity migration" is the theoretical notion that identity is both performative and dialogic and, therefore, mutable. That is, we do not act out of our innate or already formed, stable sense of self so much as we create, adjust, and fashion a self in and through specific cultural contexts or "figured worlds," a theory synthesized by Dorothy Holland and colleagues (1998) from the work of Lev Vygotsky, Mikhail Bakhtin, and Pierre Bourdieu. Figured worlds can be defined as culturally constructed discourses wherein people take up and enact socially imposed and scripted positions and roles. As Luis Urrieta Jr. (2007) explains, "People 'figure' who they are through the activities and in relation to the social types that populate these figured worlds" (108). And while that may sound grimly restrictive, it is important to note that figured worlds are not overdetermined or ever fully and finally formed themselves. Instead, the participants in any given figured world have the agency to negotiate and redefine their positions, thus creating new, potentially more liberatory possibilities for identity. Urrieta continues:

> Because figured worlds are peopled by characters from collective imaginings (e.g., of class, race, gender, nationality), people's identity and agency is formed dialectically and dialogically in them. . . . Although narratives may be used by participants as though they were pre/scriptive, they are commonly horizons of meaning against which incidents, acts and individuals are interpreted. . . . Identities are thus formed in the processes of participating in activities organized by figured worlds. (109)

This renegotiation of meanings in and through new stories is precisely what Morris (2015) sees happening in contemporary culture, at least to a point. Disparate voices are using social media as well as traditional screen and print media to put pressure on the hegemonic constraints of existing power relations to bring more forms of identity into positive social recognition through such movements as the We Need Diverse Books campaign and #ownvoices, which advocate for diverse stories told by authors who can claim similarly marginalized experiences.

What's exciting, and perhaps anxiety producing, for youth services workers is that today's teens are both the leaders and the targets for more open possibilities for identity construction. The expanded access teens have through global flows of story and image means that their figured worlds are multiple and varied, lived in both real and virtual spaces. In contemporary culture, it is undeniable that screen media are largely responsible for creating the available scripts for teens to internalize as features of the self. The carefully curated and digitally enhanced images they are bombarded with, the makeover and talent contest shows that have taken over television, and the diet trends and lifestyle hacks that pepper their feeds are all versions of the same script, exemplified in this grimly ironic motto of The Corporation from Libba Bray's (2011) *Beauty Queens*: "Because there's nothing wrong with you . . . that we can't fix" (37). Moreover, their gaming avatars often live more exciting and satisfying lives than they do, especially as teens control the screens in front of them.

In fact, these highly stylized media scripts are not only acting on teens but on adults as well. In *Identity Troubles*, sociologist Anthony Elliott (2016) argues that the unstable nature of global economies and the constant evolution of technologies create an environment where everyone who wishes to remain relevant must be, first and foremost, nimble. As a worker, you are infinitely replaceable; your worth to an organization is not gauged by your years of experience or service, but by your ability to adapt to new challenges. In other words, the self you perform today may be obsolete or devalued next week, so you need to stay plugged in and on trend. We adults may be at pains to stress the message to teens that they are just fine the way they are, but teens know better; their futures, like ours, depend on being able not just to manipulate today's software but to quickly learn the next release, and the next, and the next. This need for perpetual reinvention thus militates against the construction of a stable, coherent self; the personal malady it suborns is anxiety, or (as the cool kids were saying a couple of years ago?) the condition of having "no chill."

To offer a solution to this problem would be to participate in the very culture that created it ("7 Ways to Reduce Anxiety"—click here!). But I do think there is a role for LIS professionals to play by doing the thing they are best positioned to do: offer a space for genuine dialogue that actively engages with and talks back to cultural fictions, both in print and on screens. Since the emergence of the genre in the mid-twentieth century, much contemporary YA literature has embraced the postmodern critique that challenges normative scripts of mature adulthood and institutional power, including the idealism that David Foster Wallace (1993) attributes to early versions of postmodern irony, that "etiology and diagnosis point[s] toward cure, that a revelation of imprisonment [leads] to freedom" (183). Unlike the ways in which adult literature of the same period developed, however, YA literature never slipped into full-on nihilism with respect to the self as an empowered individual. Instead, as Roberta Seelinger Trites (2007) has argued, the adolescent character became the symbol for restless dissatisfaction with the status quo. As such, what Adam Kelly (2013) calls the trend toward "New Sincerity" in adult literature of the twenty-first century is nothing new in YA literature. Instead, with a few notable exceptions, YA texts, be they fantasies, dystopias, or realistic texts, tend most often to move their characters from "the dramatic irony of being self-aware" to "the reconstruction of belief that comes after it" (Agger 2005). In fact, I highly suspect that this is one of the reasons why adults have migrated to YA literature in droves in the early decades of the twenty-first century. As Wallace (1993) notes, postmodern irony is profoundly dissatisfying in its inability to generate a sustaining belief that humanity's problems may have even imperfect or provisional solutions. By contrast, the neo-sincere belief found in much YA fiction may be in the individual or in a social landscape that allows for more freedom in terms of how we construct and express our identities. As Timotheus Vermeulen and Robin van den Akker (2010) put it, "[I]f, simplistically put, the modern outlook vis-à-vis idealism and ideals could be characterized as fanatic and/or naïve, and the postmodern mindset as apathetic and/or skeptic, the current generations' attitude . . . can be conceived of as a kind of informed naivety, a pragmatic idealism."

In terms of youth culture in particular, "neo-sincerity" has come to refer to "a move from the ironic and detached savvy attitude to unabashed enjoyment of even 'geeky' or melodramatic texts" (Hautakangas 2015, 113). Performing identities such as these requires some degree of self-lamination and no small measure of courage, especially when they require transgressing culturally imposed boundaries of race, gender, and class. But even knowing that your neo-sincere embrace of "informed naivety" has a cool name and is part of a movement can provide the validating recognition many teens need to feel good about their identity choices. Through the development and encouragement of niche clubs and events, therefore, libraries have been and can continue to be a safe space to indulge in a deep, unapologetic love for all things Harry Potter, for instance, or Strawberry Shortcake, indie comics, cosplay, board gaming, poetry—the list goes on.

There are, of course, exceptions to this general strand of neo-sincerity in the literature. Books that leave their characters in tough spots to make their ironic points include

The Chocolate War (Cormier 1974), *Feed* (Anderson 2002), and *The Spectacular Now* (Tharp 2008). But even M. T. Anderson (2017) seems to hit a point of New Sincerity with the overly hopeful ending of *Landscape with Invisible Hand*—or does he? The key to these books lies in their ability to prompt multiple interpretations. While there are single books that encourage this sort of multivalent interpretation, another key service that librarians can provide better than anyone else is the encouragement for teens to read books that work in dialogue with another, presenting divergent ideological views on a single subject. Unfortunately, this is an extremely difficult thing to do, especially when the viewpoint of a book contradicts one's own beliefs about how an identity should be portrayed. And it has become more difficult, and thus more necessary, in an era when a few voices, magnified through viral hashtags and repostings, increasingly dominate the critical discussion.

THE DANGERS OF A SINGLE CRITICAL PERSPECTIVE

Chimamanda Ngozi Adichie's 2009 TED Talk "The Dangers of a Single Story" gently reminds listeners that a limited perspective is a universal problem; that is, we all carry within us incomplete and often stereotypical understandings of other people. This is one of the key problems that the We Need Diverse Books campaign and #ownvoices seek to address—by expanding the repertoire of stories about diverse characters by diverse authors, no one story will come to dominate as the only story, definitional of that experience. What librarians must guard against, however, is what we mean by diversity as such. As Adichie's personal anecdote demonstrates, it is not enough to share a racial or ethnic heritage if one wants to avoid the danger of a single story. In fact, all too often, our discussions of diversity focus on what anthropologists call "intermediate-level concepts: ethnic groups, values, power discrepancy, material resources, colonialism, traditional beliefs, ritual, artistic languages," rather than on the more complex and intersectional ways teens move in, relate to, and establish horizontal identities of affiliation in their various figured worlds (Schwimmer, Poirier, and Clammer 2004, ix).

The pertinent question for LIS professionals and all those concerned with helping teens form capacious and empathetic identities becomes how far we are willing to allow our teens to fall from their affiliative trees when it comes to these intermediate-level concepts, which have the tendency to lump people into identity groups based on positivist—that is, externally or positionally defined—characteristics. And how much do we trust them to be able to perform pluralistic readings of positivist representations? Put another way, can we accept diversity and challenge *within* diversity when it comes to identity? The groundswell of online conversation around diversity in youth literature not only has focused on calls for more diverse books but also has sought to control the content of such books, and to dictate who is allowed to write them. Taking full advantage of call-out culture, a handful of passionate critics have exercised a powerful and potentially chilling influence on publishing as well as on the larger critical community. Public online outrage has resulted in pre- and postpublication withdrawal of controversial books, such as e. E. Charlton-Trujillo's (2016) *When We Was Fierce*, and the sanction of certain authors for their despicable personal behavior or outspoken beliefs rather than for the quality of their books, as has been the case with Orson Scott Card and Sherman Alexie.

Alexie's case has become more complicated as noted blogger Debbie Reese (2018) cites not his personal behavior so much as his openly assimilative or "mainstream" stance with regard to Native identity, something that she presumably did not object to for the many years she promoted his work, as the reason she has removed him from her list of approved authors. As with other books she has called out as objectionable, she would rather young people not read his books at all, and her influence is such that many educators have removed them from their syllabi. But Alexie (2009) has never been cagey about how he sees his identity as culturally hybrid. In his mixed-genre piece, "Tuxedo with Eagle Feathers," for instance, he writes, "I wasn't saved by the separation of cultures; I was *reborn* inside the collision of cultures" (80). To be sure, Reese (2018) is a fierce advocate for authors whose perspectives she does not find objectionable, ones that presumably are better at "giv[ing] readers the depth of understanding to know who we are, what our histories have been, what we face on a daily basis, and what gives us the strength to carry on." But her "we" here seems both monolithic and exclusionary, focusing only on *her* ways of finding the strength to carry on rather than Alexie's (2009) unapologetic embrace of "all those damn dead white male and female writers / That first taught me how to be a fighter" (80). In other words, in her focus on a representation of Native identity that she takes issue with, she does not seem to trust teen readers' potential for pluralistic or resistant reading. Certainly, Alexie's work should not be the only thing teens read, but is a call for the elimination of his perspective the answer to understanding who indigenous people think they are in contemporary culture?

The danger here may not be so much of a "single story" as of a single critical perspective, validated by that poster's claim of positivist affiliation with a racial, ethnic, or neurodiverse identity group and then picked up and retweeted until no one dares question the uniqueness of its source or the cogency of its claims across diverse experience. All too often, the call is for absolute and total acceptance of a perspective rather than entering into what might become a mutually productive if difficult dialogue. David Brooks's (2016) comments in response to how Adichie's concept of a single story extends to political discourse seem relevant to the turn discourse about youth literature has taken online:

> Worse, the stories have become identity markers. . . . In order to express your solidarity with the virtuous team, you have to embrace the socially approved story. If you differ from the official story . . . it is not so much that you are wrong (truth is not the issue). It is a sign that you have false allegiances. You must embrace the approved story to show you are not complicit in a system of oppression.

Indeed, one too many calls for white people in particular (again a positivist categorization that privileges group affiliation over individual experience of and thinking within that affiliation) to "shut up" led to the shutting down of the child_lit electronic discussion group, which at one time existed as a forum for expressing diverse opinions about many issues and was largely responsible for advancing the professional status of research in youth literature in the academy. Objectors to the character of the discourse that ensued were accused of white fragility, but I am not speaking out of white fragility here; rather, I am mounting an argument against teen fragility, and challenging LIS professionals to consider how such online discourse, judged by its effects, accords with the fundamental ethics of librarianship to promote the free flow of ideas, even ideas we disagree with or find abhorrent. I fear that by listening to only the loudest voices in the Twitterverse, we run the risk of limiting choices rather than expanding them.

That said, I do not think we abdicate our right or our responsibility to offer guidance for teens toward more empathetic and socially positive identities when we present them with disparate ideologies. In fact, we must do everything we can to actively discourage the adoption of socially destructive identities. A stark example of the negative side of contemporary instability and choosing identity through imagistic representation comes when we consider the Parkland, Florida, case of the boy who saw being a "professional school shooter" as a viable option. This is where books can be our strongest ally, precisely because they do not rely merely on positivist visual representations. Instead, books are the best site we have for observing other minds at work. While we read, we evaluate and pass judgment on the thoughts and actions of the characters. Granted, these judgments are based on our own experiences and moral frameworks, but plots allow us to see the progression of thought to action and from action to consequence. Moreover, they offer opportunities for teens to explore diverse perspectives, especially when we challenge them to read stories that present differing perspectives against one another and in conversation with other readers. Instead of offering suggestions for "read-alikes," I propose that we should offer pairs for "reading diversely" that suggest differing ideologies with regard to people who share certain positivist identity characteristics and facilitate opportunities for follow-up discussions, either in person, in print, and/or online, so that teens can engage in their own neo-sincere, dialogic constructions of identity in these anxious times.

APPENDIX: Diverse Pairing Suggestions

The Absolutely True Diary of a Part-Time Indian, by Sherman Alexie (2007) / *X-Indian Chronicles: The Book of Mausape,* by Thomas W. Yeahpau (2006)

American Born Chinese, by Gene Luen Yang (2006) / *Picture Us in the Light,* by Kelly Loy Gilbert (2018)

Feed, by M. T. Anderson (2002) / *The End of Fun,* by Sean McGinty (2016) / *Landscape with Invisible Hand,* by M. T. Anderson (2017)

Gem and Dixie, by Sara Zarr (2017) / *Too Shattered for Mending,* by Peter Brown Hoffmeister (2017)

Haters, by Alisa Valdes-Rodriguez (2006) / *Yaqui Delgado Want to Kick Your Ass,* by Meg Medina (2013) / *Shadowshaper,* by Daniel José Older (2015)

Monster, by Walter Dean Myers (1999) / *The Hate U Give,* by Angie Thomas (2017)

Openly Straight, by Bill Konigsberg (2013) / *Simon vs. the Homo Sapiens Agenda,* by Becki Albertalli (2005)

This Side of Home, by Renée Watson (2015) / *Piecing Me Together,* by Renée Watson (2017)

PRIMARY REFERENCES

Alexie, S. 2009. *Face*. Brooklyn: Hanging Loose Press.
Anderson, L. H. 1999. *Speak*. New York: Farrar, Straus and Giroux.
Anderson, M. T. 2002. *Feed*. Somerville, MA: Candlewick.
———. 2017. *Landscape with Invisible Hand*. Somerville, MA: Candlewick.
Bray, L. 2011. *Beauty Queens*. New York: Scholastic.
Charlton-Trujillo, e. E. 2016. *When We Was Fierce*. Somerville, MA: Candlewick.
Chbosky, S. 1999. *The Perks of Being a Wallflower*. New York: Pocket Books.
Cormier, R. 1974. *The Chocolate War*. New York: Knopf.
Myers, W. D. 1999. *Monster*. New York: HarperCollins.
Rowling, J. K. 1997. *Harry Potter and the Sorceror's Stone*. New York: Scholastic.
Tharp, T. 2008. *The Spectacular Now*. New York: Knopf.

SECONDARY REFERENCES

Adichie, C. N. 2009. "The Dangers of a Single Story." TED Talk, presented at TEDGlobal 2009, July 2009. www.ted.com/talks/chimamanda_adichie_the_danger_of_a_single_story/transcript?language=en.

Agger, M. 2005. "Wilmerding Shrugged: The Political Ambitions of Benjamin Kunkel's *Indecision*." *Slate*, October 3. www.slate.com/articles/arts/books/2005/10/wilmerding_shrugged.html.

Brooks, D. 2016. "The Danger of a Single Story." *The New York Times*, April 19. www.nytimes.com/2016/04/19/opinion/the-danger-of-a-single-story.html.

Coats, K. 2013. "Dialogism, Development, and Destination: Young Adults in Contemporary Culture." In *Transforming Young Adult Services*, edited by A. Bernier, 53-75. Chicago: ALA Neal-Schuman.

Elliott, A. 2016. *Identity Troubles: An Introduction*. New York: Routledge.

Fischer, K. W. 1980. "A Theory of Cognitive Development: The Control and Construction of Hierarchies of Skills." *Psychological Review* 87, no. 6: 477-531. http://dx.doi.org/10.1037/0033-295X.87.6.477.

Hall, G. S. 1904. *Adolescence: Its Psychology and Its Relations to Physiology, Anthropology, Sociology, Sex, Crime and Religion*. New York: D. Appleton and Company.

Harter, S. 2012. *The Construction of the Self: Developmental and Sociocultural Foundations*. New York: The Guilford Press.

Hautakangas, M. 2015. "'It's OK to Be Joyful?' My Little Pony and Brony Masculinity." *The Journal of Popular Television* 3, no. 1: 111-18. https://doi.org/10.1386/jptv.3.1.111_1.

Holland, D., W. Lachicotte Jr., D. Skinner, and C. Cain. 1998. *Identity and Agency in Cultural Worlds*. Boston: Harvard University Press.

Kelly, A. 2013. "From Syndrome to Sincerity: Benjamin Kunkel's *Indecision*." In *Diseases and Disorders in Contemporary Fiction: The Syndrome Syndrome*, edited by T. J. Lustig and J. Peacock, 53-66. New York: Routledge.

King, P. E., E. M. Dowling, R. A. Mueller, K. White, W. Schultz, P. Osborn, E. Dickerson, D. L. Bobek, R. M. Lerner, P. L. Benson, and P. C. Scales. 2005. "Thriving in Adolescence: The Voices of Youth-Serving Practitioners, Parents, and Early and Late Adolescents." *The Journal of Early Adolescence* 25, no. 1: 94-112. https://doi.org/10.1177/0272431604272459.

Morris, W. 2015. "The Year We Obsessed Over Identity." *The New York Times Magazine*, October 6. www.nytimes.com/2015/10/11/magazine/the-year-we-obsessed-over-identity.html.

Reese, D. 2018. "An Open Letter about Sherman Alexie." *American Indians in Children's Literature*, February 25. https://americanindiansinchildrensliterature.blogspot.com/2018/02/an-open-letter-about-sherman-alexie.html.

Ridley, R. 2016. *Peter Pan and the Mind of J. M. Barrie: An Exploration of Cognition and Consciousness*. Cambridge, UK: Cambridge Scholars Press.

Schwimmer, E., S. Poirier, and J. R. Clammer. 2004. *Figured Worlds: Ontological Obstacles in Intercultural Relations*. Toronto: University of Toronto Press.

Solomon, A. 2012. *Far from the Tree: Parents, Children, and the Search for Identity*. New York: Scribner.

Trites, R. S. 2007. *Twain, Alcott, and the Birth of the Adolescent Reform Novel*. Iowa City: University of Iowa Press.

Urrieta Jr., L. 2007. "Figured Worlds and Education: An Introduction to the Special Issue." *The Urban Review* 39, no. 2: 107-16.

Vermeulen, T., and R. van den Akker. 2010. "Notes on Metamodernism." *Journal of Aesthetics and Culture* 2, no. 1. https://doi.org/10.3402/jac.v2i0.5677.

Wallace, D. F. 1993. "E Unibus Pluram: Television and U.S. Fiction." *Review of Contemporary Fiction* 13, no. 2: 151-94.

CHAPTER 3

Students or Learners?

Conceptualizing Youth in School Libraries

Mary Ann Harlan

This chapter interrogates the identities of youth as student and youth as learner. How does the field of LIS construct youth in school—as students or as learners? This has implications for how we approach school librarianship, including how we distribute resources such as time, money, and school librarian expertise. Beyond that, it has implications for how we work with youth related to the practices youth enact in our libraries. This chapter argues that as individuals we have a responsibility to critically examine the use of the label *student* or *learner*, to critique policy documents, and to acknowledge that those documents are perpetuating adult notions of school and library as an institution.

Imagine the teens in your library. When you think of the youth you serve, how do you define these teens or youth? More explicitly, what do you call them—what identity label do you apply when you think of the collective? Individuals inhabit many identities and perform many roles, and yet we categorize and classify people as groups through labels, sometimes attached to demographics and sometimes connected to the roles they inhabit. The teens in any library represent a wide range of demographic identities, in a plethora of combinations, and they perform a wide variety of roles. How the discipline defines teens, and the roles they inhabit in the library, impacts the experience of both patrons and librarians.

This chapter examines schools as institutions and the labels they apply to youth. Schools primarily construct youth as student. However, an emerging shift to the label *learner*, most notably in the American Association of School Librarians' *National School Library Standards for Learners, School Librarians, and School Libraries* (AASL 2018), suggests we need to examine how the discipline of school librarianship and those who work in the field understand the framing of youth as student, youth as learner, and youth as person.

STUDENT VERSUS LEARNER

Youth in the United States spend an average of 6.5 hours a day in school, 180 days a year (National Center for Education Statistics 2008). At slightly less than 50 percent of a year, youth spend a considerable amount of time in school, which therefore presents as a major role in the cultural defining of their collective identity. As an institution, the school's primary structure has not changed since the turn of the nineteenth century when public comprehensive high schools became the primary form of educational institution. Adult-dominated discussions led to decisions regarding how to learn, what to learn, how to behave, and what the school day would look like. Schools define youth as student, conveying along with that label the attendant assumptions of how to be a student. These assumptions include obeying norms of behavior in an environment shaped and controlled by adults; obtaining knowledge deemed necessary and valuable through debate within the adult community; demonstrating knowledge through systems developed by teachers, textbook and test publishers, and lawmakers; and recognizing one's place as student within the hierarchical structure. Youth find themselves negotiating these practices of *being student* with very little input into expectations of what *being student* means.

In the past 15 years, an attempt to define youth as learner rather than student developed in education communities. More accurately, the focus on learning as activity rather than student as product entered the mainstream lexicon of educational policy and cultural debate. This labeling shift suggests a different identity, with different identity practices. While this is primarily taking place within local and state circles, evidence can be found in the title of the state of Virginia's "Standards of Learning" (Virginia Department of Education 2011). At the federal level, Common Core State Standards (www.corestandards.org; adopted by 41 states) use the word *student* but focus on expected outcomes, what a student can do rather than what a student knows. While public debates have broken out regarding Common Core (Murphy 2014), practitioner resources such as the Edutopia website or the National Education Association magazine focus on student inquiry and practices of learning that include student choice and independence, including monthly articles on collaborative learning and project-based approaches to curriculum. Although when I was a student in teacher training, in the early 1990s, it was common to hear that teachers need to be a "guide on the side" rather than a "sage on the stage," this is now being adopted more broadly in state and federal policy and shared resources. What this means for the practice of *being student* is that the norms of behavior, expectations of hierarchy, and shared knowledge possibly change through a renegotiation of cultural definitions. Therefore, within educational circles, the practices of *being learner* emphasize independence, critical thinking, collaboration, and self-directed learning—all rooted in the concept of lifelong learning (Partnership for 21st Century Skills 2009; Harlan 2015; Serafini and Gee 2017).

SCHOOL LIBRARIES

School libraries are semipublic spaces within schools. They are not a conventional classroom; youth have access to library space during both class time and time designated as theirs—such as passing periods, lunch, and before and after school. As such, it has been argued within the field that they are "third spaces" (Goodin 2011; Williams 2013; AASL 2018) in which youth can develop their own interests, literacies, and expertise unencumbered by adult control. Dr. David Loertscher has spent the past 10 years advocating for his vision of a learning commons that centers youth interest, inquiry, and performance (Loertscher and Koechlin 2011, 2014).

Despite arguments within the field that school libraries should be student-centered spaces and explore individual practices as spaces, they are still housed within the schoolyard gates and, thus, youth in the library are subject to the same rules and surveillance that they face in traditional classrooms. Debates that erupt on e-mail discussion lists, at conferences, and on social media regarding policies related to resources, such as fines and restricting numbers of resources, food and drink in library space, or noise control, betray that practicing school librarians still see themselves as owning the school library space, rather than managing it collaboratively with the community. For librarians, youth in school libraries are still *students*, with all that implies regarding norms of behavior.

Just as space is controlled through institutional expectations, so is curriculum. A common understanding articulated by the American Association of School Librarians states that school libraries are a space for "on-site, personalized, and self-directed learning" (AASL 2018, 11). And yet, as the library is part of the school, its mission revolves around supporting students within the academic curriculum. Academic curriculum is decided upon through governmental policy, presented by publishers of resources and testing, and then enacted in the classroom by a teacher's pedagogical choices. In other words, academic curriculum reflects adult concerns based on Western traditions of schooling and knowledge. For practicing school librarians, this means that choices must be made in regard to priorities: Do they spend resources such as money and time supporting classroom teachers' needs or the needs of learners who seek information beyond the curriculum? Direction from the field in the form of policy documents and practitioner reports of best practices or personal successes contributes to a sense of how the field conceptualizes youth.

One of the most significant shifts in school librarianship is the spotlighting of the role of librarian as teacher. In emphasizing and encouraging collaboration with classroom teachers to implement team teaching in areas related to information literacy and course content, school librarian educators and the field as a whole define youth as their students. In doing so, they both imply and directly claim a hierarchical structure that centers the field's concerns as grounded in adult expectations of the discipline. While it should be obvious, it goes unstated that *information literacy* is a term youth have no ownership over, and the skills necessary for "career, college, and life success" (AASL 2018, 12) have been shaped by adult policy, informed by adult research questions, and performed by adults. Therefore, *students* control little of what they learn in schools, despite the urging for and stated belief of the necessity of independent inquiry found in both the Common Core State Standards (www.corestandards.org) and the AASL (2018) standards. We should question this. Should not learners (a term employed in those standards) be able to explore their own interests? Should they not leverage and develop skills within literacies they identify as necessary? What is our role as experts—is it as mentors or is it as the wisdom on the mount?

Current trends in school libraries are representative of how the field is attempting to shift to learner, to serve students beyond academic curricula. However, the adults in charge still own the choices that are made. One example of this is makerspaces. In articulating the similarities of school libraries and makerspaces, Weisgrau (2015) acknowledges both as interdisciplinary spaces of informal learning that provide equitable access while still suggesting they are distinct spaces. Given the vast range of articles and blog posts in *Knowledge Quest*, the journal of AASL, school librarians have embraced the idea of not only coexistence, as Weisgrau suggests, but also ownership of the makerspace. In discussing how to advocate for makerspaces, Rendina (2015) employs language emphasizing equitable access and independence—"every student can have the opportunity to use it and learn and grow"— while still connecting the makerspace to cultural concepts such as STEM (science, technology, engineering, and math) that are highly valued in educational policy and curricula. She advocates for play but essentially discusses it in terms recognizable to career education:

"design process, innovation, and critical thinking." These articles are representative of the practitioner debate regarding the trend of makerspaces. What is significant is that the language is consistent with the new AASL (2018) standards, the Partnership for 21st Century Learning (2009), the Future Ready Schools (2018) library framework, and other guiding documents for school librarians. And this language emphasizes youth as independent learner without questioning potential tradeoffs (focus on science at cost to art and humanities?) or why and whom the concept of makerspaces benefits. It also does not examine the cost to services, both in actual dollars and in human resources, or its impact on the mission to support curricula or basic literacy skills related to reading.

It is assumed youth benefit from makerspaces. And yet the youth perspective on makerspaces in schools remains anecdotal and unclear. Furthermore, makerspaces can be critiqued for the underlying economic privilege that is driving the messages of making (Chachra 2015). Making is built on having the time to engage with the project and the budget to provide resources and tools, and it values a product. While libraries are attempting to democratize making to challenge the economic privilege critique, they are doing so within the framework of product valuation. The field embraced makerspaces without openly engaging critique and without research. Those who advocate makerspaces do so using language constructing youth as learner combined with perpetuating cultural arguments for valued knowledge. And they only anecdotally center youth in the process. Ultimately, we, as practitioners, still own the concept, the space, and the language without engaging the underlying bias and the youth view.

CONCLUSION

My argument in this chapter is that while the field is grappling with the question of resources, we are perhaps not grappling with the assumptions guiding our choices. Assumptions related to youth should be questioned: Are youth students who need to be taught a specific curriculum in order to be successful with little input from the youth themselves? Are youth learners whose interests and literacies should be developed even if they are not part of a formal curriculum?

Perhaps I am splitting hairs regarding the difference between conceptualizing youth as student versus youth as learner. And yet it seems that if we assume an expert position in which we hold the keys to unlocking cultural knowledge through a set of skills and preferred knowledge base, then we potentially otherize youth. We perpetuate institutional notions of the practices of *being student* that are at odds with stated beliefs that youth should engage in the practices of *being learner*. Conceptualizing our role as experts in the curriculum of the library and developing programs without youth input are in conflict with language that conceptualizes youth as learner.

When we do not critically examine policy documents, when we embrace trends in the field and forego our role as facilitators in the community to engage these documents and programs, we are unconsciously perpetuating the institution of school. Simply referring to the youth who pass through our doors as learners rather than students does not inherently mean we value their knowledge and literacies. Rather, we need to engage with institutional practices, debate the implicit messages, and openly consider this: What do we call the youth who enter our school libraries?

REFERENCES

AASL (American Association of School Librarians). 2018. National School Library Standards for Learners, School Librarians, and School Libraries. Chicago: ALA Editions.

Chachra, D. 2015. "Why I Am Not a Maker." The Atlantic, "Technology," January 23. www.theatlantic.com/technology/archive/2015/01/why-i-am-not-a-maker/384767.

Future Ready Schools. 2018. "Future Ready Librarians: Empowering Leadership for School Librarians through Innovative Professional Practice." Project of the Alliance for Excellent Education. http://1gu04j2l2i9n1b0wor2zmgua.wpengine.netdna-cdn.com/wp-content/uploads/2017/01/Library_flyer_download.pdf.

Goodin, M. C. 2011. "Room to Read: Tracking the Evolution of a New Secondary School Library." Unpublished doctoral dissertation, University of California, Berkeley. http://digitalassets.lib.berkeley.edu/etd/ucb/text/Goodin_berkeley_0028E_11724.pdf.

Harlan, M. A. 2015. "Creativity, Critical Thinking, Communication, and Collaboration: Built on Information Literacy." Paper presented at the Treasure Mountain Research Retreat 22, Columbus, Ohio, November 4-5. https://sites.google.com/site/tmcolumbus2015.

Loertscher, D., and C. Koechlin. 2011. The New Learning Commons: Where Students Win. Salt Lake City, UT: Hi Willow Research and Publishing.

———. 2014. "Climbing to Excellence: Defining the Characteristics of Successful Learning Commons." Knowledge Quest 42: E1-E10.

Murphy, T. 2014. "Inside the Mammoth Backlash to Common Core." Mother Jones, "Politics," September/October. www.motherjones.com/politics/2014/09/common-core-education-reform-backlash-obamacare.

National Center for Education Statistics. 2008. "Average Number of Hours in the School Day and Average Number of Days in the School Year for Public Schools, by State: 2007-08." In Schools and Staffing Survey (SASS), "Public School Data File." Washington, DC: U.S. Department of Education. https://nces.ed.gov/surveys/sass/tables/sass0708_035_s1s.asp.

Partnership for 21st Century Skills. 2009. "P21 Framework Definitions." ERIC (Education Resources Information Center). https://files.eric.ed.gov/fulltext/ED519462.pdf.

Rendina, D. 2015. "Advocating for Makerspaces in Libraries." Knowledge Quest (blog), July 29. http://knowledgequest.aasl.org/advocating-makerspaces-libraries.

Serafini, F., and E. Gee, eds. 2017. Remixing Literacies: Theory and Practice from New London to New Times. New York: Teachers College Press.

Virginia Department of Education. 2011. "Standards of Learning." www.doe.virginia.gov/testing/sol/standards_docs.

Weisgrau, J. 2015. "School Libraries and Makerspaces: Can They Coexist?" Edutopia, "School Libraries," September 24. www.edutopia.org/blog/school-libraries-makerspaces-coexist-josh-weisgrau.

Williams, C. 2013. "Librarians as Incubators." Library Media Connection 32 (1): 28-31.

PART II

Intellectual Freedom

CHAPTER 4

Misfits, Loners, Immature Students, and Reluctant Readers

Librarianship in the Construction of Teen Readers of Comics

Lucia Cedeira Serantes

This chapter focuses on how librarianship constructs teen readers of comics. This analysis contributes to a body of work exploring denigrated materials such as series books or video games. It also makes inferences about how teen librarians understand their roles as readers' advisors. Using a social constructivist approach and applying discourse analysis to professional literature, this chapter demonstrates how librarianship collaborates in the perpetuation of stereotypes about comics reading in particular and about teen readers in general.

INTRODUCTION: SITUATING THE TOPIC

In 2002, the journal *Young Adult Library Services* published an article by a school librarian who explained her experience creating a comic book club (Halpern 2002). She claimed no expertise with these materials, recognized that comics helped her build stronger relationships with students, and focused the article on the process of recruiting students for the club. According to Halpern (2002), the potential membership for this group would most likely be

- students who were "not the popular, academic, socially mature" type and
- students who "did not care what other people thought about them" (41).

She based this target population on the one student who replied to her advertisement of the activity. Always in a general positive attitude toward the activity and her relationship with students, she described the new recruits as "misfits, loners, and kids just a little too immature to go to school dances (God bless 'em)" who "were proud to belong somewhere"

(Halpern 2002, 41). One is surprised by her confinement of comics readers to a very particular subset of the high school population: teens who are not sociable, do not have any other interests or groups to join, and essentially are not accepted anywhere else. Consequently, several questions arise: Does this group of readers represent the only group of comics readers in the school or just an actualization of how this librarian imagines comics readers? Why did she decide that comics readers were "not the popular, academic, socially mature" students? Is this a practical approach to the difficulty of recruiting teen participants for her activity? What do her descriptions say about teen readers of comics?

It is difficult to reconcile this fracture between the positive effects Halpern found using these materials in her library work and the condescending stereotype she applies to readers of these same materials. The article by Halpern (2002) is just one example of how graphic novels and their readers are currently being constructed in library and information science (LIS) professional journals. Librarians actively seek advice about acquisition, organization, and programming with these materials; graphic novels have become a "token" material to attract an evasive teenage population to the library. However, the way comics readers are presented in these same articles is harder to qualify in a positive manner.

Librarians' imagery of readers of "scorned reading materials" (i.e., series books, romance novels, comics, among others) has always been controversial. Wayne Wiegand (1997) in his widely cited article "Out of Sight, Out of Mind" alludes to the tradition in librarianship of "slighting certain kinds of reading" and points to the lack of information about the readers of these materials as a problem that sustained pejorative behavior by library professionals. He says, "We have never bothered to investigate seriously why people want to read them" (314). Is a lack of information the only problem to unfold in the way librarians present comics readers? Certainly there is a lack of research about comics readers, but through LIS professional literature one can also identify a distinctive way of constructing comics readers, one that perpetuates historical discourses and stereotypes and lacks a self-reflective approach to the understanding of teen readers specifically and teen patrons in general.

The purpose of this chapter is to analyze how recent LIS professional literature constructs teens within the context of the discourse on comics. If the construction of teen readers of comics is understood as a spectrum with positive and negative poles, the aforementioned example by Halpern (2002) would belong at the extreme negative pole. However, it is not difficult to find more moderate examples that still fall on the negative side of this spectrum. By exploring and analyzing these dominant discourses, this chapter will shed light on the question of how recent professional LIS literature is constructing young adult readers within the context of discourse on comics. These dominant discourses not only perpetuate historical stereotypes about comics reading but also construct a negative image of contemporary teen readers.

The relationship between librarianship and comics goes back to the 1930s; therefore, it is necessary to locate this study in the basic historical discourses. From this vantage, we can explore the developments, continuities, and differences in our more modern discourses. By analyzing past discourses, I hope to show how many conceptualizations of comics and their readers have stagnated and point at the need to critically engage with the way libraries construct their relationships to actual and potential teen users. The core of this chapter examines LIS professional literature from 2000 to 2008 focusing on multiple aspects of the relationship between comics as a medium and libraries—definition, content, highlighted characteristics, and roles. Many of these matters connect directly and indirectly with the examination of the teen readership of comics, thus illuminating the contemporary discourse about readers. The following section illustrates the methodology I followed to identify and narrow the professional literature. Also, since numerous approaches to discourse analysis exist, I briefly introduce the approach selected for this project.

RESEARCH DATA AND TOOL FOR ANALYSIS

First of all, two issues need to be clarified. The terminology about comics is abundant and usually confusing for beginning readers. In this chapter, the term *comics* is used as an umbrella concept for comic books, graphic novels, and other forms that employ sequential art. Also, graphic novels will be heavily used in the fourth section correlating with their heavy use in LIS professional literature. I use the term *comic books* more often in the historical section since comics books were the main form of comics production at that particular historical moment. The textual data presented in this chapter comes from a previous research endeavor (Cedeira Serantes 2010a, 2010b). The reference section provides the information for LIS professional literature cited in this chapter.

I limited my literature search to a list of journals that would help identify the prevailing definition and use of comics in libraries: *Booklist*, *Library Journal*, *Voice of Youth Advocates*, *Young Adult Library Services*, *School Library Journal*, *Children and Libraries*, *Knowledge Quest*, and *Library Media Connection*. It immediately became obvious that between 2000 and 2008 there was one major player in the development of the discourse about comics: the regular column by Kat Kan published in the journal *Voice of Youth Advocates* (*VOYA*) since 1994.

Excluding *VOYA*, one can see how the number of articles doubled between the period 2000–2004 and 2005–2008 from 41 to 93 (see table 4.1). This increase is explained in the publication of three regular columns about graphic novels in *Knowledge Quest* (2002), *School Library Journal* (2003), and *Library Media Connection* (2007). The year 2002 is clearly relevant. One hundred seventy librarians participated in the Getting Graphic @ Your Library American Library Association (ALA) preconference, becoming one of the most successful ever organized by the Young Adult Library Services Association (YALSA) ("Graphic Moments" 2002). This event proved to be a catalyst for the interest in comics among librarians and youth services librarians in particular.

In his use of discourse analysis, James Paul Gee differentiates between discourse and Discourse. The first is language-in-use, "connected stretches of language that make sense, like conversations, stories, reports, arguments, essays" (Gee 1990, 142). This discourse is always part of Discourse. In contrast, Discourse encompasses a larger meaning: "Discourse is a socially accepted association among ways of using language, of thinking, feeling, believing, valuing, and of acting that can be used to identify oneself as a member of a socially meaningful group or 'social network,' or to signal (that one is playing) a socially meaningful 'role'" (Gee 1990, 143). Because of this understanding of Discourse, Gee believes that its

TABLE 4.1 Articles on Comics in LIS Professional Journals, 2000–2008

	2000–2004	2005–2008
Voice of Youth Advocates	31	24
Rest of journals	41	93
TOTAL	72	117

analysis should go beyond the description, rather seeking to "illuminate and gain evidence for our theory of the domain" and especially to "contribute, in terms of understanding and intervention, to important issues and problems in some 'applied' area (e.g., education) that interests and motivates the researcher" (Gee 2005, 8). This research project will contribute to the understanding of how librarians construct and understand teen readers of comics, and it will support future interventions in order to increase the awareness about the overall literary value of these materials and the diversity in comics readership.

How does one apply discourse analysis according to Gee? First, it is necessary to identify a situation where language is used. As conceived by Gee (2005, 97), a situation involves a series of connected components that might be singled out through some building tasks: significance, activities, roles or identities, relationships, politics, connections, sign systems, and forms of knowledge. In the case of this project, I analyzed a sample of professional literature that offers guidance and information about comics for the library community. From these seven building tasks, four tasks have been identified as relevant for the overall purpose of this project: significance, identities, relationships, and connections. Although the questions connected to these tasks will not surface in the text of the analysis, they were pivotal during the process of interrogation, supporting the evolution and enrichment of questions and shifting perspectives. For instance, how are graphic novels understood and defined? What is their role in the library and how is this role expressed? What discourses are relevant (and irrelevant) in the construction of comics readers? How are these discourses made relevant (and irrelevant), and in what ways? What sort of relationship or relationships is this piece of language seeking to enact with others (present or not)? (See Gee 2005, 10–12.)

HISTORICAL DISCOURSES: THEIR ORIGIN AND SCOPE

The task of summarizing and highlighting relevant historical trends in the discourse about comics, especially concerning their readers, is not an easy and straightforward endeavor. The literature that informs this topic is diverse in origin and is not very extensive; however, three trends can be identified: First, one can recognize the crucial role that Sterling North and Fredric Wertham had in shaping the popular negative discourse about comic books in the period between the 1930s and 1950s. Second, the literature points not only to the strength and prevalence of this same negative opinion among librarians but also to the development of a relatively positive or at least neutral discourse. Finally, a slow process of acceptance and inclusion of graphic novels in the library is described in two secondary sources (Ellis and Highsmith 2000; Horner 2006) that examine the decades between the 1960s and 2000s.

Sterling North published "A National Disgrace" in 1940. More than 40 newspapers and magazines reprinted the editorial, and the *Daily News*, source of the article, reported receiving "twenty-five million requests for reprints of the editorial for distribution in churches and schools across the country" (Nyberg 1994, 116). North's attack was virulent and focused on cultural aspects: the quality of the comics and the repercussions of reading them for the cultural taste and habits of innocent children. North (1940) claimed that comic books' "hypodermic injection of sex and murder [made] the child impatient with better, though quieter, stories" and that the only "antidote to the 'comic' magazine poison [could] be found in any library or good bookstore" (3).

Fredric Wertham picked up the idea of innocent readers and made it central to his offensive against comic books. From the title of his main work, *The Seduction of the Innocent*

(1954), to a speech in which he addressed librarians, "Reading for the Innocent" (1955), Wertham evidenced a deep worry for the vulnerable reader. He reinforced the metaphor of reading comic books as a disease, claiming that it helped spread the general "literary avitaminosis" suffered by American children (1955, 612), and that comic books were "virulent and harbor the virus of violence" (1955, 610).

North and Wertham presented readers as passive receivers of the comics' "disease." Evidently influenced by North and Wertham along with their role as literary gatekeepers and culture guardians, librarians reinforced this hegemonic discourse about comic book reading (Beaty 2005, 106). Tilley's (2007) doctoral thesis contains a rich and detailed discussion of the relationship between youth services librarians and comic books from 1938 to 1955. She concludes that the characterization of librarians' reactions to comics as "another instance of the profession's distaste for light reading . . . obscures the complex social and cultural currents that specifically shaped librarians' responses in this instance" (244). This chapter's modest approach to the topic does not attempt to elude this contextual complexity; however, an in-depth analysis is out of scope. In order to remedy this situation to some extent, it is necessary to create a spectrum of positive and negative discourses, thus establishing a wide and solid framework that allows one to point to continuities and breaks in LIS in relation to comics readership. The examination of librarians' historical attitudes toward comics and their readers attracts researchers in LIS and other disciplines (Beaty 2005; Ellis and Highsmith 2000; Nyberg 2002; Springhall 1998; Tilley 2007; Wright 2001). Professional articles chronicling librarians' historical perspective can be divided into three groups: contrary to comics, supportive of comics, and utilitarian.

This first group of publications overwhelmingly represents a negative angle on comics. The majority of these articles are opinion pieces based on personal observations. They are rich in metaphors of disease and addiction similar to those previously advocated by North and Wertham. Often they were shocking and alarmist (Nyberg 2002, 171). Stanley Kunitz (1941a), a poet and editor of the *Wilson Library Bulletin*, called libraries to arms against the comics menace: "A child conditioned by the jerky, jiggling, inflamed world of the comics is a damaged child, incapacitated for enjoyment of the more serene pleasure of the imagination" (670). Jean Gray Harker (1948), a librarian, called upon youth services librarians to defeat comics, describing them as a cultural threat that "rob[s] our future generations of the ability to think, to talk, to read, to act with intelligence" (1705). These are just two examples of the many publications that condemned comic book reading. Numerous examples can be found in Beaty (2005), Nyberg (2002), and Tilley (2007). Librarians' writings agreed with the construction of a passive young reader who was impoverished by comics. This reader was not an agent who decides what to read but rather one whose preference for comics was highlighted as a weakness and as an example of the influence of the power of mass culture.

A second group of publications represents a much less prevalent but positive attitude toward comics. Tilley's (2007) doctoral thesis points to some positive statements made during the University of Chicago's 1943 "Conference on Reading." Frances Henne, a well-known advocate of children's librarianship, connected comic books with children's literature through picture books and asserted that "people have tended, for different reasons in different times, to consume this form of communication" (Tilley 2007, 60). Josette Frank described comics as "an expression of our times, a folk lore [sic] of today. I, for one, refuse to believe that so many millions of readers can be wrong" (Tilley 2007, 60). In contrast with North's and Wertham's conceptions of readers, Frank and Henne pointed at readers as active agents and reflected on this predilection for comic books rather than simply criticizing or ignoring it.

A third approach to comics brings a pragmatic or utilitarian approach to the relationship between comics and libraries. The goal of this approach is to reconcile practical strengths and applications of comics for the library without directly opposing the general negative discourse. This third group proves particularly insidious in the way it bridges historical and present discourses. For instance, Elizabeth Margulis (1949) in her article "The Comics Dilemma" is concerned with the violent and explicit content of comics; however, she realizes that comics attract readers who "cannot read" or are "lazy" (4). Margaret Brady's article "Comics—To Read or Not to Read" (1950) represents an effort to introduce the topic of comics in a balanced manner. On the one hand, Brady notes that comics cultivate lazy readers, and she objects to the "wild fantasy" that they embody. She also articulates a still prevalent notion about comics reading and youth: comics are something temporary for a young reader, "likely to be outgrown as older and more important interests arise" (664). On the other hand, she indicates positive attributes in comics: they teach concentration; the adaptations of classics help young readers to connect to the original work; they are good at providing an escape from reality; and in general they stimulate reading since "boys and girls read the words as well as the pictures" (665). This article exemplifies the complex and contradictory discourse around comics, reading, and libraries. These arguments are in some ways positive or supportive in light of the general rejection of comics at the time. It is intriguing to note that these same positive statements are mirrored in current articles in LIS professional literature about comics, especially the conceptualization of the comics reader as "a reader who lacks."

Historically, the discourse about comics and their readers is not an easy topic to draw defined boundaries around. This brief review of the literature shows that between the extremes of blunt criticism and unconditional support, there were many librarians who struggled with several contending ideas: the quality and value of comics as a reading material, the definitive and passionate interest from readers, and the different practical applications that comic books have in libraries. In many and less overt ways than in the past, these same struggles will be examined in the analysis of the current literature about comics.

CONTINUITIES, PRACTICES, AND CHALLENGES OF TEEN READERS OF COMICS

This section provides an analysis of LIS professional literature about comics from 2000 to 2008. This analysis examines the following aspects of the relationship between comics as a medium and libraries: definition, content, highlighted characteristics, and roles. Through the analysis of these aspects three issues emerge:

- The reader of comics is characterized as one "who lacks": a reluctant reader, a visual reader, or an English as a second language (ESL) student.
- It is difficult to reconcile a complex medium with a young readership.
- Stereotypes about the medium directly affect the image of the reader.

The following examples illustrate the general discourse that connects comics, libraries, and teen patrons/readers. Mooney (2005) sees in graphic novels a tool to hook reluctant readers "into becoming interested and enthusiastic readers" as well as to lead them down "the path to lifelong learning" (20). Those are high hopes for a reading material whose content and quality are still a major concern, as will be discussed later in this section. Wilson

(2006) insists on a connection between graphic novels and reluctant readers as well as their appropriateness for ESL students and visual learners. Crawford (2004c) comments on the experience of two librarians that reinforces the connection between reluctant readers and graphic novels: The first librarian, Kay Hones at John O'Connell High School, places graphic novels near magazines or with drawing books to create a "magnet area for reluctant readers" (26). Elaine Moskowitz from James Denman Middle School highlights the popularity of graphic novels among students with "limited English proficiency" (26). Gorman (2002) maintains that comic books are "especially attractive to reluctant readers" and, because of this, recommends that comic books be placed near "magazines, CDs, or Cliffs Notes" (47). Knop (2008) explains that her manga club offers a place to "belong" for "students who might not otherwise join an after-school club to meet with their friends and talk about a unique common interest" (41). At this point, the image of teen readers of comics projected by librarians in their articles is that of readers who lack; librarians refer to reluctant readers or nonreaders, students with limited English proficiency, or teens who do not make friends or have difficulties integrating in the school community.

A recurrent topic in LIS professional literature about comics and youth is the reluctant reader. Interestingly enough, very few authors actually attempt to set clear boundaries around this unclear term. One can certainly assume that writers and readers share the same conceptualization of what a reluctant reader is, at least in the realm of teen readers and comics. Snowball (2005) attempts to tackle this conceptual problem in her article about reluctant readers and graphic novels. This attempt points to the reality of how this term is employed, for the most part with negative implications. An alternative approach comes from the discipline of education. Reeves (2001) understands reluctant readers as those who "will not read just for the sake of reading" (13). These readers are "highly selective" in choosing their reading materials and read only when they have found something they connect with (13). This critical approach to the reading experience is often interpreted as negative in teens, assuming that their criteria or tastes are not yet adequately developed.

Lyga (2006) problematizes the reluctant reader discourse by expanding the discussion to the realm of different types of learners: those who are incapable of visualizing, those who are visually dependent, the ever-present reluctant readers, and those students who like to cross gender lines. Lyga's approach can certainly be presented as an improvement; however, three of the learners she mentions are reluctant, incapable of doing something, or dependent on the visual aspect of the comics. Again, these comments project a restrictive understanding of graphic novels and their readers.

Bergin (2005) offers a different view from the reader who lacks. Through informal observation and a survey, she explores the diversity of manga readers in her institution to find out that

- both readers and nonreaders are attracted to manga;
- students interested in anime and Japanese culture read this type of comics;
- avid readers as well as reluctant readers are attracted to titles recognizable from current anime on TV; and
- readers make reading and discussing manga part of their social experience.

According to her informal research attempt, virtually any teen can be a manga reader. One of her most revelatory reflections points at how students' self-descriptions do not match those others give to them. Bergin does not identify who these "others" are (adults in general, librarians, or maybe teachers), but it is highly relevant that she finds a dissonance between how these manga readers are constructed and perceived and how they see themselves. This idea of misrepresentation is not unique. Bauer (2001), a teenager who writes for *VOYA*'s column "Notes from the Teenage Underground," in commenting on manga, anime, and otaku culture expresses some opinions highly critical of adults' perceptions of this material. She highlights the negative portrayal that "media watchdogs" construct and transmit about manga, summarizing this negativity with the following statement: "Anime, it seemed today, [is] the New Crack" (187). In contrast, she defends its complexity and attractiveness with a passion not frequently seen. For example, about the title *Ranma ½*, she says: "the classification most often given to *Ranma ½* is 'martial arts love comedy,' a distinction giving one a pretty good idea of its gender demographic (or lack of thereof)" (187).

In many cases, graphic novels are presented as tools that solve many issues: low circulation numbers or library attendance, poor reading skills, and social inclusion issues. Gorman (2002) sees graphic novels as a material that "transcend[s] apathy and the lack of coolness" associated with reading and libraries, and so graphic novels can be used to "lure and engage" teenagers (42). Ty R. Burns, co-head librarian at Spring High School and chairperson of the YALSA 2003 Quick Pick for Reluctant Readers Committee, affirms that since his library introduced graphic novels into the collection, not only have their circulation numbers risen but also this material is "attracting students to his library who might not have otherwise stopped by to check out a book for independent reading" (Gorman 2003, 20). Other authors also highlight the connection between graphic novels and increasing circulation numbers (Ching 2005; Neace 2005). Professional literature is not just reflecting the utilitarian role that librarians have already found for graphic novels but also actively reinforcing it. Another classic example of this utilitarian role is that of graphic novels as a stepping stone to some "better reading." Dickinson (2007) uses this controversial idea in a discussion about where to shelve graphic novels; in order to support the recommendation of interfiling these materials with other forms of literature, she writes, "deep down, some of us want the reading of graphic novels to lead to 'real books'" (56).

Foster (2004) provides a rich example of this inherently contradictory position of librarians toward comics and their readers:

> [Graphic novels are] appealing to readers of all ages and intensely popular with adolescents, but they have many other redeeming qualities. Educators have discovered that comic books have proven useful in getting reluctant readers to read.... [Graphic novels] are able to teach readers about literary techniques such as plot, conflict, setting, character, and even foreshadowing and flashbacks. (32)

In this excerpt, Foster both challenges and reinforces stereotypes about comics and their readers. She presents a rather inclusive concept of comics readers, and although the connection with reluctant readers is reinforced, she justifies it based on the literary attributes of comics. However, one cannot avoid discussing the use of "redeeming" to qualify these positive characteristics; Foster seems to imply that comics are at fault and need to compensate for their intrinsic weaknesses. Indeed, library professionals like Foster seem to perpetually link comics to an imagined reluctant reader in what these professionals view as a mutually redemptive relationship: comics may redeem their readers and thereby are themselves redeemed as a medium worthy of a place in the library. In the end, what do comics need to redeem themselves for? Are they not "real books"? And if comics are not "real books," how then shall we call their readers?

Alternatively, some exceptions arise. Seyfried (2008) qualifies graphic novels as "educational heavyweights"; these texts provide his students with "rich and rewarding literary experience" at a moment when "the duration, vocabulary, and style of prose masterpieces cannot" (46). He cites a seventh-grader who says, "We didn't just read the story; we read the story behind the story" (46).

Seyfried's (2008) positive attitude is often exhibited by Kat Kan in her *VOYA* column "Graphically Speaking." Kan shares a holistic concept of what a graphic novel reader is. First, she barely talks about reluctant readers; she prefers to distinguish between young readers and mature readers, or readers familiar with the medium or not. She also connects graphic novels to other media that might interest readers, understanding reading as part of the cultural consumption patterns of teen library patrons. For instance, she recommends particular titles to readers of Roald Dahl and Lemony Snicket (Kan 2001b) or viewers of police shows like *Law and Order* and *CSI* (Kan 2004a). Beyond recommending graphic novels, Kan (1995, 1996, 2009) helps librarians to connect graphic novels with other media, supporting the reading habits of contemporary teens whose hierarchy of value and media boundaries often differ from adults'. Apart from this open conceptualization of the reader, Kan also does not confine the medium to a particular gender or age. For example, she has written articles reviewing titles for girls (Kan 2001a, 2002a, 2005), for boys (Kan 2004a), all ages (Kan 2003a, 2004b), and middle-schoolers (Kan 2001b). To summarize, Kan reviews graphic novels as any other reading material; she does not need to validate or justify the need for graphic novels but simply assesses and recommends titles that might be interesting, challenging, and appropriate for teen readers.

Librarians describe the content of graphic novels as clearly different from the classic comic books, and they consider this shift a positive one. St. Lifer (2002) situates this development in "the scope and diversity of the graphic novel [that] has broadened to include much more sophisticated subject matter." Graphic novels represent the maturity of the medium. However, this evolution crashes against the still prevalent idea that comics are a reading material for youth and all that this notion implies. Graphic novels bring a certain sophistication in art and text that does not match the expected audience's reading maturity. "Edgy" graphic novels are a regular column topic for Kan (2000, 2001b, 2002a, 2003b, 2008). She describes these titles in an extremely positive manner: they "can offer mature-minded teens a fantastic array of stories and styles to delight their minds—and perhaps their souls" (Kan 2002a).

Nevertheless, many librarians and parents are worried that mature graphic novels might end up in the hands of children or tweens. To support the selection process, most articles include some sort of bibliographic selection where reviewers tend to summarize the virtues and shortcomings of these materials. In some cases, the concern about the content is marked with visual aids added in some of these reviews. For example, Crawford has established the asterisk as a symbol to note graphic novels that have mature themes. A closer analysis of articles by Crawford (2002, 2003a, 2003b, 2004a, 2004b, 2005a, 2005b, 2005c, 2006, 2007) reveals that the section labeled "Young Adult Literature" has a higher number of titles with asterisks, becoming the unofficial section for graphic novels with mature and probably controversial titles; however, this is not made explicit in any of the articles. On the other hand, the section "All Ages" is described as "free of excessive violence, profanity, and adult situations" (Crawford 2004c). Therefore, there are comics that contain these elements in an excessive manner, and because of that, the discussion often moves to topics of age appropriateness and censorship.

Such concerns tend to be linked to the preconceived idea that comics are meant to be read only by children. This situation is described by Pawuk (2002) as an "archaic notion" and a "potential stumbling block" when both library staff and the community are "shocked" to find content that is not suitable for a young reader. Gorman (2002) extends the fear to genres of graphic novels that can potentially be a target of parental and community objections: horror, the supernatural, crime and punishment, satire, and dark humor. It seems that the profession is actively trying to reconcile the development of the comics medium with some of the lasting stereotypes about comics readers, especially young readers. The recent interest in the younger reader has also increased attention paid to the violent and sexual content in graphic novels. However, Rudiger and Schliesman (2007) offer a sound piece of advice when they say that graphic novels might present content, situations, and images that readers, parents, and teachers might find upsetting or offensive, just as some novels, picture books, or nonfiction works have dialogue, distressing images, or shocking topics (57–58). In the same way that librarians do not embrace or reject other media as a whole, they should also evaluate graphic novels individually.

In this section, one can see the multiplicity of elements impacting the discourse about teen readers of comics and how these elements in most cases contribute to creating an image of a reader who lacks. However, the possibility for change exists and should be exercised. Flagg (2003) comments on how exposure to diverse, demanding, and stimulating media "has accustomed [teen readers of comics] to more complex narratives and a less clear-cut morality" (988). This quote explores one alternative portrayal of comics and their readers and serves as an introduction to the reflection offered in the following and final section of this study.

CONCLUSION: DISCOURSE AND ITS IMPLICATIONS

In the articles analyzed for this chapter, the implicit goal of most authors was to find a role for graphic novels that validates and justifies their presence in libraries, especially in front of educational or library boards and parents. This issue is complicated, since parents and boards might not be friendly to this inclusion. Comics were born as an entertainment product for youth, but they were quickly considered a corruptor of innocent minds and were banished from any reading-sanctioning institution (i.e., libraries and schools). However, as noted in the historical review, some librarians found positive arguments for inclusion of comics in their collections, pointing to their usefulness as literacy tools for reluctant and poor readers and also as potential springboards into traditional literature. These arguments were conceived more than 60 years ago, but they are still present in the discourse about comics in libraries today.

More recently, comics have gained a certain cultural status, especially around the creation and dissemination of the idea of the graphic novel. For the general public, and many librarians, the graphic novel embodies the evolution of the sequential art from childish entertainment to serious literary form. On the one hand, the inclusion of graphic novels in the collection means that libraries and librarians support and validate the cultural and reading tastes of the current generation. On the other hand, the connection between graphic novels and validation is still made through these same ideas of evolution and maturity, in this case of the medium itself.

This idea of evolution brings a major collateral issue: the reconcilement between the challenges and tensions of a medium increasingly acknowledged as complex in content on the one hand and a young readership on the other. In this process of reconcilement, preconceptions and misconceptions about teen readers surface. Even though graphic novels are increasingly characterized as rich, complex, challenging, diverse, and multilayered reading materials, the commonplace is to present teen readers of comics as misfits, loners, reluctant readers, and patrons who lack reading skills or discriminatory taste. The richness of the material should potentially imply a similar richness in its readers, but this is not true in the literature. Teen readers—and by extension teen patrons—could be portrayed as savvy, complex, experimental, multimedia readers. They could be easily characterized as readers who have busy lives and are strategic about their reading selections; their reading agendas are packed with compulsory materials from school, and thus their reading for pleasure choices might vary tremendously from a challenging and complex novel to a satisfying and enjoyable series book.

What does need to change? The discipline's shift echoed in Wayne Wiegand's (2003) idea of "the library in the life of the user" might inform this struggle. Librarianship looks at the graphic novel as a tool to bring teen patrons to the library, as a solution to library problems. In the process, teen patrons and readers have been constructed to fit what the library needs, rather than identified by how the library fits into young readers' lives or how youth actually imagine the library. The way graphic novels are discussed in the literature symbolizes an effort to make them fit into current library practices, especially as a bait to attract teens to reading or "good reading" and to lure them into the library. Once teens are in the library, it is assumed they will discover the wealth of resources, services, and programs that the library has to offer them.

Keeping Wiegand in mind, an alternative interpretation suggests that graphic novels can be more than bait, that they can represent an actual shift. From teenagers' viewpoint, graphic novels signal a response by libraries to actual teen interests. Instead of understanding graphic novels as a panacea that remedies the difficulties between libraries and teens, graphic novels should be understood as important only insofar as they represent and intersect with teen interests. The main distinction lies in whether we want to keep problematizing teens as reluctant readers and library users or whether we shift the discourse and constructively criticize the library as not responding to teens' developments and interests.

REFERENCES

Beaty, B. 2005. *Fredric Wertham and the Critique of Mass Culture*. Jackson: University Press of Mississippi.

Brady, M. E. 1950. "Comics—To Read or Not to Read." *Wilson Library Bulletin*, no. 24: 662-67.

Cedeira Serantes, L. 2010a. "From Virus to Bait: Comic Books, Graphic Novels, and Their Readers in Library Science Professional Literature (2000-2004)." Paper presented at 3rd New Narrative Conference: Narrative Arts and Visual Media, Toronto, ON, May 6-7.

———. 2010b. "From Virus to Bait: Comic Books, Graphic Novels, and Their Readers in Library Science Professional Literature (2000-2008)." Paper presented at the Library Research Seminar V: Integrating Research into Practice, College Park, MD, October 6-9.

Ellis, A. W., and D. Highsmith. 2000. "About Face: Comic Books in Library Literature." *Serials Review* 26, no. 2: 21-43.

Gee, J. P. 1990. *Social Linguistics and Literacies: Ideology in Discourses*. New York: Falmer.

———. 2005. *An Introduction to Discourse Analysis: Theory and Method*. New York: Routledge.

"Graphic Moments from the Getting Graphic @ Your Library Preconference." 2002. *Voice of Youth Advocates* 25, no. 4: 252-55.

Harker, J. G. 1948. "Youth's Librarians Can Defeat Comics." *Library Journal*, no. 73 (December): 1705-20.

Horner, E. C. 2006. "Librarians' Attitudes and Perspectives Regarding Graphic Novels." Unpublished master's thesis, University of North Carolina at Chapel Hill.

Kunitz, S. J.. 1941a. "The Roving Eye: Libraries, to Arms!" *Wilson Library Bulletin* 15 (April): 670-71.

———. 1941b. "The Roving Eye: The Comic Menace." *Wilson Library Bulletin* 15 (June): 846-47.

Margulis, E. S. 1949. "The Comics Dilemma." *New Mexico Library Bulletin*, no. 18: 3–5.

North, S. 1940. "A National Disgrace." *Illinois Libraries*, no. 22 (June): 3.

Nyberg, A. K. 1994. "Seal of Approval: The Origins and History of the Comics Code." Unpublished doctoral dissertation, University of Wisconsin-Madison.

———. 2002. "Poisoning Children's Culture: Comics and Their Critics." In *Scorned Literature: Essays on the History and Criticism of Popular Mass-Produced Fiction in America*, edited by L. C. Schurman and D. Johnson, 167–86. Westport, CT: Greenwood Press.

Reeves, A. 2001. "Reading This and Refusing That: Case Studies of High School Students' Patterns of Reading and Resistance." Paper presented at 91st Annual Meeting of the National Council of Teachers of English, Baltimore, MD.

Springhall, J. 1998. *Youth, Popular Culture and Moral Panics: Penny Gaffs to Gangsta-rap, 1830–1996*. New York: St. Martin's.

Tilley, C. L. 2007. "Of Nightingales and Supermen: How Youth Services Librarians Responded to Comics between the Years 1938 and 1955." Unpublished doctoral dissertation, Indiana University, Bloomington.

Wertham, F. 1954. *Seduction of the Innocent*. New York: Rinehart.

———. 1955. "Reading for the Innocent." *Wilson Library Bulletin*, no. 29 (April): 610–13.

Wiegand, W. A. 1997. "Out of Sight, Out of Mind: Why Don't We Have Any Schools of Library and Reading Studies?" *Journal of Education for Library and Information Science* 38, no. 4: 314–26.

———. 2003. "To Reposition a Research Agenda: What American Studies Can Teach the LIS Community about the Library in the Life of the User." *Library Quarterly* 73, no. 4: 369–82.

Wright, B. W. 2001. *Comic Book Nation: The Transformation of Youth Culture in America*. Baltimore, MD: Johns Hopkins University Press.

REFERENCES FROM LIS PROFESSIONAL PUBLICATIONS

Bauer, M. 2001. "Anime, Manga, and Otaku Culture: A Quick Study Guide for the Uninitiated." *Voice of Youth Advocates* 24, no. 3: 186–87.

Bergin, M. 2005. "Who Is Reading Manga? One High School's Story." *Young Adult Library Services* 3, no. 4: 25–26.

Ching, A. 2005. "Holy Reading Revolution, Batman! Developing a Graphic Novel Collection for Young Adults." *Young Adult Library Services* 3, no. 4: 19–21.

Crawford, P. 2002. "Graphic Novels: Selecting Materials That Will Appeal to Girls." *Knowledge Quest* 31, no. 2: 43–45.

———. 2003a. "Beyond 'Maus': Using Graphic Novels to Support Social Studies Standards." *Knowledge Quest* 31, no. 4: 41–42.

———. 2003b. "Graphic Novels of 2002: Superheroes and More." *Knowledge Quest* 31, no. 5: 46–47.

———. 2004a. "Graphic Novels for Elementary School Libraries." *Knowledge Quest* 32, no. 3: 35–37.

———. 2004b. "Notable Graphic Novels of 2003." *Knowledge Quest* 32, no. 4: 43.

———. 2004c. "A Novel Approach: Using Graphic Novels to Attract Reluctant Readers and Promote Literacy." *Library Media Connection* 22, no. 5: 26–28.

———. 2005a. "The Fantastic Worlds of P. Craig Russell." *Knowledge Quest* 33, no. 4: 30–31.

———. 2005b. "Moving Beyond Collection Development: Recent Professional Books about Graphic Novels." *Knowledge Quest* 34, no. 1: 36–38.

———. 2005c. "Within the Realms of Faerie: Modern Fairy Tales for Older Teens." *Knowledge Quest* 33, no. 3: 50–51.

———. 2006. "Americana Popular Culture and the Comics: Studying American Culture through Comics and Graphic Novels." *Knowledge Quest* 35, no. 1: 50–53.

———. 2007. " 'Oooh! I Must Be Dreaming!' The Delightfully Strange and Marvelous Worlds of America's Great Fantasist, Winsor McCay." *Knowledge Quest* 35, no. 5: 58–61.
Dickinson, G. 2007. "The Question: Where Should I Shelve Graphic Novels?" *Knowledge Quest* 35, no. 5: 56–57.
Flagg, G. 2003. "Not Your Father's Superheroes." *Booklist* 99, no. 11: 988.
Foster, K. 2004. "Graphic Novels in Libraries: An Expert's Opinion." *Library Media Connection* 22, no. 5: 30–32.
Gorman, M. 2002. "What Teens Want: Graphic Novels." *School Library Journal* 48, no. 8: 42–44.
———. 2003. "Graphic Novels and the Curriculum Connection." *Library Media Connection* 22, no. 3: 20–21.
Halpern, J. 2002. "Ten Geeks, One League of Power, Many Butt-Kicking Comics! Francis W. Parker School Comic Book Club." *Young Adult Library Services* 1, no. 1: 41–43.
Kan, K. 1995. "Slip-Sliding through the Media . . . Novels and Movies about Superheroes." *Voice of Youth Advocates* 18, no. 3: 207–8.
———. 1996. "Slip-Sliding through the Media, Part II: About Some Favorites, Old and New." *Voice of Youth Advocates* 19, no. 3: 203–4.
———. 2000. "Strange Sojourns: Graphic Novels." *Voice of Youth Advocates* 22, no. 6: 400–1.
———. 2001a. "Girls Rule! Graphic Novels with Female Protagonists." *Voice of Youth Advocates* 23, no. 6: 418–19.
———. 2001b. "Great for Middle School." *Voice of Youth Advocates* 24, no. 4: 270–71.
———. 2001c. "Weird and Wonderful." *Voice of Youth Advocates* 24, no. 2: 116–17.
———. 2002a. "Girls Still Rule!" *Voice of Youth Advocates* 25, no. 5: 370–71.
———. 2002b. "On the Edge." *Voice of Youth Advocates* 24, no. 6: 430–31.
———. 2003a. "Fun for All Ages." *Voice of Youth Advocates* 26, no. 2: 124–25.
———. 2003b. "On the Edge." *Voice of Youth Advocates* 26, no. 5: 386–87.
———. 2004a. "Let's Hear It for the Guys." *Voice of Youth Advocates* 27, no. 2: 118–19.
———. 2004b. "More All Ages Fun." *Voice of Youth Advocates* 27, no. 5: 374–75.
———. 2004c. "Titles Too Good to Miss!" *Voice of Youth Advocates* 26, no. 6: 480–81.
———. 2005. "The Girls Have It!" *Voice of Youth Advocates* 28, no. 1: 32–33.
———. 2008. "Pirates, Zombies, Racing, and Being a Stranger in a Strange Land." *Voice of Youth Advocates* 31, no. 1: 36–37.
———. 2009. "Slip-Sliding through the Media . . . Again." *Voice of Youth Advocates* 31, no. 6: 20–21.
Knop, K. 2008. "Graphic Novels—Join the Club!" *Library Media Connection* 27, no. 3: 40–41.
Lyga, A. W. 2006. "Graphic Novels for Really Young Readers." *School Library Journal* 52, no. 3: 56–61.
Mooney, M. 2005. "Graphic Novels for the Elementary School Audience." *Library Media Connection*, 23, no. 4: 20–21.
Neace, M. 2005. "Building a Graphic Novel Collection." *Library Media Connection* 23, no. 7: 52–55.
Pawuk, M. 2002. "Creating a Graphic Novel Collection @ Your Library." *Young Adult Library Services* 1, no. 1: 30–35.
Rudiger, H. M., and M. Schliesman. 2007. "Graphic Novels and School Libraries." *Knowledge Quest* 36, no. 2: 57–59.
Seyfried, J. 2008. "Reinventing the Book Club: Graphic Novels as Educational Heavyweights." *Knowledge Quest* 36, no. 3: 44–48.
Snowball, C. 2005. "Teenage Reluctant Readers and Graphic Novels." *Young Adult Library Services* 3, no. 4: 43–45.
St. Lifer, E. 2002. "Graphic Novels, Seriously." *School Library Journal* 48, no. 8: 9.
Wilson, R. 2006. "Multicultural Graphic Novels." *Library Media Connection* 24, no. 6: 32–33.

------- CHAPTER 5 -------

Identity at Odds

The Sometimes Conflicting Viewpoints about Young Adults' Rights in Libraries

Cherie Givens

In order to effectively advocate for the intellectual freedom of young adults in libraries, librarians must be cognizant of the laws and other protections that impact young adults' ability to exercise their First Amendment rights. This chapter provides a discussion and overview of some of the professional positions on intellectual freedom, including the American Library Association's Library Bill of Rights. The legal foundation for minors' intellectual freedom under the First Amendment to the United States Constitution will be explored. Particular focus is paid to the right to receive information, limitations imposed on young adults through laws such as the Children's Internet Protection Act, and state and federal privacy and records laws impacting minors.

AUTHOR'S DISCLAIMER: *This article is for informational purposes only and does not constitute a legal opinion. Readers should consult an attorney for legal advice regarding their unique situations.*

Young adults do not shed their legal rights simply by entering the library. Laws have been passed to protect minors as they seek and receive information in library settings. Not everyone agrees that these laws are in the best interests of minors or that the laws that apply to minors in libraries should apply equally to children and young adults. Some of these laws can appear to conflict with intellectual freedom policies and positions. How then is one to support intellectual freedom while remaining mindful of applicable laws?

Understanding the legal landscape can help librarians to make informed choices and support the intellectual freedom of minors, particularly young adults, to the fullest extent possible under the law. It is important for librarians to have a basic understanding of the laws that impact the profession, and particularly those laws that apply to the rights of library users to avoid information malpractice. Knowing the legal rights of young adults in specific library settings is crucial to determining what options are available when a parent, law enforcement officer, or other interested party seeks information about a young adult patron. Understanding how the laws impact professional policies and actions is necessary to maintaining professional standards and to understanding the limitations that may be placed on young adults when they seek information in libraries. The right to information may be also be affected by the type of library environment or limitations imposed through funding sources. Certain legal limitations may be placed on libraries that receive federal funding.

The First Amendment rights of minors in public and school libraries will be explored. Particular focus will be paid to the right to receive information, the limitations imposed on young adults, and issues concerning privacy and confidentiality. This discussion is intended to serve as an introduction to some of the information policy and ethical issues library and information science (LIS) professionals need to be aware of that affect services to young adults in school and public libraries. In doing our best to advocate for intellectual freedom and considering how we should imagine today's young adults, we must be cognizant of the legal limitations and protections placed on them and of areas of disagreement and uncertainty concerning young adults' rights in libraries.

PROFESSIONAL POSITIONS ON INTELLECTUAL FREEDOM

What rights do young adults have in libraries? The American Library Association's "Library Bill of Rights" (LBOR) offers us some guidance. Libraries are places of information and should be places where intellectual curiosity is encouraged and nourished. The LBOR advises that resources should be made available for "the interest, information, and enlightenment" of everyone in a library's community (ALA 2019). This would include young adults. The LBOR supports having material available representing "all points of view" for current and historical topics and advocates libraries challenging censorship attempts in the fulfillment of these duties (ALA 2019). Most importantly, the LBOR provides that a "person's right to use a library should not be denied or abridged because of origin, age, background, or views" (ALA 2019).

Based on the LBOR, it would appear that the rights of young adults are equal to those of adults. There is a duty to treat young adults equally and to challenge censorship, which is often aimed at the materials created for or of interest to minors. Taken on its own, the LBOR stands for the ideals of librarianship. It supports what should be a key mission for all librarians, the desire to make the library a place of uninhibited inquiry where all points of view are represented, not simply the popular or best-known views. The vision proposed in the LBOR is one of freedom of inquiry and equality of service and resources for all users, including young adults.

While the Library Bill of Rights is an important document for North American library professionals, of equal importance to library professionals should be the guidance provided in the "Code of Ethics of the American Library Association" (ALA 2008). The "Code of Ethics" (COE) guides the profession, expressing the values and ethical responsibilities of librarians. The COE can also shed light on how librarians should think about young adults to whom we have a professional obligation. According to the COE, "we have a special obligation to ensure the free flow of information and ideas to present and future generations" (ALA 2008). The COE reinforces the vision of equal access and service but uncouples it from the library forum, expanding it to the profession of librarianship, which may not be strictly tied to libraries. Librarians who are members of the American Library Association (ALA) are presumed to support this ethical stance.

The eight statements forming the body of the COE serve as a "framework," giving general guidance for ethical conduct. These statements are applicable to the conduct of librarians serving users of all ages. The COE advocates for intellectual freedom and advises librarians to resist censorship of library resources. This resistance may apply beyond the individual censor or censoring school board and could be seen to apply to governmental actions that may be viewed as forms of censorship as well. We need only look to the actions of the ALA in challenging the constitutionality of requiring Internet filtering in libraries under the Children's Internet Protection Act (CIPA) for an example of resistance to perceived governmental censorship. The ALA, in advocating an anticensorship position when addressing materials for young adults, helps to define the professional vision of young adults as those deserving of uncensored inquiry and the opportunity to receive information.

The COE addresses areas of concern such as protecting privacy and confidentiality for library users of all ages. In addition to the duties to advocate for intellectual freedom and protect library users' rights to privacy and confidentiality, the COE addresses an important aspect of professionalism that has challenged some in the LIS field when addressing the needs of minors: the need to "distinguish between our personal convictions and professional duties" (ALA 2008). The COE advises librarians not to allow our personal convictions to "interfere" with our professional duties (ALA 2008). We are challenged, just as professionals in other fields such as law and medicine, to be guided by professional ethics in meeting the needs of our users. The COE offers us a vision of young adults as those deserving of equal service and protection of their intellectual freedom. When we choose to censor, as members of the library profession, we choose the personal over the professional. In law or medicine such actions have consequences, and those who would breach ethical duties can lose their right to practice. Should similar restrictions be applied to librarians who do not uphold the COE? It is an interesting question to ponder. Perhaps if similar penalties applied to individuals working in libraries who do not follow the COE the vision of equal access and service for young adults would be more widely followed.

The "Freedom to Read Statement" (FRS), a joint statement by the ALA and the Association of American Publishers, is another important document that provides guidance in addressing the challenges to service and professional duties owed to young adults in libraries. This statement, which has been endorsed by several professional organizations including the National Council of Teachers of English, advises that our freedom to read is "continuously under attack ... [by p]rivate groups and public authorities" who seek to censor reading materials in schools (ALA and AAP 2004).

According to the FRS, fear that stems from outside attempts to censor materials may lead to "an even larger voluntary curtailment of expression by those who seek to avoid controversy or unwelcome scrutiny by government officials" (ALA and AAP 2004). The truth of this statement is bolstered by several historical studies of librarians censoring materials for various reasons, including the pressure felt by outside forces (Fiske 1962; Buscha 1972; McDonald 1993). Our professional history shows that librarians have moved from the role of censors to supporters of intellectual freedom. It is not surprising then to discover that some among us may still harbor a desire to censor materials or to give in to the pressures to censor being exerted by external forces.

McDonald (1993) explains that at the time of librarianship's professional beginnings in 1876, under the national political climate, librarians "endorsed themselves as moral censors" (3). Scholars such as Geller (1984) have examined our professional history and found that the role of censor was a common one for our predecessors, noting that it was during the early 1900s that librarians took on the role of censoring (79). The ALA's position opposing censorship did not emerge until the late 1930s with the "Library's Bill of Rights," the precursor to the current "Library Bill of Rights" (Krug and Morgan 2010). Though we currently have a robust intellectual freedom presence, there remain forces seeking to restrict young adults' access to information. As librarians we are called upon professionally to resist censorship attempts in all forms, even the internal voice that may prod one to go with the majority view or to support personal views that are not in keeping with professional policies. The vision of LIS services to youth at the professional association level is one that resists internal and external efforts to censor materials and services.

The "Library Bill of Rights," the "Code of Ethics," and the "Freedom to Read Statement" provide a strong foundation of guidance that embodies our professional ethics. Those looking for more in-depth guidance from the ALA concerning interpretations of these documents should consult the Intellectual Freedom Manual (Office of Intellectual Freedom 2015), which contains interpretations and the historical backgrounds of these policies as well as essays on intellectual freedom.

The ALA has become and remains a strong advocate of intellectual freedom. This is needed in today's complex and often contentious library legal landscape that includes several laws that directly impact the rights of library users, particularly the rights of minors, such as the Children's Internet Protection Act, the USA PATRIOT Act (Patriot Act), and various state harmful-to-minors laws. The U.S. Supreme Court has also been the battleground for several struggles to clarify the First Amendment rights of minors. The limitations of these laws and the Supreme Court's ruling on minors' First Amendment rights must be considered as we determine how LIS should view young adults and how to provide them with the most effective service within the boundaries of the law.

THE LEGAL FOUNDATION FOR MINORS' INTELLECTUAL FREEDOM

The principles of intellectual freedom espoused in the ALA's "Library Bill of Rights" and "Code of Ethics" have their origins in the U.S. Constitution's First Amendment:

> Congress shall make no law respecting an establishment of religion, or prohibiting the free exercise thereof; or abridging the freedom of speech, or of the press; or the right of the people peaceably to assemble, and to petition the government for a redress of grievances.

The U.S. Supreme Court has recognized that minors have First Amendment rights, but those rights are not identical to those of adults. Several legal cases shed light on minors' First Amendment rights. In *Tinker v. Des Moines Independent Community School District* (393 U.S. 503 (1969)), the U.S. Supreme Court affirmed that students "do not shed their constitutional rights to freedom of speech or expression at the schoolhouse gate" (506). In *Tinker* student protestors of the Vietnam War were suspended for wearing black armbands of protest. The Supreme Court found that the wearing of the armbands "was entirely divorced from actually or potentially disruptive conduct . . . and as such was closely akin to 'pure speech' which is entitled to comprehensive protection under the First Amendment" (505-6). The language of the Supreme Court's opinion in *Tinker* shows a clear protection of the "pure speech" of young adults in a public school setting.

The First Amendment provides for freedom of speech, but does it provide for the corollary right to receive information? The U.S. Supreme Court has intimated on a number of occasions that the First Amendment's guarantees of Freedom of Speech and Freedom of the Press imply a corollary right to receive information. The right of minors to receive information in a public school library setting was first considered by the U.S. Supreme Court in *Board of Education v. Pico* (457 U.S. 855 (1982)). In this case the Board of Education rejected recommendations of an appointed committee of parents and staff, ordering that books the board deemed objectionable be removed from the high school and junior high school libraries. Students challenged the decision of the board in federal district court and lost. The decision was reversed on appeal. The case went to the U.S. Supreme Court, which upheld the court of appeal's ruling. The Supreme Court, in a plurality opinion, stated:

> We have held that in a variety of contexts "the Constitution protects the right to receive information and ideas." . . . This right is an inherent corollary of the rights of free speech and press that are explicitly guaranteed by the Constitution. . . . The right to receive ideas follows ineluctably from the sender's First Amendment right to send them. . . . More importantly, the right to receive ideas is a necessary predicate to the recipient's meaningful exercise of his own rights of speech, press, and political freedom. (*Pico*, 457 U.S. at 867)

The Supreme Court's opinion in *Pico* is an important one when considering how the LIS profession should envision young adults. In *Pico* the U.S. Supreme Court stated plainly that minors have the First Amendment right to receive information and ideas. The Supreme Court considers this necessary to the "meaningful exercise" of First Amendment rights. Young adults should be viewed as active participants in society with rights to information that should be restricted only in limited circumstances as determined by law.

Pico involved high school and junior high school students. The Supreme Court affirmed the right of minors to receive information. The importance of this right should not be overlooked. Young adults are just a step away from being adults. Sheltering them from unpopular ideas that they have a right to receive and may be exposed to as adults simply leaves them unprepared. Teaching information literacy and critical thinking skills can prepare young adults to competently interpret and respond to new, different, and sometimes disturbing ideas.

While the U.S. Supreme Court has affirmed the First Amendment rights of minors, it has also placed some limits on these rights in a public school environment. The Supreme Court in *Pico* cited *Tinker*, explaining that the First Amendment rights of students "must be construed 'in light of the special characteristics of the school environment'" (*Pico*, 457 U.S. at 868, quoting *Tinker*, 393 U.S. at 506). These characteristics allow materials to be restricted if the materials are "educationally unsuitable" or "pervasively vulgar" (*Pico*, 457 U.S. at 890). The school's judgment must be "based objectively on the fact that the information is 'educationally unsuitable'" (Chmara 2010b, 352). Other courts have followed *Pico*'s guidance that examining the motivation behind the action is important in book removal cases.

Although school boards enjoy broad discretion concerning questions of school curricula, provided their actions are reasonably related to legitimate pedagogical concerns, the removal of books from public school libraries implicates protected First Amendment rights. While a public school library environment presents some limitations on the First Amendment rights of minors, the U.S. Supreme Court's rulings make it clear that these limitations are few and must be based objectively on fact. They present a few caveats that temper the professional vision of service and intellectual freedom espoused by the ALA in a public school library environment.

LAWS TO PROTECT MINORS FROM THE HARMFUL AND THE OBSCENE

Material may be restricted from minors if it is obscene, harmful to minors, or child pornography. The decision of whether material fits into any of these categories is determined by state or local law (Chmara 2010a, 18). Obscene speech is not protected by the First Amendment. Under *Ginsberg v. New York* (390 U.S. 629 (1968)), "states may completely bar minors from receiving material deemed obscene for them but not for adults" (Chmara 2010b, 352). In *Ginsberg* a magazine seller was convicted under a state law of selling two "girlie" magazines to a sixteen-year-old. Courts have acknowledged limits to the *Ginsberg* holding:

> States may not simply ban minors' exposure to a full category of speech, such as nudity, when only a subset of that category can plausibly be deemed obscene for them . . . [and] states must determine *Ginsberg* "obscenity" by reference to the entire population of minors—including the oldest minors. (Chmara 2010b, 352)

According to Minow and Lipinski (2003), "States generally pattern their laws on the *Miller* decision . . . [but] may define 'obscenity' more liberally" (134). In *Miller v. California* (413 U.S. 15 (1973)), the U.S. Supreme Court developed a three-factor test to determine if a work is obscene, with works being evaluated based on the following criteria:

1. whether the "average person, applying contemporary community standards" would find that the work, taken as a whole, appeals to the prurient interest;
2. whether the work depicts or describes, in a patently offensive way, sexual conduct specifically defined by the applicable state law; and
3. whether the work, taken as a whole, lacks serious literary, artistic, political, or scientific value. (Miller, 413 U.S. at 15)

In 2001, efforts to restrict the access of minors to materials that are obscene, harmful to minors, or classified as child pornography took a leap forward when the Children's Internet Protection Act (CIPA) became law. This federal law requires libraries and schools that accept discounted services under the federal Universal Service Program for Schools and Libraries, or E-rate program, or direct federal funding through the Elementary and Secondary Education Act (ESEA) to certify that they have installed "technology protection measures" on all computers that are used to access the Internet. Under CIPA minors are considered individuals of less than seventeen years of age.

CIPA was challenged and in 2002 held unconstitutional by a federal district court. This holding was reversed by the U.S. Supreme Court in June 2003 in *U.S. v. American Library Association* (539 U.S. 194 (2003)). The Supreme Court ruled that this act does not violate First Amendment rights. The justices have provided reasons for finding this act constitutional. These include Justice Kennedy's conclusion that adults can still have unfettered access to the Internet because "a librarian will unblock filtered material or disable the

Internet software filter without further delay" upon the request of an adult patron (*American Library Association*, 539 U.S. at 214). The justices, citing *Rust v. Sullivan* (500 U.S. 173, 194 (1991)), also concluded:

> The Government is not denying a benefit to anyone, but is instead simply insisting that public funds be spent for the purpose for which they are authorized: helping public librarians fulfill their traditional role of obtaining material of requisite and appropriate quality for educational and informational purposes.

The justices go on to state that "because public libraries have traditionally excluded pornographic material from their other collections, Congress could reasonably impose a parallel limitation on its Internet assistance programs" (*American Library Association*, 539 U.S. at 211).

Libraries have the option to refuse federal funding and therefore not be subject to the requirements of CIPA, but even if libraries choose this option, they may still be subject to state laws, known as harmful-to-minors laws, that require Internet filtering in publicly funded schools or libraries. According to the National Conference of State Legislatures (2018), as of November 16, 2016, 25 states have passed laws addressing Internet filtering, requiring Internet use policies to prevent minors from accessing "sexually explicit, obscene, or harmful materials." Some states also require the installation of filtering software (National Conference of State Legislatures 2018).

Other laws also work to protect minors from harm online by regulating the collection and use of their personally identifiable information. Chief among these is the Children's Online Privacy Protection Act (COPPA) of 1998. COPPA is a federal law that is designed to protect the privacy of minors under the age of 13. The act applies to operators of commercial websites and online services including mobile applications. It applies to both those entities that target children and those that do not specifically target children but have actual knowledge that they are collecting information from minors under the age of 13. COPPA imposes rules on these entities concerning the clear posting of a privacy notice, the need for parental consent, and access to the information collected and places limits on the length of time that the information may be retained.

ARE LEGAL PROTECTIONS FOR MINORS TOO GENERALIZED?

These types of legal protective measures frequently fail to distinguish young adults from children, attaching the same standards to both, but the information needs of a 16-year-old are not the same as those of a 6- or 9-year-old. If society treats young adults like children, then we risk the possibility that they will emerge as adults without the skills and experience to prepare them for the adult world and the sometimes harmful or obscene information in it. Exposure to material that makes us uncomfortable in our youth may act to provide us with greater resilience when handling stresses in adulthood.

According to Lyons, Parker, and Schatzberg (2010), "early intermittent exposure to stress . . . enhances arousal regulation and resilience" (402). If the premise of the protective measures is to prevent harm to minors, perhaps we as a society need to reevaluate whether some limited exposure or "inoculating" is actually harmful (402). Heins (2007) advocates for "more thoughtful and finely calibrated judgments" about legal protections (259), citing the Supreme Court in *Planned Parenthood of Missouri v. Danforth* (428 U.S. 52, 74 (1976)).

She notes that "constitutional rights 'do not mature and come into being magically only when one attains the state defined age of majority'" (259).

Just as the obscenity standards are rooted in community norms, our ideas about what materials are harmful to minors stem from American culture. "Standards are relative, culturally driven, and often employed rhetorically for political ends that may have little to do with any objective showing of harm to youth" (Heins 2007, 200). Differences are readily identifiable when we compare how other cultures address sex education. "The United States . . . was the only country in the industrialized world to have, at the turn of the 21st century, legislated 'abstinence unless married' as official policy" (Heins 2007, 153).

The *Newsletter for Intellectual Freedom* has documented the active and continuing censorship efforts of sex education materials for children and young adults since the 1970s. Levine (2002) makes a powerful argument that the sexual politics of fear in the United States is what is harmful to minors (xxi). The practice of emphasizing abstinence is not shared by Western European countries, where youth are taught sex education with the assumption that during their teen years they will initiate "sex play short of intercourse" and that "sexual expression is a healthy and happy start to growing up" (xxxii).

The emphasis on abstinence-only education in the United States poses unique problems for youth who are seeking information about sex. For many, the library serves as one of the only avenues for obtaining sex education materials. As Cornog and Perper (1996) point out, parents may provide incorrect information and "sex education in schools is . . . bound up with bureaucratic concerns and agendas . . . [C]urricula may be mandated that do not tell a full story about sex" (4). This is why there is a need for sex education information to be made readily available in libraries.

Members of the LIS profession need to examine how we treat minors, especially young adults, seeking information. Young adults need intellectual freedom but often find themselves subject to the will of bureaucratic concerns and agendas. LIS professionals must fight to protect the freedom of young adults to receive information to the best of our abilities within the boundaries of the law. Librarians should examine how harmful-to-minors laws and Internet filtering practices affect the search processes and receipt of information by minors.

SCHOOLS HAVE A DUTY TO PROTECT

In addition to understanding the laws applicable to library and information resource settings, the school librarian must be familiar with the laws that apply to educational institutions. Both state and federal laws are applicable in school library settings. Some laws apply to the protection of the student and others to the student's personally identifiable information.

The Family Educational Rights and Privacy Act (FERPA) and the Protection of Pupil Rights Amendment (PPRA) are two federal laws that impose privacy protections on the personally identifiable information of students in school settings. Under FERPA, students and parents of students under the age of 18 have the right to review students' education records and request corrections for any inaccuracies. FERPA was amended in 1978 by the PPRA, which applies to educational programs that receive funding from the U.S. Department of Education.

In K–12 schools librarians assume some in loco parentis responsibilities. "In loco parentis is a legal doctrine describing a relationship similar to that of a parent and child. It refers to an individual who assumes parental status and responsibilities for another individual, usually a young person, without formally adopting that person" (Lehman and Phelps 2005, 352). This concept of legal responsibility for minors by school administrators, which stems from English common law, has shaped the responsibilities of public school teachers and has implications for the school library, which is necessarily a component of the school. Carson (2007) elaborates on these responsibilities:

> Schools have a legal duty to protect their students in a different way from public or academic libraries. . . . There is a special duty to report potentially dangerous behavior to the school guidance counselor or principal. Educators have a legal duty to report students who may have been abused, appear suicidal, or in any way appear to be at risk. (237)

These responsibilities can potentially change the dynamics of the professional relationship between a school librarian and students who are seeking information in the library. It presents a vision of young adults as a group requiring protection in all areas of the school, including the library. The role of school administrators as guardians has gained greater attention in recent years with the increased concern about school violence. School librarians must work to strike a balance when creating an environment that welcomes users and encourages information seeking while maintaining a mindfulness of the unique responsibilities school librarians undertake as part of the work environment.

Additional restrictions may be imposed on the right to seek information in school library settings based on the type of school, such as private or parochial. School libraries, in particular, are subject to school administrative controls and may be limited by the mission, funding, and priorities of their schools. Views about and support for intellectual freedom in school settings may not mirror those of the larger communities.

THE PROTECTION OF PRIVACY FOR YOUNG ADULTS

Privacy issues in libraries come in many forms. It may be an informal request from a parent or law enforcement officer for information concerning a minor user's reading choices, or it might be a more official request such as a subpoena, search warrant, or request under the Patriot Act. Decisions about how to address these matters and what rights to privacy users have in a given situation depend on who is asking and what laws govern the situation. It is important to be aware of the laws and policies that impact user privacy in libraries.

Intrusions on privacy may have a chilling effect on users if they believe information such as their reading habits, Internet browsing history, or a list of the resources they use while in the library can be made public. Neil Richards (2008) makes the case that each of us deserves to have intellectual privacy. We deserve to have protection for our records and intellectual activities. Legal protection for these records "is essential to the First Amendment values of free thought and expression" (387). According to Richards, if we want to have something interesting to say in public, we need to pay attention to the freedom to develop new ideas in private, either alone or with trusted confidants (389). This is the reason that librarians work to protect users' rights and the ALA has developed policies to address privacy in different contexts. Individual library policies should address these matters as well in order to maximize user privacy.

Every state provides some measure of protection for library circulation records through statutes, with the exceptions of Hawaii and Kentucky, which both rely on attorney general opinions. The extent to which such statutes protect these records varies by state. The following states explicitly allow parents access to the records of their minor children: Alabama, Alaska, Louisiana, South Dakota, Utah, West Virginia, Wisconsin, and Wyoming. Colorado allows access if the parent has the minor's account number. New Mexico's law allows the release of overdue notices or the release or disclosure by school libraries of the records of unemancipated minors to their guardians. Florida's law allows for the disclosing of minors' circulation records to parents for the collection of fines.

Allowing parents to access the records of their minor children, particularly the records of young adults, may have a chilling effect on information inquiry. Some controversial materials may be read only in the library, safe from parental inspection and comment. Librarians working with young adults in states where their records are accessible to parents will need to give particular thought as to how best to assist them. These library users are on the cusp of adulthood, but with limitations imposed on their rights to privacy that may make their checking out materials on certain controversial, embarrassing, or disapproved of subjects unlikely. Young adults from states that allow parents to access the library records of their minor children represent a unique subset of young adults generally and deserve special consideration to meet their intellectual needs while maintaining as much privacy and confidentiality as possible.

In addition to state laws that may impinge on privacy, librarians need to be aware of federal laws that can do the same. The USA PATRIOT Act, signed into law on October 26, 2001, following the September 11 terrorist attacks on American soil, expands law enforcement's powers of surveillance and investigation. Under the powers of the Patriot Act, federal law enforcement officers can obtain information through the use of National Security Letters (NSLs) that contain nondisclosure orders so the individuals whose information was obtained would not be notified.

The Patriot Act applies to people of all ages. It covers library users' Internet transaction records, loan history, and search history. As the powers granted through this act can impinge on young adults' privacy and confidentiality, it is important for library professionals to be familiar with the act and how it impacts patrons and library services.

CONCLUSION

Young adults are a crucial segment of the society. Their information needs are different from the needs of children with whom they are often grouped for the purposes of protection under the law. As individuals who will shortly become adults, they arguably have more in common with adults in terms of information needs and desires, but they do not share the same level of First Amendment rights. As minors they have fewer avenues to obtain information and may lack the financial power and opportunities to access needed information outside of school and public libraries.

Young adults need the support of professionals who are knowledgeable of the laws that affect libraries and the First Amendment rights of minors as well as the positions espoused by LIS professional associations. Librarians must be guided by the ethical codes of our profession and take seriously our professional duties to fight censorship and to support intellectual freedom by providing young adults with library environments that encourage uninhibited information inquiry.

As LIS professionals we must see young adults as vital members of our society who need to be prepared to understand and evaluate information, even if that information is unpopular or controversial. We must temper our vision of young adults in light of both the laws that are designed to protect minors and the rulings of the U.S. Supreme Court that specifically address and endorse minors' First Amendment rights. When thinking about how the LIS profession should view young adults, we can look to the success of other countries that provide their young adults with sex education information and have correspondingly lower numbers of teen pregnancies and STIs than are found in the United States. A closer examination is needed of the decisions made to restrict information without respect to the maturity level of the information seekers.

Society has not always considered young adults to be in need of the types of legal and moral protections currently applied to information access in school and public libraries. Are young adults being infantilized in an effort to protect them, thus hindering their transition to adulthood? What does it cost those who are kept from information? Can society afford to continue on such a path? These are questions LIS professionals must consider as we move forward in creating a comprehensive vision of young adults' rights, freedoms, and services.

REFERENCES

ALA (American Library Association). 2008. "Code of Ethics." ALA.org. Last amended January 22. www.ala.org/ala/issuesadvocacy/proethics/codeofethics/codeethics.cfm.

———. 2019. "Library Bill of Rights." ALA.org. Last amended January 29. www.ala.org/advocacy/intfreedom/librarybill.

ALA (American Library Association) and AAP (Association of American Publishers). 2004. "Freedom to Read Statement." ALA.org. Last amended June 30. www.ala.org/advocacy/intfreedom/freedomreadstatement.

Buscha, C. H. 1972. *Freedom versus Suppression and Censorship*. Littleton, CO: Libraries Unlimited.

Carson, B. M. 2007. *The Law of Libraries and Archives*. Lanham, MD: The Scarecrow Press.

Chmara, T. 2010a. "Minors' First Amendment Rights: CIPA and Schools." *Knowledge Quest* 39, no. 1: 16-21.

———. 2010b. "Minors' First Amendment Rights to Access Information." In *Intellectual Freedom Manual*, 8th ed., compiled by the Office of Intellectual Freedom, 351-60. Chicago: American Library Association.

Cornog, M., and T. Perper. 1996. *For Sex Education, See Librarian: A Guide to Issues and Resources*. Westport, CT: Greenwood Press.

Fiske, M. 1962. *Book Selection and Censorship: A Study of School and Public Libraries in California*. Berkeley: University of California Press.

Heins, M. 2007. *Not in Front of the Children: "Indecency," Censorship, and the Innocence of Youth*. New Brunswick, NJ: Rutgers University Press.

Krug, J. F., and C. D. Morgan. 2010. "ALA and Intellectual Freedom: A Historical Overview." In *Intellectual Freedom Manual*, 8th ed., compiled by the Office of Intellectual Freedom, 12-36. Chicago: American Library Association.

Lehman, J., and S. Phelps, eds. 2005. *West's Encyclopedia of American Law*. Farmington Hills, MI: Thompson Gale, 2015. PDF e-book.

Levine, J. 2002. *Harmful to Minors: The Perils of Protecting Children from Sex*. Minneapolis: University of Minnesota Press.

Lyons, D., K. Parker, and A. Schatzberg. 2010. "Animal Models of Early Life Stress: Implications for Understanding Resilience." *Developmental Psychobiology* 52, no. 5: 402-10.

McDonald, F. B. 1993. *Censorship and Intellectual Freedom: A Survey of School Librarians' Attitudes and Moral Reasoning*. Metuchen, NJ: Scarecrow Press.

Minow, M., and T. A. Lipinski. 2003. *The Librarian's Legal Answer Book*. Chicago: American Library Association.

National Conference of State Legislators. 2018. "Children and the Internet: Laws Relating to Filtering, Blocking and Usage Policies in Schools and Libraries." NCSL.org. Last updated October 30. www.ncsl.org/research/telecommunications-and-information-technology/state-internet-filtering-laws.aspx.

Office of Intellectual Freedom, comp. 2015. *Intellectual Freedom Manual*. 9th ed. Chicago: American Library Association.

Richards, N. 2008. "Intellectual Privacy." *Texas Law Review* 87, no. 2: 387–445.

CHAPTER 6

Situating Youth Voice

Moving from Understanding to Action through Critical Theory

Jeanie Austin

This chapter identifies librarians as holding specific skills and public positions that provide opportunities to address today's neoliberal turn focused on individual accounts and constructions of competitive individual success. Critical theory approaches to youth voice do increase librarians' understandings that youth always have some amount of agency. But institutional forces still shape that agency toward particular modes of culture, conduct, and comportment while marginalizing others. Greater understandings of youth should involve a situated and more complex positioning of collective voices of youth moving beyond conventional positions. In other words, librarians' views of youth must move from envisioning them within an unequal democracy in which privileged individual voices speak and toward a collective, situated, and informed sharing of knowledges, experiences, and goals with an eye toward social change.

"Youth," an adult-constructed category that is discussed as a term and as a stage of human experience, acts as a frame of reference that spans the desirable, the innocent, the untrustworthy, and the untamed. The myriad descriptive frames of youth, and the approaches that attend them, continue to hold sway over how and in what ways libraries structure and implement services and collections for young people. These influences often work to reinstate existing power structures that privilege whiteness, heterosexuality, and normative ways of belonging.[1] Library services have continued to privilege the already privileged. In recognition of this, Agosto (2013), Bernier, Males, and Rickman (2014), Braun and colleagues (2014), Kumasi (2013), and other professionals and researchers have called for "youth voice" and "youth-centered" approaches as a means to shift young adult librarianship away from historically based developmental models of youth that privilege adults as knowers. My ongoing research builds from these models by engaging deeply with youth who are held within juvenile detention facilities or, due to systemic racism, homophobia, and transphobia, are more likely to be under surveillance, policed, or incarcerated (Hunt and Moodie-Mills 2012; Meiners 2007; Sawyer and Hodge 2014).

Approaches to library services and collections have historically been deeply tied to librarians' conceptualizations of youth (as a category and in specific groupings of youth). Historical accounts relating to the formation of young adult librarianship and its early intentions reflect this occurrence (Braverman 1979). For instance, Braverman (1979) discusses a practical and ideological shift to youth services that occurred in the 1950s—a shift that moved from an emphasis on attempting to understand the circumstances of youth's lives to an object-oriented (book and learning-oriented) approach. This statement must be positioned within the nationalistic and social approaches to youth during the period. Consider that the 1950s were marked by fears of youth delinquency, intense censorship, and selection (by publishers) of materials that were related to the development of appropriate citizenship among youth (Cohen 1997). Cohen (1997) untangles the overarching ideological approaches to youth and appropriate socialization as a combination of adult fears and anxieties related to power and status quo (which, in the early years of the long Civil Rights movement, must be understood as deeply racialized anxieties). "During the 1950s," Cohen states, "fears of youthful rebellion took on added dimensions, in the midst of general internal security and prosperity, whipped up by a combination of anti-communist hysteria and racial unrest" (254). This "racial unrest" was heavily manifested through censorship, access, and mass media portrayals (Knott 2016; Robbins 2001).[2] Notably, the impulse between these anxieties often triumphed over the actual occurrence of teenage engagement in "delinquent" or "anti-social" acts. Tilley (2012) describes this in the falsification and blurring of evidence utilized by Wertham to censor and regulate the comics industry in the 1950s.[3] Adult fears were accompanied by the ramifications of histories of anxiety around youth sexuality and appropriately gendered behavior, manifested through narratives of appropriate citizenship and belonging that, at least into the 1940s, had manifested in the (literal) policing of young people's sexuality and homosexuality (Romesburg 2008). Romesburg (2008) describes this "developmental citizenship" as "persistent and troubling mechanisms linking operations of nationalism, race, gender and sexuality" (419). Adult constructions of appropriate development and of youth well-being shaped the multiple arenas in which youth found themselves during this period of time—in homes, schools, detention centers and camps, even in books and on the big screen. These ideologies influenced librarians, who were, as Braverman (1979) implies, also notably part of this project of citizenship, fostering the internationally competitive (imperial?) reading habits of white youth as an aspect of a larger project of developmental citizenship and nation building.

This brief example provides a foundation for understanding how librarians should define youth and youth services today. We must understand library services to youth as intimately bound to institutional, political, and social conceptions of youth that exist in any given period. These conceptions continue to permeate the availability, distribution, and promotion of materials as well as the creation of youth spaces and how youth behavior in the library is governed through adult intervention. This chapter concerns how, in light of the previous histories, youth who are, in this moment, created or viewed by adults and mainstream society as social and political possible delinquents—youth of color and/or LGBTQ and gender-nonconforming youth—continue to be underserved in library services due to (overt or unacknowledged) reliance on constructions of youth that relate to whiteness and normative belonging.

This analysis allows librarians to see the pitfalls created by ongoing approaches to youth as unable to express their needs and desires. But when librarians *do* incorporate or advocate for an understanding of youth voice, they rarely situate youth's statements within the lived realities of youth or what youth might mean. In this way, the results of institutional oppression are not informed by youth's ability to speak their realities. Librarians need nuanced and actionable ways to shape collections and services that attempt to meet youth, to land in conversations with youth's statements, and to be critically aware of how institutional oppression might shape the possibility that youth have had opportunities to examine their experiences as collective, ongoing, and created by powerful forces. Youth voice must be critically positioned within an understanding of these forces in order to recognize the shared, lived circumstances of institutional oppression and to creatively facilitate youth access to resources.

This chapter draws from my ongoing research on library services to youth of color and/or LGBTQ and gender-nonconforming youth—both within and outside of juvenile detention centers—to create a call for the incorporation of critical theoretical positions as a way to situate and better understand youth voice in an effort to locate the common and shared features of institutional oppression and to resist their reoccurrence. Critical race theory, research in ethnic studies, and queer and trans theories can be used to situate the statements of specific youth and to better understand how some youth get opportunities and skills to voice their needs and desires while other youth encounter silencing by systemic forces— what Fine and Ruglis (2009) describe as a logic of dispossession. Under this logic of dispossession, youth of color encounter school systems that do not acknowledge them as learners and knowers. Systems of education serving youth of color are, in this manifestation of neoliberal ideology, increasingly "colonizing dreams and overdetermining destinies of (il)legitimacy" through the furthering incorporation of police forces and surveillance into the school environment (21). Through this and overlapping systems of control and containment, youth of color, LGBTQ and gender-nonconforming youth, and other youth are categorically made "rightless" by the state—adults, often in powerful institutions, identify groups of youth as criminal by status. Cacho (2012) describes these status groups as seen without personhood. They have limited options to be valued by the state in which they are (to varying degrees) "criminal by being, unlawful by presence, and illegal by status, *they do not have the option to be law abiding*" (8). Youth navigating these forces, to the best of their abilities, may not find an obvious advantage to speaking their truths to librarians. Librarians need to be aware of these forces to better serve youth who face ongoing systemic oppression in order to push against the forces of systemic oppression that work to shape the lives of youth of color and/or LGBTQ and gender-nonconforming youth. To do this, they must see youth statements as occurring in the context of relationships to adults and to institutions. Positioning youth's statements within critical theoretical understandings of power resists the idea that youth adult librarians are inherently able to know the needs and interests of youth.

The inclusion of critical theoretical approaches into the professional education of librarians is not new (Cooke, Sweeney, and Noble 2016). Incorporating critical theoretical approaches into services for young adults is necessary in light of the intensity of state oppression that youth of color and/or LGBTQ and gender-nonconforming youth face in their day-to-day lives and how these discourses shape conceptions of youth within library practice (Bernstein 2014; Hunt and Moodie-Mills 2012). Critical theory provides a lens to better understand the positions from which youth speak and youth's perceptions of how power works against them in institutional settings—including through library services. In order to provide meaningful services for youth who have historically been excluded from library services, librarians will need to understand youth as able to speak their experiences while also understanding that speaking is always situated and shaped by powerful social and political forces. Librarians need not only to hear youth when they speak but also to have the tools that help them critically analyze youth speech and silence. In other words, librarians need youth voice as well as the professional skills provided by engagement with critical theory to actually "hear" what youth may or may not profess.

The following sections outline the various elements that contribute to the need for librarians' to critically approach youth voice. They include detail on historical approaches to youth with emphasis on how library services to youth have been influenced by constructions of youth that work through privilege and oppression. This is followed by information related to youth voice and a proposal that young adult librarians must understand youth voice as always occurring in a larger terrain of power, access, and explicit or implicit information about belonging within the space of the library.

ANALYZING HISTORICAL APPROACHES TO YOUTH

The example of how adults thought about and regulated youth in the 1950s speaks to how constructions of youth as perpetually in need of either adult-instituted punishment or guidance have found fertile soil in the interstices of power and oppression.[4] Examining the implications that historical antecedents carry forward within librarianship provides, in this moment, some footing for creating more meaningful and socially aware library services (Schlesselman-Tarango 2016). A brief review reveals that constructions of youth have historically been raced, classed, and gendered in professional approaches to youth services.[5] Racist fears of youth deviance have been a foundational aspect of professional constructions of youth development. G. Stanley Hall, for instance, held strong, eugenicist views related to the possible developmental heights available to adolescents. Hall's commitment to recapitulation theory—used here to describe the belief that individuals develop along parameters similar to those of overall human progress—led to his enthusiastic positioning of European culture as the apex of possible advancement. In Hall's construction of adolescence, the ultimate height of achievement was to become the successful, white male, model European citizen (Hall 1904; Lesko 1996).

Hall's (1904) obviously raced and gendered understanding of adolescent development continues, in various manifestations, to shape the fear that adults continuously voice about youth. In the history of librarianship, these anxieties appear in discussions of the library as a site of acculturation that took place in the early half of the 1900s (Lukenbill 2006). Librarians ushered in youth to what they deemed as appropriate development as potential, but often lacking, subjects in pursuit of white, middle-class, heterosexual belonging—or denied access to children and youth of color and other youth who were positioned, in this framework, as developmentally deviant (Hand 2012).

"Deviance" threads through historical ideologies that created and constrained youth. The raced and gendered approaches to youth within libraries must be understood within the social and moral panics adults have manufactured around youth in the past century. Youth deviance was named as the enemy to watch and used as evidence that youth needed adult control, intervention, and, at times, corporal punishment. Consider any or all of the following as brief highlights of this phenomenon: the white and disciplining violence toward Mexican and Mexican American youth during the Zoot Suit riots (Gallow 2014); the fanatical anxieties around teenage pregnancy and feminine sexuality (and the fact that men who are perpetrators or abusers rarely afford mention in these discussions) (Knupfer 2001); and the homophobic conclusion that youth would become gay by exposure to gay and lesbian adults (evident in the 1978 Briggs Initiative in California and its precedent in the passage of laws against homosexual instructors in Oklahoma and, in 2018, present as "no promo homo" laws and ordinances) (GLSEN 2017). Imagine how vastly different library education about young people might be if it included critically positioned understandings of how youth are discussed in relation to the political and social forces that work to create belonging and aberrance! The construction of specific groups of youth as "other" within library services manifests these larger projects of social control that work through the institutional structures youth encounter and navigate.

The power inherent in adult approaches to youth becomes prominent in these briefly highlighted instances of adult unease. In each of the previous instances, from Hall's (1904) conception of appropriate development to mass media panics over modern-day teen pregnancy, the construction of youth relies on the maintenance of the status quo of power relations (Luttrell-Rowland 2007; Sukarieh and Tannock 2008). Adult concerns around youth reproduced power structures that limit the chances of well-being and success for all but a select group of youth—the wealthy, or at least well-resourced, heteronormative (or, at the most, "respectfully"—quietly—gay), cisgender men. This privileging of certain types of experience bears examination when considering youth who chafe against conventional library services, those groups of youth not mentioned often or at all—those youth made vulnerable to the state, created as deviant or defiant, policed, removed from society, or under surveillance in public spaces.[6] Within librarianship, youth in these groupings arise as "underserved" populations (American Library Association 2019). These groupings of youth include homeless youth, LGBQ and especially transgender and gender-nonconforming youth, and youth of color—at times, all of these intersectional identities held by individual youth—among others (Collins 2008; Crenshaw 1991).

It is too simplistic, and incorrect, to state that librarianship always and only adheres to approaches that enhance or continue the status quo shaping of power and oppression. Rather, mainstream librarians have relied on definitions and perceptions of youth that arise outside of the profession and have been deeply influenced by social and political narratives of youth and appropriate development (Bernier 2013). This means that library and information science (LIS), as a field, has not actively involved the conceptualization of youth in regard to their information needs or desires, instead relying primarily on discipline-based definitions that have their own goals and ends. Dependence on other disciplinary perspectives, alongside the historical precedents described earlier, helps to uncover that "[t]he current (and historical) vision of youth in libraries is one that has been framed primarily by Eurocentric cultural norms and aesthetics" (Kumasi 2013, 104). Kumasi and others have offered the possibility that incorporating youth voice into library services to young adults offers a form of redress to and interruption in ongoing adult narratives that have worked to the detriment of already marginalized groups of youth. The following section provides an overview of discussions of youth voice and youth-centered library services. This discussion provides the ground for assessing the possibility of creating services that incorporate youth voice alongside critical theoretical understanding of how power shapes what youth may or may not be able to "say" in the context of the library (Li 2010).

YOUTH VOICE AS AN INTERVENTION

Young adult librarianship is slowly distancing itself from an overt reliance on developmental models as practical guides for providing collections and services or evaluating teen services. New models coalesce in "teen-centered" approaches that prioritize "increased social, intellectual, creative, and entertainment opportunities, especially for teens with economic, educational, physical, social, cognitive, and other disadvantages" (Agosto 2013, 45). Approaches to technologies, programs, literacies, and an acknowledgment of how economic precarity affects teens' lives have led the Young Adult Library Services Association to approach new ways of providing library services to and with young people (Braun et al. 2014). This alteration in the purpose and trajectory of youth services still walks the edge of several earlier pitfalls. For instance, the insistence on libraries as a safe space for teens, a concept reiterated throughout *The Future of Library Services for and with Teens*, can be viewed as a strategic engagement with funders and policy makers who ultimately determine funding allocation, playing on the existing social and political narrative of teens as helpless, confused, or in danger (Braun et al. 2014). Alternately, though, it may be read as a declaration that only those teens positioned as "victims" of dangerous situations, and not those teens perceived as dangerous or deviant, are invited to lay claim to the library. Safety, it can be perceived, implies a danger inherent in some other location—be that the danger teens face when moving through the world of adults, a nebulous "danger" of deviance or failed development (as evidenced in the previous historical analysis), or the stereotyping of youth of color (especially black youth) as dangerous subjects deserving of fear and regulation in public contexts (Haberman 2014).

Kumasi's (2013) calls for voice through the lens of critical race theory address this potential slippage and elision. Incorporating youth voice, desires, self-conception, and interests into library programming offers another challenge to the perpetuation of status quo power in library services. It offers a counter to adult-inscribed approaches to youth's need for healthy development. Yet, calls for youth voice have not always led to the adult-touted overall shifts in services to youth and speaking does not necessarily benefit youth (Conner 2016). An examination of youth voice and the nonprofit industry reveals this fact. Youth voice often features heavily in nonprofit models, and the idea of youth-centered approaches, especially for youth made vulnerable to the state, frequently recurs in that arena. For instance, in a discussion of youth of color organizing through AYPAL, Kwon (2013) notes that funders and actual youth often had very different opinions regarding the purposes of their works. These differences could account for the language of safety or of workplace development (present in Braun et al. 2014); they provide legitimacy to funders by affirming governmental bodies' conceptual definitions of teens' experiences and what teens need (Kwon 2013).

Kwon's (2013) examination stresses the tensions of youth-centered efforts in the nonprofit realm. Where nonprofit organizations often fold back in to the neoliberal order, through the specific types of projects that receive funding, nonprofits working with youth are positioned to "follow affirmative youth management strategies that shape young citizen-subjects into self-responsible and self-governing individuals who can improve their life chances in the neoliberal order" (68). In other words, nonprofits train youth into the law-abiding status quo through the nonprofit complex, giving youth little actual political power and positioning them to compete with one another—often while telling their truths from positions of marginality or vulnerability.

Critiques of the possible ramifications of youth voice as a mode of control have pointed to institutional power—from workplaces to juvenile incarceration—as the force that shapes what can be said or acted upon. Sukarieh and Tannock (2008, 2015) examine narratives of youth engagement as part of what governs youth into status quo compliance—extending a review beyond the United States to incorporate high-level governmental organization documents about youth. They identify a double-bind inherent in the calls for youth participation and voice. On one hand, "[w]hen youth stand inside this system as willing and enthusiastic participants, their identities and voices are to be welcomed and celebrated," and on the other, "standing outside this system, questioning or challenging its basic precepts and promises, they become framed instead as global society's worst nightmare" (Sukarieh and Tannock 2008, 302).

Incorporation of youth voice in library services trends toward overdependence on the perspectives of available youth in planning library programs. This results in programs and services and collections that tend to heavily emphasize the existing library users, ignoring histories of cultural whiteness in librarianship as a shaping factor in who currently trusts the library as more than a passing resource and which youth can share, or can feel comfortable sharing, their insights with librarians and staff (Schlesselman-Tarango, 2016). Many important and hopefully impactful changes have been made, evidenced in the We Need Diverse Books campaign (http://weneeddiversebooks.org), an increase in conversations about whom the library serves and why, and the ongoing, committed efforts of many librarians, caucuses, and educators. These exciting endeavors should not be forgotten, but more remains to be done. Young adult librarianship has engaged in a shift toward being youth-centered. It can now engage in a challenge to the existing status quo, a political and social order that often circumscribes the life chances of youth made vulnerable to the state (homeless youth, LGBQ and especially transgender and gender-nonconforming youth, and youth of color) in a way that can make libraries an irrelevant institution. This requires a shift within the profession and through LIS education, one that facilitates the skills needed to critically position both adult and youth voices in histories of power, privilege, and oppression in the process of creating more aware, responsive, and meaningful library services.

CRITICALLY INCORPORATING YOUTH VOICE

Youth activism and protest, as a local and international occurrence, provides some insight into how youth view the power structures that frame their lives. Activism may range from the works of FIERCE, a group of LGBTQ youth of color that began in relation to the closing of a public access space for private development (FIERCE 2017; Mananzala 2012); to student walkouts in response to intense political repression, such as the walkouts and alternative curriculum organized and implemented by students following the cancellation of the Mexican American Studies classes in Tucson (Cabrera et al. 2013); to the as yet unimagined or unrecognized (by adults) forms of resistance and claim to power that youth engage in on a daily basis (Taft 2011).

Even given the numerous instances of youth resistance and navigation of institutional forces, these examples can be used by adults to romanticize activist youth as leading young adult librarianship in its trajectory toward greater social and political equality. Two realities facilitate this romanticization. First, youth actions are often underreported (or not reported at all) or filtered through developmental models when information about them is made easily available (Conner 2016). Sukarieh and Tannock (2015) describe this adult-constructed dualism—adults alternatively view resistance as a defining characteristic of youth or as evidence that particular youth inherently engage in defiant, dangerous, or downright morally ill acts. Second, a dependence on visible youth action fails to recognize how often power structures forcefully curtail possibility for youth voice and activism. Activist youth, then, offer librarians examples of engagement and concerns, but it is incorrect to position them as the leaders of social change within librarianship. Rather, librarians need to take part in skill and knowledge building that increases our understanding of the structural and political forces that many activist youth push against in order to provide more informed services to all youth, not just those youth openly engaged in explicitly social justice-oriented endeavors.

Let me move from theoretic stances to actual instantiations of librarians' need for critical theory as part of understanding youth and youth's statements. My ongoing research hones in on an instance where some youth engage in activism yet others, due to systemic forces, find themselves positioned to be silent by analyzing when and how youth speak (or write) from their own experiences while in juvenile detention. Due to racism, homophobia, and transphobia in systems of policing, youth in detention often navigate interstitial forces of institutional and individually implemented oppression that work to place them inside of juvenile detention or other institutions (Davis 2003; Fine and Ruglis 2009; Sawyer and Hodge 2014; Spade 2011). In interviews with youth in juvenile detention and through analysis of youth's writings in *The Beat Within* (www.thebeatwithin.org), a magazine that publishes the writings of incarcerated youth, I have found that calls for youth voice often do not adequately incorporate understandings of power and oppression. This statement stands even in instances where youth hold a great deal of knowledge about the role of power in shaping the resources available to them and have what they consider to be meaningful access to library services and programs. The ability to "speak," in these circumstances, relies on several factors. Two of these factors—audience and understanding—shape how librarians serving young adults can critically engage with youth voice in order to create more meaningful library services for youth of color and/or LGBTQ and gender-nonconforming youth.

For youth who are heavily surveilled or incarcerated, "speaking" requires an audience that hears and acts in the interests of youth, an audience that holds youth statements in the context of power. Within juvenile detention, this audience rarely proves easily accessible (Bernstein 2014). Rather, I have found that youth who have the option of getting out of detention must construct their statements, and other modes of communication, to fit the functions of the institution and profess its efficacy. This means that youth might make claims to neoliberal success (such as individual personal development or a desire for mainstream education and employment) in order to appease the powers that exist over their lives. Youth successfully and knowledgeably navigate institutions and powerful forces, but, here, this does not involve youth speaking a truth of their experience. Even when individual youth *do* believe in the possibility that they will access meaningful education and achieve individual financial stability or success, youth often hold an awareness that structural forces and resource availability will mean that they face great difficulty (and little assistance) in meeting these goals. Even when making statements that appear, on the surface, to buy in to the rhetoric of institutions—including juvenile detention facilities or schools—these statements do not necessarily arise from some inherent drive toward maintaining the status quo of privilege and oppression that exists within these institutions.

Speaking, or creating a message that goes beyond the bounds of the juvenile detention or other institution, requires more than just a voice. To create a message that extends beyond the walls of juvenile detention, or is used to further its continuance, youth statements must be rebroadcast or approximated in the context of larger society. Many young adult authors engage in this effort—either through their own experiences or by sharing the information that youth entrust to them during author visits. Zetta Elliott, G. Neri, Jason Reynolds, Richard Ross, and Angie Thomas have all contributed to spreading awareness of how policing and incarceration continuously attempt to shape the lifeworlds of specific groups of youth. In these instances, youth experiences are positioned within an analysis of structural forces and are either translated or fictionalized through an adult lens. Adult voice, critical understanding, creation, and respect act as the implements through which youth voice is conveyed outside of the institution.

The statements that youth in heavily surveilled and ideologically laden contexts make must be interpreted through an informed understanding of adult institutional power, privilege, and oppression. For youth made vulnerable to state power, surveillance and policing configure their experience of the world (Skiba, Michael, Nardo, and Peterson 2000; Wald and Losen 2003).[7] Librarians working with young adults need to recognize that the forces that create populations in juvenile detention instantiate in many arenas of youth's lives; surveillance and policing happen in the communities that contain libraries. Libraries, too, are implicated within the hegemonic forces of power, privilege, and oppression. Critical understanding, through lived circumstances or the active pursuit of critical information, stands as the key element in incorporating youth voice in library projects that seek to be socially aware and responsive to the world, and the moment, in which we find ourselves. Here, Kumasi (2013) advocates for critical race theory as one of the tools for understanding youth voice. Critical theory, reflection, and understanding of how social and political forces shape the information economy reveal forces that actively privilege whiteness, English, heterosexuality (or at most subdued homosexuality), and overall complicit citizenship (Freire 2008). My own research has drawn heavily from critical theoretical approaches—present in critical race theory, queer studies, and trans studies—to examine prison, education, and the construction of youth. Notably, this research reveals that youth writings in *The Beat Within* reflected academic and scholarly understandings of the theoretical positions present in these academic traditions.[8] In speaking to the information present in critical traditions, youth simply defined it as "the system," a phrase that ultimately holds volumes of knowledge, critique, and lived experience.

There is a danger in positioning "the system" (or, in academic adult lingo, the prison-industrial complex or, in my own phrasing, the juvenile detention complex), or any other institutional force in youth's lives, as knowable only through the experience of it. This isolates youth through their experience no matter how many features of that experience reoccur. It positions youth who are or have been held in juvenile detention facilities as holding the onus for making change in their lives—failing to recognize the ongoing degradation of support systems that have issued some address, however limited, to the lived realities of institutional oppression. Narratives of youth voice that do not occur within critical understandings of the operation of power in the lives of youth run this risk.

Critically positioning youth voice is far more nuanced than trusting, or positioning, youth as ultimate sources of information. Only so much can be gleaned from youth's individual experiences or portrayals and adult interpretations of these. In looking to understand power, either in the juvenile detention facility or within librarianship, librarians need to turn from neoliberal models of individual certainty and assumed group coherence to research, practice, and patterns that occur as collective experiences (Cook-Sather 2007). Here, we need critical theoretical traditions and information from critical youth studies. Approaches to youth librarianship that seek to address privilege and oppression should be founded in understandings of youth voice that are relational and contextual rather than reinforcing the power of young adult librarians to clearly and easily discern the needs and interests of youth.

Despite the heavy restrictions, punishments, and possible consequences of youth expression within institutional contexts, youth do and can still speak to and around power. If librarians are to work to create social change and increase the well-being of those "underserved" youth (homeless youth, LGBQ and especially transgender and gender-nonconforming youth, and youth of color), not just those youth who already have some connection to the library, we will need to find guides that assist us in understanding the world that we inhabit with youth. Critical theoretical approaches offer such guidance. Youth critiques of library services offer further direction. In my research, a prominent critique youth have made of library services concerns the reiteration of racist and stereotypic understandings of youth of color. The lack of cultural awareness among librarians results in a clear and prominent message: they are not welcome in the library. This is especially painful in light of the anecdotally increased collection development focused on representation (evidenced through WeNeedDiverseBooks.org). In culturally unaware contexts, youth of color and queer and trans youth receive the message that their lives and experiences, or the lives and experiences of those like them, hold more value as representation and portrayal than as actually lived.

CONCLUSION

Recognizing youth (and ourselves) as situated through experience, privilege, oppression, individuality, and collectivity provides one way that young adult librarians can depart from frames of reference that alternately problematize or lionize youth. Critically theoretical approaches to youth and youth voice increase librarians' understandings that youth always have some amount of agency but institutional forces shape that agency. Institutional forces reward particular modes of culture, conduct, address, and comportment while condemning others. Including critical theoretical approaches goes beyond purely intellectual endeavor. Critiques present in critical race theory, ethnic studies disciplines, and queer and trans theories often contain an address to power. Critical theoretical approaches present several possibilities for young adult librarians working with youth, acting from their statements, and seeking to have a better foundational understanding of how and why life possibilities are drastically different for white, middle-class youth and homeless youth, LGBQ and especially transgender and gender-nonconforming youth, and youth of color. In order to more fully address and work against converging histories of reiterated privilege within librarianship and within discussions of youth development and deviance, librarians' understandings of youth should involve a situated, critical, and complex positioning of the many voices of youth. Critically situating youth voice allows librarians to move beyond positions that elevate the statements of those youth who do speak as library canon. It generously offers a means to recognize the collectively shared experiences of oppression of youth, to envision services beyond those already provided, and to work with youth to increase a shared awareness of how libraries might land in a conversation with youth about the realities of their lives.

Librarians hold the specific skills and public positions that provide opportunities to address the neoliberal turn toward individual accounts and individual success in constructions of youth. This involves an understanding of the constant institutional assimilation of youth voice into preexisting conduct and institutional plans by addressing the isolation constantly described within theoretical approaches to understanding power. Neoliberal models of workforce development, educational attainment, and their ilk rely on the idea of competitive individual success. Librarianship should envision, not an unequal democracy in which everyone has some room to speak, but a collective, situated, and informed sharing of knowledges, experiences, and goals with an eye toward social change. This may be what is required of librarians as we make efforts to work with, and not just for, youth. Our ability to identify relevant information can combine with the curiosity about the world that we often share with many youth to help us contextualize youth voice through an understanding of how powerful institutions, including libraries, shape what and in what ways youth may or may not speak. In doing this, we become the informed audience, that, with youth, carries forth a message of needed institutional change, of desire for a better world, and of the belief that it could still be made.

NOTES

1. See Meiners 2007, chapter 1, for a discussion of social belonging and whiteness.
2. Knott (2016) clearly states that "public libraries have contributed to the construction of race since their beginnings" (15).
3. Fredric Wertham, considered a progressive psychiatrist, is nevertheless best known for asserting that youth delinquency is caused by comic books. Wertham's (1954) *Seduction of the Innocent* led to U.S. Congressional hearings and industry reform that resulted in the Comics Code.
4. Luttrell-Rowland (2007) offers a more contemporary description of how powerful forces create categories of youth belonging and citizenship.
5. For a location-specific and more nuanced review, see Hand's 2012 description of library services in New Orleans in the early 1900s.
6. This should come as no surprise, considering that focused young adult services are a new endeavor and that recent histories of librarianship evidence an aversion to viewing any young library users as legitimate patrons (Chelton 2001).
7. Also relevant here is the work of the Children's Defense Fund, in particular its Cradle to Prison Pipeline Campaign; for the full report, see www.childrensdefense.org/reports/2007/cradle-to-prison-pipeline-2007-full-report.
8. These are traditions that, it stands to be said, were brought into the university and thereby made more respectable or legitimate through intense activism and commitment on the part of young people involved in multiple social and political movements.

REFERENCES

Agosto, D. 2013. "Envisaging Young Adult Librarianship from a Teen-Centered Perspective." In *Transforming Young Adult Services*, edited by A. Bernier, 33–52. Chicago: ALA Neal-Schuman.

American Library Association. 2019. "Outreach to Underserved Populations." ALA.org. Accessed July 22. www.ala.org/advocacy/diversity/outreachtounderservedpopulations.

Bernier, A. 2013. "Introduction." In *Transforming Young Adult Services*, edited by A. Bernier, 1–29. Chicago: ALA Neal-Schuman.

Bernier, A., M. Males, and C. Rickman. 2014. "'It Is Silly to Hide Your Most Active Patrons': Exploring User Participation of Library Space Designs for Young Adults in the United States." *Library Quarterly: Information, Community, Policy* 84, no. 2: 165–82.

Bernstein, N. 2014. *Burning Down the House: The End of Juvenile Prison*. New York: The New Press.

Braun, L. W., M. L. Hartman, S. Hughes-Hassell, and K. Kumasi. 2014. *The Future of Library Services for and with Teens: A Call to Action*. Chicago and Washington, DC: Young Adult Library Services Association and Institute of Museum and Library Services. www.ala.org/yaforum/sites/ala.org.yaforum/files/content/YALSA_nationalforum_Final_web_0.pdf.

Braverman, M. 1979. *Youth, Society and the Public Library*. Chicago: American Library Association.

Cabrera, N. L., E. L. Meza, A. Romero, and R. C. Rodriguez. 2013. "'If There Is No Struggle, There Is No Progress': Transformative Youth Activism and the School of Ethnic Studies." *Urban Review* 45, no. 1: 7–22.

Cacho, L. M. 2012. *Social Death: Racialized Rightlessness and the Criminalization of the Unprotected.* New York: New York University Press.

Chelton, M. 2001. "Young Adults as Problems: How the Social Construction of a Marginalized User Category Occurs." *Journal of Education for Library and Information Science* 42, no. 1: 4–11.

Cohen, R. D. 1997. "'The Delinquents': Censorship and Youth Culture in Recent U.S. History." *History of Education Quarterly* 37, no. 3: 251–70.

Collins, P. H. 2008. *Black Feminist Thought: Knowledge, Consciousness, and the Politics of Empowerment.* Boston: Unwin Hyman.

Conner, J. O. 2016. "Pawns or Power Players: The Grounds on Which Adults Dismiss or Defend Youth Organizers in the USA." *Journal of Youth Studies* 19, no. 3: 403–20.

Cooke, N., M. Sweeney, and S. Noble. 2016. "Social Justice as Topic and Tool: An Attempt to Transform an LIS Curriculum and Culture." *Library Quarterly* 86, no. 1: 107–24.

Cook-Sather, A. 2007. "Resisting the Impositional Potential of Student Voice Work: Lessons for Liberatory Educational Research from Poststructuralist Feminist Critiques of Critical Pedagogy." *Discourse* 28, no. 3: 389–403.

Crenshaw, K. 1991. "Mapping the Margins: Intersectionality, Identity Politics, and Violence against Women of Color." *Stanford Law Review* 43, no. 6: 1241–99.

Davis, A. 2003. *Are Prisons Obsolete?* New York: Seven Stories Press.

FIERCE. 2017. "What We Do." FIERCEnyc.org. Accessed December 19. www.fiercenyc.org/what-we-do.

Fine, M., and J. Ruglis. 2009. "Circuits and Consequences of Dispossession: The Racialized Realignment of the Public Sphere for U.S. Youth." *Transforming Anthropology* 17, no. 1: 20–33.

Freire, P. 2008. *Pedagogy of the Oppressed.* 30th anniversary ed. New York: Continuum.

Gallow, L. L. 2014. "Race as a Motivating Factor in the Zoot Suit Riots." In *The American Mosaic: The Latino American Experience.* Santa Barbara, CA: ABC-CLIO. http://works.bepress.com/lgallow/14.

Geller, E. 1984. *Forbidden Books in American Public Libraries, 1876–1939: A Study in Cultural Change.* Westport, CT: Greenwood Press.

GLSEN. 2017. "'No Promo Homo' Laws." GLSEN.org. Accessed December 18. www.glsen.org/learn/policy/issues/nopromohomo.

Haberman, C. 2014. "When Youth Violence Spurred 'Superpredator' Fear." *The New York Times,* "Retro Report," April 6. www.nytimes.com/2014/04/07/us/politics/killing-on-bus-recalls-superpredator-threat-of-90s.html?_r=0.

Hall, G. S. 1904. *Adolescence: Its Psychology and Its Relations to Physiology, Anthropology, Sociology, Sex, Crime, Religion and Education.* New York: D. Appleton.

Hand, S. 2012. "Transmitting Whiteness: Librarians, Children, and Race, 1900–1930s." *Progressive Librarian*, no. 38/39: 34–63. www.progressivelibrariansguild.org/PL/PL38_39/034.pdf.

Hunt, J., and A. Moodie-Mills. 2012. "The Unfair Criminalization of Gay and Transgender Youth: An Overview of the Experiences of LGBT Youth in the Juvenile Justice System." Brief for the Center for American Progress. https://cdn.americanprogress.org/wp-content/uploads/issues/2012/06/pdf/juvenile_justice.pdf.

Knott, C. 2016. "Introduction." In *Not Free, Not for All: Public Libraries in the Age of Jim Crow*, 1–17. Amherst: University of Massachusetts Press.

Knupfer, A. M. 2001. *Reform and Resistance: Gender, Delinquency, and America's First Juvenile Court.* New York: Routledge.

Kumasi, K. D. 2013. "'The Library Is Like Her House': Reimagining Youth of Color in LIS Discourse." In *Transforming Young Adult Services*, edited by A. Bernier, 103–113. Chicago: ALA Neal-Schuman.

Kwon, S. A. 2013. *Uncivil Youth: Race, Activism, and Affirmative Governmentality*. Durham, NC: Duke University Press.

Lesko, N. 1996. "Denaturalizing Adolescence: The Politics of Contemporary Representations." *Youth and Society* 28, no. 2: 139–61.

Li, H. L. 2010. "Rethinking Silencing Silences." In *Democratic Dialogue in Education: Troubling Speech, Disturbing Silence*, edited by M. Boler, 69–86. New York: Peter Lang.

Lukenbill, W. B. 2006. "Helping Youth at Risk: An Overview of Reformist Movements in American Public Library Services to Youth." *New Review of Children's Literature and Librarianship* 12, no. 2: 197–213.

Luttrell-Rowland, M. 2007. "Gangs, Soldiers and 'Idle Girls': Constructions of Youth and Development in World Bank Discourse." *Research in Comparative and International Education* 2, no. 3: 230–41.

Mananzala, R. 2012. "The FIERCE Fight for Power and the Preservation of Public Space in the West Village." *Scholar and Feminist Online*, no. 10.1–10.2. http://sfonline.barnard.edu/a-new-queer-agenda/the-fierce-fight-for-power-and-the-preservation-of-public-space-in-the-west-village/#.

Meiners, E. 2007. *Right to Be Hostile: Schools, Prisons, and the Making of Public Enemies*. New York: Routledge.

Robbins, L. S. 2001. *The Dismissal of Miss Ruth Brown: Civil Rights, Censorship, and the American Library*. Norman: University of Oklahoma Press.

Romesburg, D. 2008. "The Tightrope of Normalcy: Homosexuality, Developmental Citizenship, and American Adolescence, 1890–1940." *Journal of Historical Sociology* 21, no. 4: 417–42.

Sawyer D. C., III, and D. W. Hodge. 2014. "Back on the Block: Community Reentry and Reintegration of Formerly Incarcerated Youth." In *From Education to Incarceration: Dismantling the School-to-Prison Pipeline*, edited by A. J. Nocella II, P. Parmar, and D. Stovall, 227–47. New York: Peter Lang.

Schlesselman-Tarango, G. 2016. "The Legacy of Lady Bountiful: White Women in the Library." *Library Trends* 64, no. 4: 667–86.

Skiba, R. J., R. S. Michael, A. C. Nardo, and R. Peterson. 2000. "The Color of Discipline: Sources of Racial and Gender Disproportionality in School Punishment." Policy Research Report #SRS1. Indiana Education Policy Center. www.indiana.edu/~equity/docs/ColorOfDiscipline.pdf.

Spade, D. 2011. *Normal Life: Administrative Violence, Critical Trans Politics and the Limits of Law*. Cambridge, MA: South End Press.

Sukarieh, M., and S. Tannock. 2008. "In the Best Interests of Youth or Neoliberalism? The World Bank and the New Global Youth Empowerment Project." *Journal of Youth Studies* 11, no. 3: 301–12.

———. 2015. *Youth Rising? The Politics of Youth in the Global Economy* New York: Routledge.

Taft, J. K. 2011. *Rebel Girls: Youth Activism and Social Change across the Americas*. New York: New York University.

Tilley, C. L. 2012. "Seducing the Innocent: Fredric Wertham and the Falsifications That Helped Condemn Comics." *Information and Culture* 47, no. 4: 383–413.

Wald, J., and D. J. Losen. 2003. "Defining and Redirecting a School-to-Prison Pipeline." *New Directions for Youth Development*, no. 99: 9–15.

Wertham, F. 1954. *Seduction of the Innocent*. New York: Rinehart.

PART III

Confronting Convention

CHAPTER 7

Crossing Over

The Advent of the Adultescent

Michael Cart

A comprehensive collection of literature meeting the unique developmental needs of its young adult population remains a fundamental aspect of library service. This chapter addresses the question of how library professionals select these materials and how they define the term *young adult?* Furthermore, this chapter argues that reviews remain a core guide to selecting suitable materials for a dynamic young adult population that is changing as society redefines its parameters, which now extend to age 25. Reviews are also changing, migrating from print media to online sources as they become increasingly targeted at young adults themselves instead of the traditional audience of adult professionals. The impact of these changes on reviews and collections will be the major focus of this chapter.

///

> The years from 18 until 25 and even beyond have become
> a distinct and separate life stage. . . .
> —Lev Grossman (2005)

Surely the term *young adult* should be as dynamic as the population it defines. Yet since 1991 the Young Adult Library Services Association (YALSA) has continued to define young adults as young people ages 12 to 18. It is time to change this definition to recognize the rapidly changing nature of this population, for today's young adults are now widely regarded as being as old as 25. This dramatic change clearly impacts young adult library services. One area most heavily impacted is that of materials selection and collection development. In making purchasing decisions librarians need to recognize that there now are or should be three young adult literatures: (1) middle school literature for readers 10 through 14 years of age, (2) teen literature for readers 13 to 19, and (3) young adult literature for readers 19 through 25. These are not hard and fast categories, for the long-established barriers that for years rigidly defined a book's intended audience are becoming more fluid every day. That said, the new categories I propose generally define potential readerships that will guide professionals in providing materials relevant to the service population's interests and needs.

This new definition impacts not only librarians and libraries but also publishers and book reviews and reviewers. Though sometimes intimidating, change is a necessary part of library service. Recognizing and managing this redefinition of young adults and its practical implications for collection development are one of the major challenges confronting young adult librarians in the twenty-first century.

THE NEW YOUNG ADULT

The mainstream media call them "adultescents," "kidults," "twixters," or "boomerangers," but whatever you call them, they are a new generation that is redefining the traditional library meaning of young adult. For today's young adults may, it is claimed, be as old as 25. How is this so? The short answer is that they are a generation influenced by the Peter Pan syndrome: they simply will not grow up! But that is not entirely accurate. Instead, consider that nearly 20 million, or 30 percent, of America's nearly 70 million 18- to 24-year-olds are still living at home with their parents, delaying marriage until their late twenties, and often not finding a career path job until their early thirties (AP 2009).

There are a number of reasons for this: a principal one is the nature of the economy and the increasingly chronic shortage of jobs for youth, and a second is the fact that knowing their life expectancy is now 78.6 (CDC 2017) and their retirement age may be at least 68 or even 70, these young people are in no hurry to assume the responsibilities and, some might say, burdens of adulthood. Finally, today's youth are children of a generation of "helicopter parents" who are concerned for their children's well-being and have hovered over them like, well, a helicopter.

Meanwhile, these new young adults continue to be heavily invested in teen and traditional young adult (YA) popular culture, shopping at the same stores, wearing the same clothes, going to the same movies and concerts, and being similarly devoted to every aspect of the burgeoning social media. They simply will not grow up.

The prevalence of this new generation has actually inspired at least one movie, *Failure to Launch*, a romantic comedy starring Matthew McConaughey as a 35-year-old still living at home with his parents. His two best friends are also still living at home to the considerable distress of their parents. Two mainstream television programs—both comedies—illustrated this situation: *$#*! My Dad Says* and *Big Lake*. Like the McConaughey movie, both feature young men still living at home and failing to launch themselves into adulthood.

Since the early twenty-first century, a growing number of developmental psychologists, sociologists, and neuroscientists have been studying this age group (18–34), particularly the segment ages 18 to 25, and have concluded that it constitutes a new, distinct life stage that leading expert Dr. Jeffrey Jensen Arnett calls "emerging adulthood." A professor of psychology at Clark University in Worcester, Massachusetts, and author of the book *Emerging Adulthood: The Winding Road from the Late Teens through the Twenties*, Arnett, in an article in the *New York Times*, drew an analogy to what happened a century ago when social and economic changes helped create an earlier definition of "adolescence"(Henig 2010).

During that time of social and economic changes, G. Stanley Hall (1904), the first American PhD in psychology and first president of the American Psychological Association, published his massive two-volume work, *Adolescence: Its Psychology and Its Relations to Physiology, Anthropology, Sociology, Sex, Crime, Religion, and Education*. It might be said that Hall created this new category of human being; certainly his theories about the "storm and stress" that typified this season of life were enormously influential among youth services workers, educators, and developmental psychologists.

Once the idea of the adolescent was established, the concept of a specific stage of adolescence, the teenager, was not far behind. In fact, by the end of the 1930s, a youth culture was fast emerging, thanks in part to the Great Depression that had dried up the job market for youth and sent them to high school in record numbers.

With the advent of World War II, these newly minted teenagers began to acquire money of their own (in part because so many adults were involved in the war effort that new jobs for younger people were once again available). This, in turn, resulted in the establishment in the late 1940s of Eugene Gilbert's Youth Marketing Company, the first market research firm to analyze the enormous commercial potential of this group.

Meanwhile, Hall's theories continued to resonate nearly half a century later in the work of developmental psychologists Erik Erikson and Robert J. Havighurst, both of whom asserted that two of the stages of human development were (1) adolescence and (2) young adulthood. Erikson defined them as the years 12 to 18 and 19 to 40, respectively. Havighurst opted for 13 to 18 and 19 to 30. Despite these relatively small chronological differences, it is clear that both believed that full adulthood did not arrive until age 30 (Cart 2010, 7).

To attain such full adulthood, Havighurst, in the late 1940s, posited the notion that young people must successfully complete seven rites of passage, or as he called them "developmental tasks" (Cart 2011d, 61). They were (1) achieve new and more mature relations with age mates of both sexes, (2) achieve masculine or feminine social roles, (3) accept their physiques and use their bodies effectively, (4) achieve emotional independence of parents and other adults, (5) prepare for marriage and family life, (6) prepare for economic careers, and (7) acquire a set of values and an ethical system as a guide to behavior. "To accomplish the tasks," Havighurst asserted, "will lead to happiness and to success with later tasks, while failure leads to unhappiness in the individual, disapproval by society, and difficulty with later tasks" (Cart 2011d, 61).

To help young people accomplish these tasks educators turned to books for youth. A leading expert in the field, G. Robert Carlsen, led the way, equating stages of reading development with Havighurst's stages of personal development. In Carlsen's (1980) *Books and the Teenage Reader*, originally published in 1967, he identified three such stages: (1) early adolescence, or ages 11 to 14; (2) middle adolescence, ages 15 to 16; and (3) late adolescence, ages 17 to 18. He then developed a series of book categories that were appropriate to each stage and asserted that early adolescents would enjoy animal, adventure, and mystery stories; middle adolescents would prefer war stories and historical novels; and late adolescents, searches for personal values and books of social significance.

It is worth noting that Hall, Erikson, and Havighurst had all labeled as "adolescents" youth from ages 12 to 30 or even 40. Carlsen, on the other hand, limited his interest to what he called "teen-age[rs]," perhaps to signify that his classification was less inclusive than the former and was consistent with the age of high school students.

As for librarians who were discovering this population segment and beginning to develop collections and services for them, the professional term was *young adult*, one that has remained until recently. In fact, the term *young adult* appeared in library literature as early as 1944 and became formalized in 1957 with the American Library Association's formation of the Young Adult Services Division (YASD), the precursor to today's YALSA.

Like Carlsen, YASD from its beginning tacitly defined young adults as being ages 12 to 18, though it was not until 1991 that the division, in concert with the National Center for Education Statistics, formally defined young adults as "those individuals from 12 to 18 years old."

Clearly, the driving force in both Carlsen's and YASD's definitions was the age of the junior high and high school populations. The problem with this, however, was that it made youth who turned 19 into what might be called "instant adults" who were no longer eligible for young adult services. And so it remained, for good or ill, until the turn of the twenty-first century when the definition of YA once again began to broaden as many observers of the field started to argue that YA should now be regarded as youth ages 12 to 25 or even 12 to 34. How did this come about?

As is the case with so much in this material world, a root cause was economic and was vested in the bursting of the stock market bubble in 2000. The result of this fiscal disaster was a dramatic dip in the economy, which in turn caused the job market to dry up as it had in the 1930s. And so when today's high school and college graduates began entering the job market, there were not enough jobs to go around, and rather than starve (not a happy prospect) many of these young people moved back home to live with their parents. This situation can now continue even after college graduation (Wolverson 2011).

By 2004, a total of 52 percent of America's 18- to 24-year-olds were still living at home (Clifford 2005). One indication of the significance of this phenomenon is that *adultescent* was chosen by the editors of *Webster's New World College Dictionary* as Word of the Year for 2004.

A second cause of the expansion of adolescence was neurological/physiological. For years scientists had believed that the human brain was fully formed shortly after puberty (typically age 12). However, thanks to a major longitudinal study sponsored by the National Institute of Mental Health, scientists discovered—to their surprise—that the brain is in fact not fully developed until the age of 25 or older. The final areas of the brain to mature are the prefrontal cortex and cerebellum, which govern emotional control and higher-order cognitive functions. In other words, young people remain adolescents until the age of 25 or thereabouts (Henig 2010).

In addition to economic and physiological causes, at least one cultural cause should be considered—the creation of MTV in 1981. In the years since, the so-called MTV demographic—those ages 12 to 25—has become a commonplace element of branding, marketing, and, to be a bit redundant, demography. While these numbers are certainly more arbitrary than those of, say, a Havighurst or an Erickson, they do suggest a commonality of interest between 12- and 25-year-olds. "The age at which Americans reach adulthood is increasing," psychologist Robert Epstein told the magazine *Psychology Today*. "Thirty is the new twenty and most Americans now believe a person isn't an adult until age twenty-six" (Cart 2011d, 119).

While there may be some uncertainty among the general public about the age range occupied by adultescents, there is none among the members of the medical profession. Between 1994 and 2005, nearly one thousand doctors were certified in a new subspecialty: adolescent medicine. As *Newsweek* magazine observed, "The old view of adolescence was that it ended at 18 or 19. Now, with many young adults in their early twenties still struggling to find their foothold in the world, doctors call the years from 18 to 28 'the second decade of adolescence'" (Kantrowitz and Springen 2005).

During this second decade of adolescence, more and more young people seem to be taking time off from completing school and/or getting jobs to pursue interests for personal satisfaction or because they feel the experience will look good on their résumés; some of these experiences in fact consist of unpaid internships, an increasingly common phenomenon that saves employers the cost of hiring a regular employee. These life experiences are being called "gap years" or "the timeout" and may recall the nineteenth-century custom of the *Wanderjahr*, a period of wandering that typically saw wealthy young Englishmen heading to Europe to broaden their life experience (Finder 2005).

Like the first period of adolescence (12 to 18), the members of this new period have an array of developmental tasks to negotiate, though in their case only five instead of seven. They are (1) finishing school, (2) moving out of their parents' home, (3) getting a good job with benefits, (4) getting married, and (5) having a child (Henig 2010).

Offering these five choices, *Time* magazine interviewed an array of adultescents asking them, "What makes you an adult?" (Grossman 2005). A total of 22 percent said it was having their first child; another 22 percent said it was moving away from home, though surely not to buy a home of their own (the *Kansas City Star* has reported that the average age of first-time homebuyers has climbed from 29 to 33 in the past decade [Montgomery 2005]). Nineteen percent opted for getting a good job; 14 percent said it was getting married (the median age for a first marriage in the 1970s was 21 for women and 23 for men, and by 2009 it had grown to 26 for women and 28 for men); and 10 percent said it was finishing their education (though more and more students are taking five years to complete their undergraduate education and 23 percent of *Time* respondents said they were at least 24 or older before they finished).

As a follow-up question *Time* also asked, "How would you describe yourself?" (Grossman 2005). To this question 61 percent replied "an adult." However, 29 percent said they were just entering adulthood, and 10 percent said they were not yet out of school. When *Time* then asked of the 29 percent why they didn't consider themselves adults, 35 percent replied it was because they "were just enjoying life the way it is." Another 33 percent said it was because they were not yet financially independent, and 13 percent said it was because they were not out of school.

The consideration of financial independence brings us back to the economy. Going to school poses a major financial burden. A total of 52 percent of those interviewed said they owed money when they finished. How much? Well, 66 percent said it was over $10,000, 23 percent owed more than $30,000, and 5 percent owed a whopping $100,000. And that is not all; there is also credit card debt to be considered. According to public policy group Demos, credit card debt for 18- to 24-year-olds more than doubled from 1992 to 2001 (Grossman 2005). Small wonder so many of these young people are returning to the parental nest.

On the other hand, the fact that this relieves them of virtually every economic burden, including repaying student loans, means the new adultescents have a fairly significant amount of disposable income. *Time*'s survey asked these boomerangers' opinion of what they might spend more on than most people do. Their responses: 32 percent said "eating out," 26 percent said "clothes," 17 percent identified "going to or renting movies," and 12 percent said "computers and software" (Grossman 2005).

Not surprisingly, this new market has resulted in the establishment of a new market research firm called Twentysomething Inc. It is the first such company to offer research on adultescents to corporate America (shades of the 1940s' Youth Marketing Company). David Morrison, president and founder of the company, confirms the new buying power of adultescents, telling *Time*, "They are the optimum market to be going after for consumer electronics, Game Boys, flat screen TVs, iPods, couture fashion, exotic vacations, and so forth" (Grossman 2005).

On the other hand, Morrison also notes, "Young adults are the first to feel the brunt of a bad economy and the last to feel the benefits of a recovering economy" (AP 2009). It is worth noting that a firm called Twentysomething should use the term *young adult*. This appears to reinforce this writer's own redefinition of the term.

Despite this somewhat gloomy observation, and given the recent strengthening of broad economic performance, it is likely that a good number of those who are presently adultescents will increasingly assume more conventional adult responsibilities. However, according to Morrison, enough will remain to ensure that this new life stage definition continues to be a sociological, psychological, and cultural phenomenon (AP 2009). Many young people will continue to drift along enjoying life; many will remain financially dependent ("The stigma of depending on your parents is gone" [Montgomery 2005]); and many will simply remain unsettled. *Time* discovered that half of its respondents had worked at anywhere from two to six different jobs in the preceding three years (Grossman 2005). Another 25 percent had lived at three different addresses in the previous five years, while 22 percent had lived at four or more.

The existence of this new, distinct life stage surely demands new library services to meet its users' personal needs—psychological, emotional, and developmental—just as service to the new category of human being called young adult did 50-some years ago. Though there must be many different kinds of library services to meet these various needs, our focus in the remainder of this chapter will be on materials and their selection.

A NEW LITERATURE FOR A NEW CATEGORY OF USERS

Historically, library collections for young adults have been pegged at users ages 12 to 18. To expand this user base to include 19- to 25-year-olds would require a similar expansion of the collection to include what we have traditionally called adult books. Of course, there is nothing necessarily new about such inclusion. The American Library Association (ALA) has been including adult titles on its lists of best books for teenage readers since 1930 when it established its Young People's Reading Round Table (young people in this context translates roughly to today's definition of young adult). Because there was no YA literature then, the round table's annual list of best books included a sometimes uneasy mix of adult and children's books, ranging from Will James's *Lone Cowboy* to Edna Ferber's *Cimarron*.

This situation continued until 1948 when, acknowledging that the members of the new category of user called young adult had no interest in children's books, the list name was changed to Adult Books for Young People. In 1966 it was changed again to Best Books for Young Adults (BBYA), though the list continued to be one of exclusively adult books until 1973 when ALA's Young Adult Services Division (YASD) finally included young adult books (though to be fair YA literature as we know it today was still a newly minted genre, not having launched until 1967 with the publication of S. E. Hinton's *The Outsiders* and Robert Lipsyte's *The Contender*).

Since that time there has been considerable discussion (some of it heated) over the proper proportion of adult and YA titles to be included on the BBYA list. Some have suggested that adult titles should be eliminated altogether, so that the list would be exclusively YA titles, stressing the importance of YA literature in meeting the life needs of its target audience and of encouraging publishers to issue more books in the genre. While this debate has yet to be resolved, in the late 1990s, YALSA did establish a new award relevant to this discussion. The Alex Award honoring pioneering YA librarian Margaret Alexander Edwards consists of an annual list of the 10 best adult books of the year for young adults.

Adult is not the only non-YA (12–18) category to be included on the BBYA list; for some years it has also included what are now being called "middle school" books for readers in grades five through nine and ages 10 to 14. As a result—at least in BBYA terms—YA literature could theoretically if not practically be said to appeal to readers anywhere from ages 10 to 25. But this, of course, is a ridiculously broad range, impossibly broad when one considers the differences in developmental needs between a reader of age 10 and a reader of 25.

Recognizing this, I suggested in my *Booklist* column "Carte Blanche" for January 1, 2005, that we now divide YA literature into three categories. The first would be middle school literature for 10- to 14-year-olds; the second category would embrace the traditional 12- to 18-year-old readership but instead of being called young adult would be called "teen books"; and the third category for those 19 to 25 years old would now be called "young adult." These would not be rigidly fixed categories, of course, since there is always some overlapping in such arrangements, tacitly acknowledging the differing rates of development.

PRACTICAL CONSIDERATIONS: THE CROSSOVER BOOK

Adopting and implementing a new definition of young adult—turning the theoretical into reality—require attention to a number of practical considerations. Among these are the types of books and other materials that might be included as well as placing increasing importance on the selection and acquisition of reviews and review media.

If we acknowledge that 19- to 25-year-olds are indeed young adults with specific developmental needs, we also need to acknowledge that simply adding more traditional and even classic adult books to the collection will not meet those needs. Happily, however, a new kind of fiction is now available that might.

Thanks to the multigenerational popularity of J. K. Rowling's Harry Potter books, publishers have begun experimenting with the publication of other titles having similar multigenerational appeal. Called "crossover books," these titles are being published as either YA or adult, but in either case, they have intrinsic appeal to both traditional teens and to the new young adults. They are almost all coming-of-age stories and many recall Carlsen's (1980) type of novel suggested for late adolescence, though they are significantly more sophisticated in theme, language, and incident.

An early example of this type of book is Stephen Chbosky's *The Perks of Being a Wallflower*, the story of a troubled 14-year-old boy who finds his future in friendship. This was published as an adult title by MTV/Pocket Books, but in the dozen or so years since its 1999 publication, it has become a modern YA classic in the same way that J. D. Salinger's *The Catcher in the Rye* did for an earlier generation of young adults.

Another interesting early example of the crossover novel is Mark Haddon's *The Curious Incident of the Dog in the Nighttime*. Though first published in England in two simultaneous editions, one adult and the other YA, the American edition of this memorable book about a boy with Asperger's syndrome was published only as an adult title. Another example is Yann Martel's *Life of Pi*. Though published here in hardcover as an adult title, its publisher, Harcourt, recognized that the unusual survival story of a boy and a tiger had crossover appeal and subsequently published a paperback edition specifically targeted at a YA readership.

Australia is a hotbed of such simultaneous publications; some of the authors whose work falls into this category are Markus Zusak (*The Book Thief*), Sonya Hartnett (*What the Birds See*), and Margo Lanagan (*Tender Morsels*). Interestingly, unlike Haddon and Martel, all three of these authors are published in America only as YA, though the fact is they could just as easily have been published as adult. Another case in point is American author Curtis Sittenfeld's first novel *Prep*, a coming-of-age prep school story that could easily have been published as YA but instead was issued as an adult title. The opposite, however, happened to author Margo Rabb, whose first book *Cures for Heartbreak* was written as an adult novel but was published here in the United States as YA. This raises the question: What does distinguish a traditional YA novel from a crossover?

I would argue that the chief distinctions are that the crossover is character-driven rather than plot-driven; that the setting is more fully realized and far more than a static backdrop; that adult characters (those over age 25) may play significant parts, and the subject matter if not more sophisticated at least receives a more subtle treatment; and that the chances of ambiguity are greater. That said, two principal areas of commonality are the age of the protagonist relative to the readership and the coming-of-age nature of the narrative.

To demonstrate that crossovers move up as well as down, we should note that many titles that have been written and published as YA could nevertheless have been published as adult. Two examples that immediately come to mind are M. T. Anderson's two-volume novel *Octavian Nothing* and Aidan Chambers's *This Is All*.

Lastly, consider that an increasing number of established adult authors are now writing and being published for YAs, authors like Joyce Carol Oates, Francine Prose, Julia Alvarez, Alice Hoffman, and others. That these authors are now writing for YAs may attract their built-in adult audience to the dynamic exercise that literature has become.

Clearly, the long-established barriers that for years rigidly defined a book's intended audience are becoming more fluid every day. This is a great boon for readers but also a bit of a challenge to both book selectors and reviewers.

It would simplify a complexity of issues if publishers were to recognize the "new" young adult (the 19- to 25-year-old) and begin publishing books specifically targeted at this readership, but so far they have not. Librarians are not without influence in the world of publishing and therefore need to make their new needs known and apply pressure to encourage publishers to begin meeting these needs. Librarians also would benefit from a better understanding of modern publishing. Knowledge, as the old saying has it, is power. So, for example, librarians need to recognize that publishers seem to have a horror of trying anything new, a horror which rivals that of the motion picture industry. There's no surprise about that, of course, since most publishers are owned by giant conglomerates that also own motion picture studios. The ramifications, however, are widespread and explain why publishing for young readers has become "event publishing"—witness the search in the wake of Harry Potter for the next big thing that could be turned into a media event.

Another challenge to implementing a new kind of crossover book is managerial and economic: If a new YA line were to be created by a publisher, for example, the question arises of who would control it—the adult or the juvenile division? Alas, there is no opportunity for joint publication since both divisions would be in competition for profits. The same situation abounds in chain bookstores, especially Barnes & Noble, where no book can be shelved in more than one place; for example, despite its YA appeal, *The Curious Incident of the Dog in the Nighttime* could be shelved only in adult fiction. Otherwise two departments of the store would have to share profits, an impossibility since each is an independent profit center in competition for sales dollars with the other. And while we are speaking of economics, the simple answer to the often-articulated question of who decides if a book will be published as a YA title or as an adult title is the sales and marketing department of the publisher (with minimal editorial input). Often this decision may be vetted by Barnes & Noble, since the market for YA titles (old and new) has since the turn of the twenty-first century migrated from the traditional institutional market to the retail one.

The point of our brief excursion into the land of the bottom line is to point out that any book selector who is trying to establish a collection for the 19- to 25-year-old constituency will have to be familiar with both adult and juvenile publishing. This is no easy feat since upward of 5,000 YA retail titles are published each year, not to mention the equally large number of curriculum-related nonfiction titles issued by the remaining institutional publishers. And the number of adult titles is exponentially larger. To stay abreast of this avalanche of books is nearly impossible for the individual reader, and this is why reviews are more important now than ever.

REVIEWS AND REVIEWING FOR A NEW GENERATION OF READERS

The three major young adult review media—*Booklist*, *School Library Journal* (*SLJ*), and *VOYA*—all feature reviews of adult books for young adults but present them in different ways. *Booklist* adds a note to adult titles deemed to be of interest to this readership; *SLJ* features a separate section of adult books for young adults in its Book Review section; *VOYA* uses the code "A/YA" to identify "adult-marketed books recommended for YAs."

That all three review media use different methods is secondary to the fact that each does give specific attention to adult books that are suitable for and of interest to teens and young adults. There is nothing new here; all three have been providing this reader service for a number of years and it has served its purpose well. It is also a great help to those doing retrospective collection development.

Unfortunately, none of the journals identifies YA books suitable for adult readers (crossover trickles up as well as down after all). Considering the increasing number of these books, however, it would seem time for this added annotation to be considered, as it is singularly important for those attempting to build collections for the new YA reader. To understand the type of book I envision as being appropriate for this, I offer one example, Aidan Chambers's landmark novel *This Is All*. This writer happened to review this title for *Booklist* and thinking it relevant to this discussion I have included it here (Cart 2006).

This Is All BY AIDAN CHAMBERS

Nineteen-year-old Cordelia Kenn records the story of her life for the daughter with whom she is pregnant, planning to present it to the girl on her sixteenth birthday. The form Cordelia chooses for her tale is unusual: she is writing—or constructing—a pillow book (a la the tenth-century Japanese "Pillow Book of Sei Shonagon"), in which she not only records a narrative but also jots down poetry, ideas, observations, lists (she's a compulsive list-maker), musings and more. Cordelia is such an acute observer and has such a lively, inquiring mind that ultimately her pillow book becomes six books. Each one has its own structure and narrative strategy. Book 2, for example, is actually two stories—one fills the left-hand pages; the second, the right-hand pages. Readers must choose the order in which to read them. Some will complain about this; others will complain about the novel's great length. But the curious, the patient, and the adventurous will treasure the novel's challenges and savor its great rewards.

Arguably, the book offers the most complete character study in all of young adult literature, showing readers the life, mind and soul of a teenage girl, while also giving readers full-dress portraits of her baby's father, her friends, her family, and—most satisfyingly—her English teacher and mentor, Julie. Cordelia records not only her love for these people but also for Shakespeare, for poetry, for words. Unsparingly honest and candid, she never flinches from exploring the realities of her body or from recounting the sexually explicit details of her affair with an older man and her terrifying ordeal when she is kidnapped and threatened with rape. Cordelia records it all, because she wants to understand it all; she wants to know everything about herself, and her way of understanding is writing. Thus, she explores the why of things as well as the what and the how. In so doing she's by turns captivating and maddening, for she loves to analyze and to discover ambiguities.

And so her story challenges—but it will grow richer and larger with each reading. Ultimately, this ambitious and multilayered novel is more than a mere pièce de résistance; it is the masterpiece of one of young adult literature's greatest living writers.

Yes, I liked the book quite a lot, and I wouldn't hesitate to recommend it to the most sophisticated adult readers, especially since Cordelia is 19, the lower end of the new YA range.

As noted earlier, none of the review journals, like publishers, specifically identifies books for 19- to 25-year-old readers either, although since late 2004 this writer at least has been reviewing such books for *Booklist* magazine. I include two sample reviews (including their YA "tags" at the end) here (Cart 2004, 2011a).

PREP BY CURTIS SITTENFELD

"The world was so big!" 17-year-old Lee thinks in wonder as she prepares to graduate from Ault, the tony East Coast prep school that provides the setting for this bittersweet coming-of-age novel. A scholarship student from South Bend, Indiana, the relentlessly introspective and self-absorbed Lee has always regarded herself as an invisible outsider, "one of the mild, boring, peripheral girls." No wonder she's astonished when the most popular boy in class shows up in her bedroom one night, and they begin an increasingly intimate affair that lasts throughout their senior year. It's no surprise at all, however, that it should end badly. For the denouement, like so much else in this first novel, is simply too predictable. Saving the book from formula, however, are some fine writing and assorted shrewd insights into both the psychology of adolescence and the privileged world of a traditional prep school.

YA. Teens are clearly Sittenfeld's audience, despite her book being published as an adult novel. *MC*

> **The Borrower** BY REBECCA MAKKAI
>
> Lucy, a twenty-six-year-old children's librarian, has a favorite patron, a bright, book-loving ten-year-old named Ian. The trouble is the boy's fundamentalist mother insists he read only books "with the breath of God in them." When the parents enroll their son in a behavior modification program designed to "cure" him of his nascent homosexuality, the boy runs away and Lucy decides she must help. "Borrowing" (some might say kidnapping) the boy, Lucy and he—two fugitives now—hit the road. But who is really running away? Is it Ian or is it actually Lucy replicating the experience of her émigré parents who, years before, had run away from their Russian homeland? And is America, as a friend of Lucy's family claims, truly a nation of runaways but with no place left to run? Time (and considerable driving in Lucy's ancient car) may tell. An accomplished short story writer, Makkai has written a splendid first novel that cleverly weaves telling references to children's books into her whimsically patchwork plot. Larger-than-life characters and an element of the picaresque add to the book's delights. Best of all, however, is Lucy's absolutely unshakeable faith in the power of books to save. From her lips, readers, to God's ear.
>
> YA. Teen readers will identify with Lucy's desire to help Ian and will enjoy the plot's many twists and turns. MC

The Sittenfeld review—published in January 2005—was the first this writer did of a crossover novel. Note that the two reviews feature protagonists who are at either end of the adultescent stage: Lee is 17 and Lucy is 26, the outer limit of the new YA. Both novels feature female protagonists who are experiencing delayed rite-of-passage experiences, and both novels are by women. All of these factors are quite typical of the new crossover novel.

Not all crossovers are targeted at YAs. Some are simply traditional adult novels that have significant appeal to readers of all ages. I include here a review of one of those (Cart 2011b).

> **Jamrach's Menagerie** BY CAROL BIRCH
>
> When he is eight years old, Jaffy Brown, a nineteenth-century London street urchin, finds himself in the mouth of an escaped tiger. While he survives that unpleasantness, the experience does change his life when the tiger's owner, Mr. Jamrach, an importer of exotic animals, gives him a job. Seven years later the boy—along with his best friend Tim—finds himself aboard a whaler headed for the South Seas. Their assignment: capture a fabled dragon for Mr. Jamrach who will then sell it to a wealthy and eccentric collector. Things do not go as planned and the result is an almost unbearably

suspenseful story of adventure and survival. But it is also a story of madness, malevolence, and an almost palpable evil. And as the story advances, a powerfully pervasive sense of melancholy takes hold of the reader as the tiger did young Jaffy, and one wonders if it will ever let go. Though Mr. Jamrach is based on a real historical figure and Jaffy's voyage on that of the ill-fated whaler Essex, the story is entirely Birch's own and her principal characters her own wonderful invention. She is, moreover, a brilliant stylist and reading her is like Christmas, every word being a gift to the reader. Though Birch is an established writer in England, this is her first novel to be published in the U.S. One fervently hopes it will not be the last!

YA. The wonderful narrative sweep of Birch's story will captivate teen readers as will Jaffy and his friend Tim. MC

Nonfiction is an essential part of the new YA collection as well, so I include here a review of this type of book (Cart 2011c).

The Winter of Our Disconnect BY SUSAN MAUSHART

Australian journalist and single parent Maushart reports on her family's decision to take a figurative six-month voyage into an unplugged life—easier said than done when your family consists of three teenagers! No wonder she describes the "voyage" as "The Caine Mutiny" with her playing Captain Queeg. As it happens, the voyage is relatively storm free, though there are some squalls at the beginning. Maushart nearly goes through withdrawal after turning off her iPhone and finds that her work takes twice as long without a computer. In a way the kids are more adaptable (perhaps because their mother offers them various bribes). They quickly learn how to do homework without access to Wikipedia and discover such joys as playing the saxophone and having sing-alongs. Interspersed with the family's experience is a great deal of timely information about the impact of electronic technology on Generation M (8- to 18-year-olds), and not all of it is pretty. Nevertheless, the entire family is relieved when the experiment is over but delighted to discover that it has introduced them to "life itself."

YA. Though some teens will view this as a horror story, others will find it thought- and discussion-provoking. And, yes, it will be great for classroom use. MC

BOOK REVIEWING 2.0

Ironically, the growing importance of reviews comes at the same time—thanks to the economy and the migration of print to the Web—that some traditional review media are in danger of becoming extinct, newspapers being the first to feel the impact. A major reason is once again economic. Understand that as print has increasingly migrated from paper to digital form, many long-established newspapers have folded while the survivors have dramatically reduced staff and content to cut production costs. Others have created as yet unprofitable versions of their newspapers online. As a result, only one weekly book review section survives in print form in America, that of the *New York Times*; all of the others have been discontinued, though in some cases truncated versions survive online (such as those of the *Los Angeles Times* and the *Washington Post*).

Another new electronic phenomenon that is changing the world of book reviews is blogs. Though not very long ago blogs about children's and YA books were a rarity, the field has since exploded. While many blogs do not feature traditional book reviews, the highly personal, mostly unedited, idiosyncratic, sometimes controversial, sometimes ill-informed commentary they do include is changing the way many people would define reviews and reviewers. In fact, in today's wired world, everyone with a computer can become a self-styled book reviewer. Fortunately, all of the major newspapers that have launched websites include at least one blog as part of their book coverage—the *New York Times*'s "Papercutz" is one of the best—as do the major professional book review media. At least these blogs are more reliable sources of information and opinion than the self-created, independent versions.

In the meantime, the major professional review sources like *Booklist*, *SLJ*, and *VOYA* have all licensed their reviews to the two major online bookstores, Amazon and Barnes & Noble, for reprint on their sites. This is certainly convenient for librarians, who are spared searching a variety of different sources to find reviews. However, it also means that reviews originally written for professional readers are now being read by the general public, many of whom are visiting these commercial websites in search of books to purchase. Since it is the positive review that sparks sales, there is some professional concern over the influence these behemoth online sellers may bring to bear on the nature and content of reviews to drive sales, exerting economic pressure on review media (e.g., threatening the loss of their license) to make reviews more positive and books being reviewed more attractive. In late 2012, Amazon began culling reviews on its website but did not provide specific guidelines for deciding which reviews would be pulled.

Certainly, the online bookstores have already introduced another less than salutary phenomenon to the world of book reviewing: the self-posted reader review. Just as anyone with a computer can start a blog, so can anyone visit Amazon or Barnes & Noble and post a review of any book. It almost goes without saying that the quality and reliability of these reviews vary wildly, and that many of them are written by people who have not read the book, by friends of the author, or even the authors themselves posting pseudonymously.

On a more positive note, there are a number of online sites that offer a lively, reliable mix of book news, features, and reviews. Several that focus on adult books and publishing are Galleycat, Bookforum, and Bookreporter.com. Such online sources as *Salon* magazine (www.salon.com), *Slate* magazine (https://slate.com), and "Book Beast," a department of Tina Brown's *The Daily Beast* (www.thedailybeast.com), also are worth following. As for sites specializing in books for young readers, two of the best are Teenreads.com and Kidsreads.com—both services of the Book Report Network. Each offers more reliable online reviews since they are edited and written by professionals. They also offer the added benefit of being aimed at teens and young adults themselves. And being online the reviews are more likely than print reviews to be found by teens and young adults who are, famously, habitués of the online world. Finally, these online reviews can be more timely than those that have to go through a print process.

That said, the next major home for book "reviews" is now predicted to be the various social networking sites—both generic ones like Facebook.com and Myspace.com and also more subject-specific ones like Goodreads.com and LibraryThing.com. Goodreads is arguably the largest social network for readers in the world. According to its website, Goodreads hosts members who recommend books, compare what they are reading, form book clubs, and so on. LibraryThing is an online service that both helps people catalog their books easily and helps them connect with others having the same taste in books, swap reading suggestions, and so on.

But here, too, the problem remains one of reliability. Consider that if you do a Google search for the phrase *children's and young adult book reviews*, you will be overwhelmed with more than 377,000,000 hits. Learning how to select from among this surfeit of "stuff" and how to evaluate one's findings is clearly becoming a fundamental part of every nascent librarian's education. And speaking of fundamentals: this avalanche of book reviews and other book-related information on the Internet suggests that the single most important aspect of the book review today is the credentials of the reviewers themselves.

Meanwhile, the long-standing and often-criticized problem with reviews—their too brief length—may someday be resolved by the burgeoning presence of blogs, which do allow for more discursive discussion of individual books. When these blogs are features of established, creditable websites like BooklistOnline.com or PublishersWeekly.com, this could represent a positive change. For the moment, however, most traditional professional reviews remain brief (seldom longer than 200 words, if that), and they may be getting briefer as production costs continue to escalate because the number of books being published also soars. For the reviewer, this means an endless exercise in economy and self-discipline. In the world of traditional book reviewing, less really is more—particularly now when more books are being published than ever before. Thus, librarians must become more conversant with the world of publishing and with trends in the field. They must cultivate a new group of readers—the new young adults—to determine their reading tastes and interests, for there is no question that more and more books are being published for young readers than ever before in U.S. history, and the growth rate has been particularly steep in the YA area.

No matter how YA books and the young adults who read them change, one thing will surely remain constant: the essential importance of reviews. Good reviews are essential not only to ensure that good books never go overlooked but also, in a larger sense, to guarantee that by identifying and analyzing excellence in books for young readers, reviewers will stimulate young people to read better books and publishers to issue more works of enduring quality and interest to our new category of young adult, the adultescent.

CONCLUSION

Over the course of the past several years the traditional definition of young adults as individuals ages 12 to 18 has changed dramatically. Many researchers and cultural observers have concluded that young adulthood now extends to age 25. Thus far, libraries have failed to recognize this phenomenon, and as a result no new collections of materials speaking to this new group's personal, intellectual, and developmental needs have been created. It is important that librarians consider there are now three YA literatures: middle school literature, teen literature, and literature for the new young adults ages 19 to 25. In developing new collections for this new service group, librarians need to be particularly aware of crossover books, those books with multigenerational appeal. Finally, librarians need to become thoroughly familiar with new sources of reviews, many of them online.

Numerous challenges remain. The online world of information about and reviews of books can be extremely unreliable, since anyone who has a computer can become a blogger and self-styled reviewer with no credentials whatsoever. Another major challenge is determining who will be responsible for creating, organizing, and managing new collections for the new young adult. Paying for these collections is another significant challenge, as are the problem of space—where the new collections will be located and how much space can be allocated to them—and deciding how they will be introduced to the community, and so on.

Changes and challenges can be intimidating, but they are definitely worth the prize: recognizing and serving a new community of users.

REFERENCES

AP (Associated Press). 2009. "Goodbye Jobs, Hello Mom and Dad, Say Young Adults." *USA Today*, November 24. http://usatoday30.usatoday.com/news/nation/2009-11-24-boomerang-kids_N.htm.

Carlsen, G. R. 1980. *Books and the Teenage Reader: A Guide for Teachers, Librarians, and Parents*. 2nd ed. New York: HarperCollins.

Cart, M. 2004. "Prep." *Booklist* 101, no. 8: 709.

———. 2006. "This Is All." *Booklist* 102, no. 22: 66.

———. 2010. *Young Adult Literature: From Romance to Realism*. Chicago: ALA Editions.

———. 2011a. "The Borrower." *Booklist* 107, no. 17: 66.

———. 2011b. "Jamrach's Menagerie." *Booklist* 107, no. 18: 23.

———. 2011c. "The Winter of Our Disconnect." *Booklist* 107, no. 7: 8.

———. 2011d. *Young Adult Literature: From Romance to Realism*. Chicago: American Library Association.

———. 2016. *Young Adult Literature: From Romance to Realism*. 3rd ed. Chicago: ALA Neal-Schuman.

CDC (Centers for Disease Control and Prevention). 2017. "Life Expectancy." www.cdc.gov/nchs/fastats/life-expectancy.htm.

Clifford, J. 2005. "Refilling the Nest." *San Diego Union Tribune*, August 20: E1.

Finder, A. 2005. "For Some College Graduates, a Fanciful Detour (or Two)." *The New York Times*, October 23: 23.

Grossman, Lev. 2005. "Grow Up? Not So Fast." *Time*, January 16: 42.

Hall, G. S. (1904). *Adolescence: Its Psychology and Its Relations to Physiology, Anthropology, Sociology, Sex, Crime, Religion and Education*. New York: D. Appleton.

Henig, R. M. 2010. "What Is It about 20-Somethings?" *The New York Times*, August 18. www.nytimes.com/2010/08/22/magazine/22Adulthood-t.html.

Kantrowitz, B., and K. Springen. 2005. "A Teen Health Gap." *Newsweek*, December 11: 65.

Montgomery, R. 2005. "The Elastic State of Growing Up: More Young Adults Stay Longer in the Nest." *Kansas City Star*, April 24: 1.

Wolverson, R. 2011. "Now What?" *Time*, June 13. www.time.com/time/magazine/article/0,9171,2075326,00.html.

CHAPTER 8

Storytelling, Young Adults, and Three Paradoxes

Kate McDowell

The field of library and information science (LIS) as a whole has often looked beyond its own field-specific boundaries when seeking epistemological insights. While this is both unusually collegial and highly attuned to our own status as a metadiscipline (Bates 1999), librarians and LIS researchers have cultivated more ways of knowing in practice than we have yet acknowledged in our discourse. Storytelling constitutes a richer way of knowing than our field has yet embraced, particularly when it comes to the challenge of connecting with young adults in libraries today. Whether our stories are folktales based on ancient myths or tweets about the apps on our phones, storytelling is a process of communication. The historical record of storytelling in our field is based on years of practitioner wisdom, much of it unexamined outside of children's services circles. Young adults as consumers and producers enact storytelling as process of belonging.

There was a girl at a middle school library who was a steady volunteer and a serious reader, and who bantered fearlessly with teachers. One day, the middle school librarian took a moment to compliment her on her work as well as her intellectual promise. The girl was in eighth grade and had recently mentioned that she was under consideration for a place in a competitive high school. The librarian said she was sure she would do well there, presuming that the girl would soon be accepted. "I was just rejected from that school," the girl snapped. The librarian was embarrassed but quickly said that, with her talents, she would do well anywhere she went, and that whatever school she would go to for high school would be lucky to have someone as smart as her.

For any individual young person, there are many stories happening at the same time. As they struggle to live them, adults strive (and struggle) to connect, however smoothly or awkwardly. What, whether, and when young adults choose to tell the adults in their lives the stories they are living is entirely up to them. In some sense, the only power librarians have is to listen when young adults tell their stories.

For the librarians who serve them, there are many ways to envision what "young adult" means. Some of the most common ways of understanding "young adult" limit and leave us "with seemingly obvious, naturalized, assumed, and unreflexive visions of youth as a needy and marginalized population, one nearly entirely confined within a false youth/adults binary opposition" (Bernier 2013, 207). The field of library and information science (LIS) as a whole has often looked beyond its own field-specific boundaries when seeking epistemological insights. While this is both unusually collegial and highly attuned to our own status as a metadiscipline (Bates 1999), librarians and LIS researchers have cultivated more ways of knowing in practice than we have yet acknowledged in our discourse. While LIS scholarship has been well versed in the data-information-knowledge-wisdom categorization (Ackoff 1989), we too often neglect to consider librarian practices as a source for new ways of thinking and knowing. Consequently, some of our basic epistemologies in young adult librarianship remain hidden in plain sight. One of these ways of knowing, thinking, and communicating is storytelling. This chapter seeks to revisit and reclaim storytelling as a way of knowing that can add rich practical and analytical dimensions to the ways librarians and LIS researchers envision young adults.

Storytelling has been misunderstood; it is not just entertainment. Storytelling is a practice and a process that facilitates the dynamic exchange of information (Simmons 2006; Haven 2007, 2014). A great story transforms those who hear it, and a great storyteller transforms the story through the retelling. Not all librarians tell stories, of course, but storytelling continues to be taught in LIS programs (at universities including but not limited to Illinois, Simmons, and Dominican), and I argue that it constitutes a richer way of knowing than our field has yet embraced, particularly when it comes to the challenge of connecting with young adults in libraries today. Whether our stories are folktales based on ancient myths or tweets about the apps on our phones, storytelling is a process of communication.

The historical record of storytelling in our field is based on years of practitioner wisdom, much of it unexamined outside of children's services circles. Envisioning young adults requires drawing on all of our professional data, information, knowledge, and wisdom. But the long-standing practice of storytelling should factor into more than professional practices; it should also factor into our epistemological framework for understanding how librarians work and what they do.

Although this present analysis draws on historical texts about storytelling, it is not intended to be a thorough historical study. Aspects of that work have been done as part of the histories of organized storytelling to youth (Alvey 1974). Similarly, this chapter is meant to be complementary to other work on how and why to tell stories to teens. Del Negro and others in the recent book *Engaging Teens with Story* provide, at new depth, a sense of how to make storytelling work and what is at stake in using storytelling today with young adults (Del Negro and Kimball 2017). Instead, this chapter mines the professional literature about library storytelling, much as other scholars have mined the historical record of youth services librarianship to distill precepts and principles that can inform contemporary practice and research (Hearne and Jenkins 1999). From these sources, albeit with some necessary critical distance from those historical eras, this exploration draws on both current definitions and historical descriptions of storytelling with youth in order to distill paradoxes that reframe storytelling. Storytelling emerges as a process, a way of communicating, and a metaphor for thinking about how we can and should envision young adults in our libraries.

UNDEFINING YOUNG ADULTS

Current understandings of "young adult" depend more on categorization than on process, foreclosing many possibilities for communication and understanding. We use terms like *preteens, tweens, teens, young adults, new adults, adolescents, middle-schoolers, high-schoolers,* and more to describe our audiences in library settings. Some have even argued that the term *young adult* persists for the convenience of librarians (Agosto 2013). Definitions are powerful, and yet, in addition to any definitions librarians may or may not use, young people are also being defined in their daily lives. They are members of a society that ruthlessly categorizes them by race, gender, exact age, weight, appearance, and a host of other features made more immediate by the selfie vernacular, the use of one's own image as communication device (Frosh 2015). Young adults practice categorization on each other, even when simply sorting themselves using online tools that run the gamut from personality assessments to Hogwarts' house quizzes, not to mention in stereotyping or bullying.[1] Academic discourse about teens tends to presume that these identity-related behaviors are of particular import for teens, based in great part on the legacy of G. Stanley Hall's (1904) definition of adolescence.

The dynamic process of storytelling is a metaphor that offers new opportunities for understanding in the way that it challenges other common understandings of young adults. Storytelling-as-process challenges typical definitions of young adults by seeing storytellers as whole people, sufficient as they are, no matter their age. We do not need to draw strict lines around a category or categories of "young adults" in order to envision who they are and how libraries can serve them. While stepping back from categories is admittedly difficult for professionals steeped in information organization, doing so opens doors to envisioning young adults based instead on *process*.

The term *young adult* embodies the tension of these cultural definitions, tending toward the assumed finality of adulthood while pulling toward incompletion or delay. Kathryn Stockton has made similar points about the term *growing up*, unpacking its historical origins and use since 1535. Stockton (2009) critiques contemporary usages that celebrate innocence and "fetishize delay" and, in so doing, betray fear of the potency of the young alongside laments about their impending disappearance as the young due to loss of innocence. Stockton indicts the phrase "growing up" as a "short-sighted, limited rendering of human growth, one that oddly would imply an end to growth when full stature (or reproduction) is achieved" (10-11). She instead suggests that "growing sideways" is a more apt characterization, suggesting that "the width of a person's experience or ideas, their motives or their motions, may pertain at any age" (37).

Such undefinitions trouble the presumptions of developmental models that assert growth as a sequence of set stages.[2] Some scholars have made this necessary trouble by theorizing identity in terms of performativity and questioning gender, reevaluating queerness, and challenging the limited understanding afforded by binary classifications (Judith 1990; Sedgwick 1990). Others have extended this metaphor of performance to historically interrogate understandings of innocence and experience, which are relevant to librarians' long-standing informal discourse involving "protection and preparation." Recent scholarship challenges cultural norms of childhood "innocence" for their racist underpinnings and historical sanctification of white innocence in particular. As Bernstein (2011) writes, the very late nineteenth-century and early twentieth-century definitions of innocence that undergird contemporary definitions presumed "racial innocence" as "the performance of not-noticing, a performed claim of slipping beyond social categories" (6). This line of critical inquiry begs the age-old question that could be asked of social categorization: Who benefits?

In LIS, understandings of the phrase *young adult* could benefit from similar unpacking. Understandings of young adult identity typically hinge on their being "between" childhood and adulthood, in a temporal process of "growing up." "Young" implies impending growth (presumably toward "old"), and "adult" implies a kind of finality that does not, in fact, characterize the ongoing transformation of lived adult experience. This identity, implying a delayed destination of adulthood, is nonetheless a shorthand for age and the expected experiences pertaining to those teenaged years. Although "young adult" is an inexact category among other imprecise categories, it is possible to reclaim the term as long as its partial, equivocal, and incomplete aspects remain steadfastly in mind alongside its use.

An understanding of young adults, as people, citizens, and more, may require unpacking common metaphors of growth, questioning "the overlapping constructions of adolescence and the linear temporality of normative development" (Sahn 2016, 7). What models from our own professional tradition could help us to understand, accept, and work with people whose stories are temporal and temporary, whose identities are in motion, incomplete, and ambiguous? How can librarians and LIS researchers envision young adults as they actually are, evading easy classification?

Early young adult services leader and advocate Margaret Edwards wrote, "[T]here is no time in life when a greater adjustment must be made than in the transition from childhood to adolescence" (Edwards 1974, 17). How can youth services librarians carefully envision these people who are in a process of deep change in relation to their place in society? On one hand, the collected experiences and knowledge of librarians who have served many young people are invaluable. And yet these same experiences can lead to patterns of categorization based on perceptions of identity, and thus risk reifying identity categories or, even worse, stereotyping individuals based on patterns, real or perceived. Most existing approaches to envisioning young adults are limited by the idea of there being a single identity or a set of steady identities with stable patterns of preferences, desires, and interests.

When I worked in a middle school library, students showed up at the library during free periods, but the individuals and small groups in this space shifted dramatically over the course of the year. Sometimes a regular volunteer would join a sports team and stop coming during study hall. Other times a student who had been there every day for months would suddenly disappear, without explanation. I had to guess that something about their lives, from their sense of choice and self to a schedule change, had transitioned, and suddenly the library was not on their route. Or a new group of young people would discover that the library was open at lunch and take up residence there. This begs questions about adult recollections of spending "every day in the library" or having "read every book in the library." What did "every day" mean? What did "every book" actually indicate? What did that look like to the librarian, and was it different from what that felt like to the 13-year-old? What ways of envisioning young adults can account for different stories, different perspectives, different storytellers?

Although the rest of this chapter will continue to use "young adult" as the primary descriptor for these library users, the phrase is meant as shorthand for a more complex, relational, process-oriented definition. Describing what drawing from storytelling would mean is meant to work in concert with sustaining provocative questions, such as, What if we take seriously the idea that young adults are whole people in the process of living an unfolding story?

STORYTELLING AS DYNAMIC EXCHANGE

"Storytelling" here means a complex mode of dynamic exchange that draws on narrative structures and involves both telling and listening. Librarian storytellers have long-standing practical knowledge that "human beings are hard-wired for story, and respond to it at a visceral level" (Del Negro 2015, 5). In our own field, research investigating library-based storytelling performance has discovered evidence of trance states, or "enchantment," during story listening (Sturm 1999). Recently, across fields as disparate as medicine, business, and psychology, emerging research about the power of storytelling is shifting everyday communication practices in a variety of spaces and places (Haven 2007, 2014).

Though much is written about storytelling as practice, both research-based and conceptual definitions of storytelling from LIS literature are surprisingly sparse. The now-classic book *Storytelling for Young Adults* by Gail de Vos (2003) introduces the concept of storytelling by presenting a personal story of de Vos's own way of bonding and creating a "comfort zone" with young adult audiences; however, this section does not offer a definition per se. Denise Agosto offers a simple and clear definition in her research on the literacy benefits of storytelling, describing it as "telling a story from memory without the aid of a book or written script" (Agosto 2016, 22).[3] In perhaps the most complete definition, Anne Pellowski (1977) defines storytelling as "the entire context of a moment when oral narration of stories, in verse and/or prose, is performed or led by one person before a live audience; the narration may be spoken, chanted, or sung, with or without musical, pictorial, and/or other accompaniment, and may be learned from oral, printed, or mechanically recorded sources; one of its purposes must be that of entertainment or delights and it must have a least a small element of spontaneity in the performance" (18). This definition carries with it implicit connections to storytelling, folklore, and story-based programming and/or cultural events.

However, understandings of orality have changed and changed again. Walter Ong's (1982) work on "secondary orality" challenged the definition of "oral narration" in order to address forms of orality that are predicated upon and driven by technologically enabled communications. Recently, other scholars have explored the "silent orality" of digital orality, communication with the immediacy of the spoken word, facilitating rapid narrative exchange that is nonetheless never spoken (Soffer 2010). Storytelling draws from orality but is also imbued with relational spontaneity between teller and listener.

Based on his work as a storytelling coach, working with a range of storytellers from local librarians to national-stage performers (and some who qualify in both categories), Doug Lipman has crafted a conceptual definition of storytelling that is helpful in considering epistemological implications. Lipman (1999) describes storytelling as a triangle, a relationship between three entities: the storyteller, the story, and the audience. There are direct relationships between the teller and the audience as well as between the teller and the story, but he notes that the relationship between the audience and the story is not entirely within the teller's control. The teller tells a story, the audience hears a story, and the teller either hopes that the message delivered is the one received or accepts that the audience will make of the story what they will, knowing that what the teller says is never exactly what the audience takes away. This dynamism echoes another definition of storytelling, from Barre Toelken (1996), who describes it as participating in a complex process of fidelity to previous tellings along with dynamic reinvention for each new audience. While the story may be understood to be "the same," each retelling can bring an old story to life in completely new ways that depend on the teller's delivery and the audience's response (Toelken 1996).

Building on Lipman's triangle and Toelken's dynamism, we can reframe these three elements as dynamic, interacting roles (see figure 8.1). Like young adult identities, each point on the triangle is in motion, more verb than noun. For this reason, I describe this storytelling triangle as comprised of telling, listening, and story (rather than storyteller, audience, story). "Telling" and "listening" are gerunds, derived from verbs but functioning as nouns, and so they indicate acts or roles rather than entities; in terms of agency, those who engage in listening or telling are subjects rather than objects. In other words, in my definition of

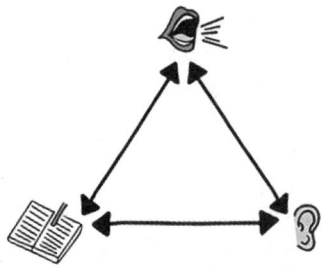

FIGURE 8.1 Storytelling Triangle
SOURCE: Courtesy of Hilary Pope, www.hipopeart.com.

storytelling, the telling and listening are at least as important as the story itself, and they both impact the story's ultimate form.

I argue that a storytelling exchange occurs when all three elements—story, listener, and teller—are transformed by the interaction. In a true storytelling exchange, the teller's way of telling shifts in relationship to the listener's responses, and thus the story is told differently in each exchange. It may be the case that the "same" story is being told, but its delivery, wording, and even content will be transformed by the particular telling and particular listening experience. This transformation may be as subtle as a "small element of spontaneity" (Pellowski 1977). Or it may be dramatic and audible, as in Elizabeth Ellis's descriptions of the "Ah ha!" audience reaction that demonstrates surprise and delight at a new understanding, or the "Ah" reaction that indicates "listening at a much deeper level of concentration" (Mooney and Holt 1996). Whatever the scale of the transformation, fundamental to this understanding of storytelling is the notion that there is a dynamic exchange involving telling, listening, and the story itself, which evolves through the telling in reaction to listening. Ultimately, this exchange is what ignites retelling, revisions, and new ways of telling the story as listeners become tellers. Storytelling as dynamic exchange of listening, telling, and story invites retelling in ways that are similar to the multivocality of jazz, rap, or improvisatory comedy, where a story, lyric, or phrase may circulate freely in the process of performance, sometimes making its way back to the originating teller and other times dissolving into group harmony or cacophony. In this sense, the extended performance of everyday life is the setting for storytelling as a living communication art form, where individual stories contribute to collectively produced stories. Ultimately, the act of storytelling is that of giving and releasing the story to those listening.

In the past decade, "storytelling" has become almost a buzzword in business settings, where the emphasis is on the narrower application of persuasive communication. Authors Annette Simmons, Stephen Denning, Paul Smith, and others have promoted the power of story to align leaders with followers and to spring an organization into action. A few librarians have written about how these business storytelling ideas could be applied to the business of librarianship (Marek 2011; Magnuson 2016). But such applications are entirely focused on persuasion as a means for other ends, not on storytelling as a shared experience of narrative that derives its power from aesthetic resonance, communicative exchange, or the possibility of story exchange. These latter approaches have been more relevant to the tradition of library storytelling. As of yet, the highly literary, aesthetic, century-long tradition of storytelling within youth services librarianship has not been part of these conversations.

Our tradition of storytelling in libraries, to young people generally and young adults specifically, may yet offer key insights into why storytelling is receiving renewed attention as a dynamic practice of communication and as what is missing from these business-driven definitions.

THREE PARADOXES

Storytelling in the library tradition is perhaps best characterized not by definitions but by paradoxes. The tradition of storytelling in youth librarianship has been documented historically, often situated in relation to similar professional storytelling traditions in education, recreation, the kindergarten movement, and more (Alvey 1974; Pellowski 1977). However, it has not been analyzed for its cultural contributions to youth librarianship and LIS more broadly. The historical record has been analyzed as a source of data and information, but the storytelling tradition has not been mined as a source of knowledge and wisdom. The folkloric knowledge that has been handed down from practitioner to practitioner (and in LIS courses) for the most part has also not been formally analyzed. Neither has this knowledge been treated as a source worth analyzing in professional literature, although, given the extreme feminization of librarianship as a profession, it is perhaps more than a little ironic that feminist epistemologies suggest that it should be (Anderson 2005). While any of these analyses at depth would require a much longer study, it is possible to look back at some of the most-well-loved handbooks on storytelling to speculate on how established ways of understanding storytelling can challenge current ways of seeing young adults.

Paradoxes demand space for seemingly opposed ideas to coexist, imbued with their own form of dynamism, as oppositions that defy resolution. Like storytelling (as a dynamic triangle), paradoxes are dynamic dyads of ideas that must be held in tension with each other. Parker Palmer (2003) describes the value of paradoxes for his pedagogical scholarship, inspired by words from Carl Jung: "Only the paradox comes anywhere near to comprehending the fullness of life" (376). Based on classic essays and textbooks for LIS storytelling courses and professional development over the past 102 years, the following three paradoxes represent my attempt to characterize the fullness of storytelling in the library tradition:

- Enchantment and Rigor
- Planning and Flexibility
- Power and Humility

The conceptualizations that these seeming contradictions represent both acknowledge and provoke the professional wisdom of library storytelling. While the wisdom of practice should inform approaches to young adults, this wisdom is also incomplete and historically contingent. Nonetheless, the ideas that are foundational to the LIS storytelling tradition should belong to all of librarianship, within as well as outside of youth services.

Enchantment and Rigor

There was enchantment at the start of storytelling in librarianship. Marie Shedlock entranced children's librarians collectively and her influence was one of the early factors that led to making storytelling central to youth librarianship for many years (Baker and

Greene 1977, 4–5; Miller 2003, 222–23). She taught librarians to think about a captivated audience by seeing the effects of enchantment on their faces: "We learn in time that want of expression on the faces of the audience and want of any kind of external response do not always mean either lack of interest or attention" (Shedlock and Davis 1936, 13). Seeing the captivation that stillness conveyed opened the door to more creative ways of understanding audience response outside of more standard reactions.

Decades later, Shedlock's practical wisdom is affirmed by research which shows that storytelling listening mimics trance states (Sturm 1999). Those states may be low affect externally, but internally the mind is actively and deeply engaged in the narrative. When considering enchantment, it is worth noting that the professional heritage of librarianship and LIS research can claim both the practice of storytelling as enchantment and the establishment of storytelling as "entrancing."

But enchantment, in this storytelling tradition, does not come without the rigor of hard work. Early children's librarians underwent rigorous training for storytelling. They were expected to practice in front of mirrors (Shedlock and Davis 1936, 144), to learn their stories aurally or through imagery, but to tell without notes and without memorizing the words (a feat that still troubles my beginning storytelling students). They were taught to develop voices that would carry "laughter, wonder, astonishment, reverence" (Sawyer 1942, 137). Ironically, the goal of making storytelling look effortless, comfortable, and even easy made it more difficult to see the rigorous training that went into storytelling.

The outward welcome of the friendly youth services librarian belies this simple truth: they were hard on each other. From generation to generation, the training for storytelling has encompassed ever increasing demands of "long contemplation" (Sawyer 1942, 142), cultural respect (Hearne 1993a, 1993b), and critical ability to select excellent stories (Greene and Baker 1996, 57). As famed storyteller (and advocate for the Black experience in children's books) Augusta Baker recalls, "It seems I did in-service for a thousand years before [Mary Gould Davis] thought I was capable of a full blown-program" (Smith 1995). That the esteemed Baker herself "had to work and wait" to be allowed to tell stories as a children's librarian is proof of the rigor of librarian storytellers (Smith 1995).

Seasoned storytellers in any profession know to expect that rigorous work will be needed to develop their stories. They also know that, if they are doing their jobs right, that work will not be at all noticeable. Their audiences will immerse themselves in the enchantment of listening intently, without any thought of the work that went into crafting the story.

Extending this paradox of enchantment and rigor, it is worth questioning how deeply professional librarians' communication skills have been or could be informed by a storytelling approach. How often have librarians allowed themselves (or been trained) to be enchanted by the young adults who communicate with us? How impressed have they been by the rigor that goes into cracking gaming codes, crafting hip hop choreography, or chatting on cell phones 24/7, sometimes outwitting adults to do so? The increasing strain of secondary education imposes rigor on young adults in ways that may make them look elsewhere for enchantment. In any encounter with young adults, librarians could imagine that they are facing rigorous challenges, whether or not they will tell us their stories.

Planning and Flexibility

The juxtaposition of planning and flexibility is fundamental to the wisdom of professional young adult librarians. Particularly for new professionals, whether published in a journal or a board on Pinterest, library programming plans are constantly evolving. Their basic contents serve as vital technical manuals for young adult librarianship: "The storytelling program must be carefully planned if it is to be successful. Flexibility and creativity are required" (Baker and Greene 1977, 88). Although such plans are often heavily prescriptive, seasoned professionals in the field know that these are the proverbial rules made to be broken. Planning is fundamental to library services that put young people at ease just as "knowing your story cold" is key to the seeming spontaneity of storytelling.

To illustrate, the specific activity of storytelling to young adults is a major challenge that takes a lot of planning. When I took storytelling with Janice Del Negro in 1997, I remember her advice on storytelling with young adults as this: scare them or gross them out. I followed her advice, and it worked; tales from Alvin Schwartz books captivated sixth-graders as I told them stories about a zombie that came back to dance at its own funeral and a romance that ended with a head falling off. As Del Negro wrote more recently, young adults enjoy "suspense and potential for danger carried by the controlled delivery of a sensational supernatural or gory tale" (Del Negro and Kimball 2017, 105). By telling them risky stories, stories right on the edge of what might be acceptable in a library context, the librarian demonstrates respect for young adults as audience. But note that Del Negro emphasizes "the *controlled* delivery." Learning a suspenseful tale and telling it with apparent spontaneity requires planning.

Flexibility puts the spontaneity into the execution of plans. Storytelling, as an art of complex presence and communication, is interruptible, often more like a conversation than a concert. Young adult librarians are used to navigating surprises, from outbursts to injuries, in ways that librarians in other contexts (academic, archival, corporate, and beyond) would benefit from understanding. All young adult librarians know that keeping plans flexible allows them to connect with the audiences before them. When the perennially popular duct tape wallet program turns into a duct tape pencil pouch or purse project, flexibility means praising creativity rather than sticking to the plan. "Storytellers are often faced with situations where any right and reasonable choice must be abandoned on the moment, and something entirely foreign to the usual story-hour must be snatched for and used" (Sawyer 1942, 158).

At the same time, that close relationship between storytelling and conversation means that the connection to the audience is deeply mutual, moment by moment. "Storytelling at its best is mutual creation. Children [sic] listen and, out of the words they hear, create their own mental images; this opening of the mind's eye develops the imagination" (Baker and Greene 1977, xii). What are the implications of envisioning young adults themselves as being actively engaged in demanding processes of planning while leaving themselves room for flexibility? One possible critique of libraries, alongside other educational settings, might be that emphasis on planning and teaching young adults to plan far outweighs any emphasis on the importance of flexibility. Perhaps looking to young adults, individually and collectively, would allow the field of LIS to better understand how they use, when they require, or when and how they prefer flexibility. How often have we discouraged flexibility and celebrated planning?

The particular kind of planning and flexibility that storytelling demands is that the telling responds to the listening, in live time and in the longer arc of retelling to multiple audiences over time. For a particular story told by a particular teller, this ongoing need for dynamic and interactive flexibility can be at odds with the fixed and less mobile quality of reusing plans (such as those for young adult stories, programs, or events) that have worked previously. How much may be missed of the dynamic emergence of a story between telling and listening by being fixated on plans? How is it possible to be flexible enough to surprise young adults by being an ideal audience for their stories, or even just their reactions? What surprises might ensue if librarians and LIS researchers were visibly flexible in the moment, listening carefully to young adults, as they engage in listening, reacting, and telling?

Power and Humility

A compelling story is a thing of power. Envision teens riveted by a ghost story around a campfire or hunched over phones texting gossip that blazes through high school halls. Folklorist and acclaimed storyteller Betsy Hearne (1993a) lauds the aesthetics of folkloric stories, with their "fast-moving, highly structured elemental plots" and "clearly delineated archetypal characters," for allowing each listener "to glean different emotional, socio-cultural, intellectual, spiritual, and physical connections with a tale" (24). The aesthetic power of an awe-inspiring story holds us in its thrall. And this has been key to the library storytelling tradition. "To be able to create a story, to make it live during the moment of the telling, to arouse emotions—wonder, laughter, joy, amazement—this is the only goal a storyteller may have" (Sawyer 1942, 148).

But power in storytelling has its limits. However intoxicating the experience, this power to enthrall is granted by the listening audience rather than created by the telling. Listeners must be paying attention, not tuned out or lost in an infinite scroll on their smartphones. As stories skip across transmedia modes and platforms, from anime to apps, from Tumblr to tweets, they may or may not translate as aesthetically powerful in every medium. Perhaps fan fiction and fan art are the ultimate indication of deep listening and the translation of aesthetic power into action (Hills 2002), but these forms have yet to demonstrate the capacity to carry that aesthetic power forward into their deliberately derivative creations (Cassandra Clare's work being a notable exception). Then again, without face-to-face interaction, it may be hard to interpret how much the aesthetic power of a story has translated across media.

In the tradition of library storytelling, the emphasis is on "the story rather than upon the storyteller, who is, for the time being, simply a vehicle through which the beauty and wisdom and humor of the story comes to the listeners" (Baker and Greene 1977, 58). The power of the librarian's story is not to aggrandize the teller: "Remember, you are the instrument; the story is the main feature" (Bishop and Kimball 2006, 28). Librarians often define the experience of storytelling. In every dimension, from place and time to power relations between (adult) teller and (young adult) audience, wielding the authority of representing the library over the public that uses it, librarians are in charge. Bishop and Kimball may issue this cautionary reminder to emphasize that the librarian is *not* in complete control of the experience. There is no telling without listening, and those who serve as listeners grant their attention to the teller. This cannot be forced without damaging the process. From another angle, for new librarians, there can be a kind of comfort in the humility of this reminder, in that stories work in service of the people we serve and the collections we steward. And yet, if the focus is not on us, then we had better be telling powerful stories, aesthetically and otherwise.

A measure of power in a story is whether it is retold, spontaneously, by those who have heard it. "Storytelling flows from a deep desire to share, the desire to be open about something that has touched one deeply" (Baker and Greene 1977, 25). Do leaders, adult or young adult, become leaders because of a single speech or story, or is it the reception and repetition of that message and meaning that bestows power from those who choose (always within the context of complex power relations) to follow? Professional leadership in libraries comes most often from people, whether librarians or community members, retelling the story of their library experiences as they are meaningful to them. If tellers are listening in turn, then they can learn from their audiences how they could reshape the library and improve services and the stories that will result from them.

As Doug Lipman (1999) describes it, there is no direct line that the teller controls between the audience and the story. "The circumstance that forces you to be humble is also what makes it so miraculous when you succeed" (Lipman 1999, 18). The triangle of teller, listener, and story is rarely static. Wielding the aesthetic power of narrative with humility means also looking for opportunities to listen. Tellers should do all in their power to become listeners, and to empower those listening to take up telling. The teller becomes the listener and the listener becomes the teller. Perhaps the real indicator of connection is not when a teenager listens to a librarian tell a story. After all, teenagers spend most of their days listening to adults. Might the real indicator of connection be when the triangle shifts, when listening becomes telling, and when young adults tell us something in return? The story then emerges between them, dynamically, at the intersection of both listening and telling in the storytelling exchange. This exchange is made all the richer for the paradoxical inheritance of the library storytelling tradition, in the tensions between enchantment and rigor, planning and flexibility, and power and humility.

STORYTELLING KNOWING

Undefining "young adult" embraces a dynamic understanding of young people as evading simple definitions of predictable identities. Similarly, the role of the storyteller, based on the humility of the library storytelling tradition, can be seen as a role through which we must be complex and not easily defined, with stories not easily anticipated, in deference to the complexity of young adult audiences. The storyteller's role is limited, indebted to the power of story, and worth sharing whenever possible. Approaching both storytelling and young adults in this way allows for the possibility of a way of knowing that is based in the storytelling exchange. Instead of seeing young adults as defined exclusively by chronological age, what if librarians envisioned them as one part of a storytelling triangle in which roles may shift? In a given moment, the young people making contact with librarians may be listeners, tellers, or the keepers of stories. Seeking connection is vital, since it is up to them whether to tell or not tell their stories.

Acknowledging an epistemology informed by storytelling as a dynamic way of communicating could mean seeing young adults in three ways. These three ways of understanding align with the previous three paradoxes derived from the historical practice of storytelling in youth services librarianship and offer metaphorically rich approaches for envisioning young adults:

1. Young adults as audience
2. Young adults as storytellers
3. Young adults as dynamic and paradoxical

Descriptions of each of these approaches follow.

Telling, or Young Adults as Audience

First, librarians might envision young adults as an audience to engage, with the expectation that it will require hard work to do so (enchantment and rigor). Since librarians have limited control over listening, the focus must be on choosing "stories," literal or metaphorical, that will connect. Positioning young adults as audience frames them as having the central interpretive power in the storytelling triangle. They determine the meaning of the library services they engage. For this reason, I propose that the young adult librarian should be rigorous in telling stories with the theme of belonging. In research on belonging based in the field of social work, researchers find that belonging exists in opposition to the disconnection of shame (Brown 2017). In the story that opened this chapter, an eighth-grader revealed to her middle school librarian that she had been rejected from a competitive high school placement. The librarian's response conveyed a message of belonging, which need not be in story form to be effective.

These "stories" may be literal or metaphorical, verbal or conveyed through furniture and signage or through other aspects of the library service profile. Thinking of stories as vehicles for shared meaning opens possibilities for considering the messages implicit in all services to young adults. Librarians should look for every indication possible of audience response. While surveys and individual dialogues are reasonable starting places, librarians need to do more. Teen advisory boards and focus groups go deeper, albeit with limited audience participation. Libraries should consider different performative strategies to reach broad audiences, perhaps inviting the kind of open-ended talk back seen at experimental theater and music performances.

Being listened to is the ultimate signifier of belonging. Librarians may tell first, but soon thereafter they must seek ways in which to yield the stage to teens themselves. Librarians may set the context, enable with collections and resources, and facilitate library use, but the message of belonging will always be best conveyed when librarians move out of the telling role and into the listening role. Young adults produce stories, messages, meanings, and by listening carefully, librarians may be able to allow the library to be a significant site for young adults' cultural productions. Let's listen.

Listening, or Young Adults as Storytellers

Hearing young adults' stories requires asking and structuring specific opportunities for them to take risks and be heard (planning). Those structures, however, should remain open to the messages young people send back along the way, so that their stories are not constrained by adult expectations (flexibility). Understanding young adults as cultural producers through their storytelling means seeing them as individuals who have unique stories to tell and whose stories encompass much more than just the parts of their lives that intersect with the library (Wiegand 2015). Young adults also come together in collective space, sharing stories at poetry slams, open mics, coffeehouses, and story slams and producing stories collectively, from planned flash mob dances to multivocal improvisatory jamming. There can be a delight in cacophony, and listening for uproarious joy may be necessary to challenge the cultural expectations of young adult library services.

One time I led a readers' theater program with middle school students as an optional lunchtime program. Long story short, it didn't work. The students were definitely interested in the props, but not especially interested in the scripts. And it was partly my fault; I hadn't accounted for varying reading levels, and readers' theater was just too hard for some of the students who wanted to participate. So I invited them to work together to come up with their own story. As they brainstormed together, somebody came up with the idea to throw the wig to symbolize the main character's head coming off. Maybe it wasn't a whole story, and it certainly wasn't the story I had envisioned when I printed out and stapled scripts to read, but we all laughed! This took planning *and* flexibility. The students left with a story to tell later, about throwing the wig in the library.

Nothing happened as planned, but what did happen facilitated genuine connections. Sometimes the ideal of "storytelling" is not useful for listening to the actual young adults who appear in our libraries. While planning for the best outcome will always be a goal, any best outcome must necessarily be flexible in order to fully engage young adult creativity in a way that serves the larger goals of listening and connecting. Letting the wig fly was a flexible way of showing them belonging.

Fundamentally, when adults and youth participate in any form of story exchange in or around libraries, the hoped-for outcome is an emergent story between them to which all involved belong. This may be simply a story held in common regard, as amusing or important. This may be an emergent sense of an untold story that needs to be told, that helps to inspire and motivate institutional change to be ever more receptive to and available for young adults. Or it may be a story of the exchange itself, as the next step in a process of continual improvement to make libraries serve young adults. But whichever way it goes, it must be an exchange, and any true exchange requires listening.

As Story, or Young Adults as Emergent, with Power and Humility

Perhaps the most important thing about hearing, reading, or watching a new story is the excitement of the unknown (power). The suspense of what will happen melds with the fascination of seeing characters grow and change. The stories of young adults in libraries are of interest to young adults themselves, and thus *should be* of greater relevance to LIS researchers than they have been in the past. Structuring any opportunity to hear them, from a focus group to a story slam, requires humility, as librarians cannot know what a young adult may tell. What we know or can understand about a young adult's experience of the library reflects just one small part of that young adult's life, which may be overflowing with equally or more important places or activities (humility).

In the telling/listening/story triangle model of storytelling, the story is unique each time it is retold because of the specific dynamics of a particular telling and listening experience. The stories that young adults "tell," directly, implicitly, or metaphorically, may require librarians and researchers to investigate new technologies for storytelling. And stories continue to exert tremendous power. To give just one example, as young people use social media to develop new forms of storytelling, such as fan role-playing based on young adult fiction-turned-films such as *The Hunger Games*, LIS researchers must change their approaches to understanding language use, literacy, literary knowledge, and ways of comprehending what young adults know (Magee et al. 2013). By being able to observe them enacting a story, through role-playing and social media, researchers can take the listening role in order to see what story emerges from young adults' telling.

Librarians and LIS researchers might look at young adults as sources of valuable and fascinating stories, as some researchers have done and more must continue to do. Centering youth knowledge in this way means, conceptually, treating young adults as living in communities with funds of knowledge that can be shared, transferred, and understood.

Thinking about young adults in the context of their communities involves considering "homes, peer groups, and other systems and networks of relationships that shape the oral and written texts young people make meaning of and produce as they move from classroom to classroom and from home to peer group, to school, or to community" (Moje et al. 2004, 38). Some have acknowledged the knowledge of young adults by exploring what young people can contribute to design as "partners in codesigning new educational technologies" (Druin 2010, 36). Storytelling as a communication practice and other forms of narrative feedback could enrich any of these approaches.

But these research practices have not yet translated to the culture of young adult librarianship at large, where contributions may be limited to the teen advisory board (TAB) at best. What if planning for the library as a whole involved imagining together in a process of welcomed telling, careful listening, and the codevelopment of an inclusive story? For example, imagine a strategic plan that was not just a nod to an administrative demand or policy requirement but a truly mutual creation between librarians and young adults. Such a plan would operate as a living, breathing, changing story that might capture the best possibilities of the spaces between young adult communities and their libraries. Young people might be invested in their libraries as a whole just as much as they invest in hearing, retelling, and co-telling hilarious or suspenseful stories, anxiously awaiting what comes next.

Truly hearing young adults' stories also requires librarians and researchers to check their assumptions and be humble in the face of power differentials. Although listening is vital, understanding young adults as storytellers does not level the playing field between LIS professionals and young adults in any simple way. The ability to switch the roles of telling and listening does not mean that those temporarily inhabiting roles wield equal power. Librarians can never forgo their professional status and power in relation to young people. To disavow or deny such power differentials would rapidly erode trust. However, librarians can embrace humility alongside their power.

Librarians may find themselves humbled when facing young adults' stories, tales told through technologies with affordances unfamiliar to older generations. Librarians must learn to embrace cultural humility as a part of cultural competence. While drawing on the library storytelling tradition can challenge assumptions about young adults, it is important to remember that this tradition was derived from a professional context that was and still remains predominantly white and female. Cultural competence is a process that can relate meaningfully to storytelling processes, but it requires several steps. Cooke (2016) points out that critical self-reflection is necessary in order to "situate ourselves in regard to our own intersectionality, privilege, and marginality" (20). As those in command of library collections and spaces, it is incumbent upon us to be humble and acknowledge our power. Cultural humility "requires practitioners to examine and identify the underlying issues that produce and exacerbate instances of inequality in the diverse communities we serve" (Cooke 2016, 24). Listening, telling, and the emergent story will help librarians and LIS researchers better understand and address the inequalities that impact young adults.

CONCLUSION

As librarians, we have inherited a story of who young adults are and what young adult services should aspire to be. Radically reclaiming and implementing perspectives based on storytelling as a model for communication, in praxis (Bernier 2013, 225) and in rich metaphorical understandings of what a storytelling process can be, may afford the kind of reframing that is necessary to enliven thoughtful, critical, inventive library services. At the most basic level, storytelling can serve as a useful metaphor for adults interacting with young adults by reminding them to serve as listeners as well as tellers.

More broadly, librarianship needs to reclaim storytelling as part of its intellectual tradition and practical knowledge. We need a folklore-inspired definition of users and a storytelling-based way of relating with them. LIS researchers and practitioners can and should theorize on the basis of rich practices, such as storytelling, in order to think more deeply and more conceptually about young adults. Extending the wisdom of our own tradition of professional storytelling conceptually, analytically, and practically is a key direction to envisioning young adults in ways that both incorporate our traditions and challenge our assumptions.

NOTES

1. Although bullying comes up frequently in discourse about young adults, it may be equally prevalent but underexamined in the adult population. Its association with young adults is another example of the limits of common definitions and connotations.
2. The developmental approach to young adults is unlike Vladimir Propp's (1968) narrative theory, which uses structuralist approaches to assert 31 tale functions in sequence.
3. Agosto (2016) adds, "Some tellers memorize their stories; others memorize the characters and events and freely tell their stories, varying them with each telling" (21). The latter form of learning the story by heart so that the teller can maximally vary the story for each audience and with each telling is key to the tradition of storytelling in LIS, as broadly addressed under Planning and Flexibility in the following Three Paradoxes section.

REFERENCES

Ackoff, R. L. 1989. "From Data to Wisdom." *Journal of Applied Systems Analysis* 16, no. 1: 3-9. https://doi.org/citeulike-article-id:6930744.

Agosto, D. E. 2013. "Envisaging Young Adult Librarianship from a Teen-Centered Perspective." In *Transforming Young Adult Services*, edited by A. Bernier, 33-52. Chicago: ALA Neal-Schuman.

———. 2016. "Why Storytelling Matters." *Children and LIbraries* 14, no. 2: 21-26.

Alvey, R. G. 1974. "The Historical Development of Organized Storytelling to Children in the United States." Unpublished doctoral dissertation, University of Pennsylvania, Philadelphia.

Anderson, E. 2005. "Feminist Epistemology: An Interpretation and a Defense." In *Feminist Theory: A Philosophical Anthology*, edited by A. E. Cudd and R. O. Andreasen, 188-209). Malden, MA: Blackwell.

Baker, A., and E. Greene. 1977. *Storytelling: Art and Technique*. New York : Bowker.

Bates, M. J. 1999. "The Invisible Substrate of Information Science." *Journal of the American Society for Information Science* 50, no. 12: 1043-50.

Bernier, A. 2013. *Transforming Young Adult Services*. Chicago: ALA Neal-Schuman.

Bernstein, R. 2011. *Racial Innocence: Performing Childhood and Race from Slavery to Civil Rights*. New York: NYU Press.

Bishop, K., and M. A. Kimball. 2006. "Engaging Students in Storytelling." *Teacher Librarian* 33, no. 4: 28-31.

Brown, B. 2017. *Braving the Wilderness: The Quest for True Belonging and the Courage to Stand Alone*. New York: Random House.

Cooke, N. 2016. "Developing Cultural Competence." In *Information Services to Diverse Populations: Developing Culturally Competent Library Professionals*, 19–30. Santa Barbara, CA: Libraries Unlimited.

de Vos, G. 2003. *Storytelling for Young Adults: A Guide to Tales for Teens.* 2nd ed. Westport, CT: Libraries Unlimited.

Del Negro, J. M. 2015. "The Whole Story, The Whole Library: Storytelling As a Driving Force—Illinois Library Association." *Illinois Library Association Reporter* 33, no. 2: 4–7. www.ila.org/publications/ila-reporter/article/52/the-whole-story-the-whole-library-storytelling-as-a-driving-force.

Del Negro, J. M., and M. A. Kimball, eds. 2017. *Engaging Teens with Story: How to Inspire and Educate Youth with Storytelling.* Santa Barbara, CA: Libraries Unlimited.

Druin, A. 2010. "Children as Codesigners of New Technologies: Valuing the Imagination to Transform What Is Possible." *New Directions for Youth Development* 2010, no. 128, 35–43. https://doi.org/10.1002/yd.373.

Edwards, M. A. 1974. *The Fair Garden and the Swarm of Beasts: The Library and the Young Adult.* Revised and expanded ed. New York: Hawthorn Books.

Frosh, P. 2015. "The Gestural Image: The Selfie, Photography Theory, and Kinesthetic Sociability." *International Journal of Communication* 9, no. 1: 1607–28. https://ijoc.org/index.php/ijoc/article/viewFile/3146/1388.

Greene, E., and A. Baker. 1996. *Storytelling: Art and Technique.* New York: R. R. Bowker.

Hall, G. S. 1904. *Adolescence: Its Psychology and Its Relations to Physiology, Anthropology, Sociology, Sex, Crime, Religion and Education.* New York: D. Appleton.

Haven, K. 2007. *Story Proof: The Science Behind the Startling Power of Story.* Westport, CT: Libraries Unlimited.

———. 2014. *Story Smart: Using the Science of Story to Persuade, Influence, Inspire, and Teach.* Santa Barbara, CA: Libraries Unlimited.

Hearne, B. 1993a. "Cite the Source: Reducing Cultural Chaos in Picture Books, Part One." *School Library Journal* 39, no. 7: 22–27.

———. 1993b. "Respect the Source: Reducing Cultural Chaos in Picture Books, Part Two." *School Library Journal* 39, no. 8: 33–37.

Hearne, B., and C. A. Jenkins. 1999. "Sacred Texts: What Our Foremothers Left Us in the Way of Psalms, Proverbs, Precepts, and Practices." *The Horn Book* 75, no. 5: 536–58.

Hills, M. 2002. *Fan Cultures.* London: Routledge.

Judith, B. 1990. *Gender Trouble: Feminism and the Subversion of Identity.* New York: Routledge.

Lipman, D. 1999. *Improving Your Storytelling: Beyond the Basics for All Who Tell Stories in Work or Play.* Little Rock, AK: August House.

Magee, R. M., M. Sebastian, A. Novak, C. M. Mascaro, A. Black, and S. P. Goggins. 2013. "#TwitterPlay: A Case Study of Fan Roleplaying Online." In *CSCW '13: Proceedings of the 2013 Conference on Computer Supported Cooperative Work Companion*, 199–202. New York: ACM Press. https://doi.org/10.1145/2441955.2442005.

Magnuson, L. 2016. *Data Visualization: A Guide to Visual Storytelling for Libraries.* Lanham, MD: Rowman & Littlefield.

Marek, K. 2011. *Organizational Storytelling for Librarians: Using Stories for Effective Leadership.* Chicago: American Library Association.

Miller, M. L. 2003. *Pioneers and Leaders in Library Services to Youth: A Biographical Dictionary.* Westport, CT: Libraries Unlimited.

Moje, E. B., K. M. Ciechanowski, K. Kramer, L. Ellis, R. Carrillo, and T. Collazo. 2004. "Working Toward Third Space in Content Area Literacy: An Examination of Everyday Funds of Knowledge and Discourse." *Reading Research Quarterly* 39, no. 1: 38–70. https://doi.org/10.1598/RRQ.39.1.4.

Mooney, W., and D. Holt. 1996. *The Storyteller's Guide: Storytellers Share Advice for the Classroom, Boardroom, Showroom, Podium, Pulpit and Center Stage.* Little Rock, AK: August House.

Ong, W. 1982. *Orality and Literacy: The Technologizing of the Word*. London and New York: Methuen.
Palmer, P. J. 2003. "Teaching with Heart and Soul: Reflections on Spirituality in Teacher Education." *Journal of Teacher Education* 54, no. 5: 376–85.
Pellowski, A. 1977. *The World of Storytelling*. New York: Bowker.
Propp, V. Y. 1968. *Morphology of the Folktale*. 2nd ed. Austing: University of Texas Press.
Sahn, S. 2016. "Fantasies of Citizenship: Adolscence and Temporality in Young Adult Literature." Unpublished doctoral dissertation, University of Illinois at Urbana-Champaign.
Sawyer, R. 1942. *The Way of the Storyteller*. New York: Viking Press.
Sedgwick, E. K. 1990. *Epistemology of the Closet*. Berkeley: University of California Press.
Shedlock, M. L., and M. G. Davis. 1936. *The Art of the Story-Teller*. Revised ed. New York and London: D. Appleton-Century.
Simmons, A. 2006. *The Story Factor: Inspiration, Influence, and Persuasion through the Art of Storytelling*. New York: Basic Books.
Smith, H. M. 1995. "An Interview with Augusta Baker." *Horn Book Magazine* 71, no. 3: 292–97, www.hbook.com/?detailStory=an-interview-with-augusta-baker.
Soffer, O. 2010. "'Silent Orality': Toward a Conceptualization of the Digital Oral Features in CMC and SMS Texts." *Communication Theory* 20, no. 4: 387–404. https://doi.org/10.1111/j.1468-2885.2010.01368.x.
Stockton, K. B. 2009. *The Queer Child, or Growing Sideways in the Twentieth Century*. Durham, NC: Duke University Press.
Sturm, B. W. 1999. "The Enchanted Imagination: Storytelling's Power to Entrance Listeners." *School Library Media Research* 2: 1–21. https://pdfs.semanticscholar.org/9d70/bdcdc34e402b5f856073df860e04b627daec.pdf.
Toelken, B. 1996. *The Dynamics of Folklore*. Logan : Utah State University Press.
Wiegand, W. A. 2015. *Part of Our Lives: A People's History of the American Public Library*. Oxford and New York: Oxford University Press.

CHAPTER 9

"The Library Is Like Her House"

Reimagining Youth of Color in LIS Discourses

Kafi D. Kumasi

In the library and information science (LIS) field, scholarly discourses and practices tend to overlook or marginalize the unique backgrounds, identities, and literacy practices of youth of color, or youth from historically underrepresented racial/ethnic backgrounds. In this chapter, I use some of the hallmark themes of critical race theory (CRT) to interrogate the ways in which the LIS field sees and positions youth of color against the backdrop of the mainstream white cultural norms and institutional practices. In keeping with the CRT theme *voice,* I argue that it is just as important for LIS scholars to understand how youth of color view and experience libraries and librarians as it is for LIS scholars to contemplate new ways of seeing and defining young adults. I conclude by offering a series of critical questions that might help LIS scholars move toward more culturally sensitive conceptualizations of youth.

If the charge of this volume is to examine the broad question of how the LIS field should define or envision young adults (YAs), then the specific goal of this chapter is to examine that query as it relates to youth of color. The repositioning of this question, I believe, helps place issues of race, power, and white privilege more squarely at the forefront of LIS scholarship, which to the present has not received such critical examinations (Honma 1995). One of the goals of this chapter is, therefore, to help LIS scholars develop a more critical, reflexive stance that would enable them to understand how whiteness and white privilege function in their own lives and ultimately how they envision youth of color in libraries. I contend that the current (and historical) vision of youth in libraries is one that has been framed primarily by Eurocentric cultural norms and aesthetics. Everything from collection development policies, rules of library usage, library programming, and hiring practices to views about what constitutes literacy has been historically constructed by and for whites (Pawley 1998).

Another goal of this work is to insert the voices and experiences of youth of color into the conversation, particularly as it relates to their experiences in libraries. Doing so will help offset an often one-sided conversation about what libraries can do for youth of color that does not include their own voices and experiences. Critical race theory (CRT) is a promising interpretive lens through which to examine this topic because it holds whiteness and white privilege up to scrutiny while foregrounding the voices of people of color as a legitimate point of entry for examining these issues (Delgado and Stefancic 2001). Therefore, in this chapter I use three hallmark themes of CRT—voice, interest convergence, and whiteness as property—to help frame a discussion about the ways in which libraries can better envision and define youth of color.

VOICE

"The library is like her house."

—Hope, 15-year-old African-American female

Sample evidence from my dissertation research with a diverse group of African-American youth confirms the notion that some youth of color experience feelings of cultural disconnect with their school and public libraries and librarians. The above quote was taken from a segment of transcript gathered during a book club conversation I helped to facilitate (Kumasi 2008). The youth were being asked some preliminary questions about their library usage and reading habits. Hope's statement that "the library is like her house" seems to capture a certain view that some library spaces reflect the cultural norms and values of the librarians who operate them. Moreover, her choice of the word *house* is significant because it carries certain implicit references to words like *ownership*, *comfortability*, and *exclusivity*.

To further dissect Hope's statement from a CRT perspective, one might ask questions such as the following: Would you ordinarily feel welcomed in her house? Are there any symbols or cultural things in her house that remind you of home? Do the rules that seem to govern her house seem similar to the rules your family keeps at home? Could your family afford a house like hers and do your neighbors look like you? Would living at her house enable you to attend a desirable school? And finally, do you think her house was ever been broken into? If so, how swift do you think the police would respond?

CRT provides the interpretive power to ask these kinds of provocative questions since it looks at the more systemic issues that underlie current racial inequalities. Through the construct of "voice," CRT scholars recognize the centrality of the experiential knowledge of people of color and view this knowledge as legitimate, appropriate, and critical to understanding, analyzing, and teaching about racial subordination. Therefore, from a CRT perspective, the statement that "the library is like her house" would not be dismissed simply as one person's subjective opinion. Rather, a CRT analysis would acknowledge the ability of a person or a group to articulate experiences in ways that are unique to that person or group (Dixson and Rousseau, 2006). Through storytelling and counter-narratives, disenfranchised people are provided the intellectual space to name their own realities in areas such as academia, where they may have been previously marginalized.

INTEREST CONVERGENCE

Interest convergence is another hallmark CRT theme that can help library scholars question the way they see (or do not see) youth of color in libraries. Interest convergence is a thesis proposed by Derrick Bell that maintains the white majority group tolerates advances for racial justice only when it suits its interests to do so. This thesis plays out subtly, often requiring multiple theoretical tools to fully unpack. It has been used most notably by leading CRT scholar Bell to explain the real impetus behind the passage of the Civil Rights Act of 1964 (Wright 2005). Through his research, Bell found that the motivating factor behind the bill's passage was to protect the national reputation of the United States amid a tense political climate during the cold war (Bell 1980). The world was watching the United States, and leaders in the U.S. government knew that they could not very well take a moral stand against other countries that were facing human rights dilemmas if their own country did not afford Black citizens basic equal rights. Therefore, the advancement of civil rights for African Americans coincided with the dominant white political interest of the U.S. government to be seen as a leader in the global political landscape. Without this convergence of interests, Bell and others argue that the so-called civil rights gains we now celebrate may not have occurred were they not also in the immediate interests of the dominant white political powers.

The question is, How does this understanding relate to the ways in which libraries envision youth of color? One way it relates is in how librarians conceptualize youth of color and their literate potential. For example, if librarians hold a cultural deficit perspective toward youth of color, they might only see their so-called problems without recognizing their unique talents and gifts. They may also hold stereotypical views toward youth of color based on representations they see in the mass media. If a librarian holds a cultural deficit perspective toward youth of color and masks this belief system but, at the same time, capitalizes on efforts to promote diversity with youth of color, then that can be seen as interest convergence. Because of the liberal ideology within the LIS profession that uncritically celebrates diversity efforts (Balderrama 2000), a librarian could benefit personally from implementing a diversity initiative with youth of color. On the other hand, no one might question how such initiatives position youth of color as objects of study and divert attention away from the roles libraries and librarians play in maintaining the status quo of racial oppression through established institutional practices and belief systems.

The interest convergence principle can help librarians take a critical look at their own perspectives about youth of color. They might ask themselves questions like these: Do I capitalize on youth initiatives that promote diversity and equality while subconsciously holding a cultural deficit perspective about youth of color themselves? Do I view youth of color as unfortunate victims in a fundamentally just society? Do I transfer the stereotypical images about youth of color that play out in the media onto those whom I might encounter in my library? Do I believe that *all* children can succeed provided the right support and opportunities?

The LIS field has traditionally taken a more pluralistic approach to diversity that avoids dealing directly with race and racial inequities. The problem with the more pluralistic or multicultural initiatives is that they seek to accommodate so many facets of diversity that they often wind up having little or no real impact on any particular group. CRT scholars have made similar critiques about the ineffectiveness of multicultural approaches. Ladson-Billings and Tate state:

> The multicultural paradigm functions in a manner similar to civil rights law. Instead of creating radically new paradigms which ensure justice, multicultural reforms are routinely, "sucked back into the system"; and just as traditional civil rights law is based on a foundation of human rights, the current multicultural paradigm is mired in a liberal ideology that offers no radical change in the current order. (quoted in Dixson and Rousseau 2006, 25)

Thus, from a CRT perspective, it is important for librarians to not just study youth of color as objects under the gaze of a predominantly white librarian workforce. Rather, it is incumbent upon librarians to look reflexively at the library's institutional policies and practices to see how they uphold certain cultural norms and worldviews that might marginalize the home and community literacy practices of many youth of color (e.g., rap, spoken word, code switching, or tagging). Or it might mean looking at how and why funding and other resources are disproportionally allocated to libraries in affluent (mostly white) suburban communities. A project such as this would not likely get agency funding, but these are the very deep-seated issues that need to be addressed if libraries and librarians are to move beyond a monolithic vision of youth of color that is based primarily on white cultural frames of reference that promote white self-interests.

WHITENESS AS PROPERTY

Understanding the CRT concept of "whiteness as property" can help LIS scholars reframe any number of questions that are taken up in LIS by critically analyzing the way that whiteness has been framed as both the preferred and normal state of being. The principle of whiteness as property maintains that people with white skin have been afforded a set of unearned rights and privileges since the period of slavery. Whiteness, as the ultimate form of property, confers upon one who "possesses" it (1) the rights of disposition, (2) the right to use and enjoyment, (3) reputation and status property, and (4) the absolute right to exclude (Ladson-Billings and Tate 1995). Thompson (2001) offers several methodological approaches for helping unmask whiteness in both professional and institutional discourses as well as on a personal level.

Related to discourses around youth in the LIS field, some questions that we might ask ourselves are the following: Do I participate in the "othering" of nonwhite youth by inadvertently assuming a white audience as the default norm in my various library practices (e.g., promotional signage, book displays, collection development, etc.)? Do the rules I support and enforce in the library primarily cater to the cultural and linguistic norms of whites (e.g., rules of noise levels, etc.)? Questions such as these help unmask whiteness as the invisible norm or reference point for thinking about any number of questions taken up in the LIS field.

The principle of whiteness as property can also be applied to examining how the concept of literacy is conceived in YA library discourses and the impact such a stance might have on how youth of color participate and are viewed in libraries. The way literacy is conceived in the LIS field tends to privilege the literacy practices of white youth, which are often rooted in cognitive and autonomous forms of knowing. This conceptual stance often comes at the expense of supporting the literacy practices of nonwhite youth, which are rooted in sociocultural frameworks of understanding (Langer 1991). The notion of whiteness itself has been linked to the development of scientific rationalist thinking, which privileges "mind over body, intellectual over experiential ways of knowing, mental abstractions over passion, bodily sensations, and tactile understanding" (Kincheloe, Steinberg, and Hinchey 1999).

Information literacy, which is the intellectual domain of librarians, falls within this cognitive and positivist tradition of learning (Kapitzke 2003). This approach begins from a standpoint that students come to the library with specific information problems that arise out of their personal, workplace, or academic concerns. The librarians' role is then to help these youth develop skills in solving these information problems by teaching them how to access the most current, reliable, and authentic information through the library's resources. Yet, this approach leaves librarians at the periphery of the learning experience and positions them more as resource providers than teachers. Thus, there is little room for librarians to help youth address anything other than mundane information problems rather than larger social and cultural concerns they may face (e.g., poverty, unemployment, racial discrimination, etc.) (Kumasi-Johnson 2007).

Yet, unless the majority white librarian scholarly base is exposed to more expansive perspectives on literacy, such as those that frame literacy as a social practice, then those newer approaches will remain on the periphery. Moreover, because there is not a critical mass of library scholars researching literacy from a sociocultural perspective, the dominant view of literacy as a cognitive skill is the only view that can take up "residence" in the LIS field—to use the metaphor of whiteness as property. This may seem like a tangential matter, but I would argue it is a very pressing issue that can have significant implications for how librarians view and engage youth of color. For example, if librarians were to expand how they define literacy to include home and community literacy perspectives, then library instruction might take on a very different form. Instead of doing activities centered on evaluating websites and other static exercises bounded to libraries, librarians might instead take up a more activist role and go into communities and help youth uncover what their real-world information concerns are and encourage them to develop skills at posing questions and finding solutions to these real-life issues.

A NOTE ON INTERSECTIONALITY

As a matter of disclosure, I write this chapter from a social location as a thirtysomething, upper-working-class Black female who is a fifth-generation college graduate. Despite being both self-identified and outwardly labeled as Black, I have probably benefited from and participated in whiteness in my daily life. The reason a person of color can participate in whiteness is because, as Thompson (2001) notes, "whiteness does not refer to a biological but to a socially constructed category" (under "Differences in Theoretical Focus and Approach," para. 6). Thompson goes on to explain that Black or other academics of color who internalize white-privileging institutional norms may be said to benefit from and participate in the promotion of institutional whiteness. Insofar as African Americans, Latinos, and other nonwhites aspire to material privileges that are coded as white *and* insofar as they see material well-being as earned through individual merit (rather than through a system that excludes all but a few people of color), they may be said to participate in material whiteness. As a Black academic who aspires to achieve a level of success in higher education, I am somewhat caught up in the trappings of whiteness. I do not, however, ascribe to the myth of "Ameritocracy" (Akom 2008), but rather I recognize that I am a fortunate exception to the implicit rule in higher education that says only so many people of color can gain access to higher-level positions at predominately white institutions. While I do believe that I have *earned* the position I occupy, I recognize that there are many more people of color who are just as deserving but who will not be given this opportunity because there are so few spaces available for faculty of color in the academy.

Similarly, we are all privileged and oppressed to differing degrees. This is what CRT scholars describe as intersectionality, or interlocking systems of oppression. Thus, white librarians who read this should not come away with a sense of guilt or shame about benefiting from and participating in whiteness. By understanding each of our layers of privilege and penalty, we can begin to locate ourselves on the stratum of race, power, and privilege as a first step toward being reflexive and self-aware, which can ultimately lead to social transformation.

Understanding one's layers of privilege can also be useful in disrupting negative stereotypes about nonwhite people. One of the first things to recognize when it comes to youth of color is that their racial identity is only *one* facet of their identity and it may *not* be the primary lens through which they view and experience the world. Still, I would argue that taking a "color-blind" stance toward seeing youth of color is not helpful. Most youth of color are aware of the way society views them and how people of color are positioned in the social stratification of society in the United States. To ignore race or to create an atmosphere in libraries that seems to minimize cultural differences and aim for a more color-blind goal could be just as damaging on a subconscious level for some youth of color. It is important to celebrate cultural differences and maintain a healthy balance between promoting mainstream color-blind perspectives and race-conscious worldviews in our work with young adults (Carter and Kumasi 2011).

CONCLUSION

The question at the heart of this chapter is, How might the LIS field better imagine youth of color in order to embrace their situated identities, their culturally based literacy practices, and their unique social histories? The answer, I believe, lies in looking reflexively at how whiteness functions in the library and scrutinizing how it is operationalized through certain institutional policies and personal belief systems. This work must occur on both the conceptual and the structural levels. Conceptually, the librarian workforce must engage in the messy and tenuous work of holding up to scrutiny our own beliefs, practices, and worldviews about people of color to see how these constructs might privilege white ways of knowing and being. Structurally, we must look at the ways libraries historically upheld (and still uphold today) whiteness through various institutional practices and policies, such as collection development, resource allocation, training, staffing, and so on. Finally, we might all benefit from keeping several questions at the forefront of our minds as we strive for a more culturally inclusive vision of youth in LIS. Some of those questions might include the following: How might I disrupt static and binary conceptualizations of youth that position white youth as the default normative cultural frame of reference? How might I avoid "othering" nonwhite youth by making them objects of study only in the context of "special" projects (e.g., closing the black-white achievement gap)? How might I help examine and transform the institutional practices of libraries that uphold racism in a profession that prides itself on being color-blind and accessible to all people? We might also direct some of our questions toward youth of color themselves and ask them:

- What would your ideal library look like?
- How would you feel when you entered it?
- What might you see and what kind of rules would you want enforced?
- What are the ways you think libraries have been organized with the needs of white youth in mind?
- What are some of the needs you see that black youth have that could be better met by libraries or librarians?

REFERENCES

Akom, A. A. 2008. "Ameritocracy and Infra-racial Racism: Racializing Social and Cultural Reproduction Theory in the Twenty-first Century." *Race, Ethnicity, and Education* 11, no. 3: 205–30.

Balderrama, S. R. 2000. "This Trend Called Diversity." *Library Trends* 49, no. 1: 194–214.

Bell, D. 1980. "*Brown v. Board of Education* and the Interest Convergence Dilemma." *Harvard Law Review* 93: 518–33.

Carter, S., and K. Kumasi. 2011. "Double Reading: Young Black Scholars Responding to Whiteness in a Community Literacy Program." In *Urban Literacies: Critical Perspectives on Language, Learning, and Community*, edited by V. Kinlock, 72–90. New York: Teachers College Press.

Delgado, R., and J. Stefancic. 2001. *Critical Race Theory: An Introduction*. New York: New York University Press.

Dixson, A. D., and C. K. Rousseau. 2006. *Critical Race Theory in Education: All God's Children Got a Song*. New York: Routledge.

Honma, T. 1995. "Trippin' over the Color Line: The Invisibility of Race in Library and Information Studies." *InterActions: UCLA Journal of Education and Information Studies* 1, no. 2: 1–28.

Kapitzke, C. 2003. "Information Literacy: A Positivist Epistemology and a Politics of Outformation." *Educational Theory* 53, no. 1: 37–52.

Kincheloe, J., S. Steinberg, and P. Hinchey, eds. 1999. *The Post-formal Reader: Cognition and Education*. New York: Falmer.

Kumasi, K. 2008. *Seeing White in Black: Examining Racial Identity among African American Adolescents in a Culturally Centered Book Club*. Ann Arbor, MI: Proquest.

Kumasi-Johnson, K. 2007. "Critical Inquiry: Library Media Specialists as Change Agents." *School Library Media Activities Monthly* 28, no. 9: 42–45.

Ladson-Billings, G., and W. F. Tate. 1995. "Toward a Critical Race Theory of Education." *Teachers College Record* 97: 47–68.

Langer, J. 1991. "Literacy and Schooling: A Sociocognitive Perspective." In *Literacy for a Diverse Society: Perspectives, Practices, and Policies*, edited by E. Hiebert, 9–27. New York: Teachers College Press.

Pawley, C. 1998. "Hegemony's Handmaid? The Library and Information Science Curriculum from a Class Perspective." *The Library Quarterly* 68, no. 2: 123–44.

Thompson, A. 2001. "Summary of Whiteness Theory." Course presentation, Whiteness in Cross-Race Classroom Relationships, University of Utah, Spring 2008. www.kooriweb.org/foley/resources/whiteness/summary_of_whiteness_theory.pdf.

Wright, S. 2005. *The Civil Rights Act of 1964: Landmark Antidiscrimination Legislation*. New York: Rosen Publishing Group.

PART IV

Emergent Roles

CHAPTER 10

Beyond Coaching

Copiloting with Young Adults

Wendy Schaetzel Lesko

> Imaginative open-minded librarians serve as catalysts and create a conducive atmosphere unlike any other environment for young adults in our age-segregated society. This chapter explores the idea that librarians who are brimming with curiosity and inquiry can engage young adults as real decision makers who can have a real impact on organizational development. Youth-led and adult-supported programs such as the Youth Activism Project and School Girls Unite serve as examples of ways that librarians can encourage minors' substantive participation in the public policy arena.

Society at large needs to put both feet in the water when it comes to seeking input, ideas, and involvement from young adults. Librarians deserve credit for sustained efforts to engage teens, but our age-segregated culture still permeates every institution. A seismic adult attitude adjustment that moves from authoritative to collegial is essential. Multiple entry points and trajectories invite a broader swath of young adults to participate in cocreating libraries. Envision truly open-minded librarians who usher in a new era of collaboration with young adults and together concoct a smorgasbord of activities and services that attract people of all ages and backgrounds.

The mantra "Don't make decisions for youth without youth" implies shared decision making but typically is limited to engaging teens on peripheral issues or parallel efforts to those of adults, often in a subordinate advisory role. The primary objectives of these programs include increasing self-esteem, real-world learning, and leadership skills. These deeply held attitudes must undergo a dramatic shift in order for young adults to assume pivotal roles in the ongoing innovation of libraries and civic engagement. The aim is for diverse young adults to be fully engaged as real decision makers who have real impact on organizational development with positive youth development as a by-product. This paradigm does not demand that new structures or initiatives be created, nor does it displace the critical job of professional librarians, but it does require intentional strategies.

The prerequisite is an adult mind-set of authentic appreciation and commitment for exchanging views with youth. The onus is on grown-ups to demonstrate their interest and intent to learn from and with teens. A can-do philosophy coupled with nimble and fast-paced strategizing are trademarks of successful multigenerational teamwork. The library universe represents one of the best community hubs to move from dabbling to copiloting with young adults. In addition to describing these opportunities, I draw other approaches for this transformative model from my firsthand experiences.

For nearly two decades, the Youth Activism Project has served as a national clearinghouse to encourage minors to participate in substantive ways in the public policy arena. We urge young people to influence their peers as well as their elected officials. For example, a tenth-grader called our toll-free hotline several times a week while he organized a successful campaign to expand the state board of education to include two student representatives. A 13-year-old wanted to start a teen center in her town and we suggested she contact several youth in another rural community who had won their mayor's support to use an abandoned movie theater. Over a period of 10 years, my two sons channeled their anger over the tobacco industry's marketing tactics and were instrumental in getting passed a county ordinance that banned cigarette vending machines and a second law requiring all tobacco products be placed behind the counters. In contrast to being the parent on the sidelines, I experienced terrific collaboration while I coauthored *Youth! The 26% Solution* with Emanuel Tsourounis, who was 19 at the time.

In 2004, my attention moved to the global south, where millions of girls are denied an education because of their sex. I shared my outrage with a half dozen seventh-graders and young African women. Together, we launched School Girls Unite, which combines philanthropy and political advocacy. Thus far, my greatest learning and most satisfying experience can be traced to working with four cofounders of School Girls Unite who were paid interns over the summer. Together, we designed all components of a national campaign for global gender equality called Day of the Girl. My role was as copilot rather than as coach.

FAVORABLE CULTURE AND CLIMATE

Libraries have several distinct advantages to shift from age-segregated traditions to new modes of interaction and operation. Librarians represent a rare species different from most adults and many teachers. Even librarians who work in school media centers offer an oasis from the classroom grind of tests and grades. Unlike most youth programs where there are unspoken boundaries when it comes to questioning authority or conventional wisdom, no such limits exist in libraries.

Openness is a hallmark of the profession. Fighting censorship is a given. Curiosity and eccentric interests are embraced. Close ties with community leaders and organizations help youth make connections to pursue their own interests and passions. Awareness of current trends in the youth culture erases the outdated stereotypes of librarians. This acceptance of free thinking and eagerness for exploration creates a truly unique environment.

Gifted young adult (YA) librarians, like most youth workers who are underappreciated and underpaid, often say one reason they do not quit is because of a special energy they gain from intergenerational exchange. There is an addictive quality derived from out-of-the-box brainstorming and the pace of action that contrasts to often sluggish adult decision-making processes. This space for freedom and exploration exists to a far larger extent in a community-based setting like a library. When a project takes off, it can be absolutely magical for all involved. For example, School Girls Unite received a minigrant to write a booklet about the reasons why millions of girls do not go to school. Soon the publication blossomed into a 100-page bilingual action guide titled *Girls Gone Activist! How to Change the World through Education* with contributions from our sister organization in Mali, West Africa. Five U.S. high school students each took responsibility for writing one chapter, another team collaborated with our graphic designer on photos and fonts, and my main role was organizing meeting spaces and managing a team of volunteer translators. Imagine this type of intergenerational project with young poets or novelists.

BUILDING ON YA PROGRAMS

Libraries are miles ahead of many youth-serving organizations in terms of giving young people opportunities to steer the ship. Youth advisory councils, reading clubs, Teen Wii, and other creative outlets translate into a core of regulars who are at home at the library. Months of shared experiences provide a collegial foundation. Assuming good group dynamics, more reticent youth become comfortable speaking their minds. Encouragement for proposing untried or wacky ideas becomes the norm. Even without a teen space complete with giant bean bags, an atmosphere charged with imaginative inquiry makes the library a hot spot.

In the youth empowerment field, typically the first step is for young adults to focus on the issues they themselves identify as paramount. This approach puts them in the driver's seat. It signals permission to abandon established programs or conventions. There are plenty of young adults eager to invent, including new ways to transform library services. This open-ended invitation is often just what it takes to unleash unorthodox thinking. Initial brainstorming should not be weighed down by a review of sacrosanct programs, library policies, or funding restrictions; however, these issues need to be discussed before blueprints for change take shape. Otherwise it may be regarded as a futile exercise. Similarly, these young architects need to understand the entire process for proposing their recommendations as well as the chain of command. This awareness of the library decision-making machine will guard against disappointment and likely cynicism if their ideas collide with existing YA services or get vetoed by the powers that be.

Another pillar of positive youth development and empowerment is peer education. The motto is that youth know best what will interest other youth. This categorical assumption denies the vast differences in every community, even towns with only one traffic signal. Luckily, librarians know there is no such thing as a monolithic generation and offer eclectic teen activities. Official structures like youth advisory boards as well as ad hoc groups are given the reins to plan events. They create the buzz and can take a lion's share of the credit for attracting people to the library.

With all the increasing demands on librarians, it makes sense to stick with a tight-knit group and put these individuals in the position of charting the future path for YA services. This comfort zone spells continuity and building on the past, but the risk is too great that the library menu will become stale and the library will fail to attract new patrons.

IMPORTANCE OF INDIVIDUAL INTERACTIONS

Even though teen space is familiar and often preferred by young and old alike, this form of quarantine has consequences. What about those youth who are not interested in YA programs or opt not to be around their near-peers who frequent the library? Think about the hordes of students who are turned off by their student government, extracurricular clubs, athletics, or other prescribed activities? In the library, do independent-minded youth feel welcome outside the teen-designated zone? Are other librarians and staff ready and eager to interact with them? What about the policies for free meeting spaces for young adults with no group affiliation? Imagine these and other situations and consider whether the library encourages freedom of movement and thought.

The shift to age-blind attitudes comes into play. Every single young adult who uses the library should feel as though he or she is a respected member of this public institution. This heightens the importance of even brief encounters with all staff from reference desk librarians to security guards. One-to-one interactions are an undervalued strategy. Without being too intrusive, chatting with people individually to learn about their interests can lead to encouraging them to share ideas, whether those ideas are about a community issue or pertain to services the library might offer. Impromptu conversations between young people and adults should be part of the library climate, as long as the adults are actively listening to what the young people are saying.

Another intuitive yet intentional strategy is for adults not to always put young people on the spot to respond to questions. The different "dance step" is to start by sharing one's own interests. If you are excited about a new graphic novel or fuming about a banned book, talk about it. Invite young adults into your circle.

The following statements from my manual, *Maximum Youth Involvement: The Complete Gameplan for Community Action* (Lesko 2006), reveal some subtleties of intergenerational collaboration in contrast to the stark labels of youth-led or adult-directed decision making. More often than not, the outcomes are due to each of the individuals involved rather than to the degree of youth independence versus adult intervention:

- "I love it when adults tell me they don't know."
- "Some adults surprise and inspire me. I am drawn to those who have not completely forgotten their adolescence and its open-mindedness."
- "Encourage us. Build on our ideas. That gives us the confidence we need."
- "Lead us to the cliff and trust us!"

Nothing beats honesty and authenticity. Young people detect insincere interest or fake praise, as described by a high school student who served on a nonprofit board: "The adult smirk is a half smile and slight nod as a young person speaks and silently thinks that the ideas being presented are unrealistic, have been tried in the past, or are plain stupid." Remember when you were young and did not reveal your opinions because of the expectation that grown-ups would dismiss your ideas. This patronizing attitude can poison the atmosphere.

Young people are not fooled when they are being asked to rubber-stamp a decision. The comment "Adults think if they feed us pizza, that's all it takes" is a telling reminder by an eleventh-grader. Imagine being put in the uncomfortable and untenable position of being the token representative to pontificate about what "kids" in the community want. Think about serving as a youth board member who is the only one not to have a vote.

We need to call out adults who speak about "using kids." Another phrase that should make us wince is "their little project." This attitude is all too common, even among well-intentioned librarians who cannot click with a challenging mix of personalities. Every mismatch undermines job satisfaction and sabotages potential youth and adult synergy.

THE SCARCE RESOURCE

Time is the four-letter word that explains why there is so little substantive youth influence with organizations, including those with a mission to empower youth. Minors have minimal control over their waking hours. Many students juggle multiple activities such as the school newspaper, a part-time job, or family responsibilities. This is one reason for erratic attendance at teen advisory group meetings or library events. Staff need to be sensitive to young people's time, and one way is not to seek input on trivial issues or ask for feedback on significant matters without providing the necessary background material or adequate discussion time. For example, the Board of Young Adult Commissioners in New Haven, Connecticut, was considering the merits of a proposed curfew and an aide to the police chief shared information he had compiled for the board that compared ordinances in dozens of other cities. This analysis enabled these high school students to rely on more than local and anecdotal information, and they proposed a modified curfew that ultimately was adopted by the city council.

Even if the mix of personalities and brainpower is awesome, there is another inevitable frustration: one or several of the most involved young adults take a break, drop out, or move. It could be something like the student is grounded or cannot miss any theater rehearsals or team practices. Snail mail, texting, e-mail, and Facebook are all strategies of patient persistence. After a one-year hiatus during the first year at college, four young adults who had started an international initiative with me back when they were in the seventh grade transitioned from volunteers to paid interns. This experience proved remarkable in several ways. All of us went up the learning curve together. We increased our efficiency by dividing into pairs and interviewing candidates for our social media manager position. Designing a website and generating content was a team effort. Daily osmosis in our campaign meant that two of the interns were completely prepared to meet with White House staff when I was out of the country. In addition to concrete accomplishments, collaborating with smart, committed young colleagues exceeded all expectations.

Providing opportunities and venues for young adults to spend time at the libraries where they are in the loop and steeped in the issues on an ongoing basis enables them to truly participate as partners. Paid internships that come with real responsibilities can be one of the best investments to get solid input, especially when it comes to cocreating libraries. Internships also provide a critical rung on the ladder of engagement. An eighth-grader can imagine such a role three to five years into the future. Part-time staff and paid internships need to become the norm to promote youth infusion with professional librarians to replace separate or parallel activities.

COMMUNITY CENTRAL

YA librarians have another distinct advantage over most adults that positions them as ideal copilots. As infomaniacs, librarians are constantly networking with community-based youth organizations, schools and universities, government agencies, advocacy groups, and so on. Electronic discussion lists, meetings, conferences, and rallies produce a stream of opportunities that might be of interest to young adults. Too often, we assume that teens will not be interested or busy schedules cause adults not to have the time to share current debates or upcoming events with teens.

Being deliberate about bringing news of community happenings, especially those beyond the school walls, can result in young adults participating in unexpected ways. I remember sharing a research study with School Girls Unite students that revealed one in seven girls worldwide is forced into marriage. An upcoming forum in the U.S. Congress on this human rights issue peaked interest more. Within the week, one student wrote an article for her high school newspaper. Several tenth-graders decided to produce a video petition in favor of legislation that would include child marriage as one of the evaluation criteria for every country in the U.S. State Department's annual human rights report. Within a two-week period, students completed a clever video with sound bites from girls and boys expressing horror at forced marriage. The video was shown at the forum and used by the students in their meetings with congressional staff, which led to their two senators and representative agreeing to be cosponsors on the bill. This example simply shows the potential of sharing information and the impact that can surprise everyone involved.

This strategy for broadening the bandwidth of young adults who depend on the library as information central can include policies and proposals that directly impact young people. In addition to battles over library funding, so many issues under consideration by the city or county council, board of education, parks and recreation, state legislature, and Congress are not on anyone's radar screen. Rarely are young people aware of when and where they could present their views and perhaps influence an outcome. Instead of taking a passive role, libraries could alert young adults to a school board hearing on changes to the zero-tolerance policy, a vote in the state senate on student voting eligibility, or immigration legislation pending in Congress. Using the library's connections to so many organizations, advocacy groups, and elected officials, this information hub could foster more meaningful civic engagement.

This approach ignores the reality that most minors believe they do not wield any influence whatsoever with decision makers, especially those who are marginalized, who are likely to feel disenfranchised well into adulthood. Storytelling, especially local history, can inspire young people to envision themselves as change agents whether in their library or the larger community. A case in point: few of the youth who visit the stunning Salt Lake City Public Library know about the East High School students who tried to start a Gay-Straight Alliance club in 2000. When initially rejected by the city board of education, students sought legal help and an antidiscrimination lawsuit forced the board to shut down all extracurricular clubs. This decision angered even more people and caused the school board to approve the student proposal. A bit of digging in every community will reveal true stories of ordinary youth accomplishing extraordinary things that prove there is no minimum age for leadership.

Another rich research area for student interns or perhaps a teen council is to survey libraries in other cities in search of innovative programming and cost-effective approaches. Browsing library websites and Facebook pages is bound to fuel fresh ideas. Following up with individual libraries to learn more details and find out the resources required gives young adults ownership of the information. This investigation also enables them to gain more equal footing with adults involved with the library's strategic planning process.

CONCLUSION

We know every young adult is not always a joy to be around, and the feeling is usually mutual. But widespread negative stereotypes can be an excuse not to engage. Another attitude that interferes with meaningful partnership involves the standard benchmarks for cognitive abilities for specific adolescents by age. Plenty of middle school students demonstrate critical thinking skills and maturity that surpass those of high school students. Online skills and social marketing savvy also are obvious reasons to tap the brains of young adults. From the standpoint of longevity, offering opportunities in the ongoing mission of revitalizing the library to very young teens can result in years of involvement, with the added benefit of valuable institutional memory.

Every organization knows the tug-of-war between continuing to deliver services that have withstood the test of time and moving beyond the comfort zone to avoid becoming obsolete. Not only do young adults need to be actively involved in transforming YA services; this multigenerational engagement also can help the entire library system be on the cutting edge. The next generation by virtue of age sees the future in ways that adults cannot fathom. It is incomprehensible not to take advantage of the ideas of a very diverse group of young adults to ensure libraries remain not only relevant but also a magnet in the community.

Combating inertia and resistance is no easy task. The common and unfortunate assumption when discussing the involvement of young people in organizational decision making is that youth are uninterested, unprepared, and uninformed. Staff time and precious resources are already stretched. As a result, most organizations involve young people only in minor volunteer roles or as program recipients. Providing paid internships for discrete projects as well as ongoing activities can begin this process in a sustained and deliberate way.

Youth infusion does not occur as an add-on or afterthought but is integral to the continual process of reinventing our libraries and community participation. Instead of asking whether young adults should be involved, the question should be, How can young adults be involved? This philosophy means valuing and respecting young people beyond an intrinsic future value and more as unique individuals who can make important contributions today.

New committees or structures are not necessary, but rather a systemic library-wide attitudinal shift. Not only do many adults need to transform their own perceptions, but also young people need to be convinced that authority figures and those in power will not be patronizing but instead genuinely seek to involve them as equal partners. Margaret Mead (1970) describes the complexity of this paradigm:

> The young, free to act on their initiative, can lead their elders in the direction of the unknown. The children, the young, must ask the questions that we would never think to ask, but enough trust must be re-established so that elders will be permitted to work with them on the answers. (73–74)

The creativity between generations has the potential to reduce our age-segregated institutions. Flexible and relentless strategies are necessary to engage young adults, including those who rarely or never use libraries. This advancement will not happen until adults—all library staff—shift their thinking from being coaches to copilots with young adults. The involvement of the next generation as architects and advocates is essential to the ongoing process of reinventing libraries to ensure their relevance and popularity as vital and irreplaceable centers in communities across America.

REFERENCES

Lesko, W. S. 2006. *Maximum Youth Involvement: A Complete Gameplan for Community Action.* Youth Activism Project. https://youthactivismproject.org/FreeDownload/MaximumYouthInvolvement/MaximumYouthInvolvement!CompleteGuidetoCommunityAction.pdf.

Mead, Margaret. 1970. *Culture and Commitment: A Study of the Generation Gap.* New York: Natural History Press.

CHAPTER 11

LIS's Vision of Young Adults

Some Historical Roots for Current Theories and Practice

Mary K. Chelton

In response to the question about a new library and information science (LIS) vision of young adults (YAs), this essay questions the degree to which a new vision is even necessary. If LIS envisions YAs as self-aware members of their community, involving an understanding of oneself in relation to others (family, friends, enemies, people from other age groups, or coworkers), there may not be a need for an LIS-specific notion for YA library users. Being part of a community demands knowledge of and respect for human interdependence, reciprocity, culture, history, values, and differences. This study thus acknowledges some qualified benefits the youth development (YD) paradigm has offered LIS, defending LIS's adoption of it but also acknowledging LIS's "fixation" on the YD paradigm to the exclusion of other approaches. In responding to conversations surfacing in LIS, this study explores notions of a dynamic YA identity already at play.

Margaret Edwards was my teacher in library school at Rutgers in 1964–1965, and I was further trained at the Enoch Pratt Free Library in Baltimore, Maryland, by her immediate successors, Sara Siebert and Linda Lapides. But even before that I was a young adult user of the Enoch Pratt Library in high school and understood what it felt like to encounter an Edwards-trained YA librarian before I became one myself. This dual perspective always left me with the proud feeling that I was following in great footsteps. I think revisiting some earlier visions experienced and internalized might inform discussions of future ones.

This is not to say that everything Edwards espoused is still completely relevant, although it could be argued that much is. For example, she never made peace with reference, finding the retrieval of facts trivial and secondary to reading promotion, when most contemporary YA librarians, myself included, understand that assisting YAs in their role as researchers for school or for personal use is probably one of the primary ways to establish a relationship with them in libraries. This has often led, however, to an overemphasis on viewing YAs as students to their exclusion as readers or anything else. In this regard, Edwards's passion for them as readers could stand a resurgence, even though their role as readers or information seekers has long since expanded into media other than books and into roles other than readers. As former ALA president Richard Daugherty (1991) once pointed out, "Kids Who Read, Succeed," and librarians who ignore the literacy needs of YAs will not be very successful in pushing information technology on them, even with the delight of the federated library systems now available, because they will not be reading literate or information literate enough to use them without major personal assistance.

This is possibly why "Reading is the core of personal and academic competency" is part of the "Common Beliefs" section of the new national standards promulgated by the American Association of School Librarians (AASL 2018). It should be noted, however, that this utilitarian view of reading is somewhat far afield from the personal enjoyment and meaningfulness of recreational reading that was espoused by Margaret Edwards.

In fact, these dual literacy deficits—reading literacy and information literacy, in combination with difficult-to-use library-based information systems, the overwhelmingness of the Internet, and YAs' lack of interest in the many ubiquitous, and often boring, school-imposed research queries—seem to be the main reasons behind young adults being viewed by many librarians as "broken." This syndrome is eloquently described by Anthony Bernier (2007) in "Not Broken by Someone Else's Schedule: On Joy and Young Adult Information Seeking." He suggests that YAs are viewed by researchers and the LIS field as "lone academic agents" with inadequate skills who find information seeking difficult, "teetering on the precipice of their own failings" (xvii). At the same time, researchers and practitioners tend to disregard literacy products created by young adults (Bernier 2007).

The YA viewed as student is exacerbated by the increased dichotomy between school and public libraries. While both institutions attempt to serve the same YAs, and even answer the same questions for them in many instances, school librarians of necessity must view YAs as students because of their curriculum support role, whereas public librarians espouse but usually do not see YAs as voluntary users with many varied personal and social interests in addition to those imposed by school. As a result, the instructional role of the librarian, the learner role of the young adult, and the institutional atmosphere are (or should be) quite different.

While I have borrowed theories I find relevant from other sources, I find the essence of Margaret Edwards's vision of young adults, especially in congruence with Gisela Konopka's views, as committed, self-conscious, and independent members of communities as relevant today as ever. It seems impossible to envision a theory of what a young adult is all by itself, when, of necessity, this vision has to be embedded in a theory of practice. Libraries, like most social institutions, do not exist in a vacuum. According to Bourdieu (1972), theories of practice offer a means of reconciling structure, agency, and human capital, that is, (1) those patterns of social life not reducible to individuals that act as rules and determinants of individuals' thoughts and behaviors, (2) individuals' freedom to act, and (3) the people who translate the two.

For just one example, in terms of structure, for all our talk about outreach, library services remain primarily building based and, as a result, are irrelevant to, or nonexistent for, YAs who do not enter the building or who use the building for nonprescribed purposes. Many practices within libraries are traditional and built into the structural assumptions of the physical plant as well as the service assumptions, and this makes it difficult for many librarians to conceptualize young adults as something other than students in a queue asking school-imposed questions, because that is traditional reference desk practice.

DISCIPLINE VERSUS PRACTICE

The other problem with theorizing about young adults without context, besides the general antipathy toward theory among library practitioners (Crowley 2005), is the intellectual vacuum created by the lack of agreement on whether LIS is a discipline from which theories originate or a practice in which theories are only applied. Even when viewed as a discipline, there are arguments over whether it is part of information science or the humanities. Like William Crowley, I favor the latter view, that LIS is a practice and part of the humanities; hence my interest in a theory of YAs being part of a theory of practice. Crowley (2007) has defined the LIS field as

> concerned with understanding and advancing learning throughout the human lifecycle, with a particular emphasis on the processes of reading and other forms of communicating story, information, and meaning through library and library-related contexts. The emphasis on human learning, content and meaning distinguishes library science from the newer field of information science.

Since public librarians do not see themselves as teachers (despite the irony of seeing most YAs as students), they have an assumption built into their service for everyone not deemed to be a "child" that users can help themselves. I call this the unspoken self-help assumption of LIS practice. Children need help, but everyone else gets it only if they ask for it.

This assumption can add to the perception of young adults as "broken" because YAs can easily flounder in such an atmosphere, if in fact they are in the library for any library-ordained uses. They may need help but not know it, or they may not know how to ask for it, or they do not want to ask for it. Furthermore, if they are there only to socialize with friends, do homework together, or wait for transportation, their needs collide with structural expectations and they are seen as an irritant, even though, as I have argued elsewhere, YAs are only problems that libraries have created themselves, for themselves (Chelton 2002). Reconciling YAs' needs for assistance with libraries' structural assumptions is a formidable task.

GROUP PROGRAMMING

One way in which public libraries have straddled the divide between structure and individuals is through group programming, of which YA services generally should be proud. Quality YA programs take advantage of real YA interests and talents and offer opportunities for participation, a social means for dispensing information, plus intergenerational interaction. Every issue of *VOYA* (*Voice of Youth Advocates*) offers examples of this in practice.

Although books and reading and reading advising were the heart of Edwards's vision for YA services, it is important to remember that she saw these activities as a means toward a highly communitarian end. As repeated in the celebration of the one hundredth anniversary of Edwards's birth,

> [L]ibrarians working with teenagers aim to introduce books to young people which will help them to live with themselves as citizens of a democracy and to be at home in the

world. Our goals are a progression from self-realization to responsible American citizenship to belief in the brotherhood of all men. . . . What really mattered . . . was not "appreciation of literary style" but "the understanding of man, of yourself and your relation to all men." (Lapides 2002)

Edwards's service philosophy was codified in a manual for YA librarians used by the Enoch Pratt Library, which I was unable to locate despite intervention and corroboration from Deborah Taylor there, but my memory of it is as clear today as it was then. YA services existed to help young adults feel at home with themselves, their families, their peers, their communities, and the world. This was easily visualized as a series of expanding concentric circles with the individual YA in the center and the largest outside circle representing the world and encompassing all the others.

POSITIVE YOUTH DEVELOPMENT

Edwards's vision for YA services is the one that I internalized early in my career, and it is also one of the reasons that subsequent external influences, those from youth development in particular, so derided by Bernier (2013) in the previous edition of *Transforming Young Adult Services*, never bothered me very much. I never viewed the research on positive youth development so much as a theory, but rather as a service outcome that helped practitioners set service objectives and explain to others what they were trying to do. It arrived on the scene around the time that government programs were trying to evaluate themselves to show that they were accomplishing something.

The National 4-H Council did a longitudinal study of their programs with Tufts University, for example, that found that 4-H'ers were four times more likely to make contributions to their communities; two times more likely to be civically active, and so on (Lerner et al. 2013). In 1990, the Search Institute published research that identified a set of skills, experiences, relationships, and behaviors that enable young people to develop into successful and contributing adults (Scales and Leffert 1999). The idea was that the more of these developmental assets young people acquired, the more likely they would succeed in school and become healthy, happy, and contributing members of their communities. Patrick Jones took the asset framework and used the developmental assets in presentations, followed by an article titled "Why We Are Kids' Best Assets: The Role of Librarians in Youth Development" (Jones 2001), and he also included them in a YALSA publication, *New Directions for Library Service to Young Adults* (Jones 2002). Given his reputation, YALSA's imprimatur, the eternal quest of YA services to explain and justify itself, and reinforcement from the field of youth work outside libraries, it is obvious in retrospect why we probably got fixated on the developmental assets framework, to the exclusion of other relevant ideas and theories.

BORROWED THEORIES

The initial editorial that Dorothy Broderick wrote for *VOYA* suggested the usefulness of such influences:

> Our primary goal in producing *Voice of Youth Advocates* is to demonstrate that library service to young adults in schools, public libraries and institutions has a valid theo-

retical basis. The theory does not come from librarianship, but from disciplines with strong components devoted to the study of adolescence and containing highly qualified personnel whose life work is the study of adolescents. (Broderick 2013, 37)

This did not mean, however, that I was devoid of my own theory of practice, but rather that I saw young adults as social beings who could use library services to understand themselves, those who came before them, and those around them. "Borrowed theories" from other fields helped me understand young adult behavior in a library setting as well as when that setting was not congruent with their needs, and I tried to apply insights from these borrowed theories to my own practice. Obviously, libraries are not psychologists' offices, but behaviors described in developmental psychology play out in front of us in library settings every day. It also helped that I was a well-grounded, Edwards-trained YA librarian, so external theories were add-ons, not gap-fillers.

There are problems with borrowed theories of which to be aware. Such theories can contradict each other, but librarians may not know enough about the other fields to understand when this happens. The other problem is a tendency for all theories to assume some sort of "normalization" which results in an overgeneralization to all YAs that is neither accurate nor appropriate. Carol Kuhlthau's (2004) information search process theory is an example of such overgeneralization because, despite any intuitive elegance it may seem to have and despite its popularity, the sample on which it is based cannot be stretched beyond academic white YAs, despite all attempts since she first published it to ignore this fact.

Because of my exposure to research on risk factors for adolescent suicide, I began to understand how libraries had unwittingly created environments designed for sick kids—no friends, no noise, and so on. This was before Bernier's work on YA spaces, which has tried to put an end to that deficient model in many libraries (Bernier, Males, and Rickman 2014).

Michael Lipsky's (1976, 1980) theory of street-level bureaucracy (SLB) has helped me understand a variation of the "broken" YA syndrome as a form of self-serving "client definition" libraries (and other SLBs) use, not only to limit role expectations for certain client segments, but also to absolve themselves from responsibility and ascribe "worth" and otherness to those client segments. This attitude of young adults as "problems" is perfectly summarized in the following e-mail post in which the librarian describes a mythical client instead of the ones in front of her:

> I'll be happy to tell you why I find this age group "problematic." So many come to the reference desk with no idea of why they are there. They shove a sheet of paper in my face and say "This is my homework. Where can I find this?" When I ask them what the assignment is, they appear to be looking at it for the very first time. Or they simply mumble "I don't know." It's the total lack of concern and the assumption that I'll figure it all out for them and go fetch the materials that irritates me. (Chelton 1997, 193)

I met Joan Lipsitz, the founder of the Center for Early Adolescence at the University of North Carolina, and became familiar with her research review on the variability and velocity of all the developmental changes in early adolescence, as well as her refrain that most kids grow up healthy in spite of us. Only a small percentage are troubled or "at risk." The center's multidisciplinary work can be explained as an attempt to enlighten adults in many professions about ways we might facilitate teens' maturing without lumping them all together or getting in their way. Lipsitz (1979) also regularly made the point that many important life decisions with serious and often irrevocable consequences, such as becoming sexually active or girls deciding to drop math classes, are made in early adolescence, and that adult influences on such decisions might be beneficial.

I also find Gisela Konopka's (1973) "Requirements for the Healthy Development of Adolescent Youth" still relevant to YA services, in particular, her statement that

> we do not see adolescence purely as preparation for adulthood. Rather we see it as one part of the total developmental process—a period of tremendous significance distinguished by specific characteristics. Basic to our view is the concept that adolescents are growing, developing persons in a particular age group—not pre-adults, pre-parents, or pre-workers, but human beings participating in the activities of the world around them. In brief, we see adolescence not only as a passage to somewhere but also as an important stage in itself. (7-8)

Her proposed conditions for healthy development, which sound remarkably like Margaret Edwards's vision for YA services, were to provide young people with these opportunities:

- To participate as citizens, as members of a household, as workers, as responsible members of society
- To gain experience in decision making
- To interact with peers and acquire a sense of belonging
- To reflect on self in relation to others and to discover self by looking outward as well as inward
- To discuss conflicting values and formulate their own value system
- To experiment with their own identities, with relationships to other people; with ideas, to try out various roles without having to commit themselves irrevocably
- To develop a feeling of accountability in the context of a relationship among equals
- To cultivate a capacity to enjoy life (Konopka 1973)

If librarians are not working consciously to help provide such opportunities for YAs, I think they are a pretty miserable excuse for librarians in terms of this clientele, even if struggling within inhospitable or indifferent library structures.

SERVICE PROVIDERS

Another factor in a theory of practice is the human capital involved—the translators between structure and individual. This brings us up against the professional conflicts about where and by whom young adults should be served: specialist versus generalist, children's versus adult versus young adult department, or, in some places, school or public library. There are also conflicts about who should be educating these practitioners about what, with no standardization (even if that should be desirable) anywhere.

Even if the LIS field could agree on desirable personality characteristics for librarians serving YAs, the ideal service provider would then come up against structure, with the resulting conflict threatening to destroy any coherent theory of practice. *Connecting Young Adults and Libraries* has some great examples of this problem (Jones 1998, 26-29), and as a personal example, one of my Rutgers PhD classmates, who had been a superb YA librarian, left the library field because her success with YAs made her so suspect in her public library that she was too uncomfortable to stay there.

WHAT NOW?

Having suggested that a theory of YAs cannot easily be divorced from a theory of practice that also accounts for library structures and the human capital straddling both, I think we need a return to the Edwards and Konopka visions of YAs as self-aware and committed members of interdependent communities.

In 1992, I was asked to contribute to an ALA publication called *Your Right to Know: Librarians Make It Happen*, and in addition to knowing that one is valued, how to communicate, how to learn, how to work, how to make choices, how to protect oneself, and how to be a moral person, I included "How to be part of a community." This assumes that knowledge of community was something that could be learned and that libraries could help in the process. It also assumes that for young adults, being part of a community is important. I did not realize that I was channeling Margaret Edwards again, but I was. I think her vision is as valid today as it was when she first stated it.

Another reason to revisit and reiterate Edwards's vision is because identity, which many feel is the primary work of adolescence, we now know to be "constituted interactively within ordinary contexts through communication" (Mokros 2002). In other words, identity is both a gift and a product of social interaction. It is impossible to know who one is in isolation, so it can be argued that helping young adults become members of communities also helps them form coherent identities.

Envisioning young adults as self-aware members of communities involves understanding oneself in relation to others, whether they are family, friends, enemies, other age groups, or coworkers. Being part of a community demands knowledge of and respect for human interdependence, reciprocity, culture, history, values, and differences. Knowing how to make friends and resolve conflicts is important, as is the knowledge that the rights and privileges granted by community membership demand particular responsibilities. Understanding how to take, counter, defend, and gain support for a political position is also part of being engaged in a democratic community.

The knowledge and skills outlined in this chapter offer a rich conceptual background against which YA librarians can interact with YAs and offer collections and services to them within the library context. I am not sure we need new visions of young adults when we already have perfectly good ones.

REFERENCES

AASL (American Association of School Librarians). 2018. "Common Beliefs 4." In *AASL Standards Framework for Learners*. Chicago: American Library Association. https://standards.aasl.org/framework.

Bernier, A. 2007. "Not Broken by Someone Else's Schedule: On Joy and Young Adult Information Seeking." In *Youth Information-Seeking Behavior: Theories, Models, and Issues*, edited by M. K. Chelton and C. Cool, xiii-xxvii. Lanham, MD: Scarecrow Press.

_____. 2013. "Historical Contexts and Consequences of the LIS Youth Consensus." In *Transforming Young Adult Services*, edited by A. Bernier, 207-38. Chicago: ALA Neal-Schuman.

Bernier, A., M. Males, and C. Rickman. 2014. "'It Is Silly to Hide Your Most Active Patrons': Exploring User Participation of Library Space Designs for Young Adults in the United States." *Library Quarterly* 84, no. 2: 165-82.

Bourdieu, P. 1972. *Outline of a Theory of Practice*. Translated by R. Nice. Cambridge, UK: Cambridge University Press.

Broderick, D. M. 2013. *The Collected Wit and Wisdom of Dorothy M. Broderick: The VOYA Editorials and More*. Edited by A. Bernier. Lanham, MD: Scarecrow Press.

Chelton, M. K. 1992. "What Should Youth Know? Some Observations." In *Whole Library Handbook: Current Data, Professional Advice, and Curiosa about Libraries and Library Services*, edited by G. M. Eberhart, 248-50. Chicago: American Library Association.

———. 1997. "Adult-Adolescent Service Encounters: The Library Context." Unpublished doctoral dissertation, Rutgers University, New Brunswick, NJ.

———. 2002. "The Problem Patron Public Libraries Created." *The Reference Librarian* 36, no. 75/76: 4-11.

Crowley, W. 2005. *Spanning the Theory-Practice Divide in Library and Information Science*. Lanham, MD: Scarecrow Press.

———. 2007. "Don't Let Google and the Pennypinchers Get You Down: Defending (or Redefining) Libraries and Librarianship in the Age of Technology." Presentation at British Columbia Library Association Conference, Beyond 20/20: Envisioning the Future, Burnaby, BC, Canada, April 19-21.

Daugherty, R. M. 1991. "The Opportunity to Empower: ALA, Children, and Reading." *American Libraries* 22, no 2: 176-79.

Jones, P. 1998. *Connecting Young Adults and Libraries: A How-To-Do-It Manual*. 2nd ed. New York: Neal-Schuman.

———. 2001. "Why We Are Kids' Best Assets." *School Library Journal* 47, no. 11: 44-47.

———. 2002. *New Directions for Library Service to Young Adults*. Chicago: YALSA/ALA.

Konopka, G. 1973. "Requirements for Healthy Development of Adolescent Youth." *Adolescence* 8, no. 3: 1-26.

Kuhlthau, C. 2004. *Seeking Meaning: A Process Approach to Library and Information Services*. 2nd ed. Santa Barbara, CA: Libraries Unlimited.

Lapides, L. F. 2002. "Margaret Alexander Edwards, 1902-1988." In "Celebrating the Centennial of Margaret Alexander Edwards' Birth," special section of *Journal of Youth Services in Libraries* 15 (Summer): 45-49.

Lerner, R. M., J. V. Lerner, and Colleagues. 2013. *The Positive Development of Youth: Comprehensive Findings from the 4-H Study of Positive Youth Development*. Boston: Institute for Applied Research in Youth Development, Tufts University.

Lipsitz, J. S. 1979. "Adolescent Development: Myths and Realities." *Children Today* 8, no. 5: 2-7.

Lipsky, M. 1976. "Toward a Theory of Street-Level Bureaucracy." In *Theoretical Perspectives on Urban Politics*, edited by W. D. Hawley, 196-213. Englewood Cliffs, NJ: Prentice-Hall.

———. 1980. *Street-Level Bureaucracy: Dilemmas of the Individual in Public Services*. New York: Russell Sage Foundation.

Mokros, H. B. 2002. *Identity Matters: Communication-Based Explorations and Explanations*. New York: Hampton Press.

Scales, P. C., and N. Leffert. 1999. *Developmental Assets: A Synthesis of the Scientific Research on Adolescent Development*. Minneapolis, MN: Search Institute.

PART V

From Citizenship to Membership

CHAPTER 12

Tribalism versus Citizenship

Are Youth Increasingly Unwelcome in Libraries?

Mike Males

> Young adult spaces, which are populated by racially and ethnically diverse youth, challenge the assumption that libraries can accommodate only traditionally narrow "tribal" uses. This chapter addresses the question of whether these generational divisions between young adults and elder society members are so irreconcilable that libraries must physically separate young people from older patrons, perhaps to the point of restricting or banning youth from library spaces. In addition, this chapter explores how the fear-based movement in the larger society creates barriers between older Americans and young people and complicates notions of library citizenship.

Startling demographic and technological changes have combined to shake traditional views of libraries as passive cellulose (i.e., book and printed material) repositories occupied by patrons whose shared citizenship valued quiet studiousness, the ordered partitioning of specialties, and segregation of child from adult. As will be discussed in detail, libraries are a microcosm of larger society's increasing refusal to reconcile elders, still viewing society through their tribal lens, with emerging, multicultural youth adept in global technology. Segregative movements, wielding threats to defund libraries along with other publicly shared institutions, are likely to become more intense as age demographics continue to diverge. One counterforce—modern young adult (YA) library spaces populated by more racially and ethnically diverse youth populations and equipped with activist, integrated technologies—challenges these segregative forces and assumptions that libraries can enforce such traditionally narrow "tribal" uses, ironically, by segregating youth from adults!

Are generational divisions so irreconcilable that libraries must physically separate young people from older patrons, perhaps to the point of restricting or banning youth from adult library spaces or libraries themselves? The fear-based movement in larger society to create barriers between older American "citizens" and younger "invaders" complicates notions of library citizenship as well. While I advance the argument that in an era of rapid change, young people now make better citizens than older adults, my larger thesis is that the theoretical underpinning of library policy should recognize that the general features of old and young are not oppositional, but symbiotic; that is, libraries are in a unique position to boldly lead the way to redefine youth as genuine citizens.

GENERATIONAL DECORUM

The legacy of my dozen years of working with youth in community and wilderness programs is that I have scores of photos of teenagers. There are pictures of teens sitting around campfires, celebrating work project completions, watching rangers' evening talks, wrapped in sleeping bags on the porch of a remote cabin, perched on high mountain ledges, standing in lines, saying hello, saying goodbye. Where there are teens in groups, their most striking feature is their physicality. They tend—not universally but as a general rule—to cram closer together than adults do even in the most routine circumstances.

Teenagers' physicality bothers many grown-ups, who confuse it with sexuality. This has led to infamous "two feet apart" and "anti-PDA" (public displays of affection) rules mandating corporeal distance. In libraries, the rule emerges in so many words as "one butt to a chair." One library banned patrons, clearly meaning young ones, from "grooming each other" (Kelly 2007).

One could ask how the mere fact of chair-sharing—which has practical utility when, say, maximizing eyes on a computer screen during busy hours—or brushing someone else's hair thwarts any important library goal. But such behaviors clearly offend many elders' sense of what is "appropriate" in shared library culture. Few libraries have gone to the extremes of Maplewood, New Jersey's, which simply closed its doors during after-school hours until the mostly black, allegedly rowdy middle-schoolers had dispersed (an edict later reversed after negative publicity) (Kelly 2007). While libraries may not originally have intended to use separate teen/young adult spaces to address generational decorum rifts, the soberly considered placement of a YA space today would be away from the sight lines of aging patrons.

Why are such dramatic generational rifts occurring at this time? Step back and consider America's gathering "demographic revolution." The concern that age segregation is a sign of more serious demographic fear is an extension of Margaret Mead's (1970) conclusion in *Culture and Commitment* (and, less starkly, Alvin Toffler's popular *Future Shock*) 40 years ago: adults, bound to tradition, cannot handle the jolting pace of modern racial and technological change and become irrationally alienated from younger generations they see as embodying an unwanted present and future. "In this new culture it will be the child—and not the parent and grandparent—that represents what is to come. . . . The alienation of the young is emphasized, while the alienation of their elders may be entirely overlooked" (Mead 1970, 62, 68).

While Mead (1970) argued the modern, post-1960 "generation gap" was "deep, new, unprecedented" (63), few seem to appreciate just how this simple-sounding idea foretold an accelerating evolutionary shift. Prior to the modern era, elders held power by virtue of harboring the knowledge and skills necessary to the survival of their tribe, and elder and younger generations were tied by the common kinship, race, customs, and traditions derived from homogeneity and assurance that the future would be much like the present and past. But in diversifying, fast-changing modern societies, the grown-ups "do not know how to teach these children who are so different from what they themselves once were, and the children are unable to learn from parents and elders they will never resemble" (Mead 1970, 66).

Today's generation gap, whose ominous implications are just now being perceived in mainstream discussion, has a stark fault line. The 2010 census details the demographic revolution. Among children, youth, and young adults ages 19 and younger, 47 percent are nonwhite: Hispanic, African-American, Asian-American, or Native American, or of other or mixed race. By the 2020 census, American youth will have no racial majority. Among adults ages 50 and older, just 25 percent are of color. Compare this to the 1950 census, when approximately 85 percent of youth and over 90 percent of elders were white of European origin; that is, the kids looked like the parents (U.S. Bureau of the Census 2011).

The United States is rapidly becoming an all-minority country, with the arrival of a nonwhite majority predicted by the 2030s (U.S. Bureau of the Census 2017). Most cities have already undergone the transition, and states herald the multicultural future. In 2010, Texas, Florida, Arizona, Nevada, Georgia, and Mississippi joined California, New Mexico, and Hawaii with all-minority youth populations. New York, Illinois, Delaware, Oklahoma, Colorado, Louisiana, North Carolina, and South Carolina will soon follow suit, and then a dozen other states.

This hypothalamus-rattling demographic revolution has occurred in the space, not of centuries, but within a single individual's life span—indeed, dramatic changes have and will continue to take place during the professional lives of most librarians today. The color wave is rising from young ages upward. The trend is setting off evolutionary alarm bells, and the reaction against it—though coded—has been virulent. Efforts to restrict immigrants, reverse advancements in minority rights, and banish young people from private and public spaces have burgeoned as nativist movements led by the Tea Party, heavily comprised of aging whites, gain influence. Generational conflicts, coextant with racial and ethnic rifts, were most evident in states like Arizona, Florida, and California, where unusually large aging white populations confront unusually large minority youth populations. Libraries situated at the intersections of inner cities and old-wealth districts, in increasingly minority older suburbs and newly gentrifying neighborhoods, and in rural communities where employers have brought in Hispanic and other migrant laborers—in short, everywhere where races are in flux—are likely to face pressures to shield older patrons from younger ones of varying colors, speaking unknown languages, and presenting the visible menace of difference.

One largely noncontroversial result—in that it has proven popular among both conservative and liberal officials—has been a sweeping movement to banish young people from public spaces, especially where older folks gather. Our studies at the Center on Juvenile and Criminal Justice and research reviews of juvenile curfews find they are not effective at their ostensible goals of enhancing crime control or public safety (Males and Macallair 1998). Curfew advocates, however, do not seem to care about research findings. Rather, they gain momentum in gentrifying areas such as Minneapolis's Mall of America, Oklahoma City's Bricktown, Pasadena's Old Town, and suburbs gaining minority populations, where black and brown youth are alarmingly visible in districts attempting to attract and maintain older, mostly white clientele.

Along with efforts to get darker youth out of sight, traditional measures to separate white youth from base underclass influences are being pushed with renewed vigor. As an information-dispersing and globally socializing force, the Internet is seen as a major threat to preservation of distinct, elder-controlled tribal cultures. Thus, the Internet is now being depicted in a cascade of identical press articles and interest-group forums as the font of dangerously ungoverned youth interaction and, therefore, atrocities. Libraries, as nodes of Internet technology as well as information-dispensing institutions in their own right, are subject to similar suspicions and retribalizing efforts.

Is, then, age segregation by means of youth spaces—a permutation of the sequester-youth impetus of larger American society reflected in juvenile curfews, mall and store banishments, separated venues founded in alcohol, pornography, or other "adults only" settings—the direction libraries ultimately want to go? My Youth in Transition class at the University of California-Santa Cruz, addressed that question to library youth-space specialist and Los Angeles Public Libraries Teen'Scape designer Anthony Bernier (see Bernier 2011; Bernier et al. 2005). His response was framed as a question of practicality: How can services to youth be maintained and expanded in the face of the growing desire on the part of elders to avoid young people? If forcing generations to occupy the same space results in conflicts leading to severe restrictions or even banishment of young people from libraries, how can libraries continue to serve youthful populations—at least for now, during the difficult transition from tribal to multiracial society—other than by benign, temporary age apartheid?

While to some extent youth spaces fulfill traditional library goals of organizing special collections and service areas around the interests of distinct populations, is their main function to get young people, with their generally darker skins and allegedly freer verbal and physical expressions, away from the gaze of nervous elders? If so, their proliferation raises troubling questions.

UNRULY TRENDS

In formulating my idealism for libraries to boldly lead the way to redefine youth as full-fledged citizens rather than an object demographic whose status is defined by the metric of fear and disdain adult constituencies feel toward them, I had expected to make a standard pitch. To begin, I would concede: Look, we have learned too slowly and painfully to put aside what sociologist William Julius Wilson (1997) calls "statistical bigotry" and to admit to more or less full equality minority races, multiplying varieties of gender, and even statuses based on lifestyle. That is, because an African-American 40-year-old has a gun-homicide rate nine times higher than a corresponding white does not mean we should penalize 999 out of 1,000 middle-aged black men who will not be involved in gun murder for the one who is. Of course, Wilson should have said "selective statistical bigotry"; if the index were drug abuse instead of homicide, older white men might be saddled with the sundown curfew.

I had expected to continue by pointing out that the case for segregating adolescents and young adults from adults under a system of unique restrictions relies largely on statistical claims, along with "developmental" and "cognitive" (more crudely, "teen brain") arguments assembled to provide biological explanations for the statistics, of the type that would be rejected as prejudicial if applied to adult populations. Thus, the argument I expected to make was that even if teenagers as a class are statistically "worse" than adults, this would no more justify mass age-based partition than the even larger statistical differences between males and females, or between races, would justify gender or racial bigotries. Such a "civil rights for teens" case would carry the validity of banality, since no one to my knowledge argues for restricting men, older whites, or Mississippians because their group statistics tend to be alarming.

But it turns out that the actual argument against teen apartheid is stronger and stranger. First, the statistical and developmental arguments advanced to justify special restrictions and banishments of young people were dubious to begin with; resurrected psychobabble about teens' supposedly innate volatility, criminality, impulsiveness, and egocentrism disappears once the elementary stratum of socioeconomics is considered. Put a 40-year-old in the higher poverty brackets typically suffered by adolescents, and suddenly the middle-ager generates serious statistics regarding traffic crashes, guns, and alienation of the magnitude we typically blame on angsty kids (Males 2010a). In fact, boomers are showing some dismaying behavior problems even though we are the richest demographic ever. Perhaps libraries should establish special boomer spaces stocked with that 1970 Sonny-Bono-on-Quaaludes video and rehab-retirement posters.

To add insulting trend to injurious behavior, recent decades have brought distinct improvements in a wide variety of youth behaviors as the youth population has become more racially diverse and technologically interconnected—even as behaviors among much less diverse middle-aged and older adults have deteriorated alarmingly. Perhaps the most startling relevant statistic is that the FBI (2019) *Uniform Crime Reports* shows more adults in their forties are arrested for murder, rape, felony assault, drunken offenses, and all crimes than all juveniles under age 18, a truly shocking development given the distinct economic advantages midlife adults enjoy compared to youth. This renders statistical arguments that youth must be isolated and custodialized as a uniquely unpredictable, dangerous, "crime prone" population invalid on their face.

Marrying standards of basic equality to the force of modern trends, then, the argument for making young people full citizens is stronger than ever. But the argument for calling young people forth into citizenship and leadership roles is, to my mind, the most compelling of all when we consider what that actually might mean.

ARE AGE- AND GENERATION-BASED QUALITIES IRRELEVANT?

Pin down the two general, interrelated features of young people that are typically seen as negative: *inexperience* with complex tasks due simply to having lived fewer years and *inefficient thinking* due to the proliferation of wide-open neural pathways in developing brains. In some situations, these are disadvantages. There are not many 16-year-old National Football League (NFL) quarterbacks or high-specialty surgeons; in traditional societies, being old and versed in the traditional skills confers great power. But the trade-off, well discussed by social scientist Howard Sercombe (2010) and neuroscientist Tomas Paus, is that aging brains' rigidifying neural pathways result in narrower efficiencies at the expense of flexibility, openness to learning, and meeting new challenges.

As Mead (1970) pointed out more than 40 years ago, young people enjoy major advantages in a rapidly changing society. They grow up with the latest culture and technologies and do not tend to view change with the reflexive trepidation of their elders. Today's younger people also are more comfortable with diversity, displaying more racially integrated dating and friendship patterns and levels of tolerance appropriate to emerging multicultures. Youthful attitudes on immigration, gay rights, interracial marriage, religious tolerance, and the need for shared social investments are far more progressive than those found among the over-30 ages, as we have documented from analysis of numerous surveys (YouthFacts.org 2010).

It is not just that elders are succumbing to more reactionary attitudes, including majority support for far-right-wing candidates who openly seek to dismantle shared public investment and concentrate wealth in older and richer cohorts, even to the point of threatening gunplay and secession. We are seeing massive deteriorations in the *personal behaviors* of older Americans, led by explosions in drug abuse, criminal arrest, imprisonment, and family disarray. Mead (1970) warned that the "alienation of the old" from their society, manifest in both attitudes and behaviors, would become more of a crisis than that of the young, and the rise of the modern Tea Party and reactionary politics driven heavily by over-45 white constituencies seem powerful evidence for concern.

The result, perhaps the temporary product of a wrenching transition from traditional, homogeneous population groups (tribes) to a global multiculture in which America harbors major representation from all five inhabited continents, means that young people now make better citizens than do older people. That is, on balance, I suspect that the young today possess more skills necessary to the continuity of our society as it evolves into a worldly polyglot than do the old. This is unprecedented.

I do not propose a public campaign headlining this point, especially if a library's ultimate goal, like mine, is a more integrated approach and the organization of services around the most appropriate categories rather than around those dictated by fear and prejudice. To the extent that youth spaces are the products of ephebiphobia (the irrational fear of adolescents) rather than ideal allocation of library space, they need to be reexamined in terms of their integrative rather than segregative potential. This potential can be segregative in that as youth become more unwelcome in "adult" zones, the adult who uses a children's or YA space is likely to come under suspicion under the growing paranoia over pedophilia. An example of this dualized fear occurred in the San José, California, system when a citizen's group complained that children who ventured into adult library areas were glimpsing "secondhand porn" on computer screens (Bernier 2011; KCBS 2007)—a panic that symbolized the larger fear of young people having uncontrolled access to information as the result of their presence in "adult" spaces and the corresponding access of adult pedophiles to children.

YA spaces are also justified on the professional grounds that adolescence, being a distinct and bounded time of life, has its own informational culture. There is a category dubbed YA literature, magazines that serve younger teens and grade-schoolers, and singular entry-level job, college preparatory, and other materials in which older adults presumably would have little interest. Seemingly, few adults would buy Miley Cyrus CDs or peruse *Tiger Beat* (and those who did would generate watchful anxiety). There may be some intersections of interest; for example, in today's market, adults are going back to school and exploring entry-level jobs in tandem with youth.

No, indeed, integrative pressures are not emanating from the oldsters. The big problem is seen as teen and tween precocity. While teens may form a distinct informational demographic, they also spill into adult library realms by consuming "adult" literature, visuals, research holdings, and other references too vast and varied to be maintained in a YA space. In fact, the teen "invasion" of adult territories is occurring across a wide spectrum of society, from having sex, drinking alcohol, and choosing independent lifestyles to checking out R-rated movies, steamy novels, racy magazines, and who knows what Internet sites.

Teenage incursions into adult spaces are generating society's greatest panics over "kids growing up too fast," followed by the harshest repressions. Yet, again, panic and repression are unrelated to the best measures of how teens are handling themselves as the invading force, which show young people are safer, healthier, and expressing better attitudes than ever before. This conclusion is based on our analysis of a wealth of long-term statistics on such topics as crime, violence, violent mortality, unwanted sexual outcomes, school performance and graduation, surveyed attitudes and behaviors, and other standard indexes, nearly all of which indicate most teenage "badness" is at or near all-time lows (Males 2006). Emotional efforts to suppress teenage precocity and repel their invasion of adult life—typically founded on salacious anecdotes and panicky quips rather than on sober evidence—seem related more to the difficulties of a graying generation in a culture of change than to manifest youth troubles.

Are YA spaces functioning as cog in a systemic effort to maintain the juvenilization of adolescents then? At this juncture, several conclusions can be reached. Libraries' inadvertent contribution to the latest phase in a century-long effort to create a segregated teenage stage—ironically, one that contributed to the cementing of the very "youth culture" adults would fear as much as the prospect of teens lurking on the street corners of adult culture

(Kett 1977; Hine 1999)—includes primitive efforts to separate adolescent from adult access to information via Internet filters, age-based restrictions on materials checkout, and more censorious policies on which items can appear in YA spaces rather than on adult shelves.

I do not mean to imply that the YA space functions as some kind of holding tank, only that it represents libraries' own version of resolving the tribal demand for generational separation. The ecology of the teen/YA space has recognized adults as the dominant species, allocated grown-ups the fullest library range in which to forage and graze on their interests as individual citizens. The child and adolescent niche species are given smaller, separate reserves with narrower ranges of materials on the assumption that their appetites are more uniform and circumscribed. Of course, few if any libraries actually fence the young out of adult spaces, though there have been some rumblings in that direction that are likely to grow louder as the demographic chasm between teen and grown-up becomes more pronounced over the next 25 years before receding. Left to themselves, the emotional "incident," the calls to "protect children" from adult materials, the intervention of herd journalism (which reflexively champions every new restriction on teens), and notions of "cognitive development" that insist adolescents generically are incompatible with adults will continue to dominate. Assumptions (using curfews as a model) that the mere discomfort and fear of older patrons (the dominant species) toward the presence of young people (the unwanted vectors) justifies the latter's banishment are likely to be cited in favor of formal enforcement of age barriers within libraries. That libraries may not enforce the age divide as strictly as other institutions does not negate the utility of YA spaces and youth-specific polices in maintaining adolescent apartheid.

More practically, then, I would suggest that the theoretical underpinning of library policy recognize that the general strengths of old and young are not oppositional, but symbiotic, and that individuality, not demographic determinism, remains the salient characteristic of individuals of all ages. The biggest revolutionary advance is not just to treat teenagers as individuals—my impression in this regard is that libraries already are more advanced than, say, schools, police, the media, and mental health interests (damnation by faint praise, perhaps)—but actually to *see* teens as individuals. That is, if a 50-year-old drunk man sprawls in the restroom, we do not crusade to lock the doors against citizen middle-agers or citizen males; we see him as a singular miscreant unreflective of his larger demographic. But it remains a venture into uncharted tolerance for us to accord a citizen 15-year-old the same reflexive respect.

But does this mean teens are comfortable with adults in "their" space? Here we have to rely on the always unreliable anecdote and its connection to survey findings. On the one hand, *Monitoring the Future* (Bachman, Johnston, and O'Malley 2011) finds, over its 35-year history, that fewer teens are spending or feel the need to spend more time with adults 30 and older. It is not that teens hold negative stereotypes about grown-ups the same way as grown-ups hold about the young; when asked, as in Public Agenda polls, large majorities of youth seem to see adults as individuals, most good, some bad. Is, then, the fact that modern teens spend more time around peers and less with adults the result of a natural separation, a reactive one, or an artifact introduced by segregative policies?

WHAT WOULD "YA SPACE" MEAN?

What, then, might libraries look like if more survey-indicated youth values were incorporated, and would these values necessarily be incompatible with age integration? As noted, age and race are conflated, so that simplistic bigotry against youth is often framed in the same terminologies and remedies as those based on race. However, it still remains hard to reconcile patrons who like quiet and order with those who favor noisier, more-butts-to-a-chair library usage. Thus, one could imagine libraries more practically organized around styles of usage—contemplative versus collaborative, for example—rather than age alone.

Or it may turn out that libraries will continue to find YA spaces the most efficient service mode because general differences between teen and young adult patrons compared to older adults remain the most important organizing factor. An excellent ethnography by Herb Childress (2000) contains a systematic critique by young people of the human ecology of their small town. Childress found young people favored gathering areas that promoted centripetal values—that is, ones whose design features

- created a centralizing public focus;
- afforded easy views of comings and goings;
- were not internally divided or separated from other areas by barriers, hard angles, wide corridors, or broad open areas;
- created a sense of density, comfort, and motion with people present at all hours;
- contained both a "centerpiece" to concentrate users for unifying functions and multiple points to "stop and lean" to facilitate mingling;
- included natural elements (presumably plants, or even access to outdoor flora) that were clearly distinct from man-made areas; and
- incorporated diverse uses within easily walkable distances and accessibility to wide varieties of users.

It is hard to imagine a design that looks less like a typical suburban community, where sprawl, decentralization, strip malls, heavily trafficked roadways dividing districts, sparsely populated areas, car dependency, restrictive covenants, privatized rather than public gathering points, and zoned single-use functions predominate, than the one its teenagers wanted. With a stretch of imagination, one can correlate the public spaces teenagers advocate with their political attitudes favoring diverse nodes within larger community, tolerance, and shared public investment (see Bachman, Johnston, and O'Malley 2011).

HARNESSING SYNERGY

Are these values libraries can build on? In suggesting the leadership of libraries in inaugurating young people as citizens, I argue for three basic premises.

First, I believe from empirical evidence that the global demographics, attitudes, behaviors, skills, and "vision" (if so pompous a generality can be used) of America's young people today generally constitute a far more promising foundation for building the emerging multicultural society than the fearful, tribal anachronisms of the old. These general views and wide varieties of thought exist among all ages. Today's situation did not apply in static, traditional cultures in which the accumulated wisdom of the old was crucial to the survival and continuity of cultures. But in today's rapidly changing and diversifying societies, the recency and flexibility of youth provide a leadership edge.

As young people got more diverse, their attitudes and conduct improved, even as the best traditional sciences would have predicted deterioration. Synergy—in this case, the evolution of a population in directions more beneficial than would be predicted from the sum of the characteristics and trends of its subpopulations—is a uniquely dynamic development. As American kids got darker, they got better, against all odds. Why? Understanding this youthful synergy would yield a leg up in contemplating and realizing the library of the future.

Second, libraries as inherently progressive institutions—that is, as democratizing through the promotion of universal information—are better placed than others to host this generational synergy. This may strike many in the field as dubious or even risible, but consider the alternatives: it is not likely that schools, municipalities, businesses, churches, or government will lead the way to a more age-egalitarian framework, since most at the moment thrive on the fears of an aging society. Universities and university communities are probably the only other, also uncertain, sites of progressive innovation. Even if these institutions did reverse current trends by investing more heavily in younger and future generations, it is likely that this would come with continued age apartheid on the unspoken grounds that darker-skinned teenagers and white elders are not a good mix—along with an unspoken "duh!"

Yet, because youth have decisive potential to facilitate the transition to a more global, variegated culture, I would contend that maintaining age separation is a devastating mistake. Generational integration is not just desirable but also vital. If you think I am idealistic, listen to Mead's (1970) exuberance: "We can change into a prefigurative [youth defined] culture, consciously, delightedly, and industriously rearing unknown children for an unknown world" in which "the young, free to act on their own initiative, can lead their elders in the direction of . . . a viable future" (73, 75).

Third, given the invasion of teens into adult realms of information, popular culture, and cybersocializing to the point that many of these are becoming youth dominated—and evidence of some oldsters taking a shine to certain aspects of youth cultures—the potential of information-disseminating institutions such as libraries to naturalize interactions between old, middle, and young is an easier task than it would be, say, in the church or the Supreme Court. Young people do not have to be forced into the adult world; they are already there. All that is necessary is to stop trying to force them out of it.

To that end, I would suggest some initial steps for those interested in generational integration, divided into "nonnegative" and "positive." In the nonnegative category, libraries' programming and publicity should consciously treat youth the same as adult groups. An after-school reading program for middle-schoolers should not be advertised as a way to "get kids off the streets" or "prevent after-school crime" any more than a senior citizens' function should be advertised as a way to keep a leash on granny. Demands by the police and schools for library collaboration in arresting youth for curfew violations and truancy or abrogating teens' Internet communications privacy for various law enforcement schemes, such as criminalizing "sexting," should be strenuously resisted. Censorware and restrictive policies should be scaled back so that youth are afforded the same freedom of access to library materials that adults enjoy. Negative generalizations about young people, which often occur after the occasional media-inflamed incident, should be regarded with the same disdain as ones stigmatizing race or gender.

In the positive arena, teens' leadership roles should be expanded past advisory panels and toward active administration, as some libraries now seem to be doing. But the implications of affirming young people as true citizens in library culture challenge traditional assumptions held over from the cellulose-repository era. Teens in general (repeating the caveat that "general" does not mean "universal" or "exclusive") favor a more wide-open, collaborative, technologically fluid, communal, centered, yet busy (in the sense that multiple uses are available in one space) environment. This vision clashes radically with the notion of libraries as enthroning contemplative, individual quiet and order where the inner mind feeds in one's own one-butt chair.

Teen apartheid may be a necessary phase given today's attitudes, but it is not the ideal as a permanent vision. The gossamer of American adulthood—a developmental artifact currently being reified and canonized as the glorious endpoint of human development (indeed, all of evolution) by more sensational "teen brain" and "psychological stage" disciples even as empirical evidence finds it barely distinguishable in practice—does not benefit from continued fortification against the adolescent "invasion." As a graphic example, laws in 43 states allow adults all the way up to geezerhood to have sex legally with 16- and 17-year-olds (presumably those needing lots of money or eye exams); it makes no sense to ban high-schoolers from perusing their own choice of "unnannied" websites.

Still, new technologies and youth-created institutions continue to be depicted as threats even if provable damage remains rare, while traditional institutions such as the family and the church remain "Teflonned" from their sins. The Crimes against Children Research Center's nationwide survey of police agencies found only 25 documented cases of rape, physical violence, abduction, or other harm to youth inflicted by people they met online in 2005 (Wolak, Finkelhor, and Mitchell 2007), a year in which child maltreatment authorities substantiated more than a quarter-million cases of physical and sexual violence against youths within families, nearly all inflicted by parents. More than 5,000 sexual abuses of children by church personnel have been admitted by the Catholic Church alone in recent decades (see Males 2010b). Yet, check incessant evening news and "expert" warnings about the "dangers of the Internet" to young people, combined with only occasional mentions of traditional institutions as representing dangers many magnitudes worse.

So, I readily acknowledge the difficulties. Libraries are subject to outside political forces demanding censorware and age segregation, and even a handful of save-our-children vigilantes can wreak years of administrative misery. These segregative forces armed with the power to defund libraries along with other publicly shared institutions are likely to strengthen as age demographics continue to diverge. In contrast, libraries' provision of YA spaces—that is, expending funds and real estate on young people—already seems insurrectional in a larger America increasingly bent on banishing youth from public and on dismantling teens' private territories, both physical and virtual, seen as promoting unregulated peer interactions (see Bernier 2011; Bernier et al. 2005).

CONCLUSION

Libraries, another microcosm of larger society's failure to reconcile the tribal elders with emerging, multicultural youth, are positioned to lead the way to redefine youth as full-fledged citizens. Should they accept the challenge, their ally is the biggest counterforce to age and generational apartheid: the rising pressure by teens seeking to move into adult society (or, more correctly, to exercise the privileges of adults to choose their society as individuals). The progress in dismantling segregation based on race as minorities gained political power has intensified, not weakened, the pressure to segregate by age, since adolescents as a "temporary minority" are unlikely to accumulate the political power necessary to prevent discrimination. In that light, one particularly stunning manifestation is the surge in the percentage of high school seniors of both sexes telling the annual *Monitoring the Future* survey they want to assume leadership positions in their communities, up from around one in five in 1975 to nearly half today (Bachman, Johnston, and O'Malley 2011).

Teenage leadership motivations—another precocity now being treated as a dire threat to the developmental order and demanding of suppression by isolation of youth and by application of special restrictions—are another force countering today's tribal clamor seeking to thwart generational synergy. Though seldom formulated this way, tribal imperatives seek to head off the dangerous intersection of precocious youth with those geezer gatekeepers who have not gotten the memo and might see merit in youthful initiative. (President Barack Obama was once seen in that light; no longer.) Adults who accord adolescents adult privileges are particularly condemned for endangering young people by facilitating their premature entry into a dangerous grown-up world—like pedophiles do!—though the real, unspoken fear is that adolescents are succeeding there all too well.

Libraries, along with dozens of other major institutions and thousands of minor ones, consistently fail to respond to historical moments such as these. That is understandable, since interpretations of the ongoing history of the present, to borrow a position from social philosopher Michel Foucault, are inevitably trapped within limited perceptions of alternatives dictated from the past. So long as the stroll to the future represented a leisurely plodding up a gentle trail that diverged only gradually and predictably from generation to generation, then the flaws of past-dictated alternatives would be obscured by their comforting familiarity. For a relevant example, one small step from the original Carnegie Library blueprint of bifurcated adult and children's wings has been to pencil in a logical trifurcation, space for the teen/young adult. Libraries effectively endorsed the larger psychological construct that while an adult from ages 20 to 120 is an adult and a child under age 12 or so is a child, a teenager is something yonder.

I suggest that libraries consciously lead in a different direction justified by the advantages the institution enjoys compared to others in society. First, libraries have more experience than most with teen advisory panels that actually advise (and, in some libraries, actively influence resource allocation), a necessary but insufficient step toward generational integration. By providing references and connective technologies needed by low-income youth in particular, libraries are in a position both to be relevant to a wide variety of young people and to expand their institutional power.

Second, libraries fulfill an information dispersion function, an inherently democratizing force. Libraries have (mostly) opposed popular censorship demagoguery such as Congress's Communications Decency Act; censorious ideology is a special case of age-based apartheid. It does not simply involve compartmentalizing adolescents and deterring them from accessing the full range of "adult" information; it also more subtly prevents adolescents from subverting adult library culture with more collaborative, diverse, centripetal styles ("more butts to a chair") amplified by their keener technological savvy. The most subversive threat is not the stereotypical "rebellious teen" against whom grown-ups have marshaled statutes, security, and dismissive "science," but the undeniable manifestation of the reality that youth, indeed, might well make better citizens in a dynamic new era to which grown-ups are refusing to adapt.

REFERENCES

Bachman, J. G., L. D. Johnston, and P. M. O'Malley. 2011. *Monitoring the Future: Questionnaire Responses from the Nation's High School Seniors, 2010.* Ann Arbor, MI: Institute for Social Research, University of Michigan. www.monitoringthefuture.org/datavolumes/2010/2010dv.pdf.

Bernier, A. 2011. "Representations of Youth in Local Media: Implications for Library Service." *Library and Information Science Research* 33: 158–67.

Bernier, A., M. K. Chelton, C. A. Jenkins., and J. B. Pierce. 2005. "Two Hundred Years of Young Adult Library Services: A Chronology." *Voice of Youth Advocates* 28, no. 2: 106–11.

Childress, H. 2000. *Landscapes of Betrayal, Landscapes of Joy: Curtisville in the Lives of Its Teenagers*. Albany: State University of New York Press.

FBI (Federal Bureau of Investigation). 2019. *Uniform Crime Reports*. https://ucr.fbi.gov/crime-in-the-u.s.

Hine, T. 1999. *The Rise and Fall of the American Teenager*. New York: Avon Books.

KCBS. 2007. "Blocking Second-Hand Porn in San José." Radio broadcast, October 20.

Kelly, T. 2007. "Lock the Library! Rowdy Students Are Taking Over." *The New York Times*, January 2, B2.

Kett, J. 1977. *Rites of Passage: Adolescence in America, 1790 to the Present*. New York: Basic Books.

Males, M. 2006. "Youth Policy and Institutional Change." In *Beyond Resistance! Youth Activism and Community Change*, edited by S. Ginwright, P. Noguera, and J. Cammarota, 301–18. New York: Routledge.

———. 2010a. "Is Jumping off the Roof Always a Bad Idea? A Rejoinder on Risk Taking and the Adolescent Brain." *Journal of Adolescent Research* 25, no. 1: 48–63.

———. 2010b. *Teenage Sex and Pregnancy: Modern Myths, Unsexy Realities*. New York: Praeger.

Males, M., and D. Macallair. 1998. "The Impact of Juvenile Curfew Laws in California." San Francisco: Center on Juvenile and Criminal Justice. www.cjcj.org/uploads/cjcj/documents/the_impact.pdf.

Mead, M. 1970. *Culture and Commitment: A Study of the Generation Gap*. Garden City, NY: Natural History Press/Doubleday.

Sercombe, H. 2010. "The Gift and the Trap: Working the 'Teen Brain' into Our Concept of Youth." *Journal of Adolescent Research* 25, no. 1: 31–47.

U.S. Bureau of the Census. 2011. "2010 Census Data." Census.gov. Accessed July 5. www.census.gov/programs-surveys/decennial-census/data/datasets.2010.html.

———. 2017. "Projected Population by Single Year of Age, Sex, Race, and Hispanic Origin for the United States: 2016 to 2060." Census.gov. Accessed July 25. www.census.gov/data/datasets/2017/demo/popproj/2017-popproj.html.

Wilson, W. J. 1997. *When Work Disappears: The World of the New Urban Poor*. New York: Vintage.

Wolak, J., D. Finkelhor, and K. Mitchell. 2007. "Trends in Arrests of 'Online Predators.'" Crimes against Children Research Center, University of New Hampshire, Durham, NH. www.unh.edu/ccrc/pdf/CV194.pdf.

YouthFacts.org. 2010. "Elder Meltdown Threatens America." Updated September 20. www.youthfacts.org/?page_id=982.

———. 2011. "All Part I (Index) Felony Arrests." www.youthfacts.org/?page_id=144.

CHAPTER 13

Imagining Today's Young Adults in LIS

Moving Forward with Critical Youth Studies

Paulette Rothbauer

The psychological "storm and stress" model of adolescence advanced by G. Stanley Hall and others continues to underpin the conceptions of teen library users and teen readers. This chapter questions the ways in which this model has become essentialized in library and information science discourses concerned with public library services to young adults and offers alternative frameworks for conceptualizing young adults. Moreover, this chapter investigates the possibilities offered by critical youth studies to disrupt and complicate ideas about a universal experience of adolescence and how these might work to transform young adult services.

Asked to consider the question "How should library and information science imagine today's young adults?," I knew in an instant that I wanted to explore our taken-for-granted understanding of those people we call young adults, youth, adolescents, and teenagers as simply belonging to a bracketed age classification, usually between 12 and 19 years of age. In this chapter, I explore a body of work that is sometimes called "critical youth studies" and consider what it offers to the conceptual project that underpins this collection of chapters on transforming young adult (YA) librarianship. Before I go any further, however, it is necessary to be clear about what this chapter *is not*. It is not a critique of YA librarianship or YA librarians, nor is it a critique of advocacy for young adults and YA library services. I am a strong supporter of the efforts of organizations like the Young Adult Library Services Association (YALSA) and Canadian Libraries Are Serving Youth (CLASY) that are composed of groups of individuals who are keenly committed to improving library services to teenagers and young adults in North America and, by so doing, enhancing the lives of teenagers and young adults. However, I intend to examine closely the logic of the discourses we use to explain and justify what it is we do in libraries with youth and why we think we should be doing it (or doing more). Further, I want to explore whether and how such work might be informed by critical youth studies perspectives. The ideas in this chapter are tentative, exploratory, and offered respectfully as part of the ongoing conversation among researchers, library school students, library workers, library users, and others concerned with youth services librarianship.

CONSEQUENCES OF DOMINANT STEREOTYPES OF YOUTH

When we examine more closely the general representations of teenagers and young adults in contemporary North American society, we can begin to see the ways in which dominant stereotypes of teenagers also become entrenched in library discourses. Many others have warned of the dangers of reducing young adults to stereotypes (see, for example, Chelton 2001; Gorman and Suellentrop 2009, 25-26; Jones and Shoemaker 2001), but I want to go one step further here. One of the major assumptions underpinning this chapter is that there is no naturally occurring entity in the world called a "young adult," but rather there are competing and changing discourses on what constitutes young adulthood. While many stereotypes exist, some of the most dominant and enduring characterizations of teenagers are described by Nancy Lesko (2001, 4-5) in her book *Act Your Age!* on the cultural construction of adolescence. Each is described in turn.

Adolescents "Come of Age" into Adulthood

The idea that adolescence is a transition from childhood to adulthood is one of the most enduring conceptualizations. It is usually further conceived of as a series of discrete and unidirectional stages or steps with physical, cognitive, and emotional milestones where adulthood is judged to be the more rational and reliable state (Raby 2007, 40-41). Developmental milestones suggest that on the one hand all youth, regardless of their own situations in the world, progress toward adulthood in the same ways, and on the other hand that if a particular young person, or groups of young people, get stopped or even worse move backward, that there is something wrong, deficient, inadequate, immature, incomplete, and so on. Critical youth scholars contest such claims for an "essential" stage of human development when they argue that its scientific identification is a recent phenomenon dating only to the early 1900s with the popularization of G. Stanley Hall's so-called discovery of adolescence. Studies like Margaret Mead's anthropological study *Coming of Age in Samoa* are used to argue that adolescence is a product of culture, and as such its meanings vary across cultural contexts (see Côté and Allahar 2006, 4-5).

Adolescents Are Controlled by Raging Hormones

In the master of library and information science (MLIS) class that I teach on youth, information, and library services, like many other instructors, I often begin the term with a discussion of stereotypes—those held by teens about adults and those held by adults about teens. The conceptualization of young adults as people buffeted about by raging hormones in a "storm and stress" framework is often one of the first models of adolescence to be voiced. In this formulation, young adults are seen to be subject to impulses that are uncontrollable, potentially dangerous, and certainly distasteful. Consequent to this idea of youth is the biological inevitability of adolescence—that if we just wait long enough, it will soon be over, but in the meantime young people need to be monitored and controlled by adults.

Adolescents Are Peer Oriented

That adolescents are strongly influenced or pressured by their peers seems like an essential truth about teenagers and young adults, perhaps even more so in the present era of socially mediated communication and entertainment. As Lesko (2001) tells us, the subtle consequences of this idea are to take away the individual's ability to determine or judge for himself or herself, to discount his or her full autonomy, and to assume the conformity of youth as young people are socialized to peer norms.

Adolescence Is Signified by Age

For many of us, adults and young people alike, biological or chronological age (e.g., 13 to 19 years of age) and generational age (e.g., millennials, generation Y) have become main entry points for thinking about young adults. Age-graded education is now the norm in most schools in North America, as are age-graded library collections and services in public libraries. Age intersects with all other conceptualizations of young adulthood and operates as a powerful way to eliminate diversity and differences among cohorts of youth. In other words, the statement that "Jane is 15 years old" signifies a great deal to those who read it without any need for further elaboration.

Lesko (2001) helps us to understand why we need to pay attention to these dominant characterizations. It is worth citing her at length:

> These four confident characterizations of adolescence operate within and across numerous fields, including education, law, medicine, psychology, and social work, as well as in popular culture, such as movies, television, and literature. They declare the nature of youth and they incite us to find instances of their truth in new encounters. In theoretical terms these confident characterizations tell us what adolescents will be like, help us interpret our personal experiences of being teenaged in their light, and inform future observations by telling us what is important and enduring in adolescent lives. We believe that youths are under peer pressure, we understand our own experiences in these terms, and we see new situations in these terms. Thus these characterizations move both into our pasts and into our futures, helping us to shape individual subjective experiences but also objective knowledges. (4–5)

These characteristics of youth are so prevalent and so taken for granted that we no longer tend to question their validity or see them as stereotypes. There is, however, a growing body of theoretical and empirical research that helps us to interrogate such stereotyping of youth. Along with Lesko, several scholars call into question the idea that adolescence is a transitional period between childhood and adulthood that can be solely explained by biological factors, the raging hormones thesis chief among them (see Jones 2009; Best 2007; Côté and Allahar 2006). Some point to evidence that shows how economic forces dictated the need for youth labor and then later activated a need for new markets that took account of increased earning power of young adults. At the same time, schooling became compulsory for longer periods of time, which kept young people in school, at home, and out of the labor force and by extension deferred the possibility of being granted an adult status in society.

The basic counterargument to developmental discourses on youth is that over time social demographics and economic trends have as much explanatory power for the frustrations experienced during the coming-of-age period. For example, critical youth scholars James Côté and Anton Allahar (2006) explain the nature of adolescence in the late twentieth century and early twenty-first century as being the result of the decimation of the youth labor markets where meaningful work is replaced by low-paying, temporary service jobs (e.g., so-called McJobs), the rise in credentialism leading to prolonged postsecondary education (despite the depressed outlook for attainment of meaningful professional jobs), and the related extended dependency on parents and caregivers. All of these factors lead to a deferral of so-called adulthood and its associated characterizations (e.g., a rewarding job, marriage, child rearing, mortgages, and so on) and result in prolonged young adulthood well beyond the teenage years and upward even to 30 years of age and older. The persistence of the age bracketing of youth, along with the concept of youth as immature adults even as they approach their thirties, has certain consequences for our interaction with teenagers and young adults. Defining youth by age—one of the most "epidemic" (Lesko 2001, 4) definitions in library and information science (LIS)—carries the tendency to erase differences among youth related to class, gender, ethnicity, and other social variables. It follows that such erasure leads to the conceptualization of youth as a homogeneous demographic group, allowing us to think of teenagers and young adults in universal or essentialist terms.

Biology-based explanations for youthhood carry similar universalizing consequences. As discussed earlier, despite continual challenges to his ideas (see Griffin 1993), Hall is often cited as "discovering" adolescence as a unique stage in human development. Hall is recognized as an early proponent of the "storm and stress" model of adolescence that defines it as a period of rebellion, conflict, and discord with authorities. Adolescent turmoil then is seen to be responsible for the perceived social phenomenon of misbehaving youth (see Côté and Allahar 2006, 16-17). More recently, neuropsychology and brain mapping efforts have been used to explain youth behavior. Evidence garnered from brain mapping efforts is used to argue that the adolescent brain is different from adult brains, resulting in impulsive behavior, lack of foresight, and the inability to exercise both sound judgment and rational decision making among teenagers and young adults (see Côté and Allahar 2006, 17-18).

One consequence of biology-based explanations of adolescence can be the pathologization of youth by which negative stereotypes come to represent universal truths of human development that posit youth *are by their very nature* imperfect, inadequate, or abnormal. Another consequence is an undue focus on the individual, which some say leads to a kind of victim blaming where young people are themselves seen to be the cause of their marginalization, disenfranchisement, or disengagement. This in turn results in a drive to "fix" the teenager rather than attend to underlying social, economic, and cultural factors (Côté and Allahar 2006, 31). A third consequence of this line of thinking is the notion that because young adults are incapable of good judgment and are ruled by their emotions, and thus their actions are dictated by hormone levels, adult guidance is required and, further, autonomy is put off until the transition to adulthood is achieved. These "consequences" are also visible in LIS discourse and practice: we need only look to debates related to age-appropriate collections and programming and policies on Internet use and other teen conduct in libraries.

When we design services based on the logic of biology-based theories of adolescence, we may unintentionally propagate some of the damaging trajectories of such logics. Dominant ideologies regarding the roles of education and employment in young adulthood support the victim-blaming thesis as well. Academic achievement among youth is uniformly lauded as desirable, as is the attainment of post-secondary schooling in colleges and universities. Indeed, libraries have always been positioned as partners in school readiness training and lifelong learning initiatives. Participation in schooling is one of the milestone markers of young adulthood, and there is a clear stepping-stone model for success in life that is based on a certain progression through the ranks: elementary, then secondary school, then college or university, increasingly postgraduate degrees, and then ongoing upgrading of credentials or continuing education. Such educational attainment is seen to further one's chances in life for a fulfilling, rewarding, and suitably compensated career.

However, trends in educational and workplace opportunities can be seen to undermine the promise of education for contemporary cohorts of young adults. In fact, some go so far as to say that without a careful scrutiny of realistic education and job opportunities, we do little more than offer false promises of the future to youth by encouraging them to pile credential upon credential and school debt upon school debt (Côté and Allahar 2006). There are further potentially damaging consequences of the mainstream psychologized discourses on adolescence. In particular, the tendency to represent individual young people and certain groups of youth as "deviant" or "deficient" or otherwise inadequate can lead to certain moral panics about the same groups of youth. In her book *Representations of Youth*, Christine Griffin (1993) provides an insightful examination of the moral panics or "constructed crises" over young people, such as teenage sexuality (e.g., teen pregnancy, homosexuality) and youth leisure and unemployment (e.g., hooliganism, delinquency). We also have certain youth crises within LIS discourse. For example, Anthony Bernier (2011) illustrates that the overwhelmingly dominant media representation of youth as deviant, criminal, and dangerous has critical implications for service and policy responses related to youth in libraries. Other panics about youth in libraries, some of the most enduring, concern the "reluctant" library nonuser; the resistant, mostly male reader; and the unruly, disruptive, in-house library users. In her work, Mary K. Chelton (2001) has shown the damaging consequences of our reliance on stereotypes of youth in the provision of customer service to them in libraries, most notably in the construction of teens as problem patrons.

The universalizing logic of developmental discourses on youth and the stereotyping related to moral panics about certain groups of youth can have serious consequences on how we conceive of young adults in LIS. Before I turn to a discussion of alternative ways to consider youthhood, it is important to reiterate that processes of human development are not being questioned here. It would be foolish to argue that young adults do not experience physical, emotional, mental, and social changes related to maturation, but these processes on their own cannot offer robust explanations for young adult behavior, nor therefore should they be used uncritically in our service initiatives, research projects, and training objectives or, indeed, in how we envision youth in LIS.

ALTERNATIVE FRAMEWORKS FOR THINKING ABOUT YOUNG ADULTS

Scholars and theorists working in the general area of critical youth studies are concerned with actively improving the condition of young people's lives, while at the same time acknowledging youth agency, autonomy, and abilities. Critical youth studies resist the essentializing discourses that posit young adulthood as a stable and universal category of human development that holds steady across time as well as cultural and social contexts. There are two intersecting methodologies for understanding the experiences of adolescence or young adulthood in this framework: political economy and cultural studies.

Critical youth studies is a perspective informed by political economy. Scholars and researchers working in this tradition are critically concerned with the unequal distribution of power and, like cultural theorists, with the marginalized status and institutionalized powerlessness of young adults in contemporary society. Educational systems, the media, and other social institutions work to both control and indoctrinate young people into being willing participants in their systematic oppression (Tyyskä 2009, 10). Further, political economists are motivated to uncover the "false consciousness" of youth in society that works to permit and enable young people to undermine their own interests and their own social power. They call for critical consciousness raising by educating young people to be aware of their systematic oppression within the currents of power that affect their lives: the economy and various youth markets, employment and labor, media, and education infrastructures. The goal of this consciousness raising is to reverse both young people's economic and political disenfranchisement and to support meaningful youth participation in civil society. By taking a macro approach, political economy perspectives on youth bring to light deep structural inequities in society.

In cultural studies of youth, the diversity of human experience cannot be erased. Culture is front and center in any analysis of youth experience, and theorizing reflects the particularities of race and ethnicity, gender, class, sexuality, and other cultural and social variables. Furthermore, the agency and autonomy of youth are privileged. Young adults are viewed as competent, thoughtful, rational, and capable. The very idea of *youth* is seen to be an embodied space constituted of contested and dynamic meanings and constructed through social relations of power. In other words, the concept of youth is not a naturally occurring category of humanness—its meaning has been and is continually negotiated. We observe this contestation even when we look at some common ways to describe youth: Does young adulthood begin with puberty? With gainful employment? With marriage? With the establishment of an independent household?

The cultural studies perspective takes serious account of young people's own perspectives on their lives and often privileges their accounts and voices over adult and expert interpretations. One of the overarching goals of many cultural studies of youth is to give voice to those young people who are marginalized from mainstream popular and scholarly discourses and in that way to disrupt universalizing, essentialist, and deterministic understandings of youth.

These two well-established frameworks for understanding youth can compete, resulting in tensions in projects that seek to conceptualize young adulthood. The cultural studies perspective is critiqued for its individualizing analysis, while political economy is often seen as overly deterministic. Nancy Lesko (2001) proposes alternative conceptions in her attempts to privilege youth as "always active, social beings" and at the same time to allow for collective social practices. Lesko recommends thinking about conceptions of growth and change based on contingency and recursive sense making. She also asks us to reject a priori frameworks based on development, which is rejected for its legacy of racism, sexism, and classism and its inability to account for contexts, or on socialization, which is rejected despite its attempt to account for group and social processes for its unidirectionality and its basic assumption on the passivity of youth (Lesko 2001, 194–95). Lesko (2001) also encourages us to think of youth (and everyone) as "holding seemingly opposing identities *simultaneously*" (197)—by, for example, allowing young adults to be both "old" and "young" at the same time. Lesko further claims that if the concept of adolescence emerged to help "identify and create a vision of the modern citizen who would be equipped for the challenges of the new social, economic, and world arrangements" (Popkewitz 1998, cited in Lesko 2001, 197), new conceptions of adolescence should emerge alongside the "articulation and popularization of different problems" (Lesko 2001, 198). This articulation may in turn change how we conceive of youth needs in changing social, economic, educational, and cultural conditions affecting youth experience. Finally, Lesko (2001) calls for advocacy that "undermines the monolithic view of adolescents as supposedly all the same and as fundamentally different from adults" (199).

TOWARD A CRITICAL YOUTH STUDIES FRAMEWORK FOR LIS

There is a strand in LIS research on YA librarianship and YA library services that dovetails with some of the major dimensions of a critical youth studies framework. Perhaps one of the ways in which critical youth studies differs most from developmental models of adolescence is in its explicit political motivation to increase the social and at times economic power of young adults as they participate in the currents of society. While it is not possible to provide an exhaustive review, it is instructive and illuminating to revisit some of the historical studies of young adults and libraries to see that we have had, from time to time, cogent articulations of more politicized conceptualizations of youth and youth services within LIS. These studies take a different methodological approach to the conceptualizations of youth and youth services that rely solely on developmental frameworks for adolescence.

In LIS, there is a well-known genealogy associated with the emergence of public library services for young people, but as Christine Jenkins (2000, 107) wrote in her review of youth services librarianship, the histories of a distinct set of library services to teenagers and young adults in North America make up a scant field of scholarship; a decade or so later, this would still seem to hold true. However, LIS scholars have provided templates for thinking about teenagers and young adults in libraries that depart from developmental theories of adolescence to take account of the social factors affecting both how adult librarians think about youth but also how services are conceived of and designed to meet their needs. In their respective studies, Jenkins (2000) and Jane Anne Hannigan (1996) provide feminist analyses of youth services librarianship. Jenkins analyzes the work—the mission—of the female librarians who built strong foundations within the profession for a child-centered philosophy of service. A few years earlier, Hannigan also situates the emergence of YA librarianship in the United States within a feminist analysis of the work of several prominent female librarians, from Mabel Williams in the early 1900s through to Mary K. Chelton and her ongoing advocacy for young adults and YA services in libraries. Jenkins is concerned with the emergence of both children's and YA librarianship, while Hannigan focuses primarily on YA services and teen advocacy. By examining the roles played by prominent female librarians in the development of YA library services in the United States, both Jenkins and Hannigan provide insights into how to conceptualize collective action across individual accounts. Young adults are situated in their work as subjects within conceptual frameworks that respect their diversity, autonomy, and ability to participate in the design and development of library spaces, collections, programming, and services.

In the 1970s, Miriam Braverman examined the larger contexts for youth services librarianship. In her landmark study (Braverman 1979), she compares the development and provision of YA library services in five prominent public libraries and chronicles what she calls the cultural and social cycles of YA librarianship in the United States from the 1920s through the 1970s. Braverman makes a distinction between the cultural work of librarians she saw as oriented to books, collections, and reading promotion and the social work of librarians who responded with programming and services that addressed the daily lived experiences of teenagers in the community. Further, she claims that it was a "flawed humanism" that led to a professional "retreat" to books and reading rather than a continued commitment to the ongoing development of socially responsible and socially conscious programming designed to provide information for youth to learn about issues that affect them personally in their lives. Braverman's work is an important history of the emergence of YA services and is notable for its attention to social and cultural factors.

In a similar vein, Lukenbill (2006) examines the emergence of youth librarianship in the United States and looks at how it intersected with various social reform movements in the late 1800s through the twentieth century. Lukenbill reminds us that from the earliest reform movements, the educative function of various social institutions, including the library, was seen to

> address problems of immigrant assimilation, crime, vice, pauperism and juvenile delinquency. Above all, this particular arm of the reform movement stressed the importance of the eradication of the urban slum where most of the working class lived, and the Americanisation of immigrants. These movements emphasized the idea that, through education, every individual could be "uplifted" from the limits of their social roots and environments. (202)

Lukenbill nicely demonstrates how certain ideas about young adults as "youth at risk" fueled library reform and development. Lukenbill ends with a call for youth librarianship that is conscious of its politics. Following Braverman, Kathleen Craver (1988) looked at how library programming to teens and young adults and collections work continued through the 1960s. Both Braverman and Craver note that at different times librarians in the United States were effective outreach workers, bringing an awareness of library services and collections to communities of young people who might not have opportunities to visit libraries on their own. However, the division between books, collections, and reading, on one side, and programming and outreach services, on the other, has become entrenched in our understanding of YA librarianship today.

We see the division inscribed in LIS curricula that offer separate courses on YA materials and YA library services and in job descriptions that feature collections work and outreach and programming as distinctly different positions. This division is sometimes colloquially described as the difference between people who love to work with books and people who love to work with teens. There are important consequences for this divide between books and services. It is a somewhat arbitrary split that artificially pits books and reading against other kinds of engagement with other types of library materials and library services. It also continually re-inscribes age-based divisions by following age-based schooling categories for outreach and age-based reading levels for texts. Further, when we consider the ways in which YA materials and services are separated from those developed for children and adults, we begin to see how age-based conceptions of human experience are deeply entrenched in libraries. The idea that youth are different from others, especially adults, becomes a strong rationale for developing specialized collections, designing specialized services and spaces, and fighting for specialized staff.

By the 1970s, the pioneering work of several youth advocates created a stable and enduring foundation for our current understanding of what it means to provide committed service to teenagers in libraries—an understanding, moreover, that has been inscribed into national guidelines for service to teens. Margaret Edwards's (2002) book *The Fair Garden and the Swarm of Beasts* represents one of the first book-length articulations of codified library practice regarding teen services. In 1969, Edwards famously adopted the construction of teenagers as "the beasts" in the "fair garden" of the library for her book, exhorting her colleagues, based on her observations of 30 years of working with young people in libraries, to recognize, as she writes in her closing sentence, "It is time to let them in" (89). *The Fair Garden and the Swarm of Beasts* and other works like it continue (and should continue) to inspire cohorts of library students and YA librarians. There is immeasurable value in their calls to duty that challenge librarians to be creative, sensitive, politically savvy, and tireless in their efforts to carve out dedicated space and resources for young adults, and to be ever vigilant in protecting and promoting their rights to free and unfettered access to information. The histories of youth services in public libraries have consistently shown that the (mostly) female library leaders disrupted developmental discourses inherited to some degree from protectionist philosophies of service for much younger children based on the need to limit access and to create age-appropriate collections and programs.

So, what does this brief review of some landmark studies tell us? As youth services librarians and LIS scholars, our work fits within the paradigm of critical youth studies. Our heavy reliance on theories of human development is, perhaps, unwarranted. Furthermore, there can be real benefits to expanding our understanding of what it means to be a young adult by adopting some of the positions found within a critical youth studies framework.

CONCLUSION: HOW SHOULD LIS ENVISION YOUTH?

The first answer to this question is to seriously consider a critical youth studies framework and its several claims about young adulthood, including the following:

- As a concept, adolescence is socially constructed and is not a stable, universal, naturally occurring phase of human life. It is always changing, and its meanings must be continually negotiated.
- What it means to be a young adult is contingent on many factors, including race and ethnicity, gender, sexuality, geographic location, and class; therefore, these variables must be addressed in our work.
- Any understanding of young adults must allow for their participation in meaning-making exercises; their voices and perspectives are as important as any adult-observed interpretations of their experience.
- Individual perspectives are critically important to our understanding, but we must also find ways to take account of the influences of collective action.
- Young adults, like adults, are in a position both of "becoming" and of "being," and one does not trump the other.
- Youth participation is of paramount importance in a critical youth studies framework. It is both a method of understanding youth and a goal for our interactions with youth.

All of these claims work to disrupt the biology-based theories of adolescence that rely on definitions of youth derived from age categories. Biological age or chronological age is seen to be a kind of straw horse figure in imagining what is possible in a reconceptualization of young adults. In other words, the numbers of years that a person has been alive can really only ever tell us how many years a person has been alive. In particular when it comes to young adults, we should not rely too much on what age can tell us about them. Whereas the claims just listed allow us to give full play to the already existing as well as developing abilities and interests of young adults, I would challenge readers to consider each point in the context of a specific teen library program or service, or for researchers to examine each in the context of your research problem. How do these ideas change the ways in which you think of teens and your work with teens?

The second answer to the overarching question is again to take our cue from critical youth studies by moving between micro and macro perspectives on the issues that concern us in YA librarianship as we recognize that young adulthood is a social and cultural construction that relies on particular and changing ideologies. When we acknowledge that there are competing ideologies (e.g., the difference between liberationist and protectionist stances on adolescence), we can respond to or harness the power of particular sets of discourses and use them to serve the library's interests. On the face of things this may seem cynical, but I would argue that it puts discourses in their proper place: they can be disrupted and challenged, and, further, there is no need to "throw the baby out with the bathwater"! For example, when making proposals to conservative library boards about the establishment of special youth programs, collections, or spaces, it can be in our interest to use ideas from developmental discourses to make our pitches. There are still many good reasons for this kind of segregation in services and collections, as in many communities it may signal, for the first time, that youth are being seriously considered as members of a library deserving of services for that reason alone. But at the same time we should work to disrupt such discourses from making a stranglehold on our own conceptualizations of our patron group.

This line of thinking, of course, gives rise to an immediate tension: on the one hand, I am calling for us to jettison age-based and biology-based understandings of youth, but on the other hand, I am saying use the discourses to support the establishment of specialized collections and services for youth. This effort points to the necessity, I think, at this particular juncture in time, to allow competing conceptualizations to coexist, recognizing the role each plays in terms of its influence and effects on our practices and research. If critical youth studies tell us anything, it is the necessity of constantly interrogating the ways in which we define young people. In the early decades of the twenty-first century, there is mounting evidence to suggest that we need to extend services, to account for prolonged dependency on parents, and give credence to the concept of the emerging adult, without creating an insoluble age boundary. Honoring this tension helps us to honor the complexity of our work practices as well. For example, in a developmental framework, the promotion of YA literature can be seen as little more than prescription or developmental aid for that discrete phase of human life called adolescence. A framework that sees adolescence as socially constructed, its meanings unstable, contextual, and constantly negotiated, supports the concept that YA literature carries symbolic, cultural, and social freight for its young adult (and older adult) readers at the same time that these same readers contribute to the possible meanings of YA literature—what it is, how it is read, why it is valued, and how it changes.

A critical youth studies approach holds much promise for the study of young adults and their information, library, and reading practices within LIS. The slate of research questions that could be informed by this rubric is quite literally completely open. Interesting work could be done right away by considering how existing research findings related to information-seeking behavior, reading practices, and library use can be reinterpreted by dispensing with developmental frameworks for analysis and discussions of implications of the research—to be replaced instead by the axioms of critical youth studies. For example, rather than construct young people as novices, students, or otherwise inadequate information seekers, we could reframe them as users who are defined by their already existing position in the world as young adults who are seeking information in ways that are wholly appropriate to that position. The point is, we need to understand that reframed position by looking at more than just developmental milestones. Critical youth studies' insistence on the negotiated meaning of young adulthood demands consideration of class, gender, race and ethnicity, sexuality, and geography, and we need more research in LIS (and all its cognate areas) that matches this demand. Youth participation has long been valued in youth services librarianship (Tixier Herald and Monnier 2007), and it is one of the areas of librarianship that corresponds most closely to some of the ideas from critical youth studies. We can do more work to allow young adult voices and perspectives in meaning-making exercises within LIS to inform practice and research. Such perspectives support our efforts to involve youth meaningfully in the governance of libraries: youth membership in library boards, teen-run programs, meaningful and respectful use of teen labor in paid and volunteer positions, and youth participation at the levels of state and provincial, national, and international library associations. Furthermore, this framework calls for our ceaseless advocacy for full participation of youth in society, as a critical youth studies framework encourages us to renew our, decidedly nonneutral, commitment to the idea of libraries as participating members of civil society and as agents in the creation of a just society for all people, young adults among them.

REFERENCES

Bernier, A. 2011. "Representations of Youth in Local Media: Implications for Library Service." *Library and Information Science Research* 33: 158–67.

Best, A. L., ed. 2007. *Representing Youth: Methodological Issues in Critical Youth Studies.* New York: New York University Press.

Braverman, M. 1979. *Youth, Society and the Public Library.* Chicago: American Library Association.

Burek Pierce, J. 2006. "The Borderland Age and Borderline Books: The Early Practice of Reader's Advisory for Youth." *Young Adult Library Services* 5, no. 1: 42–47.

Chelton, M. K. 2001. "Young Adults as Problems: How the Social Construction of a Marginalized User Category Occurs." *Journal of Education for Library and Information Science* 42, no. 1: 4–11.

Côté, J. E., and A. L. Allahar. 2006. *Critical Youth Studies: A Canadian Focus.* Toronto, ON: Pearson Prentice Hall.

Craver, K. W. 1988. "Social Trends in American Young Adult Library Service, 1960–1969." *Libraries and Culture* 23, no. 1: 18–38.

Edwards, M. 2002. *The Fair Garden and the Swarm of Beasts: The Library and the Young Adult.* Centennial ed. Chicago: American Library Association.

Gorman, M., and T. Suellentrop. 2009. *Connecting Young Adults and Libraries: A How-To-Do-It Manual.* 4th ed. New York: Neal-Schuman.

Griffin, C. 1993. *Representations of Youth: The Study of Youth and Adolescence in Britain and America.* Cambridge, UK: Polity Press.

Hannigan, J. A. 1996. "A Feminist Analysis of the Voices for Advocacy in Young Adult Services." *Library Trends* 44, no. 4: 851–74.

Jenkins, C. 2000. "The History of Youth Services Librarianship: A Review of the Research Literature." *Libraries and Culture* 35, no. 1: 103–40.

Jones, G. 2009. *Youth.* Cambridge, UK: Polity Press.

Jones, P., and J. Shoemaker. 2001. *Do It Right: Best Practices for Serving Young Adults in School and Public Libraries.* New York: Neal-Schuman.

Lesko, N. 2001. *Act Your Age! A Cultural Construction of Adolescence*. New York: Routledge.

Lukenbill, W. B. 2006. "Helping Youth at Risk: An Overview of Reformist Movements in American Public Library Services to Youth." *New Review of Children's Literature and Librarianship* 12, no. 2: 197-213.

Raby, R. 2007. "Across a Great Gulf? Conducting Research with Adolescents." In *Representing Youth: Methodological Issues in Critical Youth Studies*, edited by A. L. Best, 39-59. New York: New York University Press.

Tixier Herald, D., and D. P. Monnier. 2007. "The Beasts Have Arrived." *Voice of Youth Advocates* 30, no. 2: 116-19.

Tyyskä, V. 2009. *Youth and Society: The Long and Winding Road*. Toronto: Canadian Scholars' Press.

CHAPTER 14

Moving Beyond YAs as "Citizens"

The Promise of Membership

Anthony Bernier

While the previous edition of *Transforming Young Adult Services* contained arguments advocating that the field of library and information science (LIS) begin constructing a notion of young adults (YAs) as citizens (especially in contrast to notions of young adults as objects of a dated "youth development" regime), this new chapter attempts to respond to more immediate political circumstances. Rather than provoking continued and unproductive conflict over the term *citizen*, this chapter builds instead on constructive qualities contained in the notion of young adult identity shaped by *membership in local community*. Among the many applicable benefits of this identity for YAs is how it better assists LIS to envision young people as having more in common with adults than conflict.

As referred to in the introduction to *Transforming Young Adult Services*, and sprinkled throughout the text, LIS's broad and lingering avoidance of social theory continues to indulge the century-long deficit assumptions inherent in what I call today's youth development industrial complex (YDIC). More specifically, LIS's historic consensus on youth has consequently failed to reflect upon or develop its own normative vision of youth, one consistent with its own institutional mission, its professional obligations, one reflective of its own values. LIS relies instead almost entirely on other disciplines to define its vision of the young adult audience and consequently leaves unexplored more relevant, creative, theoretical, strategic contexts to measure its own professional contributions. This is, to borrow the metaphor inaugurated by LIS historian Wayne Wiegand, the field's "blind spot" with regard to YA services.[1] LIS students, practitioners, and scholars should squarely address this blind spot.

Reliance on dated and borrowed approaches leaves LIS in general, and YA services in particular, with seemingly obvious, naturalized, assumed, and unreflexive visions of youth as a needy and marginalized population. This view renders LIS confined within a false youth/adult binary opposition—a marginalization rooted largely in assumptions and overemphasis on difference and conflict.[2] LIS discourse thus continues to concentrate chiefly on a model of youth inadequacy—youth in the life of the library while neglecting the potential value the library might otherwise play in the life of today's actual youth.[3] Yet LIS continues on—indifferent to its responsibility to articulate a vision of its own.

Further, as true a half-century ago as today, if libraries take YA service data seriously at all, they continue to do so almost entirely rooted in institutionally defined and age-segregated output measures: How many YAs attended the YA program? How many joined the teen advisory group? How many signed up for the summer reading program?[4]

Negative consequences for LIS spring from these legacy assumptions and practices. One negative consequence for LIS's legacy practice extends the cliché about library school itself being "too theoretical." This sentiment rehearses LIS's traditional allergic reaction to social theory when it should be an ardent student.[5] In order to benefit from and keep pace with insights and interventions advancing in many other disciplines and fields, such as those in general youth studies, researchers and YA practitioners must strive to better link the theoretical/conceptual to daily practice and action. Theory calls this linkage "praxis."[6]

Beyond its allergy to incorporating social theory, LIS faces a second consequence of maintaining its current youth consensus: a conceptually banal approach to service assessment and evaluation that encourages and reproduces success bias; "success" is declared simply because something happened. The same holds true for common claims of "best practices." The mere occurrence of something does not qualify it as a model. Simply counting heads or circulation statistics (though useful to some degree) does not demonstrate a persuasive defense during the present neoconservative onslaught on the very notion of public service itself.[7] More importantly, these superficial output metrics ignore user experience, meanings, or value.

This chapter of *Transforming Young Adult Services* asks the following question: How can theory combined with practice produce a rich service praxis—alternatives to LIS's otherwise derived youth consensus—to transform the current vision of YAs and thus YA services? After contextualizing a turn toward critical social theory, this chapter will investigate and problematize several distinct "paths" on which LIS might begin to debate and come to articulate its own specific vision of young adult library users to inform a transformative YA service praxis.

At least part of the answer to this question about how to combine theory and practice emerges most explicitly in part V of this collection, "From Citizenship to Membership." One response resides in exploring an LIS-specific vision of YAs as fully entitled end users. Before considering a variety of specific implications or "paths" on which to pursue this notion of LIS praxis, this chapter first probes the critical social theory landscape for a vision of YAs conceived as local community members.

How might this notion influence various aspects of the library's daily and applied service profile? How, for example, might imagining YAs as entitled and active local community members transform collection management to serve ordinary YAs? How might this LIS-specific vision influence library space design? What new opportunities arise to connect libraries to YAs outside of library buildings? How might envisioning YAs as community members deepen intergenerational library services? When LIS critically engages important theoretical interventions and applies them to creating its own vision of YAs in our daily postmodern world powerful possibilities of praxis emerge.

IN DEFENSE OF THEORY: PRAXIS

Among the defining characteristics professions offer society are critical self-reflections and theoretical groundings in a field's respective foundational concepts. Ironically, one of the enduring clichés about graduate library school training is that it is *"too* theoretical."

Unfortunately, abundant evidence demonstrates just the opposite: LIS's refusal of theory remains deeply ingrained in the professional culture.

As long ago as 1933, for instance, Lee Pierce Buttler, then Dean of the University of Chicago library school, noted, "Unlike his colleagues in other fields of social activity the librarian is strangely uninterested in the theoretical aspects of his profession."[8] More recently, LIS scholar John Budd has observed, "Within library and information work there is a fairly long-standing antipathy toward 'theory.'"[9] There is also ample evidence that youth-serving fields share this aversion.[10]

These professional predispositions notwithstanding, conceptual foundations exist and have always existed in the "background" of LIS. They appear as assumptions about what the field perceives as "true" and "false." They articulate what it values and what it does not. The profession badly errors, however, when confusing current assumptions with timeless and universal truths. This and the other chapters in this collection conceptually engage YA services to provoke debate and deliberations to differentiate the enduring from the fleeting. They urge differentiating between practices rooted in mere glad tidings, testimonials, and traditions versus contextualized, defensible, and evidence-based practice.

Thus does appear the question of why LIS needs critical theory. LIS needs critical theory because the nature of the profession's obligations to society, to libraries, and most particularly to young people requires critically engaging practice *and* research. This obligation for conceptual vigilance goes far beyond the mere annual rituals of reviewing, ranking, and awarding fiction titles. It extends as well to how the profession envisions its users, its institutional interventions, and how professionals contribute to society. If LIS advances a notion of professionalism about "youth services," then it must also accept an obligation to offer coherent and relevant conceptual justification for its expertise, including its notions of how it constitutes "youth."

This obligation for assessing and applying theory necessarily contains a degree of ambiguity if not humility. With different formulations of theory the same phenomena or data can plausibly describe and explain different interpretations, understandings, and meanings. Also, at base, theory permits professionals to interpret data and relationships to render higher quality, more creative, more relevant, more confident, and better applied decisions.

Critical engagement with theory advances the field as a consequence of examining learning, scrutinizing, debating, modifying, applying, and evaluating alternative paradigms or models.[11] In contrast, technicians, paraprofessionals, and clerks repetitively apply uncontested methods fitting preconceived circumstances.

Without theory librarians remain merely trained employees. Without theory viable professional volition cannot exit. Without theory LIS cannot meet its profession's obligations to remain relevant.

LIS's best option for beginning a conversation about this widely shared and observed antipathy to theory resides in pursuing "praxis." Praxis represents the actionable intersection of theory, education, and daily practice. Praxis belies pedestrian assumptions about "theory" and "practice" existing in simplistic opposition to one another. Praxis seeks to understand and explicitly teach the relationship between professional activity and theory so that practice does not function as mere unrelated sequences of isolated or repetitive procedures. As John Budd observes, "Praxis refers to action that carries social and ethical implications and is not reducible to technical performance of tasks."[12]

Praxis also, however, provides LIS an opportunity to apply conceptual rigor to the design of a new project. This new project, employing a new interpretation of data, field experience, and the critical engagement of legacy practices, can result in the emergence of an LIS-specific vision of its YA end users.

This is not a study of theory for theory's sake. Praxis furnishes the profession with legitimizing criteria by which to assess practice beyond pedestrian or paraprofessional-level interventions. Instituting praxis rejuvenates theory as a legitimate professional obligation and contribution. On the other hand, without theory, LIS surrenders its claim to the "S" in library and information *science*.

FROM POSITIVISM TO POSTMODERNISM

Modernist analysis traditionally boasts confidence in its universal truth claims rooted in positivist notions of "objective" and universal knowledge. Postmodernism, on the other hand, finds a more complex, contingent, situated, and diverse world. G. Stanley Hall and Emmett L. Holt, for instance (see this book's introduction), claimed discovery of the "crisis" and "turmoil" at the root of all youth for all times, cultures, and places. Postmodernism's inquiry enjoins those concerns over, among other things, such claims of universal applicability.

More specifically, positivism focuses broadly on the nature of experience. Positivism manifests its concerns, in the instance of YA services, as largely focused on "behavior." Thus, and because LIS has reclined on developmental psychology for its vision of YAs, it should come as no surprise that the questions driving its research agenda have concentrated on such topics as information behaviors, search behaviors, reading behaviors, antisocial behaviors, and "the needs" of YAs.[13]

A particular institutional vision of the YA library user emerges from these assumptions. Such concerns, on the one hand, by definition, reduce youth to a deficient, needy "other" contrasted exclusively against perceived differences with adults and adult-defined expectations. This traditional LIS master narrative pursues a vision of service only about how youth fit into the life of the existing institution. What do libraries offer, for instance, that YAs need? What learning and skills and capacities address YA challenges? The answers point back only to institutional resources (mainly books), access (to information), and skills (chiefly bibliographic and curricular in nature).[14]

Defining the notion of these library users only by their deficits and differences with adults thus also precludes envisioning them by any other criteria—such as their abilities, interests, or capacities. Consequently, LIS responses orbit nearly exclusively around what libraries might offer rather than what users may want, enjoy, contribute, or produce.

In greater contrast to positivism, however, postmodern theory advances an entirely different set of questions and concerns. Postmodern inquiry is rooted in questions of dynamic meanings and situated power relations rather than static concerns for experience or behavior.[15] What *meanings* of library resources and uses do YAs know, define, and create? How do they create these meanings? Why? Moreover, what can libraries do, or do better, to help them pursue these meanings? What power relations connect (or disconnect) YAs, information, and libraries? Thus, dramatically new questions emerge from this theoretical trajectory and offer LIS a transformative praxis.

In order for this transformation to emerge, however, LIS must change the ways in which it uncritically derives its vision of YAs. The driving assumptions, borrowed notions of inadequacy and difference, enact a vision from nineteenth-century adultist ideals and models. Instead, LIS can become more aware of how these long-standing views about the library's larger role in society chafe against the cultural meanings of the young people libraries seek to serve today.

LIS could begin such self-reflection by reimagining youth, not as deficient blank slates suffering from a lack of bibliographic behaviors or skills, but, rather, as fully entitled users in a democratic culture to which libraries putatively aspire, represent, and help define. Framed this way new questions emerge through praxis: How can today's youth better gain access to and contribute their own meanings toward democratic culture in their libraries? How, and under what circumstances, do different YAs enact, derive, and manifest variant meanings of democratic culture? For library school students and researchers questions emerge about facilitating and studying all of this.

These are not remotely the questions posed by LIS's positivist legacy and deficit vision of youth—rooted in either the "youth at risk" approach or its kissing cousin youth development.[16] These questions do not emerge from envisioning YAs sentimentally as timeless innocents in crisis, condescendingly as depraved threats, or merely as preadults. Postmodern questions, however, do begin to point the way to a different institutional imagination of young people and thus a much-needed transformation in YA librarianship.

Without the benefit of future LIS research, such as that inaugurated in this collection, any particular innovation, beyond this present century-old master narrative consensus, can provoke only speculation for future debate. But postmodern theory can certainly assist LIS to identify and better cultivate a more measured confidence than positivism has historically.

Critical social theory can help LIS more clearly recognize how its past tethers the field to a focus on oppositions and differences between young people and idealized notions of adulthood. Critical theory can also, in combination with insights and energies gained from daily practice, generate and identify a new categorical praxis in serving young people and thus help discover new institutional relationships to and with them. These concerns carry the potential of influencing LIS work with youth not on a piecemeal basis but systematically across the entire LIS institutional footprint.

FROM CITIZENSHIP TO MEMBERSHIP

So, how to re-envision young adults specifically for LIS? What steps can LIS take, better informed by critical social theory, to create alternatives to the prevailing consensus on deficits and difference? What praxis can emerge for a more relevant and LIS-specific vision of young people in diverse and contemporary society?

As suggestively unfurling in several chapters of *Transforming Young Adult Services*, one possible vision of youth emerging from these essays considers YAs as citizens. There are, of course, many definitions and meanings of *citizen*. The term certainly and immediately begs a raft of questions in applying such a term to youth. But among its assets is that the term is rooted in the present as well as the past. It is flexible and capable of being sculpted for particular purposes. It is a term informed by postmodern inquiry about meaning and power. Further, the term intimately and deeply connects to a familiar LIS institutional mission within civil society.[17]

Recent political circumstances have, however, renewed highly contested arguments about what constitutes the definition of *citizen* or *citizenship*. Nevertheless, some uncontested features of the term might help LIS envision a more creative notion of YAs. In terms of building design, for instance, architectural critic Alexandra Lange argues, "Our built environment is making kids less healthy, less independent, and less imaginative. Treating them as citizens . . . can break that pattern . . ."[18]

A creative approach could recognize that the state (government) does not hold a monopoly on the idea of citizenship. Civil society, too, and civic institutions such as libraries, as well as the people who interact with them, also embody sufficient cultural power to define their own forms and contours of what *citizen* means.

Another argument in favor of reimagining and applying this notion to an LIS-specific vision of youth is that the term *citizen*, beyond some essays in this collection, has recently gained currency in the broader fields of youth studies.[19] While acknowledging the current debate about its application and definition, it could also be argued that this very fact offers LIS a rare opportunity to join and contribute to these broader debates. In contrast to the ways LIS traditionally shrinks from broader debates, adopting this term suggests that LIS could assert its own definition of youth as citizen.

On the other hand, a crafted LIS-specific vision of the YA as citizen does not come without challenges. While a hopeful notion, advancing it under current political conditions, especially in the United States, presents many obstacles and liabilities. The better part of wisdom may suggest that the field avoid potential confusion and strife especially if other creative options present themselves. Nevertheless, if *citizen*, however defined, does not offer a strong possibility for an LIS-specific vision of YAs, what does?

Out of the recent and increasingly hostile political debates regarding illegal immigration status and citizenship a small but growing body of scholarship has emerged specifically to address the implication of these policies and definitions as they impact young people. There is potential in this emerging scholarship to offer creative possibilities for LIS.[20]

Federal government policy today considers over two million young people ("minors") residing in the United States as "illegal." The day these young people turn 18 years of age their lives and status change: the day before they become eighteen they lead lives of relative "normality" (i.e., comparable to native-born U.S. citizens); the day after that they become defined as "criminal" and subject to deportation. The fearful implications for young people coming of age under such circumstances, of being suddenly outcast and transported to a country they have never known, are well documented in Roberto G. Gonzales's excellent study *Lives in Limbo: Undocumented and Coming of Age in America*.[21]

The aspect of Gonzales's study relevant to evolving an LIS-specific vision of YAs lies in the experiences of youth *prior* to turning 18 years old. Although some of these young people grow increasingly aware of the insider/outsider lives they lead, others sustain sudden shock to discover how radically their status changes upon turning the age of majority. "Almost overnight," Gonzales's research reveals, "feelings of inclusion and belonging were replaced by experiences of rejection and a heightened awareness of their unauthorized status."[22]

Nevertheless, prior to turning 18, before experiencing this stigmatized transition to illegality, many of these young people grow up much as native-born youth do. They build social capital within families, at school, and in neighborhoods. They move about the community freely and enjoy public spaces and the resources of civil society. They develop feelings of belonging and inclusion. Gonzales refers to this period in the life of these youth as "integrated community membership."

Herein lies the potential for a new LIS vision for *all* YAs. LIS could create a vision of YAs as *members of local community* integrated as civic members. A creative definition of YAs as community members might include dynamic and multidimensional features of participation at the local community or neighborhood level. This notion of membership recognizes anyone who participates in or contributes to making community, culture, or society; anyone who takes part in the practice of *organized memory as conducted in the library*; anyone appearing in the presence of others, assuming a degree of responsibility for one's actions and community, negotiating the rights and obligations of a shared resource.[23]

This notion of age-integrated community membership is predicated on connecting with strangers in ways libraries already and normally aspire to in building upon the trust of strangers in civic culture. Participation here might include not simply joining those prescribed and approved endeavors emanating from the YDIC, for instance, forever preparing for the future, but, rather, pursuing current interests in and a share of responsibility for contributing to the present public sphere through any number of wide-ranging civic engagements. This evocative notion of YA identity resides within a broad and active civil society while at the same time avoids conflicting with narrow and contentious liabilities currently connected to weaponized political terms like *citizen*.

Community membership does not question *whether* or *if* youth should have power in civil society. It does not delay granting power or status until some arbitrarily defined date or age—suddenly hitting the adult power switch on one's eighteenth birthday. Further, envisioning YAs as entitled local community members adheres to much of the library's historical aspirations for not discriminating against or withholding service from users from particular national groups, races, faith traditions, or gender orientations.[24]

Libraries do not require presenting passports or national identification cards or scrutinizing travel visas or birth certificates. There are currently no documented incidents of raids by ICE (Immigration and Customs Enforcement) or INS (Immigration and Naturalization Service) on summer reading programs.

Nor does the notion of local community membership perpetuate the nagging conceit inherent in the assumed scope of the current LIS reliance on youth development in which professionals bestow "empowerment" unto youth. Librarians beneficently seeking to "empower" youth implicitly constitute them, by definition, as power*less*. Adults feeling the need to empower youth effectively deny that youth already possess power and agency.[25] Indeed, they may even seek to block the use of that power if YAs deploy it in unauthorized ways.

Viewing YAs as already fully entitled community members within a broader civic culture acknowledges they already possess power. The question thus shifts from *if* youth have power to asking *how* their power is defined, negotiated, navigated, exercised, documented, manifested, and recognized.

Community membership already assumes, envisions, and legitimizes local participation of youth in a way that, driven by the YDIC agenda, LIS cannot, being claustrophobic, static, and universally delimited to fields of action and agency based merely on age-based demographics (age segregation) and highly adult circumscribed criteria. If LIS were to constitute youth as participants within local community membership, it would become easier to conceive of them as not only consuming but also *contributing* to and producing culture and less defined by LIS's historic marginalization of them.

Participation, however, remains only one facet of local membership. The notion of community membership also refocuses the prevailing conceptualization of youth as "other." It concentrates more on the *commonalities* youth share with the larger adult community. In this regard, not every aspect of youth experience or meaning becomes interpreted as "different" or "alien" or compared always only negatively to putatively high-functioning adults.

Further, envisioned as entitled community members, youth do not become relegated to a condition of ever and always only *becoming*. They can also be recognized and valued for their *present* circumstances, concerns, interests, contributions, and even responsibilities in the here and now.

Informed by core postmodernist concern with meaning and power, the notion of YAs as local community members imagines a transformative YA service praxis for LIS and libraries. The next four subsections explore in more detail key features of this contemporary YA service praxis. Each subsection respectively addresses the question about how praxis, informed by the vision of YAs as community members, can transform prevailing services and cultivate better connections between youth, libraries, and, by extension, society.

The first subsection examines the fundamental aspects of collection development and management. The second addresses library YA spaces. The third explores incorporation of YA services across intergenerational library service. The last subsection moves analysis beyond the physical walls of library buildings (outreach). Together these topics, and the questions emanating from them, demonstrate a capacity to launch rich discussions and debates about transforming YA services from their dated and moribund model and toward an approach capable of reinvigorating LIS with robust research and relevant praxis.

Membership, "Sweet Frauds," and Collection Management

How might an LIS view of YAs as engaged local community members, instead of as deficient preadults, transform collection management? Rather than continuing to privilege books (mostly fiction), curricular experience, and a construction of youth as subpar information consumers, a vision of YAs as community members might more easily recognize the multiplicity of ways in which young people produce their own literacy enactments.

This notion moves well beyond literacy experiences conventionally published between mass-produced book covers or delivered digitally through commercial publications, databases, and websites. It also moves far beyond imagining YAs as mere reading consumers.

Considering YAs a community members systematically includes the myriad of cultural forms youth increasingly produce themselves to express and document their own meanings *as* youth. This sentiment emerges from broad observations of LIS history such as those registered by Richard Rubin: "Our current concept of information provision has been historically conditioned by a traditional preoccupation with the collection rather than people."[26]

An ethical collection management process informed by a vision of YAs as community members also requires that LIS reposition itself with respect to the historically anointed and disproportionate energy currently devoted to book selection, book reviews, book promotions, book awards, and book lists especially *at the expense* of all the other ways youth enact literacy.[27]

It goes without saying that conventional publications have their place in libraries. Given the exclusive reliance on the youth-as-deficit paradigm, however, LIS has traditionally privileged commercial collections over the literacy enactments and meanings produced by local young people in their own communities.

In imagining youth as community members, immediate and additional questions present themselves. What do they produce?[28] What meanings do youth derive from the cultural forms they produce themselves? How do young people produce these cultural meanings through their literacy enactments? Where do these meanings appear and how do they use them? Other than the literacies they produce themselves, what other cultural forms do they value? How does youth culture and community membership manifest meaning in literacy enactments?[29] Note, too, how these questions share fundamental concerns that LIS addresses in envisioning adult service, rather than exclusively focusing on what differentiates YA service.

Perhaps LIS would do well, too, to consider YA collection practices more seriously as harbingers of future information practice. What can LIS students, practitioners, and researchers do to value and promote these YA literacy enactments? They may well prefigure future library usage—valuing YAs as resources for libraries to learn about their own future rather than trying to determine or direct the future of young people. Further, what steps can libraries take to better document, collect, organize, store, preserve, curate, exhibit, promote, evaluate, and serve as an access conduit for the literacy acts produced and valued by YAs as community members? Finally, historical questions: What positions did LIS take in the past regarding the literacy acts and artifacts of YAs? How did this history advance (or inhibit) access to service, library collections, or YAs?[30]

LIS's possible responses could include, for example, creating evaluation diagnostics more similar to how libraries cultivate, build, and evaluate the performance of adult collections. Adults create cultural meaning in their use of libraries. Libraries document, collect, organize, store, preserve, curate, and make accessible this cultural record. Libraries have historically collected nearly every type, mode, technique, method, style, and format of how adults capture, create, and represent their experiences in the world. Libraries accomplish making the adult record accessible by taking the processes of adult culture creation seriously. They take the products of these practices seriously. And libraries deploy all of these professional skills and commitments because they understand that it is in the collection, organization, preservation, and curation of the products of adult culture where they demonstrate upholding their mission to make the human record accessible in a democratic society.[31]

Other collection responses to an LIS vision of YAs as local community members would include taking their own preferred domains of meaning creation seriously. Such a concentration would better emphasize topics such as friendship, exploration, self-expression, play and fun, passion, idealism, the building of social capital, and community.

Changes like these require shifting from a deficit vision of YAs as poor information users, a vision derived exclusively from a focus on difference from adults, to one grounded in a contemporary definition of culturally productive community membership. They require shifts in institutional attention toward taking youth's social worlds, self-directed experience, independence, *inter*dependence, and peer experiences seriously rather than continuing to marginalize or ignore them.

Among the many possibilities of literacy enactments meaningful for youth, libraries could begin taking seriously (systematically) formats of cultural production emerging in the past quarter-century, such as the new youth journalism, that promote "youth voices" and perspectives.[32] Many other forms of youth literacy enactments too: Consider YA zine culture. Consider student newspapers and yearbooks (current as well as historical, in paper as well as digital formats). Consider local youth sports culture; prom culture; social organizations; public performance (film, poetry, music, art, dance programs and drama playbills, rap and hip-hop culture, coming-of-age rituals from the diversity of racial and ethnic experiences); among many other cultural forms that constitute and document the daily and lived meanings of ordinary youth in the here and now. Often these manifestations of YA literacies will be assembled informally from what resources young people find at hand or bend to their own will from their insurgent communities, bootlegged technologies, pirate media, and rebel outposts.[33]

In terms of its obligation to collection management, an LIS vision of YAs as local community members would eschew the pedantic and dogmatic YDIC practices concentrating exclusively on the *differences* between youth and adults. It would build more upon *similarities* with LIS's core values and aspirations traditionally reserved for serving adults.

Author Tobias Wolff captures the adult world's common quick dismissal of youth meanings as "a series of sweet frauds" in a passage from his short story "Smorgasbord":

> We're supposed to smile at the passions of the young, and at what we recall of our own passions, as if they were no more than a series of sweet frauds we'd fooled ourselves with and then wised up to. Not only the passions of boys and girls for each other but the others, too—passion for justice, for doing right, for turning the world around. All these come in their time under our wintry smiles. Yet there was nothing foolish about what we felt.[34]

This is not a sentiment LIS should emulate.

Valuing the scope and breadth of literacy enactments created by YAs as community members promises new expectations, practices, and visions of the role the library can play in the lives of youth in their here and now. Doing so would dramatically lower traditional barriers previously considered impenetrable due to assumptions rooted in a vision of merely tolerating or teaching or marginalizing youth.

By cultivating and facilitating new interests, in tinkering and "messing around" not simply with new forms of media (i.e., a broader view of collections), youth acquisition of today's technical and media literacy skills would number among their present cultural expressions as well as offer libraries insights for what value they perhaps may hold for the future. Further, their growing expectations for immediate feedback from/with others they select would be institutionally respected as a cultural outcome—not dismissed as the exotic or unrealistic or immature white noise of youth.

Professionals could build new and exciting relationships with young people in implementing these new collection development roles, geared more to their current lives as productive information and culture creators than to a current and self-reverential institutional vision of itself.

Why have libraries found such core values, forever vaunted and trumpeted for adult users and culture, so difficult to apply to its younger users? How might an institution, so dedicated to a dated vision of young users as inherently "other," less-than, and needy (always compared to only a mythical, self-actualized future adult), come to recognize the value of youth's own cultural meanings? Given the assumptions hard-wired into LIS legacy practices and the YDIC agenda, the answer is simple: How could it be otherwise?

LIS can learn, however, from the questions proffered by postmodern analysis. LIS teaching, practice, and research can acknowledge the degree to which prior commitments to a vision of the end user, not of the field's own making, debilitate the profession's ability to realize its public value with young people. Not doing so makes a higher practice conceptually and institutionally impossible.

An aspirational vision of YAs as community members, however, demands of LIS answers to new questions. It drives collection development and management through different assumptions. These new assumptions would, in turn, drive the taking of youth meaning making no less seriously than that of adults. First, however, this new vision must value the cultural products and enactments of these practices by treating them systematically. Currently, there is no evidence that libraries systematically regard *any* of the cultural artifacts young adults produce. Their own experiences and meanings about the world do not appear in library collections.

All of these LIS concerns about collections percolate as a product of envisioning YAs as community members rooted in daily praxis. They represent a new path, an expanded civic diagnostic, for executing a vision of young people that avoids their assumed universal and demographic deficiency and difference from adulthood. Such praxis would extend an LIS discipline dedicated to thriving with rich cultural legacy, values, and institutional resources libraries already possess and thus invite making more of the human record accessible and useful.

Membership and Young Adult Space

What difference would an LIS-specific vision of YAs as local community members produce for library space design? Because libraries continue to devote more space and design consideration to restrooms than to YA users, they inherit a long legacy of denying young people public space equity.[35] Vast potential for transforming YA services appears nowhere more visibly than in how libraries inscribe their public spaces.

Of course, libraries ideally serve the entire public within a single facility. Once inside, however, library space becomes immediately segregated (commonly bifurcated: adult/children).[36] Today, even after over a decade of robust conversation and innovation, libraries continue to understudy, undertheorize about, and relegate YAs to leftover, surplus, or afterthought spaces.[37] This afterthought aesthetic includes the nation's signature YA library spaces.[38]

Libraries continue to underperform in this regard because they fail to address their YA audiences as entitled community members. Offering an adequate and equitable share of a library's public space from the beginning, through original design, requires that libraries incorporate a more participatory vision of YAs from the initial conceptual and design stages. Libraries, contrary to simply reproducing prevailing spatial competition between young people and adults (a competition rarely if ever won by youth), could then well stand as an institutional role model for reducing the seemingly inexorable segregation and erasure of youth from public space. As historian Steven Mintz observes, "More than ever before, children are segregated in a separate world."[39]

In imagining youth with an entitled right to library space, on equitable footing with other members of the community, LIS would necessarily serve as a more democratic foil to a broader and growing age-based Jim Crow Junior aesthetic.[40] LIS would achieve this through actually expanding the public sphere and incorporating young people into the true "third space" of the entire community rather than following prevailing trends to invent evermore-effective ways in which to marginalize, discourage, or prohibit them.[41] Envisioning young people as community members, however, opens up a vast terrain in which the broader community might come to see the library as an exemplar not an afterthought or self-proclaimed "safe" island in another wise dangerous land.[42]

As space manifests power, youth clearly understand how libraries marginalize them. Young people realize how little power libraries confer upon them. This perhaps explains why, decade after decade, YAs tell how libraries number among their least desirable public places.[43]

Many previous LIS perspectives on the YA service profile manifest this spatial inequity. Youth-at-risk is one approach; YDIC represents a slightly different paradigm; and YA as community member a third. The first two are rooted in hegemonic nineteenth-century deficit approaches predicated exclusively on youth-as-different-from-adult assumptions. The third envisions YAs as current, productive, entitled civic actors within today's local community.

More specifically, libraries institute meaning and power in the design of YA spaces. Space design evolves one way when they view youth as "at risk" (focus on surveillance). Libraries institute meaning and power in another way when they envision YAs as projects of "youth development" (focus on skills)—as in "homework centers" or "makerspaces." Finally, libraries enact space entirely another way when they envision YAs as entitled members of the community (focus on the production, consumption, and meanings youth culture manifests through various creative forms).

Unfortunately, lacking a basis in research, LIS frequently confuses these positions. Note the common conflation of curricular goals with the YDIC agenda evident in the following grant award announcement to build a new YA library space: "This competition was announced in answer to President Obama's 'Educate to Innovate' campaign, a nationwide effort to bring American students to the forefront in science and math, to provide the workers of tomorrow with the skills they need today."[44]

Here postmodern concerns about meaning and power (instead of experience and behavior) can help LIS generate an entirely new agenda of YA spatial praxis. How would library space, defined with a vision of YAs as community members, transform spatial design values, aesthetics, processes, criteria, practice, evaluation, and research?[45] What process or method would help LIS incorporate YAs as community members into library design? Further, because even the most progressive libraries limit youth involvement to "the YA space," how might LIS expand YAs' civic experience of contributing to the design of the entire library by incorporating them as members of the local community?

How might libraries incorporate, for instance, YA participation in the selection of an architecture firm for a new public library design process or building? Such a vision would necessarily require the library to consider the contributions of YAs on equal footing with those of adult participants, architects, administrators, and designers. Doing so would not privilege YA contributions but include them in the mix of all the many considerations required of a new building design.

Aided by a praxis acknowledging YAs as community members it is easier to understand how different YA service truths would percolate up variously from within the local and situated, under particular circumstances, in specific places, and at specific times. Such an approach represents a core departure from grand truths about all youth, such as those issuing from the YDIC. With a new YA service praxis such assumptions, generalizations, and conceits cannot simply flow down wholly conceived from on high. Instead they build up from the daily and lived relationships between libraries and actual users.

Envisioning YAs as community members establishes and enacts library space as a discernable democratic entitlement. It represents spatial equity about a public resource in ways quite similar to how LIS changed to gradually incorporate white middle-class women in the late nineteenth century and African American and Latinx community members after the middle of the twentieth. Until such time arrives, however, when libraries can envision YAs as contributing members of the community, they will remain, especially for ordinary youth, increasingly irrelevant and avoidable—merely adult "temples of youth improvement" and hostage to the YDIC.[46]

Membership and Young Adult Outreach

Discovering how a vision of YAs as local community members can transform LIS practice on the inside of library buildings into potentially flourishing new relationships (through developing more complex collections or offering better space designs) does not nearly exhaust the possibilities of a new service praxis. Library buildings clearly represent, of course, the largest institutional environment in which LIS professionals seek to serve young people.

But LIS professionals also possess skills particularly valuable to institutions and service environments that either directly or indirectly serve YAs beyond and outside library buildings as well. These skills range broadly across a variety of capacities, commitments, principles, and proficiencies. Such competencies include advanced education preparation, training, and records management skills, for instance. LIS professionals understand the nature of applying research and delivering professional presentations, and they increasingly understand how best to exploit an expanding tool kit of communication technologies, among other abilities.

All of these skills and competencies can deliver value in serving young people and connecting them with information, both directly and indirectly, and to institutions beyond the library. In one instance, LIS skills led a strategic planning process to build a special library's collection for a nonprofit law firm representing a county agency's foster youth.[47] An educational advocacy office, fighting for the rights of special education youth, could benefit from an LIS professional capable of developing information and records processing protocols. The editor of a journal or the director of a professional association supporting youth work would also benefit from the capacities contained in LIS training and experience. A nongovernmental organization dedicated to community development through constructing youth libraries internationally in impoverished urban centers benefits from LIS skills in building relationships with local educational, governmental, and other civic organizations (both in physical and virtual spaces).[48] A special international youth library offers professional staff to serve scholars from all over the world.[49]

None of these scenarios can thrive, however, through perpetuating a lesser-than-adult view of youth; nor by marginalizing them in the social hierarchy; nor by impugning them as necessarily oppositional to normative (idealized) adulthood. Stated differently, maintaining a near religious dependency on YDIC hegemony makes youth service difficult in urban Zambia, for foster youth advocates in the United States, and for international youth studies researchers. Not all youth are served by the same universal assumptions.

Nevertheless, a praxis infused with critical social theory, combined with professional excellence and volition, can make strong, positive, and valuable contributions to the well-being of youth and their caregivers. Such efforts can succeed because they work more consciously with local circumstances and situated knowledges, within the context of a particular time and place, and for actual and ordinary youth. Working in otherwise "alternative" environments outside of library buildings affords such perspective-expanding opportunities to help sharpen critical distance on LIS's historic and fatigued youth consensus. At the same time, doing so delivers professional capacities and competencies in wide-ranging and impactful venues.

Programming and Intergenerational Membership versus After-School Apartheid

YAs now possess many independent ways in which to communicate, create, and distribute information—thus increasingly circumventing traditional adult and institutional scrutiny. With this new capacity, perhaps in response to the continuing segregation of young adults from public space, YAs can now also often dictate more of the terms of that separation.

Where does this leave the library in the life of young people? What difference would a new YA service praxis offer relationships between YAs and library programming efforts? How would envisioning YAs as local community members matter?

Despite the seemingly inexorable separation (segregation) of YAs from the public realm, the library can still serve a critically important role as a space of intergenerational mediation. Libraries can do this by collecting, curating, and exhibiting cultural production in a public space when few other civic institutions can or will.

Thus, in addition to a new LIS trajectory on collection management, library space, and outreach, yet another promising path toward a praxis envisioning youth as community members might better explore and exploit the library's meaning as a nearly unique intergenerational public resource within contemporary civil society. As Wendy Lesko's essay in this collection certainly illustrates (see chapter 10), many intergenerational questions for attentive LIS professionals arise.[50] LIS can achieve intergenerationality, however, only if it eschews envisioning YAs as "other," as deficient, and defining young people only by their differences with adults.

The vast majority of young people experience de facto age-segregated educational facilities all day in school and then find themselves increasingly remanded to additional age-based after-school programming as well. This pattern abides the prescriptions as promulgated by the YDIC. This results, however, in youth's physical sequestration from the community's mainstream to a degree unimaginable even a few decades ago. I refer to this pattern as *after-school apartheid*. In expanding on the late-nineteenth-century view of youth-as-other, the cultural imperative not only has removed them from the dangers of the industrial workplace but increasingly erases them from public life altogether.[51]

Libraries envisioning YAs as community members offer the opportunity to preserve and even *extend* access to civic life on equal footing with other members of the community. In daily practice, however, LIS frequently does quite the opposite. Libraries nominally serve all generations equally, but in practice, they do so largely confined within age-based service silos in which YAs seldom receive equitable attention and service. Indeed, the rather recent manufacturing of the term *tween* suggests that LIS intends to segment youth into evermore thinly sliced silos.[52] This "new" category, despite its growing popularity in some LIS quarters, remains unjustified in evidence-based scholarship.

Until LIS more critically engages its philosophical approaches, it will continue to reproduce age-based segregation (wittingly or not). On the other hand, envisioning youth as entitled members of an age-integrated community requires rethinking the roles currently confining them: criminal intruders in our quiet and orderly world at worst; marginalized library users in most instances; or, under the best circumstances, the few hand-picked volunteers for the teen advisory group.

Beyond the most obvious manifestations of narrow age-based collections, afterthought YA spaces, and unimaginative outreach efforts, programming philosophy remains even more age segregated. Here, justified by either the implementation of a strict youth development catechism of skill enhancements for the future or the more lax and ill-defined YA "interest" criteria (with developmental "assets" and measures always lurking just off-stage), YA programming rarely extends beyond the bounds of age segregation.[53] Documented evidence for this observation dates back to the dawn of library YA programming itself.[54]

Teen advisory groups and summer reading programs (the nearly ritualized sine qua non of YA librarianship), by definition, demographically limit by age, as do gaming nights, so-called "maker" programs, and, indeed, nearly all manner of group program offerings. Along with YA literacy enactments and cultural productions, intergenerational models of programming rarely attract research or experimentation.[55]

What difference would an LIS-specific community membership vision for YAs produce for intergenerational library programming? Answering this question lies chiefly in the outcomes of future debates. Upon first blush, however, this notion might include systematic youth representation, visibility, and active YA roles at *all* library public events—not simply as passive audience members, but as hosts, guest introducers, ushers, or even content contributors to some portion of the events themselves. YAs would routinely serve as members of library boards, commissions, and Friends groups. YAs would attend, along with adult community members, annual legislative days to enable elected officials and policy makers to hear directly from young advocates. YAs might contribute to the content and assembly of library annual reports with their meanings and experiences represented. Formal and systematic YA appearances at city council and subcommittee meetings—at times other than simply to testify against budget cuts—would no longer raise eyebrows in surprise. YAs would appear as panelists at local, regional, and national library conferences as "normal" library users—not simply to perform as age-defined exemplars.

COMMUNITY MEMBERSHIP WITH ADULTS

The principle point here is simple. It would be foolish, of course, to deny that no differences exist between young people and adults. However, it is even more foolish, if not detrimental, never to examine LIS assumptions that there are no commonalities. As with other areas of LIS interventions, YA services should focus more on building meanings that young people *share* with adults, rather than limit a conception of them as merely, ever and only, different and subadults.

Again, answers to this question, of how to imagine YAs as members of the community, as with questions about other topics covered and not covered in this volume, contribute to a comprehensive praxis of institutional age-*integrated* operations and professional practice. These responses offer answers other than what LIS has advanced in relegating YAs decade after decade to silos exclusively defined by difference.

NOTES

1. W. A. Wiegand, "Tunnel Vision and Blind Spots: What the Past Tells Us about the Present; Reflections on the Twentieth-Century History of American Librarianship," *Library Quarterly* 69, no. 1 (1999): 1-32. The observation Wiegand lodges here about the entire LIS research tradition certainly applies to YA services: "contemporary LIS discourse is plagued with tunnel vision and blind spots that greatly limit the profession's ability to understand the role of the American library in the present accurately, and thus seriously affect the profession's efforts to plan the library's future" (1).
2. F. Gabriel, *Deconstructing Youth: Youth Discourses at the Limits of Sense* (New York: Palgrave Macmillan, 2013); G. Dimitriadis, *Studying Urban Youth Culture* (New York: Peter Lang, 2008).
3. W. A. Wiegand, "To Reposition a Research Agenda: What American Studies Can Teach the LIS Community about the Library in the Life of the User," *Library Quarterly* 73, no. 4 (2003): 369-82.
4. This undervaluing of YA service data inhibits the conduct of professional program evaluation as much as it inhibits more generalizable YA service research. Even when libraries do collect basic output measures, there is seldom evidence that they use the data for program evaluation or reform. See A. Bernier, "Young Adult Volunteering in Public Libraries: Managerial Implications," *Library Administration and Management* 23, no. 3 (2009): 95-112.

5. G. J. Leckie, L. M. Given, and J. E. Bushman, eds., *Critical Theory for Library and Information Science: Exploring the Social from across the Disciplines* (Santa Barbara, CA: Libraries Unlimited, 2010).
6. Praxis is referred to herein as the process by which theory, ideas, and skills are enacted together in daily practice.
7. Success bias and unsubstantiated "best practice" claims persist, however, despite our Eliza Dresang's urgings to systematically evaluate by measuring outcomes—things that actually change as a consequence of service interventions—not simply what libraries report doing. Granted, YA librarianship has largely pioneered the incorporation of technology into public service discourse. But technology offers a delivery system, not a service vision, and certainly not a vision of its end user. See E. T. Dresang, M. Gross, and L. E. Hold, *Dynamic Youth Services through Outcome-Based Planning and Evaluation* (Chicago: American Library Association, 2006). Further, no matter how powerful and plentiful individual accounts are, the plural of "anecdote" is not systematically collected "scientific data" and analysis.
8. L. P. Buttler, *An Introduction to Library Science* (Chicago: University of Chicago, 1933), xi-xii.
9. J. M. Budd, "The Library, Praxis, and Symbolic Power," *Library Quarterly* 73, no. 1 (2003): 19-32. The long-standing antipathy toward critical social theory echoes throughout youth studies. See B. Belton, *Radical Youth Work* (Lyme Regis, Dorset, UK: Russell House, 2010), 65-66.
10. "In many fields of academic research, the actual experiences of youth are not always considered important sites for developing theory and methodology and are seen as secondary in importance to the actions and imaginations of adults." See S. Maira and E. Soep, eds., *Youthscapes: The Popular, the National, the Global* (Philadelphia: University of Pennsylvania, 2005), xv.
11. The term *paradigm* used in this essay means dominance of a totalizing and grand scheme of thought analogous to ideology.
12. Budd, "Library, Praxis, and Symbolic Power," 20. See also J. Budd, "Phenomenological Critical Realism: A Practical Method for LIS," *Journal of Education for Library and Information Science* 53, no. 1 (2012): 69-80.
13. YALSA, "YALSA National Research Agenda: On Libraries, Learning, and Teens, 2017-2021," ALA.org, accessed November 2018, www.ala.org/yalsa/guidelines/research/researchagenda; V. A. Walter, "Public Library Services to Children and Teens: A Research Agenda," *Library Trends* 51, no. 4 (2003): 571-89.
14. A. Bernier, "Not Broken by Someone Else's Schedule: On Joy and Young Adult Information-Seeking," in *Youth Information-Seeking Behavior: Theories, Models, and Issues*, ed. M. K. Chelton and C. Cool (Lanham, MD: Scarecrow Press, 2007), xiii-xxvii.
15. F. Gabriel, *Deconstructing Youth: Youth Discourses at the Limits of Sense* (New York: Palgrave Macmillan, 2013); J. Deodato, "Becoming Responsible Mediators: The Application of Postmodern Perspectives to Archival Arrangement and Description," *Progressive Librarian* 27 (2006): 52-63; M. Foucault, *The Archaeology of Knowledge and the Discourse on Language* (New York: Pantheon, 1972); M. Foucault, *Power/Knowledge: Selected Interviews and Other Writings, 1972-1977* (New York: Pantheon, 1977); M. Foucault, *The History of Sexuality*, vol. 1, *An Introduction* (New York: Random House, 1978).
16. From among many examples, see G. Neri, "Safe Havens: Public Librarians on the Rigors and Rewards of Working with At-Risk Teens," *School Library Journal* 61, no. 11 (2015): 51; J. Ahn, "The Effect of Social Network Sites on Adolescents' Social and Academic Development: Current Theories and Controversies," *Journal of the American Society for Information Science and Technology* 62, no. 8 (2011): 1435-45; H. Julien, "Adolescent Career Decision Making and the Potential Role of the Public Library," *Public Libraries* 37, no. 6 (1998): 376-81; D. Callison, "Evolution of Methods to Measure Student Information Use," *Library and Information Science Research* 19, no. 4 (1997):

347-57; E. Howe, "Using Surveys to Build and Evaluate an Information Skills Program," *School Libraries Worldwide* (1997): 68-77; D. Neuman, "High School Students Use of Databases: Results of a National Delphi Study," *Journal of the American Society for Information Science* 46, no. 4 (1995): 284-98.

17. The approach percolating from this collection, however, does not, it must be pointed out, endorse qualifying the notion with a term like *"youth" citizenship* or *"junior" citizenship*. Contemporary democratic culture does not qualify this notion with diminutive labels or demographic qualifications. We do not use, for instance, the term *female citizenship* or *elder citizenship*. For an excellent historical treatment of this "junior" form of citizenship emanating in the Progressive Era's city improvement movement (complete with assumptions about "distracting" youth from presumed negative predispositions to urban ills, "preparing" them for adult life, as well as easily recognizable avoidance of the distinctions in social and material conditions), see J. S. Light, "Building Virtual Cities, 1895-1945," *Journal of Urban History* 38, no. 2 (March 2012): 336-71.

18. A. Lange, *The Design of Childhood: How the Material World Shapes Independent Kids* (New York: Bloomsbury, 2018), 10.

19. While the United States numbered among only three countries out of 193 that were not signatory to the United Nations Convention on the Rights of Children (ratified in 1989), the growing discourse on a vision of youth as citizens specifically stipulates that young people should "participate fully in family, cultural and social life." From among many sources demonstrating recent interest in this discourse, see Lange, *The Design of Childhood*; J. Kennelly, *Citizen Youth: Culture, Activism, and Agency in a Neoliberal Era* (New York: St. Martin's Press, 2011); L. Burnett and A. Spelman, "Creative Citizenship: Building Connection, Knowledge, Belonging and Leadership in Young People," *Aplis* 24, no. 1 (2011): 23-31; L. R. Sherrod, J. Torney-Purta, and C. A. Flanagan, eds., *Handbook of Research on Civic Engagement in Youth* (Hoboken, NJ: John Wiley & Sons, 2010); C. A. Flanagan, *Teenage Citizens: The Political Theories of the Young* (Cambridge, MA: Harvard University Press, 2013); and M. Torres, I. Rizzini, and N. Río, *Citizens in the Present: Youth Civic Engagement in the Americas* (Urbana: University of Illinois Press, 2013). See also D. Buckingham, ed., *Youth, Identity, and Digital Media* (Cambridge, MA: MIT Press, 2008).

20. As of this publication, there are several particularly pertinent scholarly studies: S. Costanza-Chock, *Out of the Shadows, Into the Streets! Transmedia Organizing and the Immigrant Rights Movement* (Cambridge, MA: MIT Press, 2014); R. G. Gonzales, *Lives in Limbo: Undocumented and Coming of Age in America* (Oakland: University of California Press, 2016); V. S. Katz, *Kids in the Middle: How Children of Immigrants Negotiate Community Interactions for Their Families* (New Brunswick, NJ: Rutgers University Press, 2014); and W. J. Nicholls, *The DREAMers: How the Undocumented Youth Movement Transformed the Immigrant Rights Debate* (Stanford, CA: Stanford University Press, 2013).

21. Gonzales, *Lives in Limbo*.

22. Ibid., 33.

23. The public realm in general has drawn the attention of many critical social theorists in the late twentieth and early twenty-first centuries. One example is Hannah Arendt. "For Arendt the public sphere comprises two distinct but interrelated dimensions. The first is the *space of appearance*, a space of political freedom and equality which comes into being . . . in concert through the medium of speech and persuasion. The second is the *common world*, a shared and public world of human artifacts, institutions and settings which separates us from nature and which provides a relatively permanent and durable context for our activities. Both dimensions are essential to . . . providing the spaces where it can flourish, the latter providing the stable background from which public spaces of action and deliberation can arise. For Arendt the reactivation of . . . the modern world depends upon both the recovery of a common, shared world and the creation of numerous

spaces of appearance in which individuals can disclose their identities and establish relations of reciprocity and solidarity." See M. P. D'Entreves, *The Political Philosophy of Hannah Arendt* (London: Routledge, 1994), 15.

24. It should not go unnoted; library history includes various forms of racial segregation. For a rapidly growing scholarship on the history of library racial segregation, particularly against African Americans, and the young adult activism that led to its demise, see W. A. Wiegand and S. A. Wiegand, *The Desegregation of Public Libraries in the Jim Crow South: Civil Rights and Local Activism* (Baton Rouge: Louisiana State University Press, 2018); C. Knott, *Not Free, Not for All: Public Libraries in the Age of Jim Crow* (Amherst: University of Massachusetts Press, 2015); D. M. Battles, *The History of Public Library Access to African Americans in the South, or Leaving the Plow Behind* (Lanham, MD: Scarecrow Press, 2009); P. T. Graham, *A Right to Read: Segregation and Civil Rights in Alabama's Public Libraries, 1900–1965* (Tuscaloosa: University of Alabama Press, 2002).

25. N. Eliasoph, *Making Volunteers: Civic Life After Welfare's End* (Princeton, NJ: Princeton University Press, 2011).

26. R. E. Rubin, *Foundations of Library and Information Science*, 2nd ed. (New York: Neal-Schuman, 2004), 33.

27. Numerous and formidable interests invested in legacy and unreflective practice would likely take issue with this vision: fiction publishers, publishing agents, writers, curriculum-only advocates, and ALA selection and awards committees, among many others.

28. Evidence exists that the adaptation to personal information devices is being taken seriously. See Denise E. Agosto's chapter 1 in this collection. For studies on the literacy enactments of YAs, see J. R. Vickery, *Worried about the Wrong Thing: Youth, Risk, and Opportunity in the Digital World* (New York: MIT Press, 2017); H. Jenkins, S. Shresthova, L. Gamber-Thompson, N. Kligler-Vilenchik, and A. M. Zimmerman, *By Any Media Necessary: The New Youth Activism* (New York: New York University Press, 2016); d. boyd, *It's Complicated: The Social Lives of Networked Teens* (New Haven, CT: Yale University Press, 2014); for one more geared to youth activism, see Costanza-Chock, *Out of the Shadows, Into the Streets!*.

29. For a more thorough treatment of what libraries commonly refer to as "ephemera," what I have termed YA "fugitive literacies," see Bernier, "Not Broken by Someone Else's Schedule."

30. See Cedeira Serantes and Kumasi, chapters 4 and 9, respectively, in this collection.

31. K. Haycock and M. Romaniuk, eds., *The Portable MLIS: Insights from the Experts* (Santa Barbara, CA: Libraries Unlimited, 2018); S. Hirsh, ed., *Information Services Today: An Introduction*, 2nd ed. (Lanham, MD: Rowman & Littlefield, 2018); K. de la Peña McCook and J. S. Bossaller, eds., *Introduction to Public Librarianship*, 3rd ed. (Chicago: American Library Association, 2018); R. E. Rubin, *Foundations of Library and Information Science*, 4th ed. (Chicago: American Library Association, 2017).

32. Youth Communication in New York and Pacific News Service's youth journalism arm, "Youth Communications Team," in San Francisco are just two examples.

33. To my knowledge, no library in the country systematically values even conventionally printed student newspapers, let alone "zines" and other forms of what I call the "fugitive literacies" of young adults. LIS must learn to value YA user relationships and manifest these relationships in what libraries collect. The facts contained in current library holdings betray a legacy of ignoring YAs' literacy enactments.

34. T. Wolff, "Smorgasbord," in *The Night in Question* (New York: Alfred A. Knopf, 1996), 162.

35. Historically, LIS has not deemed young adults entitled to space of their own, an equitable share of common library environments, nor produced research on the connections between YAs and space. For important historical texts focused on YA services that omit treatments of YA spaces, see M. A. Edwards, *The Fair Garden and the Swarm of Beasts: The Library and the Young Adult*, centennial

ed. (Chicago: American Library Association, 2002); M. K. Chelton and J. M. Rosinia, *Bare Bones Young Adult Services: Tips for Public Library Generalists* (Chicago: Public Library Association/Young Adult Library Services Association, 1993); E. V. LiBretto, ed., *New Directions for Young Adult Services* (New York: R. R. Bowker, 1983); J. V. Rogers, ed., *Libraries and Young Adults: Media, Services, and Librarianship* (Littleton, CO: Libraries Unlimited, 1979); D. M. Broderick, *Library Work with Children* (New York: H. W. Wilson, 1977); A. Bernier, "On My Mind: Young Adult Spaces," *American Libraries* 29, no. 9 (1998): 52.

36. Public library history is, it should also be remembered, replete with examples of defining, redefining, and overcoming spatial prohibition or segregation based on demographic categories such as sex, race, language, and social class.

37. A. Bernier, "Spacing Out with Young Adults: Translating YA Space Concepts Back into Practice," in *The Information Needs and Behaviors of Urban Teens: Research and Practice*, ed. D. E. Agosto and S. Hughes-Hassell (Chicago: ALA Editions, 2010), 113–126; A. Bernier, "'A Space for Myself to Go': Early Patterns in Small YA Spaces," *Public Libraries* 48, no. 5 (2009): 33–47; G. Cranz, "Body Conscious Design in a 'Teen Space': Post-occupancy Evaluation of an Innovative Public Library," *Public Libraries* 45, no. 6 (2006): 48–56; S. A. Lee, "Teen Space: Designed for Whom?," unpublished doctoral dissertation, University of California, Los Angeles, 2009; A. E. Pusey, "Public Library Teen Space Design: An Evaluation of Theory in Practice," unpublished master's thesis, University of North Carolina at Chapel Hill, July 2008.

38. For some signature examples, see San Francisco Public Library, Los Angeles Public Library, Phoenix Public Library, Chicago Public Library, and New York Public Library. Each of these examples, among others, despite undergoing either major renovation or new construction, implemented YA spaces in previously underutilized or repurposed spaces—none implemented YA space equity in their original, new, or renovation designs.

39. S. Mintz, *Huck's Raft: A History of American Childhood* (Cambridge, MA: Harvard University Press, 2004), 383.

40. There is excellent critical theory here, too, to expand how libraries imagine the spatial resources they represent. See H. Lefebvre, *The Production of Space*, trans. D. Nicholson-Smith (Oxford, UK: Blackwell, 1991); H. Lefebvre, "The Right to the City," in *Writing on Cities*, ed. and trans. E. Kofman and E. Lebas (Oxford, UK: Blackwell, 1996), 63–181.

41. Previous references to the library as a "third space" too narrowly perpetuate a false "safe haven" cliché that libraries, as an actual public place, cannot deliver. For reference to the "safe place" cliché, see K. Kendal, "YA Spaces of Your Dreams: Teen Central—Safe, Structured, and Teen-Friendly," *Voice of Youth Advocates* 26, no. 5 (December 2003): 380–381. For scholarly treatments of the "third space" metaphor, see E. W. Soja, *Thirdspace: Journeys to Los Angeles and Other Real-and-Imagined Places* (Cambridge, MA: Blackwell, 1996).

42. A. Bernier, "No Safe Space Haven in a Public World," *Voice of Youth Advocates*, "YA Strike Zone," April 2017, http://voyamagazine.com/2017/03/20/ya-strike-zone-april-2017.

43. As Richard E. Rubin has noted, the ways in which young people have experienced libraries is "aristocratic, authoritarian, unfriendly and unresponsive." See Rubin, *Foundations of Library and Information Science*, 2nd ed., 46. See also D. Agosto and S. Hughes-Hassell, *Urban Teens in the Library: Research and Practice* (Chicago: ALA Editions, 2010), 9–24; J. Abbas, M. Kimball, K. Bishop, and G. D'Elia, "Why Youth Do Not Use the Public Library," *Public Libraries* 47, no. 1 (2007): 80–85; S. L. Cook, S. Parker, and C. E. Pettijohn, "The Public Library: An Early Teen's Perspective," *Public Libraries* 44, no. 3 (2005): 157–61; DeWitt-Wallace-Readers Digest Fund, *Public Libraries as Partners in Youth Development* (New York: The Wallace Foundation, May 1999), www.wallacefoundation.org/knowledge-center/pages/public-libraries-as-partners-in-youth-development.aspx; Benton Foundation, *Buildings, Books, and Bytes* (Washington, DC: Benton Foundation, 1996).

44. Institute for Museum and Library Services (IMLS), "National Competition Selects 12 Libraries and Museums to Build Innovative Learning Labs for Teens," IMLS news release, November 17, 2011, www.imls.gov/national_competition_selects_12_libraries_and_museums_to_build_innovative_learning_labs_for_teens.aspx.
45. For a rare scholarly engagement with several of these issues, see P. Williams and J. Edwards, "Nowhere to Go and Nothing to Do: How Public Libraries Mitigate the Impacts of Parental Work and Urban Planning on Young People," *APLIS* 24, no. 4 (December 2011): 141–52.
46. H. Childress, *Landscapes of Betrayal, Landscapes of Joy: Curtisville in the Lives of Its Teenagers* (New York: State University of New York, 2000), 248.
47. I supervised a graduate LIS student in doing this very thing. Consequently, the law firm is currently considering hiring a part-time YA professional librarian.
48. One library school places semester-long digital interns with this organization; see Lubuto Library Partners, www.lubuto.org.
49. S. Hirsh, M. Simmons Holschuh, P. Christensen, M. Sellar, C. Stenström, C. Hagar, A. Bernier, D. Faires, J. Fisher, and S. Alman, "International Perspectives in LIS Education: Global Education, Research, and Collaboration at the SJSU School of Information," *Journal of Education for Library and Information Science* 56, supp. 1 (2015): S27–S46.
50. For an additional example of successful intergenerational collaboration, see E. Soep and V. Chavez, *Drop That Knowledge: Youth Radio Stories* (Berkeley: University of California Press, 2010).
51. S. Lincoln, *Youth Culture and Private Space* (New York: Palgrave Macmillan, 2012); M. Gutman and N. de Coninck-Smith, eds., *Designing Modern Childhoods: History, Space, and the Materials Culture of Children* (New Brunswick, NJ: Rutgers University Press, 2010); M. Miranda, *Homegirls in the Public Sphere* (Austin: University of Texas Press, 2003); S. C. Aitken, *Geographies of Young People: The Morally Contested Spaces of Identity* (New York: Routledge, 2001); I. Borden, *Skateboarding, Space and the City* (Oxford, UK: Berg, 2001); Childress, *Landscapes of Betrayal, Landscapes of Joy*; D. Sibley, *Geographies of Exclusion: Society and Difference in the West* (London: Routledge, 1995); R. White, *No Space of Their Own: Young People and Social Control in Australia* (New York: Cambridge University Press, 1990).
52. K. Fisher, E. Marcoux, E. M. Meyers, and C. F. Landry, "Tweens and Everyday Life Information Behavior: Preliminary Findings from Seattle," in *Youth Seeking Behaviors II: Context, Theories, Models, and Issues*, ed. M. K. Chelton and C. Cool (Lanham, MD: Scarecrow Press, 2006), 1–26.
53. C. Rogers-Whitehead, *Teen Fandom and Geek Programming: A Practical Guide for Librarians* (Lanham, MD: Rowman & Littlefield, 2018); K. Fitzgerald, *Successful Summer Reading Programs for All Ages: A Practical Guide for Librarians* (Lanham, MD: Rowman & Littlefield, 2018); T. McLees, *YALSA's Top Reads: STEM and Making* (Chicago: American Library Association, 2017); A. J. Alessio and K. A. Patton, *A Year of Programs for Teens*, 2nd ed. (Chicago: American Library Association, 2011); L. B. Alexander and N. Kwon, eds., *Multicultural Programs for Tweens and Teens* (Chicago: American Library Association, 2010); M. Gorman and T. Suellentrop, *Connecting Young Adults and Libraries: A How-To-Do-It Manual*, 4th ed. (New York: Neal-Schuman, 2009); A. Alessio, *Excellence in Library Service to Young Adults*, 5th ed. (Chicago: American Library Association, 2008); P. Brehm-Heeger, *Serving Urban Teens* (Westport, CT: Libraries Unlimited, 2008).
54. M. Braverman, *Youth, Society, and the Public Library* (Chicago: American Library Association, 1979), 96–100.
55. The obvious exceptions are the involvement of youth in the children's reading program and the teen volunteers who help elders learn how to navigate computer technology. However, it should be pointed out that these exemplify only youth involved with preconceived programming processes. And in both of these instances, YA meaning and experience are subsumed under the needs of the other groups. This must be distinguished from more truly reciprocal intergenerational program content development, execution, and evaluation.

CONCLUSION

Membership's Promise for Praxis

Anthony Bernier

> I am alarmed that when we aim to control young people, we miss out on opportunities to instead guide teens as co-creators and fellow citizens.
>
> —Jacqueline Ryan Vickery, Worried About the Wrong Things (2017)

LIS has maintained a "tunnel vision" legacy with respect to critical social theory, particularly regarding the professional practice of YA librarianship. The same, however, is not true for other youth studies disciplines. There is a gathering new discourse in the scholarship on youth informed by theoretical sophistication that can meaningfully contribute to a much-needed debate over an LIS-specific vision of young people. The degree to which LIS engages a fitful debate about its own vision of YAs is the degree to which a praxis geared more to contemporary youth can emerge.

The concept quickly gaining purchase among academic youth scholars and allies calls for nothing less than "the end of adolescence" as it has been known.[1] This notion advances that contemporary culture, with its deficit-only views, imagines young people based not upon their capacities but exclusively upon their differences with adults and a misleading, arbitrary, and superficial age-based demographic profile. Scholars advancing the end-of-adolescence suggest that this age-based vision unalterably and fundamentally renders youth infantilized and incompetent subadults.

By altering the current proscriptive and reductionist view of young people to incorporate more complexity and diversity, by focusing on their respective and demonstrated capacities (rather than fetishizing only their limits), and in granting them rights and responsibilities based upon their capacities, youth would flourish, these advocates claim, at much higher levels of accomplishment.

Youth activism in American history, to consider only one area of youth competency, dates to the founding of the Republic. History demonstrates all the capacities claimed by the youth development industrial complex (YDIC) as lacking in youth but without its hegemonic and dogmatic lists and dictates. Youth pressing for social justice in the early 1960s, such as the founders of Students for a Democratic Society, insisted that their celebrated and founding document begin with the powerful and collective referent "we."[2] History teaches that there is no need to limit a view of youth's cultural contributions to incompetence and difference.

Even from LIS's own history, witness young peoples' volition in repeatedly calling each other forward into civic participation. Historian Patterson Toby Graham, for instance, documents one such call, from 1961–1963, in cities throughout racially segregated Alabama. Young adults (adolescents) led, staged, and ultimately succeeded in desegregating public libraries through "read-ins."[3] This is, of course, in addition to a long and continuing string of more recent youth activism on such public policy issues as the various waves of youth-led immigration reform efforts, the Occupy and Me Too Movements, gun policy reform, activism on environmental change, youth enfranchisement—young people are, as usual, at the center of the essential issues of our time.[4]

These examples illustrate ways of envisioning young people not simply as autonomous or individual agents but as interdependent and collective actors. Time after time youth have entered the public square to weigh in on policy to change the institutions and circumstances influencing their lives and our culture. Adults played important roles in these events, of course. But neither can it be denied that it was youth, individually and collectively, fueling the fires and asserting broad and active community membership, many times at the risk of their own safety.

While there are many such stories in youth history, the YDIC does not know a vocabulary describing or acknowledging being civic-minded through advancing social justice. Preoccupied with its own ideological commitments, about what youth lack and how they differ from adults, the YDIC does not even attempt to explain how youth become active without instruction from its hegemonic prescriptions.

On the other hand, a competency-based youth vision closely mirrors the vision of youth as already active local community members. This is an important concept percolating in the essays of *Transforming Young Adult Services*.

If adopted, such a vision would enable LIS to better incorporate youth capacities as members of situated communities within the library's larger civic context. A vision of young people as community members emphasizes more of what youth share and contribute *with* adults, rather than ever and only emphasizing the differences and deficiencies when compared to idealized adults. If this vision is achieved, LIS may well find it easier to grant youth commensurate acknowledgment, rights, privileges, and opportunities. A possible consequence might then arise for LIS to take youth seriously for their cultural contributions more on their own terms rather than as institutionally marginalized, deficient, and needy preadults.

The debate now before LIS is this: In what ways can praxis (the combination of critical theory and reflective practice) help reimagine today's young people as active, engaged, and contributing members of their respective communities? The notion of "membership" aligns, it bears repeating, much more closely with LIS's expansive historical, institutional, and ethical aspirations in promoting intellectual freedom and information access. Appropriately applying this concept to young people, however, requires LIS's critical engagement and reconciling its legacy of systematic and institutional marginalization.

Table C.1 begins to feather out some of the more obvious aspects of YA services grounded in the dated and borrowed vision of youth from the YDIC. It also charts language to inform an emerging LIS vision of YAs as community members. It is important to observe how a different vision of YAs produces different praxis in nearly every aspect of a professional YA service profile.[5]

In daily practice, applying a vision of YAs as community members within a civic culture and considering them as subjects in their own rights would become systematic not episodic.

TABLE C.1 Common Touchstones Applying Different Visions of Young Adults to Library Services

CONTRASTING VISIONS OF YOUNG ADULTS IN LIBRARY PRACTICE		
	YAs as Objects of Youth Development	**YAs as Local Community Members**
Collections	• Privilege conventionally published materials (particularly proscriptive and curricular literature and celebrated fiction)	• Emphasis on youth-produced literacy enactments documenting contemporary experience • Youth creative forms curated and featured systematically
YA Space	• Unused/spare space • Librarian choices • Houses collection • Homework/tutor space • Computer or learning lab • "Makerspace" • Matching tables and task chairs • Necessarily separated as far as possible from children's space • Competition with adult spaces/purposes	• Purpose-built designed space • Deeper participatory roles in design processes (including non-YA spaces) • Privileges social experience, community building, sharing • Wide variety of seating options and configurations • Better understanding of how, in some communities, parents rely on older youth to take care of younger children, thereby suggesting distinctive (but not necessarily distant) spaces • Reduced competition with adult spaces/purposes • Greater awareness of environmentally sustainable design features • More liberal food/drink policies
Atmosphere	• Quasi-academic, curricular • Rule-centric behavior	• Conviviality of a school hallway between classes • Socially enforced behavior
Participation	• Largely individualistic • Teen advisory group helps with YA collection development • Reproduced bureaucratic culture • Volunteers help with summer reading program	• Group/peer-centered • Teen advisory group integrated into all public library operations (not just YA activity) • Socially determined and enforced organizational culture • Volunteers exposed to tasks throughout the entire institution (including administration)

[CONTINUED ON FOLLOWING PAGE]

TABLE C.1 [CONTINUED]

	CONTRASTING VISIONS OF YOUNG ADULTS IN LIBRARY PRACTICE	
	YAs as Objects of Youth Development	**YAs as Local Community Members**
Programming	• Youth Development and skill enrichment programs determined and produced by library (rarely evaluated) • General library programming contains no youth component	• Program content determined and delivered by youth (constantly evaluated) • All library programs contain youth component
Staffing	• Job descriptions designed by legacy administrative practice	• Job descriptions of staff periodically reviewed by informed youth panel (note: differs from formal staff evaluation from youth)
Security	• Receives no YA-specific coaching or instruction • Largely relied upon to address YA "behavior" issues • Rarely documents disciplinary actions	• Greater social enforcement cultivated • YAs participate in sensitivity training for security personnel • Rules enforced within context • Problems documented and analyzed for patterns and policy implications

It means acknowledging them in their present moment as opposed to objects upon which to pour unexamined and dated assumptions and future-oriented adultist agendas.

In research, this requires methodologically developing an LIS research agenda and protocols *with* young people. It means more than merely conducting research simply "on" young people and how their needs are/are not met on institutional terms.[6]

This transformative vision characterizes the difference between youth representing value for the life of the library versus the library offering its value for the life of young people.

Answers to questions about defining the granular features and contours of an LIS YA local community member vision remain a key challenge before the profession generally and YA students, practitioners, and researchers in particular. But while the debate emerging in these pages may not yield "neat and clean" maps to so-called "best practices," it does promise to help build better relationships with young people than will trafficking in a century-old economy of deficits and difference.

Imagining transformative paths toward meaning with youth, viewed foremost as fully entitled members of local community, also immediately begs questions about power relations between young people and the libraries ostensibly funded to serve them. Thus, whatever debate ensues would necessarily involve more discussion at the nexus of culture, libraries, and youth as institutional actors, rather than simply asserting the prevailing prescriptive focus on what libraries think youth should be or become someday.

How do youth, viewed as entitled community members, interpret, create, negotiate, evolve, and navigate their own volition and the institutional meanings contained in libraries? What are the competing and cooperative circuits and levers of power YAs engage and encounter in libraries? How do they manifest and negotiate those institutional circuits? How do libraries respond to, study, deploy, and evaluate their institutional power with/on youth when not envisioning them as interlopers or needy less-than adults?

Engaging these questions might well result in reducing LIS's legacy preoccupations and emphasize more of the meanings ordinary youth reach for every day. It could mean less library-determined prescriptive programming content, reducing traditional collection management prerogatives, and more avoidance of perpetual preoccupation with so-called "teen behavior."

Conversely, reimagining YA users offers the potential for more youth-centric initiatives in creating, collecting, exhibiting, preserving, curating, and promoting their own literacy enactments. It could mean less youth avoidance of libraries and more expectations of genuine welcome, discovery, acceptance, affinity, community, and the flourishing of a broader civic identity.[7]

Indeed, the debate over how an LIS-specific vision of YA community member comes about offers opportunities for the entire profession. It nominates a particularly important question, of course, for LIS students at the beginning of their careers. Further, it remains an essential debate for experienced researchers and practitioners floundering in decades of uncritical consensus and YDIC hegemony.

A transforming debate toward defining an LIS-specific vision of young adults affords many positive outcomes. Critical youth studies scholar Greg Dimitriadis is correct: "No one has felt the brunt of neoliberalism, the withering of the public sphere, or the rise of rampant worldwide capitalist logics more than young people."[8] Thus, this new debate offers an opportunity to both create a flexible and dynamic new LIS-specific vision of youth and consequently move it beyond historic reliance on other disciplines.

LIS requires concepts fit for its own purpose. It will not arrive at these concepts, however, by remaining confined to or complicit with the agendas of therapists, counselors, or "soft cops."

A fitful debate over a new YA service praxis also potentially contributes something meaningful to emerging interdisciplinary conversations and inquiry in the broader field of youth studies.[9]

Finally, an LIS-specific vision of young adults as members of local community offers a comprehensively transformative opportunity. It would leave a more positive, contemporary, and dynamic institutional legacy for future LIS professionals to inherit than one forever grounded in century-old static assumptions of deficits and preadult candidacy. A YA community membership vision positions the library in the here and now of youth meanings and power.

LIS's "tunnel vision" and "blind spots" remain the lingering consequences of the ways in which it has adopted, integrated, reproduced, and institutionalized a nineteenth-century vision of young adults. On the other hand, by turning attention toward postmodern concerns about the power and meanings community members make themselves, a new LIS-specific YA services praxis stands to add new value to the lives of today's ordinary youth.

LIS students should debate, argue over, and then take this professional vision forward into their new careers. They should then apply their visions to the particular circumstances in which they serve with the particular young people they find there. The authors contributing to this collection have certainly attempted to launch and propel this discussion into future professional interventions. They welcome the coming debate.

NOTES

1. See Michael Cart's chapter 7 in this collection; G. Dimitriadis, *Studying Urban Youth Culture* (New York: Peter Lang, 2008); R. Epstein, *The Case against Adolescence: Rediscovering the Adult in Every Teen* (Sanger, CA: Quill Driver Books, 2007); R. C. Savin-Williams, *The New Gay Teenager* (Cambridge, MA: Harvard University Press, 2006); P. Graham, *The End of Adolescence* (Oxford, UK: Oxford University Press, 2004).
2. T. Hayden, "Participatory Democracy: From Port Huron to Occupy Wall Street," *The Nation* 294, no. 16 (April 2012): 11-23.
3. P. T. Graham, *A Right to Read: Segregation and Civil Rights in Alabama's Public Libraries, 1900-1965* (Tuscaloosa: University of Alabama Press, 2002). For more recent treatments of young peoples' frontline activism in desegregating southern public libraries, see W. A. Wiegand and S. A. Wiegand, *The Desegregation of Public Libraries in the Jim Crow South: Civil Rights and Local Activism* (Baton Rouge: Louisiana State University Press, 2018); C. Knott, *Not Free, Not for All: Public Libraries in the Age of Jim Crow* (Amherst: University of Massachusetts Press, 2015); D. M. Battles, *The History of Public Library Access to African Americans in the South, or Leaving the Plow Behind* (Lanham, MD: Scarecrow Press, 2009).
4. There is an entire and growing critical youth studies historiography, on the twentieth century alone, documenting the strong civic roles youth have assumed. LIS would do well to begin incorporating some of its wisdom into praxis. See, from among many examples, B. Haas, *Fighting Authoritarianism: American Youth Activism in the 1930s* (New York: Fordham University Press, 2017); J. Helgren, *American Girls and Global Responsibility: A New Relation to the World during the Early Cold War* (New Brunswick, NJ: Rutgers University Press, 2017); H. V. Scott, *Younger Than That Now: The Politics of Age in the 1960s* (Amherst: University of Massachusetts Press, 2016); J. Conner and S. M. Rosen, eds., *Contemporary Youth Activism: Advancing Social Justice in the United States* (Santa Barbara, CA: Praeger, 2016); S. Blumenthal, "Children of the 'Silent Majority': Richard Nixon's Young Voters for the President, 1972," *Journal of Policy History* 27, no. 2 (2015): 337-63; M. Blackwell, *¡Chicana power! Contested Histories of Feminism in the Chicano Movement* (Austin: University of Texas Press, 2011); M. Forman-Brunell and L. Paris, eds., *The Girls' History and Culture Reader: The Twentieth Century* (Urbana: University of Illinois Press, 2011); E. Soep and V. Chavez, *Drop That Knowledge: Youth Radio Stories* (Berkeley: University of California Press, 2010); W. R. Jorae, *The Children of Chinatown: Growing Up Chinese American in San Francisco, 1850-1920* (Chapel Hill: University of North Carolina Press, 2009); E. Luhr, *Witnessing Suburbia: Conservatives and Christian Youth Culture* (Berkeley: University of California Press, 2009); L. Alvarez, *The Power of the Zoot: Youth Culture and Resistance during World War II* (Berkeley: University of California Press, 2008); C. Munoz, *Youth, Identity, Power: The Chicano Movement* (New York: Verso, 2007).
5. It should go without saying that not every aspect or service idea generated with a youth development perspective is "wrong" or useless. A reflective and critical professional practice makes these distinctions. Without a self-aware praxis to recognize the differences, however, the challenge to do so becomes that much more difficult.
6. Chin cites a number of examples of research that are child-centered in which young people control the research. One example of this methodological approach is Youth Participatory Action Research (PAR) as implemented at the Institute for Community Research (ICR). "The ICR's philosophy is that youth are citizens too and that they are capable of research." See E. Chin, "Power-Puff Ethnography/Guerrilla Research: Children as Native Anthropologists," in *Representing Youth: Methodological Issues in Critical Youth Studies*, ed. A. L. Best (New York: New York University Press, 2007), 269-83. See also N. Mirra, A. Garcia, and E. Morrell, *Doing Youth Participatory Action*

Research: Transforming Inquiry with Researchers, Educators, and Students (New York: Routledge, 2016); E. Tuck and K. W. Yang, eds., *Youth Resistance Research and Theories of Change* (New York: Routledge, 2014); E. J. Ozer and D. Wright, "Beyond School Spirit: The Effects of Youth-Led Participatory Action Research in Two Urban High Schools," *Journal of Research on Adolescence* 22, no. 2 (2012): 267–83; M. Kellett, *Rethinking Children and Research: Attitudes in Contemporary Society* (London: Continuum International, 2010); T. M. Brown and L. F. Rodriguez, *Youth Participatory Action Research* (San Francisco: Jossey-Bass, 2009); J. Cammarota and M. Fine, eds., *Revolutionizing Education: Youth Participatory Action Research* (New York: Routledge, 2007); B. Kirshner, "Supporting Youth Participation in School Reform: Preliminary Notes from a University-Community Partnership," *Children, Youth, and Environments* 17, no. 2 (2007): 354–63; V. Caputo, "Anthropology's Silent 'Others': A Consideration of Some Conceptual and Methodological Issues for the Study of Youth and Children Cultures," in *Youth Cultures: A Cross-Cultural Perspective*, ed. V. Amit-Talai and H. Wulff (London: Routledge, 1995), 8–27.

7. So-called "teen behavior," and how to deal with it, has been and remains one of LIS's most popular YA topics for decades—particularly in blogs, webinars, and ALA association documents. For a recent example, see J. Velasquez, "A Place of Their Own: Creating Spaces Where Teens Can Thrive," *American Libraries*, September 1, 2016, https://americanlibrariesmagazine.org/2016/09/01/library-teen-spaces-place-of-their-own; see also YALSA, "Teen Space Guidelines," ALA.org, accessed November 2018, www.ala.org/yalsa/guidelines/teenspaces; M. K. Chelton, "The 'Problem Patron' Public Libraries Created," *The Reference Librarian* 36, no. 75/76 (2002): 23–32; M. K. Chelton, "Young Adults as Problems: How the Social Construction of a Marginalized User Category Occurs," *Journal of Education for Library and Information Science* 42, no. 1 (2001): 4–11. This approach to the literacy enactments, documents, and meanings created by YAs as local community members would necessarily take YA social behavior more seriously as well. It would include reconsidering and reorienting library service philosophy, ethics, practice, space, and the other dimensions of service by designing them with YAs' social norms as a legitimate dimension of the process, not something added, inconvenient, or peripheral. See also A. Bernier, "The Damaging Myth of 'Teen Behavior,'" *Voice of Youth Advocates*, "YA Strike Zone," February 2018, http://voyamagazine.com/2018/02/05/ya-strike-zone-february-2018.

8. Dimitriadis, *Studying Urban Youth Culture*, 17.

9. In few scholarly works on youth are libraries even mentioned. See, for example, Conner and Rosen, *Contemporary Youth Activism*; N. Lesko and S. Talburt, eds., *Keywords in Youth Studies: Tracing Affects, Movements, Knowledges* (New York: Routledge, 2012); C. Macleod, *"Adolescence," Pregnancy and Abortion: Constructing a Threat of Degeneration* (London: Routledge, 2011); J. K. Taft, *Rebel Girls: Youth Activism and Social Change across the Americas* (New York: New York University Press, 2011); M. E. Thomas, *Multicultural Girlhood: Racism, Sexuality, and the Conflicted Spaces of American Education* (Philadelphia: Temple University Press, 2011); C. Wright, P. Standen, and T. Patel, *Black Youth Matters: Transitions for School to Success* (New York: Routledge, 2010); E. Luhr, *Witnessing Suburbia: Conservatives and Christian Youth Culture* (Berkeley: University of California Press, 2009).

About the Editor

ANTHONY BERNIER, PHD, is professor at California's San José State University School of Information. As a critical youth studies scholar, Dr. Bernier explores the administration of library services with young people as his primary field of research. The iSchool has awarded him Distinguished Service, Outstanding Professor, and Outstanding Researcher Awards. He received two National Leadership Grants from the Institute of Museum and Library Services (on library spaces for young people), one from ALA's Diversity Research Committee, and another from the Association for Library and Information Science Education (ALISE) in support of his research on first-generation graduate students. He also served a four-year term on ALA's Committee on Accreditation, chaired several national professional and academic associations, was recently elected chair of ALA's Library History Round Table, and currently writes the regular "YA Strike Zone" column for *Voice of Youth Advocates* (*VOYA*). A practicing YA specialist librarian and administrator for 15 years, he designed the first purpose-built library space for teenaged youth, the Los Angeles Public Library's acclaimed Teen'Scape, and produced nationally recognized youth outreach and programming models. Dr. Bernier's doctoral dissertation at the University of California examined changing notions of public space in twentieth-century America.

About the Contributors

DENISE E. AGOSTO, PHD, is Professor in the College of Computing & Informatics at Drexel University and Director of its Master's of Library and Information Science Program. Her research focuses on young people's use of social media and the implications for public library services. She has won many awards and grants for her research and teaching, and for her more than 100 scholarly publications. Her most recent book is *Information Literacy and Libraries in the Age of Fake News* (2018).

JEANIE AUSTIN is a librarian with San Francisco Public Library's Jail and Reentry Services program. Their interests include the provision of library services to people held in state custody and the gendered, racialized, and ability-centric political and social systems that surround this work. Jeanie received their PhD in Library and Information Science from the University of Illinois, Urbana-Champaign.

JOHN M. BUDD is Professor Emeritus in the School of Information Science and Learning Technologies at the University of Missouri-Columbia. Winner of the 2002 Highsmith Library Literature Award (formerly the G. K. Hall Award for Library Literature), he has authored numerous publications and articles in professional and scholarly journals and has given presentations at national and state conferences.

MICHAEL CART, former director of the Beverly Hills (CA) Public Library, is the author or editor of 21 books. He is a columnist and reviewer for the American Library Association's *Booklist* magazine and a past president of both the Young Adult Library Services Association (YALSA) and the National Council of Teachers of English's Assembly on Literature for Adolescents (ALAN). Mr. Cart is the recipient of the 2000 Grolier Award and in 2008 became the first recipient of the YALSA/Greenwood Publishing Group Service to Young Adults Achievement Award. Before his relocation to the Midwest, he taught young adult literature at UCLA. Mr. Cart received the 2018 ALAN Award, and his work has appeared in *The New York Times*, *The Los Angeles Times*, *The San Francisco Chronicle*, and *Parents* magazine.

LUCIA CEDEIRA SERANTES, PHD, works as Limited-Duties instructor at the Faculty of Information and Media Studies, The University of Western Ontario (Canada). Her primary research lies at the intersection of young adults, reading, and public libraries, with an emphasis on the reading experience from the reader's perspective. She has also provided contributions to *Plotting the Reading Experience: Theory/Practice/Politics* (2016) and *Young People Reading: Empirical Research across International Contexts* (2018). Her last publication is the minigraph *Young People, Comics, and Reading: Exploring a Complex Reading Experience* (2019).

MARY K. CHELTON, PHD, is Professor Emeritus at the Graduate School of Library and Information Science, Queens College, City University of New York, where she taught for 20 years. Her PhD is from Rutgers University (1997), where she did the award-winning dissertation "The Adult-Adolescent Encounter in the Library Context," the culmination of years of having been a young adult librarian in public libraries in New York, Maryland, and California. She has published more than 65 articles in library literature and was a cofounder, with Dorothy Broderick, of the journal *Voice of Youth Advocates* (*VOYA*). She is a recipient of both ALA's Grolier Award for service to youth and YALSA's Lifetime Achievement Award. Dr. Chelton is enjoying retirement reviewing military romances for *Booklist* and playing with her three Vizsla dogs on Long Island.

KAREN COATS, PHD, is Professor of English at Illinois State University, where she teaches children's and young adult literature. She publishes widely on how children's and young adult literature showcases, examines, and helps form identity in youth culture. Her most recent book is *The Bloomsbury Introduction to Children's and Young Adult Literature* (2017).

CHERIE GIVENS, JD, PHD, CIPP, is an attorney, certified information privacy professional, and author. She holds a doctorate in Library, Archival, and Information Studies from the University of British Columbia and a JD from Louisiana State University. Dr. Givens is the author of *Information Privacy Fundamentals for Librarians and Information Professionals* (2014). She works in the Washington, DC, area where she advises and writes about information privacy, cybersecurity, and information governance. Her other professional interests include the First Amendment, intellectual freedom, and legal and policy issues affecting information environments and their users.

MARY ANN HARLAN, PHD., is Assistant Professor at San José State University School of Information where she oversees the Teacher Librarian Program. She teaches courses in school library programs, materials, and fieldwork. Her research interests include information practices of youth and girlhood representations in young adult literature. She is particularly interested in examining statements from those in the field regarding youth experience with reading young adult literature related to what they "learn" by working with youth to examine the information practices of reading fiction. Her most recent publication is *The Girl Positive Library: Inspiring Confidence, Creativity, and Curiosity in Young Women* (2018).

KAFI D. KUMASI, PHD, is Associate Professor in the Graduate School of Information Sciences at Wayne State University. She teaches in the areas of school library media studies, urban librarianship, multicultural education, and research methods. Her research interests revolve around issues of literacy, equity, and diversity, particularly in urban environments spanning K–12 and graduate-level educational contexts. Her publications include book chapters and journal articles in (among others) *Journal of Education for Library and Information Science*, *The Journal of Research on Libraries and Young Adults*, *Library and Information Science Research*, *School Libraries Worldwide*, *School Library Media Research*, and *Urban Library Journal*.

WENDY SCHAETZEL LESKO is President of the Youth Activism Project, a national nonpartisan clearinghouse that encourages those not yet of voting age to be agents for policy change. In 1998, she coauthored and self-published *Youth! The 26% Solution* with 19-year-old Emanuel Tsourounis. Lesko has written training manuals designed for adults on effective multigenerational advocacy, including *Youth as Equal Partners* (2002) for United Way of America. In 2004 she launched School Girls Unite with a group of seventh-graders in the United States and the Youth Activism Project became a nonprofit organization. In 2009 these American teens with their sister organization in Mali wrote the bilingual action guide *Girls Gone Activist! How to Change the World through Education*, and in 2011 they led the successful campaign to mobilize U.S. support to establish the United Nations International Day of the Girl Child. Anika Manzoor, one of the 12-year-old cofounders, became executive director immediately following her graduation from the Harvard Kennedy School of Government in June 2018.

MIKE MALES, PHD, is a senior researcher for the Center on Juvenile and Criminal Justice, San Francisco; former sociology instructor at the University of California, Santa Cruz; author of five books and numerous journal and periodical articles on youth issues; and a consultant to the San José State University Library and Information Science research team on young adult library spaces.

KATE MCDOWELL, PHD, is Associate Professor and Interim Associate Dean for Academic Affairs at the School of Information Sciences at the University of Illinois at Urbana-Champaign. She is the recent recipient of UIUC's Excellence in Online and Distance Teaching Award and has been teaching storytelling since 2007, helping graduate professional students explore how their stories can help them succeed in libraries and beyond. She has worked as storytelling consultant to Advancement at the University of Illinois, to the Illinois statewide Prairie Rivers Network, and to various nonprofits. Her workshops in troubleshooting storytelling, data storytelling, and storytelling for fund-raising bring the tools of storytelling to many areas, including career preparation, business, and public service. Her current research project is on storytelling at work, and she is working on a book called *Storytelling Thinking for Professionals*.

PAULETTE ROTHBAUER, PHD, earned her doctorate in library and information science from The University of Western Ontario where she is an associate professor with the Faculty of Information and Media Studies. For about 20 years, she has been studying reading, readers, and public libraries. Her overarching research questions remain the same: What do readers make of what they read? How does reading (and, by extension, how do libraries) help people to fashion their identities, their resistance, their resilience, their pasts, their futures? She is coauthor with Catherine Ross and Lynne McKechnie of *Reading Still Matters: What the Research Reveals about Reading, Libraries and Community* (2018) and coeditor of a collection of contributed essays called *Plotting the Reading Experience: Theory/Practice/Politics* (2016).

Index

A

AAP (Association of American Publishers), 51
AASL
    See American Association of School Librarians
Abbas, J., 12
The Absolutely True Diary of a Part-Time Indian (Alexie), 25
abstinence-only education, 56
academic achievement, 154-155
academic curriculum, 29
access
    censorship, resistance to, 51, 52
    LBOR/COE on, 50
Ackoff, R. L., 94
Act Your Age! (Lesko), 152
activism
    capacities of youth for, 183-184
    youth activism, 67-68
    Youth Activism Project, 122
Adichie, Chimamanda Ngozi, 23, 24
adolescence
    affective-cognitive development during, 19-20
    alternative frameworks for vision of young adults, 155-157
    coming-of-age into adulthood idea, 152
    end-of-adolescence, call for, 183
    expansion of, 79-80
    G. Stanley Hall on, xxvii
    idea of, 78-79
    LIS vision of youth, 159-161
    signified by age, idea of, 153-155
Adolescence: Its Psychology and Its Relations to Physiology, Anthropology, Sociology, Sex, Crime, Religion, and Education (Hall), 78
adolescent medicine, 80
adolescents
    See teens
adult books
    on BBYA, 82-83
    crossover books, 83-85
    for young adults, reviews of, 85-88
Adult Books for Young People, 82
"adult" status, xi-xii

adult-centered perspective
    literature in library services for teens, analysis of, 4-8
    in professional library literature, 13
    teen-centered perspective and, 4
    of YA services, 3
    Young Adult Library Services articles, analysis of, 8
adult-constructed dualism, 67
adultescents
    new young adult, 78-82
    YA literature for new category of users, 82-83
    young adult definition, changing, 77-78
adulthood
    coming-of-age into, 152
    deferral of, factors leading to, 154
adults
    age-/generation-based qualities for citizenship, 143-145
    alienation of old people from society, 143
    comics, perceptions of, 42
    copiloting with young adults, 121-122, 124
    generational integration at library, 146-148
    generational synergy, thwarting of, 149
    in Holt's "power and control" theory, xxvii-xxviii
    LIS vision of YAs as community members and, 171-172
    logic of dispossession and, 63
    stereotypes about teens, 152-155
    teens as individuals, focus on, 11-12
    youth, conceptualizations of, 61-62
    youth, difference from, xxxii
    youth in comparison to "adulthood," xl
    youth/adult binary opposition, 163-164
African-American youth, 112
after-school apartheid, 176
age
    adolescence signified by, 153-155, 159-160
    of adolescence/young adulthood, 79-80
    of adultescents, 81
    age segregation at libraries, 139
    generation gap, 140-141

age *(cont.)*
    generational integration at library, 146-148
    graphic novels and, 43-44
    growing up and, 95
    intergenerational membership, 175-177
    of new young adult, 78
    YA space design and, 146
    of young adults, 77
Agger, M., 22
Agosto, Denise E.
    digital natives discourse, 12
    "Envisaging Young Adult Librarianship from a Teen-Centered Perspective," 3-14
    life/work of, 193
    overview of chapter by, xiv
    storytelling definition of, 97
    on YA librarianship, 65-66
    on "young adult" term, 95
    on youth voice, 61
"Ah ha!" audience reaction, 98
Akom, A. A., 115
ALA
    See American Library Association
Albertalli, Becki, 25
Alex Award, 82
Alexie, Sherman
    The Absolutely True Diary of a Part-Time Indian, 25
    censorship of books by, 23-24
Allahar, A. L.
    on education/job opportunities, 155
    on nature of adolescence, 154
    on stereotypes of adolescence, 153
alternative frameworks, 155-157
Alvarez, Julia, 84
Alvey, R. G., 94, 99
Amazon, 89
American Association of School Librarians (AASL)
    learner, use of term by, 27
    on reading as core of competency, 130
    on school libraries, 29
    standards, shift to learner term and, 29, 30
American Born Chinese (Yang), 25
American Library Association (ALA)
    as advocate for intellectual freedom, 52
    CIPA, lawsuit against, 54-55
    G. Stanley Hall at 1919 conference, xxvii
    Getting Graphic @ Your Library ALA preconference, 37
    on groupings of youth, 65
    on intellectual freedom, 50-51
    Young Adult Services Division, 9
    Young People's Reading Round Table, 82
American Library Association, U.S. v., 54-55
Anderson, E., 99
Anderson, Laurie Halse, 19
Anderson, M. T.
    Feed, 23, 25
    Landscape with Invisible Hand, 25
    Octavian Nothing, 84
anime, 42
Arnett, Jeffrey Jensen, 78
Aronson, M., 9
articles, 4-8
Associated Press
    on new young adults, 78
    on young adults and economy, 81, 82
Association of American Publishers (AAP), 51
assumptions, 30
    See also stereotypes
"at risk" programs, xxx-xxxi
atmosphere, 185
audience
    connection to audience in storytelling, 101
    enchantment/rigor paradox, 99-100
    in storytelling triangle, 97-98
    young adults as, 104
Austin, Jeanie
    life/work of, 193
    overview of chapter by, xv
    "Situating Youth Voice: Moving from Understanding to Action through Critical Theory," 61-71
Australia, 83-84
authenticity, 18

B

Bachman, J. G., 145, 146
Baker, A.
    on enchantment/rigor paradox, 99-100
    on planning/flexibility paradox, 101
    on power/humility paradox, 102
    on storytelling training, 100
Bakhtin, Mikhail, 21
Balderrama, S. R., 113
Barnes & Noble, 84, 89
Bates, M. J., 93, 94
Bauer, M., 42
Baxter, Kent, xxxiv
BBYA (Best Books for Young Adults), 82-83
The Beat Within (journal), 68, 69
Beaty, B., 39

Beauty Queens (Bray), 21
behavior
    adolescent brain and, 154
    positivism and, 166
    youth as student and, 28
    youth behavior, focus on, xxxvii
    youth behavior, statistical bigotry and, 142-143
Bell, Derrick, 112-113
belonging
    citizenship status and, 168
    historical approaches to youth, 64, 65
    normative, 62
    stories with theme of, 104, 105
    storytelling as process of, 93
    teen readers of comics and, 35-36, 41
Bergin, M., 41
Bernier, Anthony
    on children in adult library areas, 144
    digital natives discourse, 12
    on library perceptions of youth, 65
    on library youth spaces, 142
    life/work of, 191
    on LIS's views of YAs, 130
    on media representation of youth as deviants, 155
    "Membership's Promise: Toward a New Young Adult Praxis," 183-187
    "Moving Beyond YAs as 'Citizens': The Promise of Membership," 163-177
    overview of chapter by, xviii
    preface, xi-xx
    on storytelling, 106-107
    transformation, case for, xxv-xli
    on YA spaces, 133, 148
    on young adult, ideas about, 93
    on youth voice, 61
Bernstein, N., 63, 68
Bernstein, R., 95
Best, A. L., 153
Best Books for Young Adults (BBYA), 82-83
best practices, xii, 164
betweenness
    identity, diverse, 17-25
    overview of chapters on, xiv
    YA librarianship from teen-centered perspective, 3-14
    youth as students/learners in school libraries, 27-30
"Beyond Coaching: Copiloting with Young Adults" (Lesko), xvii, 121-127
Big Lake (television program), 78
Biladeau, S., 12

Birch, Carol, 87-88
Bishop, K., 102
blogs, 89, 90
Board of Education v. Pico, 53
Board of Young Adult Commissioners (New Haven, Connecticut), 125
The Book Thief (Zusak), 83
Booklist (journal)
    comics articles in, 37
    licensing of book reviews, 89
    reviews for new YA reader, 85-88
books
    crossover book, 83-85
    division of books/services, 158
    LIS focus on, 12-13
    practice-based articles on, 6-7
    teen input in practice/research articles, 7-8
    YA librarianship and, 3
Books and the Teenage Reader (Carlsen), 79
borrowed theories, 132-134
The Borrower (Makkai), 87
Bourdieu, Pierre, 21, 130
Brady, Margaret, 40
brain
    full development of, 80
    mapping of adolescent brain, 154
    of young people/older people, 143
Braun, L.W., 61, 66
Braverman, Miriam
    on shift to youth service, 62
    on YA librarianship, xxxviii-xxxix, 157-158
Bray, Libby, 21
Briggs Initiative (California), 64
Broderick, Dorothy, 132-133
Brooks, David, 24
Brown, B., 104
Budd, John M.
    foreword, vii-ix
    life/work of, 193
    on praxis, 165
Burns, Ty R., 42
Buscha, C. H., 51
Buschman, John, xxvi
Buttler, Lee Pierce, 165

C

Cabrera, N. L., 67
Cacho, L. M., 63
California, Miller v., 54
call-out culture, 23
Canadian Libraries Are Serving Youth (CLASY), 151

Card, Orson Scott, 23
Carlsen, G. Robert, 79, 83
Carson, B. M., 57
Cart, Michael
    on adolescence/young adulthood, 79
    on adulthood, 80
    book reviews by, 85-88
    "Crossing Over: The Advent of the Adultescent" (Cart), 77-91
    life/work of, 193
    overview of chapter by, xvi
    on "young adult" term, 9
Carter, S., 116
The Catcher in the Rye (Salinger), 83
categorization, 94-96
Catholic Church, 148
CDC (Centers for Disease Control and Prevention), 78
Cedeira Serantes, Lucia
    on librarianship in construction of teen readers of comics, 35-45
    life/work of, 193
    overview of chapter by, xv
censorship
    challenge of, 50
    First Amendment rights of minors and, 53-54
    of graphic novels, 43-44
    librarian resistance to, 51
    in 1950s, 62
    opposition to, 149
    professional positions on intellectual freedom, 51-52
    of sex education materials, 56
Center on Juvenile and Criminal Justice, 141
Centers for Disease Control and Prevention (CDC), 78
Chachra, D., 30
chair-sharing, 140
Chambers, Aidan, 84, 85-86
Charlton-Trujillo, E., 23
Chbosky, S., 19, 83
Chelton, Mary K.
    advocacy for YA librarianship, 157
    life/work of, 194
    "LIS's Vision of Young Adults: Some Historical Roots for Current Theories and Practice," 129-135
    overview of chapter by, xvii
    on stereotypes of young adults, 152, 155
    YA's needs for library assistance, 131
child pornography, 54-55

child rearing
    nineteenth century views of, xxvi-xxix
    twentieth century views of, xxix-xxxii
child_lit electronic discussion group, 24
Children and Libraries (journal), 37
Children's Internet Protection Act (CIPA)
    ALA resistance to Internet filtering, 51
    impact on rights of library users, 52
    Internet filtering requirement, ruling on, 54-55
Children's Online Privacy Protection Act (COPPA), 55
Childress, Herb, 146
Ching, A., 42
Chmara, T., 53, 54
The Chocolate War (Cormier), 23
Cimarron (Ferber), 82
CIPA
    See Children's Internet Protection Act
circulation, 42
citizenship
    adult fears/anxieties about youth and, 62
    age-/generation-based qualities, 143-145
    library citizenship, notions about, 139
    LIS vision of youth as citizens, 167-170
    of young people, synergy and, 146-148
    youth as full-fledged citizens, 148-149
citizenship to membership
    imagining today's young adults in LIS, 151-161
    overview of chapters of, xvii-xviii
    tribalism *vs.* citizenship, 139-149
    young adults, membership in local community, 163-177
Civil Rights Act of 1964, 113
Civil Rights movement
    anxieties about youth during, 62
    youth activism in, 183-184
civilizing, of youth, xxvii
Claes, J., 3
Clammer, J. R., 23
CLASY (Canadian Libraries Are Serving Youth), 151
Clifford, J., 80
Coats, Karen
    "Diverse Identity in Anxious Times," 17-25
    life/work of, 194
    overview of chapter by, xiv
"Code of Ethics of the American Library Association" (ALA), 50-51
cognitive development, 19-20
Cohen, R. D., 62
collaboration
    copiloting with young adults, 121-127

intergenerational, 124
librarian/teacher collaboration, 29
collection development
    adult-centered perspective on, 3
    crossover book, 83-85
    vision of YAs as community members and, 170-173
    visions of YAs in library practice and, 185
    YA literature for new category of users, 82-83
    young adult definition and, 77-78
Collins, P. H., 65
comic book club, 35-36
comic books, 37
comics
    comics readers, librarian attitudes about, 35-36
    conclusion about, 44-45
    continuities, practices, challenges of, 40-44
    historical discourses about, 38-40
    research data/tool for analysis, 37-38
    use of term, 37
"The Comics Dilemma" (Margulis), 40
"Comics—To Read or Not to Read" (Brady), 40
Coming of Age in Samoa (Mead), 152
coming-of-age
    adolescence signified by age idea, 153-155
    adolescents "come of age" into adulthood idea, 152
    stories in crossover books, 83-84
Common Core State Standards, 28, 29
community
    community membership with adults, 177
    library ties with, 122
    networking for copiloting with young adults, 125-126
    programming/intergenerational membership *vs.* after-school apartheid, 175-177
    young adults as self-aware members of, 135
community membership
    collection management and, 170-173
    vision of youth as members of local community, 167-170, 184-187
    YA outreach and, 174-175
    YA space and, 173-174
competencies, 183-184
confidentiality, 51
Connecting Young Adults and Libraries (Jones), 134
Conner, J. O., 66, 67
The Contender (Lipsyte), 82
control, 66-67
convention, confronting
    overview of chapters of, xvi
    storytelling, 93-107

YA literature for new YA definition, 77-91
youth of color, reimagining in LIS discourses, 111-116
Cooke, N., 63, 106
Cook-Sather, A., 69
copiloting with young adults
    aim of/prerequisites for, 121-122
    community networking for, 125-126
    conclusion about, 126-127
    culture/climate for, 122-123
    individual interactions, 123-124
    School Girls Unite, 122
    time for, 124-125
    YA programs, building on, 123
    Youth Activism Project, 122
COPPA (Children's Online Privacy Protection Act), 55
Cormier, R., 19, 23
Cornog, M., 56
Côté, J. E.
    on education/job opportunities, 155
    on nature of adolescence, 154
    on stereotypes of adolescence, 153
court cases
    Board of Education v. Pico, 53
    Ginsberg v. New York, 54
    Miller v. California, 54
    Planned Parenthood of Missouri v. Danforth, 55
    Tinker v. Des Moines Independent Community School District, 52
    U.S. v. American Library Association, 54-55
Craver, Kathleen, 158
Crawford, P., 41, 43
Crenshaw, K., 65
Crimes against Children Research Center, 148
critical race theory (CRT)
    for examination of LIS discourses on youth of color, 111-112
    interest convergence, 112-114
    on intersectionality, 115-116
    whiteness as property, 114-115
    youth voice and, 112
critical social theory
    LIS "tunnel vision" legacy, 183
    LIS's need for praxis with, 164-166
    for new praxis in YA librarianship, 167
    for vision of YAs as local community members, 164
critical theory
    for understanding of youth, 63-64
    for understanding youth activism, 68
    for understanding youth voice, 69-71

critical theory *(cont.)*
    youth voice through lens of critical race theory, 66
critical youth studies
    alternative frameworks for thinking about young adults, 155-157
    dominant stereotypes of youth, consequences of, 152-155
    for evaluation of vision of youth, 151
    framework for LIS, 157-159
    LIS vision of youth, conclusion about, 159-161
"Crossing Over: The Advent of the Adultescent" (Cart), xvi, 77-91
crossover books
    examples of, 83-85
    reviews of YA literature, 85-88
Crowley, W., 131
CRT
    See critical race theory
cultural competence, 106
cultural fictions
    identity formation in figured worlds, 21-23
    as mirror of identity anxiety, 18
cultural production, 170-172
cultural studies, 155-157
culture
    affective-cognitive development and, 19-20
    cultural differences, 116
    identity construction and, 17-19
    influence on ideas about appropriate materials, 56
Cures for Heartbreak (Rabb), 83-84
curfew
    advocates, 141
    assumptions about young people and, 145
    youth influence on, 125
The Curious Incident of the Dog in the Nighttime (Haddon), 83
curriculum, 29

D

Daily News, 38
Danforth, Planned Parenthood of Missouri v., 55
"The Dangers of a Single Story" TED Talk (Adichie), 23
Daugherty, Richard, 130
Davis, A., 68
Davis, M. G., 100
de Vos, Gail, 97
decision making
    copiloting with young adults and, 123
    intergenerational, 124
    shared decision making with young adults, 121
    by young adults, 133-134
    young adults' involvement in YA services, 126-127
Del Negro, J. M.
    on storytelling, 94, 96
    storytelling planning, 101
Delgado, R., 112
Demos (policy group), 81
Denning, Stephen, 98
Des Moines Independent Community School District, Tinker v., 52
development
    See human development; youth development industrial complex
developmental psychology
    dominion over LIS, xxxvii-xxxix
    LIS vision of YAs based on, xxv
    LIS vision of youth based on, 166
    LIS's dependence on, xxxiv
    youth as ever "other," xxxvi
developmental theories, 11-13
deviance
    stereotypes of adolescents as, 155
    youth deviance, ideas about, 64-65
    youth voice as intervention, 66
"Dialogism, Development, and Destination: Young Adults in Contemporary Culture" (Coats), 18
Dickinson, G., 42
difference
    cultural differences, 116
    honoring individual differences, 13
    teen-centered approach and, 12
    visible menace of, 141
digital natives, 12
Discourse, 37-38
discourse
    about comics, historical, 38-40
    alternative frameworks for thinking about YAs, 155-157
    comics, recent literature about, 40-44
    Discourse *vs.*, 37-38
    LIS vision of youth, 159-161
    stereotypes of youth, consequences of, 152-155
discourse analysis, 38
disease, 39
diverse identity
    See identity
Diverse Identity in Anxious Times: Young Adult Literature and Contemporary Culture" (Coats), xiv, 17-25

diversity
- diverse pairing suggestions, 25
- LIS pluralistic approach to, 113–114
- single story, dangers of, 23–25
- young people's attitudes about, 143

Dixson, A. D., 112
Druin, A., 106
dynamic exchange, 96–99

E

economy
- adolescence signified by age idea, 153–154
- book reviews and, 89
- criminal behavior and, 142–143
- young adults and, 81

education, 154–155
Edwards, Margaret Alexander
- Alex Award, 82
- *The Fair Garden and the Swarm of Beasts*, 158–159
- on goals of librarians, 131–132
- as Mary K. Chelton's teacher, 129–130
- on transition from childhood to adolescence, 96
- vision of young adults, 130, 135

Elliott, Anthony, 21–22
Elliott, Zetta, 68
Ellis, A. W., 38, 39
Ellis, Elizabeth, 98
emergent roles
- copiloting with young adults, 121–127
- LIS's vision of young adults, 129–135
- overview of chapters of, xvi–xvii

Emerging Adulthood: The Winding Road from the Late Teens through the Twenties (Arnett), 78
empowerment, 169
enchantment/rigor paradox, 99–100
The End of Fun (McGinty), 25
Engaging Teens with Story (Del Negro & Kimball), 94
Enoch Pratt Free Library, Baltimore, Maryland, 129, 132
Envisaging Young Adult Librarianship from a Teen-Centered Perspective" (Agosto), xiv, 3–14
Epstein, Robert, 80
Erikson, Erik, 79
ethics
- ethical action, ix
- intellectual freedom, professional positions on, 50–52

F

Failure to Launch (film), 78
The Fair Garden and the Swarm of Beasts (Edwards), 158–159
Family Educational Rights and Privacy Act (FERPA), 56
Far from the Tree (Solomon), 17
FBI (Federal Bureau of Investigation), 143
fear
- of adolescents, 144
- age segregation and, 140, 145, 147
- anxieties about youth in 1950s, 62
- censorship and, 51
- sexual politics of, 56
- tribalism *vs.* citizenship, 139
- of youth, 64–65
- of youth deviance, 64
- of youth of color, 66

Federal Bureau of Investigation (FBI), 143
Feed (Anderson), 23, 25
Ferber, Edna, 82
FERPA (Family Educational Rights and Privacy Act), 56
FIERCE, 67
figured worlds, 21–23
Finder, A., 80
Fine, M., 63, 68
Finkelhor, D., 148
First Amendment
- legal foundations for minors' intellectual freedom, 52–54
- librarian knowledge of, 58–59
- minors' intellectual freedom under, 49
- protection of privacy, 57
- rights of minors in public/school libraries, 50

Fischer, Kurt W., 19
Fiske, M., 51
Flagg, G., 44
flexibility
- planning/flexibility paradox, 100–102
- young adults as storytellers, 104–105

Flowers, S., 14
"40 Developmental Assets" (Search Institute), xxxvi
Foster, K., 42
Foucault, Michel, 149
frameworks
- alternative frameworks for thinking about young adults, 155–157
- critical youth studies framework for LIS, 157–159
- LIS vision of youth, 160

Frank, Josette, 39
Fraser, Sandy, xxxvii
freedom
    See intellectual freedom
"freedom and intimacy," xxvi–xxvii
"Freedom to Read Statement" (FRS) (ALA & AAP), 51, 52
Frosh, P., 95
future, xxxvii
The Future of Library Services for and with Teens (Braun et al.), 66
Future Ready Schools, 30

G

Gallow. L. L., 64
Gee, E., 28
Gee, James Paul, 37–38
Geller, E., 51
Gem and Dixie (Zarr), 25
gender
    equality, 122
    identity construction and, 17–18, 19
    youth, historical approaches to, 64, 65
    See also LGBTQ_/gender-nonconforming youth
generation gap, 140–141
generations
    age-/generation-based qualities for citizenship, 143–145
    generational decorum, 140–142
    generational integration at library, 146–148
Getting Graphic @ Your Library ALA preconference, 37
Gilbert, Eugene, 79
Gilbert, Kelly Loy, 25
Gilmore-See, J., 12
Ginsberg v. New York, 54
Girls Gone Activist! How to Change the World through Education (School Girls Unite), 122–123
Givens, Cherie
    "Identity at Odds: The Sometimes Conflicting Viewpoints about Young Adults' Rights in Libraries," 49–59
    life/work of, 194
    overview of chapter by, xv
GLSEN, 65
Gonzales, Roberto G., 168
Goodin, M. C., 28
Goodreads.com, 90
Gorman, M.
    on comic books, 41
    on fear of graphic novels, 43–44
    on graphic novels, 42
    on stereotypes of young adults, 152
government
    censorship, ALA's resistance to, 51
    citizenship, idea of, 168
    role in LIS, xl
Graham, Patterson Toby, 184
Graham, Philip, xx
graphic novels
    acceptance/inclusion of, 38
    conclusion about, 44–45
    librarians' ideas about, 36
    LIS literature on, 40–41, 42–44
    use of term, 37
Greene, E.
    on enchantment/rigor paradox, 99–100
    on planning/flexibility paradox, 101
    on power/humility paradox, 102
    on storytelling training, 100
Grossman, Lev, 81
"growing up," 95

H

Haberman, C., 66
Haddon, Mark, 83
Hall, G. Stanley
    on adolescence, xxxiv, 78–79, 152
    adolescence, definition of, 95
    adolescent development, ideas about, 65
    child-rearing theories of, xxvi–xxvii
    "discovery" of adolescence, 154, 166
    Emmett L. Holt and, xxviii
    "freedom and intimacy" strategy of, xxix
    "storm and stress" model of, xxxii, 20, 151
    youth, views of, 64
    youth as biologically flawed specimens, xxxvi
Halpern, J., 35–36
Hand, S., 64
Hannigan, Jane Anne, 157
Hardesty, C., 12
Harker, Jean Gray, 39
Harlan, Mary Ann
    on learner, use of term, 28
    life/work of, 194
    overview of chapter by, xiv
    "Students or Learners? Conceptualizing Youth in School Libraries," 27–30
harmful materials, 54–55
harmful-to-minors laws, 55
Harris, C., 12

Harter, Susan, 19, 20
Hartnett, Sonya, 83
#ownvoices, 21, 23
The Hate U Give (Thomas), 25
Haters (Valdes-Rodriguez), 25
Hautakangas, M., 22
Haven, K., 94, 97
Havighurst, Robert J., 79
Hearne, B., 94, 100
Hearne, Betsy, 102
Heins, M., 55-56
Henig, R. M., 78, 80
Henne, Frances, 39
Highsmith, D., 38, 39
Hilbun, J. W., 3
Hills, M., 102
Hinchey, P., 114
Hine, T., 144-145
Hinton, S. E., 82
Hodge, D. W., 61, 68
Hoffman, Alice, 84
Hoffmeister, Peter Brown, 25
Holland, Dorothy, 21
Holt, D., 98
Holt, Emmett L.
    child-rearing theories of, xxvi
    "discovery" of adolescence, 166
    "power and control" strategies of, xxvii-xxviii, xxix
    youth as biologically flawed specimens, xxxvi
homosexuality, 64-65
Hones, Kay, 41
hormones
    consequences of adolescent stereotypes, 154
    idea of adolescents controlled by, 152
    raging hormones thesis, 153
Horner, E. C., 38
Hughes-Hassell, Sandra, 10
human development
    adolescence signified by age idea, 153-155
    adulthood as endpoint of, 148
    biology-based explanations of adolescence, 154
    critical youth studies and, 155
    LIS reliance on, 159
    teen development, focus on, 10-11
    See also developmental psychology; youth development industrial complex
humility
    power/humility paradox, 102-103
    young adults' stories and, 106
Hunt, J., 61, 63

I

idealism, 22
identity
    cultural identity migration, 17-18
    dialogic identity formation, contexts for, 19-23
    diverse pairing suggestions, 25
    single critical perspective, dangers of, 23-25
    in YA literature, 18-19
    young adults, undefining, 94-96
    youth as students/learners in school libraries, 27-30
"Identity at Odds: The Sometimes Conflicting Viewpoints about Young Adults' Rights in Libraries" (Givens), xv, 49-59
identity formation
    affective-cognitive development, 19-20
    figured worlds, 21-23
Identity Troubles (Elliott), 21-22
"Imagining Today's Young Adults in LIS: Moving Forward with Critical Youth Studies" (Rothbauer), xvii-xviii, 151-161
immigration status, 168
in loco parentis doctrine, 56-57
incarceration, 68-70
income inequality, xxxix
individual interactions, 123-124
individuals
    focus on teens as, 11-12, 13
    undue focus on individual, 154
individuation, xxxviii
inexperience, 143
information, right to receive
    First Amendment rights of minors, cases on, 53
    privacy protections for young adults, 57-58
    in school libraries, 57
information literacy
    whiteness as property and, 114-115
    youth as students/learners and, 29
Information Privacy Fundamentals for Librarians and Information Professionals (Givens), xv
information resources, 12-13
information search process theory, 133
innocence, 95
intellectual freedom
    legal foundations for minors' intellectual freedom, 52-54
    legal protections for minors, evaluation of, 55-56
    librarianship in construction of teen readers of comics, 35-45
    overview of chapters on, xiv-xvi
    privacy protections for young adults, 57-58

intellectual freedom *(cont.)*
    professional positions on, 50–52
    school library laws, 56–57
    of young adults, conclusion about, 58–59
    young adults' rights in libraries, 49–59
    youth voice, situating, 61–71
intergenerational membership, 175–177
intergenerational partnership, xii, xvii
Internet
    book reviews on, 89–90
    as major threat to youth, 141
Internet filtering
    ALA resistance to censorship, 51
    U.S. Supreme Court ruling on, 54–55
internships, 125
intervention, youth voice as, 65–67

J

James, Allison, xxxvi
James, Will, 82
Jamrach's Menagerie (Birch), 87–88
Jenkins, Christine A.
    on LIS research on YA services, xix
    on storytelling, 94
    on YA services, history of, 157
job opportunities, 155
Johnston, L. D., 145, 146
Jones, G., 153
Jones, P.
    on assets, 132
    Connecting Young Adults and Libraries, 134
    on stereotypes of young adults, 152
Journal of Research on Libraries and Young Adults, 8
journals, 37–38
Judith, B., 95
juvenile detention, 68–70

K

Kan, Kat, 37, 43
Kantrowitz, B., 80
Kapitzke, C., 114
Kelly, Adam, 22
Kelly, T., 140
Kennedy, Anthony, 54–55
Kett, J., 144–145
kids, 10
"Kids Who Read, Succeed" (Daugherty), 130
Kidsreads, 89–90
Kimball, M. A.
    on stories for young adults, 101
    on story as feature, 102
    on storytelling, 94
Kincheole, J., 114
King, P. E., 20
Knop, K., 41
Knott, C., 62
knowing, 103–106
Knowledge Quest (journal), 37
Knupfer, A. M., 64
Koechlin, C., 28
Konigsberg, Bill, 25
Konopka, Gisela, 130, 134
Kozol, Jonathan, xxxvii
Krug, J. F., 52
Kuhlthau, Carol, 133
Kumasi, Kafi D.
    on critical race theory for youth voice, 69
    on cultural differences, 116
    "The Library Is Like Her House: Reimagining Youth of Color in LIS Discourses," 111–116
    life/work of, 194
    overview of chapter by, xvi
    on youth voice, 61, 65
    youth voice through lens of critical race theory, 66
Kumasi-Johnson, K., 115
Kunitz, Stanley, 39
Kunzel, B., 12
Kwon, S. A., 66

L

labels, 27–28
    See also stereotypes
Ladson-Billings, G., 113–114
Lanagan, Margo, 83
Landscape with Invisible Hand (Anderson), 23, 25
Lange, Alexandra, 167–168
Langer, J., 114
Lapides, Linda, 129, 131–132
laws
    intellectual freedom, professional positions on, 50–52
    intellectual freedom protections for minors, 49–50
    legal foundations for minors' intellectual freedom, 52–54
    legal protections for minors, evaluation of, 55–56
    privacy protections for young adults, 57–58

to protect minors from harmful/obscene
materials, 54-55
school library protection laws, 56-57
leadership
calling YAs to, 143
copiloting with young adults, 121, 126
stories of, 103
teen leadership roles at library, 147-148
teenage leadership motivations, 148-149
learner
shift to use of label, 27, 28
youth as students/learners in school libraries,
27-30
Leckie, Gloria, xxvi
Leffert, N., 132
Lehman, J., 57
Lesko, Nancy
on adolescence signified by age, 153, 154
on alternative conceptions of youth, 156-157
on Hall's construction of adolescence, 64
on stereotypes of teenagers, 152
Lesko, Wendy Schaetzel
"Beyond Coaching: Copiloting with Young
Adults," 121-127
life/work of, 195
overview of chapter by, xvii
Levine, J., 56
LGBTQ/gender-nonconforming youth
library services to, 62, 63
youth groupings in library, 65
youth voice in library, 67
youth voice of juveniles in detention, 68-70
librarians
comic book readers, historical discourses about,
39-40
comic book readers, ideas about, 35-36
copiloting, community networking for, 125-126
copiloting with young adults, 121-127
critical youth studies framework for LIS,
157-159
crossover books and, 84
First Amendment rights of minors and, 58-59
graphic novels, perceptions of, 41-44, 45
individual interactions with young adults,
123-124
intellectual freedom, professional positions on,
50-52
LIS vision of youth, 159-161
privacy protections for young adults, 57-58
service providers for young adults, 134-135
storytelling, conclusion about, 106-107
storytelling, paradoxes of, 99-103

storytelling as dynamic exchange, 96-99
storytelling as richer way of knowing, 93-94
storytelling knowing, 103-106
vision of youth, blind spot in, 163-164
whiteness, intersectionality of, 115-116
whiteness as property, literacy and, 114-115
YAs as community members, YA outreach and,
174-175
young adult, use of term, 79
young adults, undefining, 94-96
youth, conceptualizations of, 62
youth, historical approaches to, 64-65
youth as students/learners in school libraries,
28-30
youth of color, interest convergence, 113-114
youth voice and, 61, 62-64
youth voice as intervention, 65-67
youth voice, critical theory for understanding,
70-71
youth voice, critically incorporating, 67-70
librarianship
in construction of teen readers of comics, 35-45
critical youth studies framework for LIS,
157-159
Library Bill of Rights on intellectual freedom,
50
LIS vision of youth, 159-161
YA librarianship from teen-centered
perspective, 3-14
libraries
collection responses to LIS vision of YAs as
community members, 170-173
copiloting, community networking for, 125-126
copiloting, favorable culture/climate for,
122-123
generational integration at, 146-149
interest convergence, 112-114
LIS vision of YA services and, xxv-xxvi
new young adult praxis, movement toward,
183-187
privacy protections for young adults, 57-58
sex education materials in, 56
state's role in LIS, xl
storytelling, paradoxes of, 99-103
YA space, design of, 145-146
YAs as community members, programming/
intergenerational membership, 175-177
YAs as community members, YA outreach and,
174-175
YAs as community members, YA space and,
173-174
YAs' involvement in YA services, 126-127

libraries *(cont.)*
    young adults' rights in libraries, 49-59
    youth, historical approaches to, 64-65
    youth as students/learners in school libraries, 27-30
    youth services, twentieth century views of youth and, xxix-xxxii
    youth voice as intervention, 65-67
library and information science (LIS)
    comics, historical discourses, 38-40
    comics, recent literature about, 40-44
    comics articles in LIS professional journals, 37-38
    comics readers, librarian attitudes about, 35-37
    crossroads of practice/theory, xviii-xix
    debate, instigation of, xix-xx
    imagining today's young adults in, 151-161
    liabilities based on YDIC reliance, xxxv-xl
    literature in library services for teens, analysis of, 4-8
    new young adult praxis, movement toward, 183-187
    storytelling as richer way of knowing, 93-94
    theory, critical engagement with, 164-166
    Transforming Young Adult Services (Bernier), xiii-xviii
    twentieth century views of youth and, xxix-xxx
    vision of youth as members of local community, 167-177
    vision of youth, legacy practices and, 163-164
    YA services, relationship to, xi-xii
    YAs, vision of, xxv-xxvi
    youth, perceptions of, 65
    youth as students/learners in school libraries, 27-30
    youth consensus, critical look at, xxxiv-xxxv
    youth consensus/"path dependency," xxxii-xxxiv
    "youth" definition of, xiv
    youth development paradigm, adoption of, xxxi-xxxii
    youth of color, reimagining in discourses, 111-116
library and information science (LIS), vision of young adults
    borrowed theories, 132-134
    conclusion about, 135
    discipline *vs.* practice, 131
    group programming, 131-132
    Margaret Edwards, view of, 129-130
    overview of, 129
    positive youth development, 132
    service providers, 134-135
    YA services, outreach, 130
"The Library Is Like Her House: Reimagining Youth of Color in LIS Discourses" (Kumasi), xvi, 111-116
Library Journal, 37
Library Media Connection (journal), 37
"Library's Bill of Rights" (ALA), 52
LibraryThing.com, 90
Life of Pi (Martel), 83
Lipinski, T. A., 54
Lipman, Doug, 97, 103
Lipsitz, Joan, 133
Lipsky, Michael, 133
Lipsyte, Robert, 82
LIS
    See library and information science
"LIS's Vision of Young Adults: Some Historical Roots for Current Theories and Practice" (Chelton), xvii, 129-135
listening
    power/humility paradox, 102-103
    to stories of young adults, 106
    by storyteller, 102
    in storytelling triangle, 97-98
    young adults as storytellers, 104-105
literacy
    collection responses to LIS vision of YAs as community members, 171-172
    views of YAs and, 130
    whiteness as property and, 114-115
literature
    comics, historical discourses, 38-40
    comics, recent literature about, 40-44
    comics articles in LIS professional journals, 37-38
    crossover book, 83-85
    identity focus in YA literature, 18-19
    intellectual freedom, professional positions on, 50-52
    in library services for teens, analysis of, 4-8
    resource-centered view of, 12
    on storytelling, 96-99
    teen-centered approach and, 13-14
    YA literature for new category of users, 82-83
    See also young adult (YA) literature
Lives in Limbo: Undocumented and Coming of Age in America (Gonzales), 168
Locke, John
    view of young people as subadults, xxviii
    view of youth as inherently damaged, xxxiv
    on young people, xxvi

Loertscher, D., 28
logic of dispossession, 63
Lone Cowboy (James), 82
Losen, D. J., 69
Lukenbill, W. B., xxx, 64, 158
Luttrell-Rowland, M., 65
Lyga, A. W., 41
Lyons, D., 55

M

Macallair, Daniel, xxxiii, 141
Magee, R. M., 105
Magnuson, L., 98
makerspaces, 29-30
Makkai, Rebecca, 87
Males, Mike
    on age and behavior problems, 142
    on banishing young people from public spaces, 141
    life/work of, 195
    overview of chapter by, xvii
    on "at risk" youth, xxxi
    "Tribalism versus Citizenship: Are Youth Increasingly Unwelcome in Libraries?," 139-149
    work on YA spaces, 133
    on youth voice, 61
malpractice, 49
Mananzala, R., 67
manga readers, 41-42
Maplewood Library, New Jersey, 140
Marek, K., 98
Margulis, Elizabeth, 40
Martel, Yann, 83
material circumstances, xxxix
Maushart, Susan, 88
Maximum Youth Involvement: The Complete Gameplan for Community Action (Lesko), 124
McConaughey, Matthew, 78
McDonald, F. B., 51-52
McDowell, Kate
    life/work of, 195
    overview of chapter by, xvi
    "Storytelling, Young Adults, and Three Paradoxes," 93-107
McGinty, Sean, 25
Mead, Margaret
    on advantages of young people, 143
    Coming of Age in Samoa, 152
    on generation gap, 140
    on leadership by young people, 127
    on youth defined culture, 147
meaning
    Discourse *and*, 37-38
    LIS vision of YAs and, xix
    renegotiation of, 21
    storytelling and, 103, 104, 106
    YAs as local community members and, 186-187
    YDIC and, xxviii, xli
media scripts, 21-22
Medina, Meg, 25
Meiners, E., 61
membership
    collection management and, 170-173
    community membership with adults, 177
    LIS vision of youth as members of local community, 167-170
    programming/intergenerational membership *vs.* after-school apartheid, 175-177
    vision of youth as members of local community, 184-187
    YA space and, 173-174
    young adult outreach and, 174-175
"Membership's Promise: Toward a New Young Adult Praxis" (Bernier), xviii, 183-187
middle class, xxxix
Miller, M. L., 99-100
Miller v. California, 54
minorities, 140-141
    See also race
minors
    intellectual freedom of, conclusion about, 58-59
    intellectual freedom, professional positions on, 50-52
    intellectual freedom protections for, 49-50
    laws to protect minors from harmful/obscene materials, 54-55
    legal foundations for minors' intellectual freedom, 52-54
    legal protections for, evaluation of, 55-56
    privacy protections for young adults, 57-58
    school library laws, 56-57
    See also teens; young adults
Minow, M., 54
Mintz, Stephen, xxix
"Misfits, Loners, Immature Students, and Reluctant Readers: Librarianship in the Construction of Teen Readers of Comics" (Cedeira Serantes), xv, 35-45
Mitchell, K., 148
Moje, E. B., 106

Monitoring the Future (Bachman, Johnston, & O'Malley), 145, 148–149
Monnier, D. P., 161
Monster (Myers), 25
Montgomery, R., 81
Moodie-Mills, A., 61, 63
Mooney, M., 40
Mooney, W., 98
moral panics, 155
Morgan, C. D., 52
Morris, Wesley, 17–18
Morrison, David, 81–82
Moskowitz, Elaine, 41
mothers, xxviii
"Moving Beyond YAs as 'Citizens': The Promise of Membership" (Bernier), xviii, 163–177
MTV, 80
multiculturalism
    criticism of multicultural approach, 114–115
    young people's attitudes about, 143
Murphy, T., 28
Myers, Walter Dean, 19, 25

N

naiveté, 22
Nardo, R. S., 69
narratives, 21
    See also storytelling
"A Nation at Risk" (U.S. presidential report), xxx
National 4-H Council, 132
National Center for Education Statistics, 27, 79
National Conference of State Legislatures, 55
National Council of Teachers of English, 51
"A National Disgrace" (North), 38
National Institute of Mental Health, 80
National School Library Standards for Learners, School Librarians, and School Libraries (AASL), 27
Native identity, 23–24
Neace, M., 42
needs, of teens, 12–13
Neri, G., 68
New Directions for Library Service to Young Adults (Jones), 132
New Sincerity, 22–23
New York, Ginsberg v., 54
New York Times, 89
Newsletter for Intellectual Freedom, 56
newspapers, 89
nineteenth century, views of YAs in, xxvi–xxix
Noble, S., 63

nonprofit industry, 66
North, Sterling, 38, 39
"Not Broken by Someone Else's Schedule: On Joy and Young Adult Information Seeking" (Bernier), 130
Nyberg, A. K., 38, 39

O

Oates, Joyce Carol, 84
Obama, Barack, 149
obscene materials, 54–55
Octavian Nothing (Anderson), 84
Ojala, M., 12
O'Malley, P. M., 145, 146
"One Butt to a Chair" rule, xxviii, 140
Ong, Walter, 97
online bookstores, 89
Openly Straight (Konigsberg), 25
orality, 97
"other"
    othering of youth of color, 114
    YAs as community members and, 169
    youth as ever "other," xxxvi
    youth as students/learners and, 30
"Out of Sight, Out of Mind" (Wiegand), 36
outreach, 174–175
The Outsiders (Hinton), 82

P

Palmer, Parker, 99
panics, moral, 155
paradoxes
    enchantment/rigor, 99–100
    planning/flexibility, 100–102
    power/humility, 102–103
    of storytelling, 99
parents
    of new young adult, 78
    privacy protections for young adults and, 57–58
    young adults living with, 80
Parker, K., 55
Parkland, Florida, 25
participation
    benefits of teen participation, 10–11
    visions of YAs in library practice and, 185
    YA's as community members and, 169
    in youth services librarianship, 161
Partnership for 21st Century Skills, 28, 30
Paus, Tomas, 143
Pawley, C., 111

Pawuk, M., 43
pedophilia, 144
peer education, 123
peers, 153
Pellowski, Anne
    storytelling definition of, 97
    on storytelling in library, 99
    on storytelling transformation, 98
Perkins, Frederick, xxx
The Perks of Being a Wallflower (Chbosky), 83
Perper, T., 56
personal convictions, 51
personally identifiable information, 56–57
perspective, 23–25
Peterson, R., 69
Phelps, S., 57
physicality, 140
Pico, Board of Education v., 53
Picture Us in the Light (Gilbert), 25
Piecing Me Together (Watson), 25
Planned Parenthood of Missouri v. Danforth, 55
planning, 106
planning/flexibility paradox, 100–102, 104–105
Poirier, S., 23
political economy, 155–157
positive youth development (PYD)
    embrace of, 20
    peer education, 123
    research on, 132
    teen participation in programs and, 10–11
    youth consensus and, xxxv
positivism, 166–167
postmodern irony, 22
postmodernism, 166–167
power
    political economy, 156
    "power and control" strategies, xxvii–xxviii
    power/humility paradox, 102–103
    of stories, 105
    storytelling and, 106
    YA's as community members and, 169, 186–187
power structures
    adult concerns around youth and, 65
    LIS scholarship on youth of color and, 111
    youth activism/protest and, 67
    youth voice, critically positioning, 69
    youth voice of juveniles in detention, 68
PPRA (Protection of Pupil Rights Amendment), 56
practice-based articles, 5–7
praxis
    for LIS vision of youth, 167
    LIS's need for, 164–166
    new young adult praxis, movement toward, 183–187
    YA outreach and, 174–175
    YAs as local community members, 170–177
Prensky, M., 12
Prep (Sittenfeld), 83, 86
privacy
    COE on protection of, 51
    COPPA, 55
    laws protecting students, 56–57
    protections for young adults, 57–58
privilege, 115–116
process, 95
professional literature, 4–8
    See also discourse; literature
programming
    intergenerational, 175–177
    visions of YAs in library practice and, 186
property, whiteness as, 114–115
Prose, Francine, 84
Protection of Pupil Rights Amendment (PPRA), 56
protest, 67–68
Prout, Alan, xxxvi
provisionality, 18
public libraries
    group programming, 131–132
    roles in teens' lives, 11
    YA viewed as student, 130
public schools, 52–54
public spaces
    design features of, 146
    YA space, 173–174
publishers, 84–85
Pulliam, J., 9
Putnam, Robert, xxxix
PYD
    See positive youth development

R

Rabb, Margo, 83–84
Raby, R., 152
race
    diversity in YA literature and, 23–24
    generation gap and, 140–141
    identity construction and, 17–18
    intersectionality, 115–116
    racial innocence, 95
    whiteness as property, 114–115
    youth of color in libraries, interest convergence, 112–114

race *(cont.)*
    youth of color, library services to, 63
racism
    anxieties about youth and, 62
    youth, historical approaches to, 64
Ragged Dick series (Alger), xxxiv
Ranma 1/2 (Takahashi), 42
readers
    of comics, conclusion about, 44–45
    of comics, historical discourses about, 38–40
    of comics, librarian views about, 35–37
    of comics, recent literature on, 40–44
    librarianship in construction of teen readers of comics, 35–45
    reluctant readers, comics and, 40–42
readers' advisory, 20, 35
reading
    librarianship in construction of teen readers of comics, 35–45
    stages of reading development, 79
    views of YAs and, 129–130
"Reading for the Innocent" (Wertham), 39
"read-ins," 184
Reese, Debbie, 23–24
Reeves, A., 41
reform, 158
reluctant reader
    comics and, 40–42
    comics as literacy tools for, 44
Rendina, D., 29–30
Representations of Youth (Griffin), 155
"Requirements for the Healthy Development of Adolescent Youth" (Konopka), 134
research
    comics readers study, 37–38
    LIS liabilities based on YDIC reliance, xxxv–xxxvi
    LIS's dependence on developmental psychology, xxxiv
    new young adult praxis and, 186
    research-based articles, 5–6
    teen-centered perspective, 8–14
    YA researchers, xii
    on YA services, lack of, xi
    Young Adult Library Services articles, analysis of, 5–6
reviews
    book reviewing, changes to, 89–90
    of graphic novels, 43
    of YA literature, 85–88
Reynolds, Jason, 68

rhetoric, xxxiii
Richards, Neil, 57
Rickman, C., 61, 133
Ridley, Rosalind, 19
right to receive information
    First Amendment rights of minors, cases on, 53
    privacy protections for young adults, 57–58
    in school libraries, 57
rights
    First Amendment rights of minors, 52–54
    intellectual freedom, professional positions on, 50–52
    laws to protect minors from harmful/obscene materials, 54–55
    whiteness as property, 114–115
    young adults' rights in libraries, 49–59
rigor, 99–100
rites of passage, 79
Robbins, L. S., 62
Romesburg, D., 62
Ross, Richard, 68
Rothbauer, Paulette
    "Imagining Today's Young Adults in LIS: Moving Forward with Critical Youth Studies," 151–161
    life/work of, 195
    overview of chapter by, xvii–xviii
Rousseau, C. K., 112
Rousseau, Jean-Jacques
    G. Stanley Hall and, xxvii
    view of young people as subadults, xxviii
    on young people, xxvi
Rowling, J. K., 19, 83
Rubin, Richard, 170
Rudiger, H. M., 44
Ruglis, J., 63, 68
Rust v. Sullivan, 55

S

Sahn, S., 96
Salinger, J. D., 83
Salt Lake City Public Library, 126
Sawyer, D. C., III, 61, 68
Sawyer, R., 100, 102
Scales, P. C., 132
Schatzberg, A., 55
Schlesselman-Tarango, G., 64, 67
Schliesman, M., 44
school administrators, 57
School Girls Unite
    as example, 121

forced marriage, research on, 125-126
Girls Gone Activist! How to Change the World through Education, 122-123
    launch of, 122
school libraries
    laws of, 56-57
    YA viewed as student, 130
    youth as students/learners in, 28-30
School Library Journal (*SLJ*)
    comics articles in, 37
    licensing of book reviews, 89
    reviews for new YA reader, 85
schools
    school library laws, 56-57
    youth as student, 27-28
Schwartz, Alvin, 101
Schwimmer, E., 23
science, xxvi-xxix
screen media, 21-22
Search Institute, xxxvi, 132
security, 186
Sedgwick, E. K., 95
The Seduction of the Innocent (Wertham), 38-39
segregation
    after-school apartheid, 175-177
    by age, rise in, 148-149
    age segregation at libraries, 139, 140, 147
    age-/generation-based qualities and, 143-145
    generational integration at library, 146-148
    statistical bigotry, 142
    YAs as community members, YA space and, 173-174
self
    affective-cognitive development and, 20
    identity formation in figured worlds, 21-23
    sense of self, 19-20
Serafini, F., 28
Sercombe, Howard, 143
service
    division of books/services, 158
    LBOR/COE on, 50
    YA service providers, 134-135
sex education, 56
sexual abuse, 148
sexual content
    laws to protect minors from harmful/obscene materials, 54-55
    legal protections for minors, evaluation of, 56
sexuality, 62
Seyfried, J., 42-43
Shedlock, M. L., 99-100
$#! My Dad Says* (television program), 78

Shoemaker, J., 152
Siebert, Sara, 129
Simmons, Annette, 94, 98
Simon vs. the Homo Sapiens Agenda (Albertalli), 25
sincerity, 22-23
single critical perspective, 23-25
Sittenfeld, Curtis, 83, 86
"Situating Youth Voice: Moving from Understanding to Action through Critical Theory" (Austin), xv, 61-71
Skiba, R. J., 69
SLB (street-level bureaucracy) theory, 133
Smith, H. M., 100
Smith, Paul, 98
"Smorgasbord" (Wolff), 172
Snowball, C., 41
social class, xxxix
social identity, xxxix-xl
social media, 105
social networking sites, 90
social power, 156
social theory
    identity formation through figured worlds, 21-23
    LIS's allergic reaction to, 163, 164
    See also critical social theory
society
    adolescence signified by age idea, 153-154
    age-/generation-based qualities for citizenship, 143-145
    alternative frameworks for thinking about young adults, 155-157
    whiteness, intersectionality of, 115-116
    See also culture
Soffer, O., 97
Solomon, Andrew, 17
spaces
    See young adult (YA) spaces
Spade, D., 68
Speak (Anderson), 19
The Spectacular Now (Tharp), 23
speech, 52-54
    See also youth voice
Springen, K., 80
Springhall, J., 39
staffing, 186
"Standards of Learning" (Virginia Department of Education), 28
state, role in LIS, xl
states
    harmful-to-minors laws, 55
    privacy protections for young adults, 57-58

statistical bigotry, 142-143
Stefancic, J., 112
Steinberg, S., 114
stereotypes
    about comics, 40
    about comics readers, 35, 36, 42, 44
    avoidance of, 13
    media portrayals of teens, 12
    single critical perspective, dangers of, 23
    of YAs, xviii
    of YAs held by librarians, 96, 126
    of youth, consequences of, 152-155
    of youth of color, 66, 70, 113, 116
Stockton, Kathryn, 95
"storm and stress" model
    conceptions of teen library users and, 151
    of G. Stanley Hall, xxxii, 78, 154
    rejection of, 20
    as stereotype of adolescents, 152
story
    dangers of single story, 23-25
    power/humility paradox, 102-103
    in storytelling triangle, 97-98
    of young adults, 105-106
storytelling
    conclusion about, 106-107
    as dynamic exchange, 96-99
    knowing, 103-106
    for minors' engagement in decision making, 126
    as richer way of knowing, 93-94
    three paradoxes of, 99-103
    undefining young adults, 94-96
    voice of youth of color, 112
"Storytelling, Young Adults, and Three Paradoxes" (McDowell), xvi, 93-107
Storytelling for Young Adults (de Vos), 97
storytelling triangle
    story, 105-106
    young adults as audience, 104
    young adults as storytellers, 104-105
street-level bureaucracy (SLB) theory, 133
students
    debt of, 81
    privacy laws protecting, 56-57
    Transforming Young Adult Services (Bernier) and, xiii
    YA viewed as, 130
    youth as students/learners in school libraries, 27-30
Students for a Democratic Society, 183
"Students or Learners? Conceptualizing Youth in School Libraries" (Harlan), xiv, 27-30
Sturm, B. W., 97
success, 164
Suellentrop, T., 152
Sukarieh, M., 65, 66-67
Sullivan, Rust v., 55
Sweeney, M., 63
synergy, 146-148

T

Taft, J. K., 67
Tannock, S., 65, 66-67
Tate, W. F., 113-114
Taylor, Deborah, 132
teaching, 29
technology
    identity construction and, 18
    identity formation in figured worlds, 21-22
teen fragility, 24
teen-centered approach
    changing thinking to, 8-13
    conclusion about, 13-14
    literature in library services for teens, analysis of, 4-8
    meaning of, 3-4
    YA librarianship from, 3-14
Teenreads.com, 89-90
teens
    age-/generation-based qualities for citizenship, 143-145
    alternative frameworks for thinking about, 155-157
    comics/graphic novels, conclusion about, 44-45
    copiloting with, 121-127
    focus on teens as individuals, 11-12
    generational integration at library, 146-148
    identity anxiety among, 18-19
    identity construction of, 17-19
    identity formation, contexts for, 19-23
    input in *Young Adult Library Services* articles, 7-8
    new young adults, 78-82
    single story, dangers of, 23-25
    stereotypes of youth, consequences of, 152-155
    as students/learners in school libraries, 27-30
    teen readers of comics, librarianship and, 35-45
    in teen-centered approach, 3-4
    teen-centered perspective, changing thinking to, 8-13
    use of term, 8-10

YA space, design of, 145-146
See also adolescence; young adults
teller
    power/humility paradox, 102-103
    in storytelling triangle, 97-98
telling
    in storytelling triangle, 97-98
    young adults as audience, 104
Tender Morsels (Lanagan), 83
Tharp, T., 23
theories of practice
    borrowed, 132-134
    discipline *vs.* practice, 131
    positive youth development, 132
    service providers for young adults, 134-135
    vision of young adults and, 130
theory
    positivism/postmodernism, 166-167
    praxis, 164-166
    See also critical race theory; critical social theory; critical theory
This Is All (Chambers), 84, 85-86
This Side of Home (Watson), 25
Thomas, Angie, 25, 68
Thompson, A., 114, 115
Tilley, C. L., 39, 62
time, 124-125
Time magazine, 81-82
Tinker v. Des Moines Independent Community School District, 52
Tixier Herald, D., 161
Toelken, Barre, 97
Too Shattered for Mending (Hoffmeister), 25
training, 100
Transforming Young Adult Services (Bernier)
    final word about, xix-xx
    overview of chapters of, xiii-xviii
    who should read, xiii
    YA services, examination of, xii
tribalism, 149
"Tribalism versus Citizenship: Are Youth Increasingly Unwelcome in Libraries?" (Males), xvii, 139-149
tribalism *vs.* citizenship
    age segregation in libraries, 139
    age-/generation-based qualities for citizenship, 143-145
    conclusion about, 148-149
    generation gap, 140-141
    library youth spaces, segregation and, 141-142
    synergy, harnessing, 146-148
    YA space, design of, 145-146
    youth crime/behavior statistics, 142-143
Trites, Roberta Seelinger, 22
Tsourounis, Emanuel, 122
Tuccillo, D. P., 4, 10-11
Tufts University, 132
"Tuxedo with Eagle Feathers" (Alexie), 24
tween, 176
twentieth century, views of young adults in, xxix-xxxii
Twentysomething Inc., 81
"Two Hundred Years of Young Adult Library Services History" (Bernier et al.), 9
Tyyskä, V., 156

U

Uniform Crime Reports (FBI), 143
University of California-Santa Cruz, 141-142
Urriete, Luis, Jr., 21
U.S. Bureau of the Census, 140-141
U.S. Supreme Court
    First Amendment rights of minors, cases on, 52-54
    U.S. v. American Library Association, 54-55
U.S. v. American Library Association, 54-55
"us versus them" narrative, 12
USA PATRIOT ACT (Patriot Act), 52, 58

V

Valdes-Rodriguez, Alisa, 25
van den Akker, Robin, 22
Vermeulen, Timotheus, 22
Vickery, Jacqueline Ryan, 183
victim blaming, 154-155
Vietnam War, 52
Virginia Department of Education, 28
vision
    alternative frameworks for vision of young adults, 155-157
    LIS's vision of youth, xxv-xxvi
    LIS's vision of youth, legacy practices and, 163-164
    LIS's vision of youth, self-reflection on, 167
    LIS's youth consensus, 163-164
    new young adult praxis, movement toward, 183-187
    praxis for changing LIS vision of youth, 164-166
    of YAs as local community members, 167-177

voice
    See youth voice
Voice of Youth Advocates (VOYA)
    comics articles in, 37
    "Graphically Speaking" column, 43
    licensing of book reviews, 89
    "Notes from the Teenage Underground" column, 42
    reviews for new YA reader, 85
Vygotsky, Lev, 21

W

Wald, J., 69
Wallace, David Foster, 22
Watson, Renée, 25
We Need Diverse Books campaign
    diverse stories, need for, 23
    teen identity construction and, 21
    youth voice and, 67
Webster's New World College Dictionary, 80
Weisgrau, J., 29
Wertham, Fredric, 38-39, 62
What the Birds See (Harnett), 83
When We Was Fierce (Charlton-Trujillo), 23
white privilege, 111-112
whiteness
    function in library, 116
    intersectionality, 115-116
    as property, 114-115
whites
    demographic revolution and, 141
    interest convergence and, 112-114
"Why We Are Kids' Best Assets: The Role of Librarians in Youth Development" (Jones), 132
Wiegand, Wayne
    comics/graphic novels, shift in, 45
    on LIS blind spot, 163
    "Out of Sight, Out of Mind," 36
    young adults as storytellers, 104
Wilde, Oscar, xxvi
Williams, C., 28
Williams, Mabel, 157
Wilson, R., 41
Wilson, William Julius, 142
The Winter of Our Disconnect (Maushart), 88
Wolak, J., 148
Wolff, Tobias, 172
Wolverson, R., 80
Wright, B. W., 39

X

X-Indian Chronicles: The Book of Mausape (Yeahpau), 25

Y

YALSA
    See Young Adult Library Services Association
"YALSA's Competencies for Librarians Serving Youth" (YALSA), 14
Yang, Gene Luen, 25
Yaqui Delgado Want to Kick Your Ass (Medina), 25
YAs
    See young adults
YASD (Young Adult Services Division), 79, 82
YDIC
    See youth development industrial complex
Yeahpau, Thomas W., 25
"The Year We Obsessed about Identity" (Morris), 17
young adult
    change in definition of, 77-78
    use of term, 8-10
Young Adult Library Services Association (YALSA)
    efforts of, 151
    Getting Graphic @ Your Library ALA preconference, 37
    library services for young people, change in, 66
    teen-centered focus advocated by, 14
    teen-centered research, 4
    YA services, ideas about, xii
    young adult, definition of, 77
    Young Adult Library Services articles, analysis of, 4-8
    "young adult" term, use of, 9
    youth development paradigm and, xxxi
Young Adult Library Services (journal)
    article on comic book club, 35-36
    articles published in, analysis of, 4-8
    comics articles in, 37
Young Adult Services Division (YASD), 79, 82
young adult (YA) literature
    book reviews on, 89-90
    comics, conclusion about, 44-45
    comics, historical discourses about, 38-40
    comics, recent literature about, 40-44
    crossover book, 83-85
    diverse pairing suggestions, 25
    diversity of stories, need for, 23-25
    identity focus in, 18-19
    identity formation and, 20
    identity formation in figured worlds and, 22-23

new YA definition and, 90–91
reviews for new YA reader, 85–88
YA literature for new category of users, 82–83
young adult definition and, 77–78
young adult (YA) services
as building based, 130
critical youth studies framework for LIS, 157–159
examination of, xii
group programming, 131–132
LIS and, xi–xii
LIS vision of youth, blind spot in, 163–164
from teen-centered perspective, 3–14
Transforming Young Adult Services (Bernier), xiii
twentieth century views of youth and, xxix–xxxii
vision of YAs as community members and, 183–187
YA literature for new category of users, 82–83
young adult definition and, 77–78
young adult (YA) spaces
age-/generation-based qualities for citizenship, 143–145
design of, 145–146
visions of YAs in library practice and, 185
YA community membership and, 173–174
young adults (YAs)
age-/generation-based qualities, 143–145
alternative frameworks for thinking about, 155–157
book reviews, 89–90
as community members, YA outreach and, 174–175
as community members, YA programming and, 175–177
as community members, YA space and, 173–174
copiloting with, 121–127
crossover book for, 83–85
generation gap and, 140–141
generational integration at library, 146–148
identity construction of, 17–19
identity formation, contexts for, 19–23
imagining today's young adults in LIS, 151–161
intellectual freedom of, conclusion about, 58–59
intellectual freedom of, laws protecting, 49–50
intellectual freedom, professional positions on, 50–52
legal foundations for minors' intellectual freedom, 52–54
LIS vision of, positivism/postmodernism, 166–167

LIS vision of, praxis for, 164–166
LIS's vision of, xxv–xxvi, 129–135, 159–161
as local community members, 167–177
new young adult praxis, movement toward, 183–187
new young adults, 78–82
nineteenth century views of, xxvi–xxix
privacy protections for, 57–58
reviews for new YA reader, 85–88
segregation of youth from adults in libraries, 139, 141–142
statistical bigotry, 142–143
stereotypes of, consequences of, 152–155
storytelling as dynamic exchange, 96–99
storytelling knowing, 103–106
tribalism *vs.* citizenship, 139–149
twentieth century views of, xxix–xxxii
undefining, 94–96
YA literature for new YA definition, 90–91
YA space, design of, 145–146
youth of color, reimagining in LIS discourses, 111–116
See also youth voice
Young People's Reading Round Table, 82
Your Right to Know: Librarians Make It Happen (ALA), 135
youth
alternative frameworks for thinking about, 155–157
difference from adults, xxxii
doctrines about, xxv–xxvi
LIS liabilities based on YDIC reliance, xxxv–xl
LIS vision of, 159–161
LIS vision of, blind spot in, 163–164
LIS vision of youth as members of local community, 167–170
LIS's definition of, xiv
nineteenth century views of, xxvi–xxix
rhetoric of youth consensus, xxxiii
stereotypes of, consequences of, 152–155
as students/learners, 27–30
twentieth century views of, xxix–xxxii
Youth Activism Project, 121, 122
"youth always of the future" liability, xxxvii
"youth as ever "other" liability, xxxvi
"youth at risk" approach
library reform and, 158
LIS vision of youth, 167
at-risk programs of libraries, xxx–xxxi
view of youth, xxxiv
YA space and, 173
youth development model and, xxxii

youth consensus
    assumptions of, xxxii–xxxiii
    critical look at by LIS, xxxiv–xxxv
    LIS liabilities based on YDIC reliance, xxxv–xl
    rhetoric of, xxxiii
youth development
    crossroads of practice/theory, xviii–xix
    LIS vision of youth, 167
    positive youth development, 132
youth development industrial complex (YDIC)
    Anthony Bernier on, xviii
    assumptions about youth inherent in, 163–164
    birth of, xxvii
    critical look at, xxxv
    LIS liabilities based on reliance on, xxxv–xl
    LIS's implementation of, consequences of, xli
    questioning, xix
    YA outreach and, 175
    YA space and, 173–174
    youth activism and, 183, 184
    youth consensus, xxxiv
youth development industrial complex (YDIC), liabilities of dependence on
    developmental psychology's dominion, xxxvii–xxxix
    introduction to, xxxv
    material circumstances, xxxix
    social identity, xxxix–xl
    state's role in LIS, xl
    summary about, xli
    youth, comparison to adults, xl
    youth always of the future, xxxvii
    youth as ever "other," xxxvi
    youth for all time, xxxvi
youth development paradigm
    discussion of, xix
    LIS adoption of, xxxi–xxxii, 129
    LIS mired in, xi–xii
    youth as "partners" in, xxxiv

youth empowerment, 123
"youth for all time" liability, xxxvi
youth labor, 153–154
Youth Marketing Company, 79
youth of color
    interest convergence, 112–114
    intersectionality, 115–116
    library services to, 63
    reimagining in LIS discourses, 111–116
    voice of, 112
    whiteness as property, 114–115
    youth voice of juveniles in detention, 68–70
Youth! The 26% Solution (Lesko & Tsourounis), 122
youth voice
    conclusion about, 70–71
    critically incorporating, 67–70
    in cultural studies of youth, 156
    librarian understanding of, 62–64
    vision of YAs as community members and, 171
    youth, conceptualizations of, 61–62
    youth, historical approaches to, 64–65
    of youth of color, 111–112
    youth voice as intervention, 65–67

Z

Zarr, Sara, 25
Zeller-Berkman, Sarah, xxxviii
Zoot Suit riots, 64
Zusak, Markus, 83